DESIGNING REFORM

COLE ROSKAM

DESIGNING REFORM

Architecture in the People's Republic of China, 1970–1992

Yale University Press
New Haven and London

For Diana, Clay, and Maizie

Published with assistance from the Graham Foundation for Advanced Studies in the Fine Arts.

Graham Foundation

Versions of Chapters 3, 6, 7, 8, and 9 were published as "Non-Aligned Architecture: China's Designs on and in Ghana and Guinea, 1955–92," *Architectural History* 58 (2015): 261–91; "Practicing Reform: Experiments in Post-Revolutionary Chinese Architectural Production, 1973–1989," *Journal of Architectural Education* 69, no. 1 (March 2015): 28–39; "Envisioning Reform: The International Hotel in Postrevolutionary China, 1974–1990," *Grey Room* 58 (Winter 2015): 84–111; "Expanding Architectural Discourse in Early Reform-Era China, 1978–89," in *Second World Postmodernisms: Architecture and Society under Late Socialism*, ed. Vladimir Kulić (London: Bloomsbury Visual Arts, an imprint of Bloomsbury Publishing, 2019); and "Building Reform: The Block and the Wall in Late Mao-Era China," in *Neoliberalism on the Ground: Architecture and Transformation from the 1960s to the Present*, ed. Kenny Cupers, Catharina Gabrielsson, and Helena Mattson, © 2020, reprinted by permission of the University of Pittsburgh Press.

Page 22: Train Station, Ministry of Railways Third Design Institute, Dar es Salaam (detail of fig. 19)
Page 94: Exhibition opening, *Everyday Life in China*, Pompidou Centre, Paris (detail of fig. 36)
Page 178: Metropolitan Hotel, Beijing, proposal (detail of fig. 69)

Cover and interior designed by Jeff Wincapaw
Set in Akagi Pro
Printed in Singapore
International Limited

Library of Congress Control
Number: 2020952888
ISBN 978-0-300-23595-1

A catalogue record for this book is available from the British Library.

This paper meets the requirements of ANSI/NISO Z39.48–1992 (Permanence of Paper).

10 9 8 7 6 5 4 3 2 1

Cover illustration: Shanghai Centre, John Portman & Associates, Shanghai, 1985–90. Elevated view. Photo © 1991 Michael Portman, the Shanghai Centre collection, courtesy the Portman Archive.

Contents

Acknowledgments

Numerous individuals and institutions were vital to the completion of this project. Initial research was supported by the University of Hong Kong (HKU) and the Research Grants Council (RGC), under the aegis of the University Grants Committee (UGC) in Hong Kong. A significant portion of this book was completed during my appointment as an Ailsa Mellon Bruce Visiting Senior Fellow at the Center for Advanced Study in the Visual Arts (CASVA) at the National Gallery of Art in Washington, D.C. This book's publication was supported by a grant from the Graham Foundation for Advanced Studies in the Fine Arts.

Conference travel-related funding provided by HKU allowed me to present parts of this project at several international conferences and workshops, including the Society of Architectural Historians, the College Art Association, Asian Studies in Africa: Challenges and Prospects of a New Axis of Intellectual Interactions, Harvard University Graduate School of Design, and King's College London. I was also very fortunate to have had the opportunity to present this work at a number of invited lectures.

I want to thank all of the people who agreed to meet and speak with me in relation to this project. I also received much-appreciated encouragement from colleagues at HKU and numerous friends, acquaintances, and scholars around the world. John Carroll, Zeynep Çelik Alexander, Jiat-Hwee Chang, Kenny Cupers, Catharina Gabrielsson, Timothy Hyde, Vladimir Kulić, Helena Mattsson, and Łukasz Stanek all read portions of the work in progress and provided valuable feedback. Two anonymous reviewers read the entire manuscript multiple times; their suggestions and comments helped me improve the manuscript in numerous ways. Katherine Boller, Raychel Rapazza, and the editorial, production, and design team at Yale University Press have been incredibly helpful throughout the publishing process. I'm also grateful to Laura Hensley for her copy editing.

Finally, and most important, I want to thank Diana, Clay, and Maizie for all of their love and patience over the course of this project. This book is dedicated to them.

Introduction

In 1970 the Chinese Communist Party (CCP) approved plans for the design and construction of the tallest building in Beijing—an eighteen-story addition to the Beijing Hotel, then the city's most prominent destination for overseas visitors. The completed hotel, which involved the country's most advanced structural technology and several of its most senior architects, soared at least twice as high as its neighboring buildings, including the Forbidden City, transforming the capital's skyline in the process (fig. 1). It anchored a sprawling, citywide development scheme that included the construction of a new national airport, diplomatic housing projects, the International Club, the Friendship Store, and a long-distance telephone building. China's architectural ambitions were not limited to Beijing, however. In Guangzhou, a series of new structures were concurrently launched to expand the city's famous import and export trade fair facilities.

At the same moment, halfway around the world, construction was also underway on China's most expensive foreign aid project, and the third-largest infrastructure initiative in Africa: the nearly 1,800-kilometer-long, Chinese-designed and -financed Tanzania-Zambia Railway Authority (TAZARA) Railway (fig. 2). Officially launched in 1970, and composed of twenty-two tunnels, ninety-three train stations, and 320 bridges, the five-year initiative required the movement of millions of dollars' worth of Chinese technology, equipment, and thousands of Chinese workers laboring in tandem with their Tanzanian and Zambian counterparts.

These endeavors occupy uncertain space and time in the architectural history of the People's Republic of China (PRC). The country's state-run media outlets eagerly depicted the projects as evidence of the manifold diplomatic and economic successes achieved by "the uninterrupted progress of Chairman Mao Zedong's revolution"—a reference to the then-active Cultural Revolution (1966–76), which was a sociopolitical movement launched by the CCP chairman and others to reassert their authority over the party by rooting out and punishing perceived elites through prolonged class warfare.[1]

But such production departed from many of the aesthetic, programmatic, and technological norms associated with the aggressive struggle for proletarian empowerment supported by Mao, and in that sense, the ideological contours at work in these projects remained unclear. The Beijing Hotel, for example, was designed with foreign tourists and businesspeople in mind; indeed, to prepare for the project, its architects had

Fig. 1 East wing, Beijing Hotel, Zhang Bo, Cheng Delan, and others, Beijing Institute of Architectural Design, Beijing, 1970–74.

embarked upon a clandestine study tour to the Portuguese and British colonies of Macau and Hong Kong to study international hotel design trends. The hotel featured prefabricated wall panels and prestressed, reinforced concrete beams and purlins—existing but relatively uncommon production and structural technologies in China at the time, and materials that required a certain degree of professional expertise. Such technology, coupled with bands of balconies projected from its façade, imbued the edifice with a light, thin form relative to the drab concrete and brick housing blocks that dominated much of the country's communist-era construction.

The TAZARA Railway, which Chinese and international press alike described as emblematic of socialist China's efforts to foment revolution throughout the developing world, was also a logistical and ideological divergence from party precedent. Prior to their departure from China, for example, participating technicians were purportedly warned by PRC Premier Zhou Enlai to avoid excessive propaganda and set aside ideology to focus on the work of construction itself.[2] These examples suggested the emergence of another sociopolitical mission at work in China—one largely antithetical to the ideological aims of Mao's revolution and intended to transform the country's existing relationship to both the capitalist and socialist worlds.

Designing Reform examines the Beijing Hotel, the TAZARA Railway, and other buildings, environments, designers, discourses, practices, and institutions involved in the country's pivot away from the violent fervor of the Cultural Revolution and toward what would eventually become the conjoined projects of China's Four Modernizations and Reform and Opening Up (1978–92). Both campaigns promoted China's rapid internationalization in the name of advancing the country's agriculture, industry,

Fig. 2 TAZARA Railway, Xinhua, 1970–75. Republished in Richard Hall and Hugh Peyman, *The Great Uhuru Railway* (1976).

defense, and science and technology and improving national economic output, which had grown significantly under Mao but remained behind the production levels of countries such as the United States, the Soviet Union, and Japan.

Over the course of the 1980s, China emphasized growth in these sectors while opening itself to foreign investment and ideas and experimenting with new economic policies intended to improve living conditions for millions of its residents. Despite the tangle of domestic and international forces at play, the party was keen to promote the notion that economic liberalization could be launched as a secure and collectively shared struggle—an all-encompassing objective that touched upon each and every facet of China, from "every short story in China, every novel, play, or movie, and every poem" to "every shoe in China, every tree, every television set, cartwheel, flywheel, airplane, [and] ditch."[3]

This book argues that buildings were also vital to reform, which entailed a reconfiguration of China's diplomatic outreach in the Global South, a strategic reassessment of the country's geopolitical standing relative to both its Cold War–era allies and enemies, and a dramatic and experimental reorientation toward capitalism. Collectively, these labors roiled internal party politics and the country at large, consequently altering Chinese society in the process. In transforming China, they also transformed the world.

As important as the built environment was to the Reform and Opening era, architecture has not previously been considered instrumental to the party's diplomatic and economic mission during the period. However, and as the following chapters reveal, architecture proved consequential to the changes taking place. Architecture's inherent and visible physicality seemed to offer a means by which the country's leaders could project the benefits of reform to all without jeopardizing their governing authority. Such an aim ultimately proved impossible to realize, and the government acknowledged that some people would benefit before others.[4] Nevertheless, buildings helped in conveying, if not completely delivering, the party's promises both to urban residents and the country's large, predominantly rural population.

Architecture provided much more than a series of physical tributes to the political and economic fluctuations taking place, however. New practices, terms, images, and ideas emerged that departed significantly from the fervent proletariat-oriented design and construction exercises that had been implemented throughout the country just years prior under Mao.[5] These elements stimulated public discourse regarding the built environment and normalized the physical and psychological effects of new flows of varied forms of capital in and out of the country, even as they also aggravated the procedural and ideological inconsistencies courted by reform itself. These influences circulated within and beyond China, composing new kinds of knowledge that affected the country's architectural culture, its design and construction work in other parts of the world, and global architectural production more generally.

Such knowledge did not derive exclusively from the Chinese government itself, but rather through a mixture of sources, including objects, various forms of media, individualized experiences abroad, cooperative ventures with foreign investors, firms, and other corporate entities, and the intellectual efforts of an empowered professional class of Chinese designers, among other influences. The complex and international dimensions of such information challenged the Communist Party's control over the discipline and, in so doing, broadened the very notion of architecture in China itself, even as many within the design community remained committed to the party's ideals for social betterment through architectural production, despite its limitations. Architects became key figures in the production of one socioeconomic reality within another by imagining buildings that enabled new, more market-friendly practices and modes of thinking to take root in physical environments otherwise designed for and defined by socialism.

As the country lurched toward an uncertain future shaped by more speculative economic, social, and cultural possibilities, architecture's perceived ability to both induce change and limit its potential pitfalls and adverse effects was understood to be a valuable, moderating influence on liberalization's unpredictable effects—a belief, as this book argues, that had an effect on China's political, cultural, and economic life.[6] Over time, the appearance of multiple, occasionally conflicting conceptions of architecture, coupled with the refashioning of architectural methods and expression across the PRC, rendered visible new truths often anathema to established party principles, and thus perplexing for China's citizenry.

Such confusion posed risks for the party and the project of reform itself. These risks became reality on June 4, 1989, in a violent assertion of CCP authority so damaging to the national spirit it necessitated the party's reformulation of its own reform project beginning in 1992. Official anxiety over these events and the economic, political, and social concerns that fueled them remains acute today and continues to reverberate through multiple aspects of Chinese architecture. In revisiting the roots of contemporary Chinese design, *Designing Reform* thus attends both to China's recent past and the innumerable intersections between buildings, cities, materials, ideas, and people still reshaping life in China and the world at large.

AN ARCHITECTURAL PREHISTORY TO REFORM

Appreciating architecture's contributions to post-Mao China warrants a brief overview of the discipline's development in China under Mao. All architecture designed and constructed in the PRC after 1949 must be read politically, and through the lens of the governing authority responsible for its production, that is, the CCP. Following the socialist nation's establishment by the party in 1949, the country's guiding architectural principles were organized around themes of "Utility, Economy, and if possible, Beauty."[7] Architectural design and construction processes were restructured as exercises in collective action that fulfilled a range of economic, political, and social goals particular to the construction of a new China.

The country's preexisting private design firms and architectural departments were consolidated into state-run design institutes—massive bureaucratic organs responsible for all of the country's architectural thinking and design. Organizationally, they composed systems of architectural labor responsible for shaping built space at the municipal, provincial, and national levels. Emphasis was placed on collaboration in ways that seemed to deliver on the promises of socialism—a shared pursuit across teams of designers, engineers, and workers with tangible benefits to citizens and the country at large that made architecture an important instrument in demonstrating the state's ability to effect change. Acts of design and construction were themselves understood to be contributing forces to the country's modernization, which was assessed primarily in material terms.

Architecture itself thus fulfilled both practical and representational purposes. It was expected to aid the government in meeting certain economic and social goals by improving efficiency, reducing inequality, and transforming people's lives through the production of new spaces—spaces that, in turn, gave rise to new behaviors, and, by extension, new socialist Chinese subjects. Architecture also created physical monuments to progress that helped to rally the masses around the party, eradicate contradiction within society, combat enemies of the state, and give form to the country's collective aspirations.[8]

China's desire to develop required both domestic capacity building and outside assistance, and over the course of the 1950s, the Soviet Union and other socialist allies contributed to the production of a new, socialist Chinese landscape. The subsequent deterioration of the Sino-Soviet relationship by 1960, however, prompted the CCP to intensify its industrialization efforts at home while also pursuing opportunities for diplomatic and architectural engagement abroad. As China's reliance upon foreign technology emerged as a logistical and political liability, campaigns to spur domestic industrial production such as the Great Leap Forward (1958–62) proved disastrous.

China's technical constraints at home also resonated through its architectural production abroad, which over the course of the 1960s included the financing, design, and construction of temporary exhibition halls, government buildings, stadiums, factories, and small-scale infrastructural works in a number of recently decolonized countries throughout Southeast Asia, the Middle East, Latin America, and Africa. China's international design work served as forms of architectural and infrastructural aid designed to support socialist revolution abroad, curry diplomatic favor by distinguishing the PRC as the rightful heir to China's political identity relative to the Republic of China (Taiwan), and evince China's sensitivity to the postcolonial challenges facing numerous decolonizing nations around the world.[9] Over time, such work helped ingratiate the PRC's socialist revolutionary credentials to local populations through structures that implicitly acknowledged socialist China's own humble but dogged industriousness.

The PRC's economic precariousness in the wake of its arduous efforts at modernization made material and structural thrift essential—a liability that CCP leadership eventually reframed as national policy in part through large-scale mobilization strategies to transform architectural production such as Mao's 1964 Mass Design Revolution movement, which called for the implementation of a new, proletarian-oriented national building program. Using acts of design and construction to project the party's abstract political and social goals posed risks, however. For all of the collaborative potential inherent in architecture, it was also vulnerable to charges of elitism, material excess, and undue bourgeois sentiment—accusations that were, in fact, leveled against a number of the country's most established architects and architectural thinkers at several points during the 1950s and the 1960s. Such claims prefigured the discipline's marginalization during the Cultural Revolution as one technical cog in a national grassroots operation paradoxically engineered by the state and devoted to the construction of a truly socialist society from the ground up.

By the late 1960s, the PRC's shift toward more proletarian approaches to design influenced perceptions of Chinese architecture, its production, and its history. Following the launching of the Cultural Revolution in

1966, architecture was understood as a physical encapsulation of China's "Four Olds"—old ideas, old customs, old culture, and old habits—in need of reconsideration. Thousands of foreign churches, temples, commercial establishments, and homes of intellectuals and so-called class enemies were closed, ransacked, or destroyed around the country.[10] Supposedly nonhierarchical, on-site building practices known as "Three Combinations" involving workers, cadres, and technicians were implemented throughout the country, with the resulting projects framed as physical refutations of anti-revolutionary theories privileging tropes of individual architects as possessing "innate genius" or the notion that singular "heroes make history."[11] Both buildings and workers were presented as embodiments of Chairman Mao's "unified struggle" against class enemies through constant revolution.[12] Manufacturing techniques such as prefabrication remained active through the Cultural Revolution but were adapted to shifts toward decentralization. The physical results of these efforts—simple brick infill construction and relatively raw concrete formwork—embodied Mao's vision of modernization through socialist collectivity.

The attention paid to localized, on-site building techniques disrupted the flow of building expertise both within the country and with respect to China's international relations. Many professionally trained architects, engineers, and other technical experts were forced to leave their homes and jobs and were reassigned to reeducation facilities known as "May Seventh Cadre Schools"—labor camps established in accordance with Mao's May 7, 1966, directive to subject intellectuals and other professionals to thought reform as part of the government's "Down to the Countryside" initiative. "Experts in waterproofing material became public toilet attendants," noted architect Wang Zhili, "while heating ventilation specialists became purchasing agents for their resident communes."[13] Many of the country's state-run design institutes were forced to curtail design and construction activity, and though the country's largest institutes remained open, large segments of China's design and construction industry struggled to operate at full capacity.

Modifications in standard design and construction practices were accompanied by corresponding shifts in architectural education. China's university examination system was suspended in 1966; that same year, a new architectural educational model was established at Tongji University in Shanghai and replicated around the country. It reduced the major to a three-year program reoriented around on-site construction collaborations intended to contribute to the social and political upheaval taking place.[14] These and other pedagogical changes were designed to translate Mao's egalitarian goals into physical reality, though the resulting buildings revealed the atrophied state of China's design education and its construction industry, which posed long-term problems for the country's future development (fig. 3).

Fig. 3 Elementary school project, Tongji University "5.7" cadre school, No. 72 graduate school group, Shanghai, 1975. Originally published in *Architectural Journal* (*Jianzhu Xuebao*), no. 4 (1975).

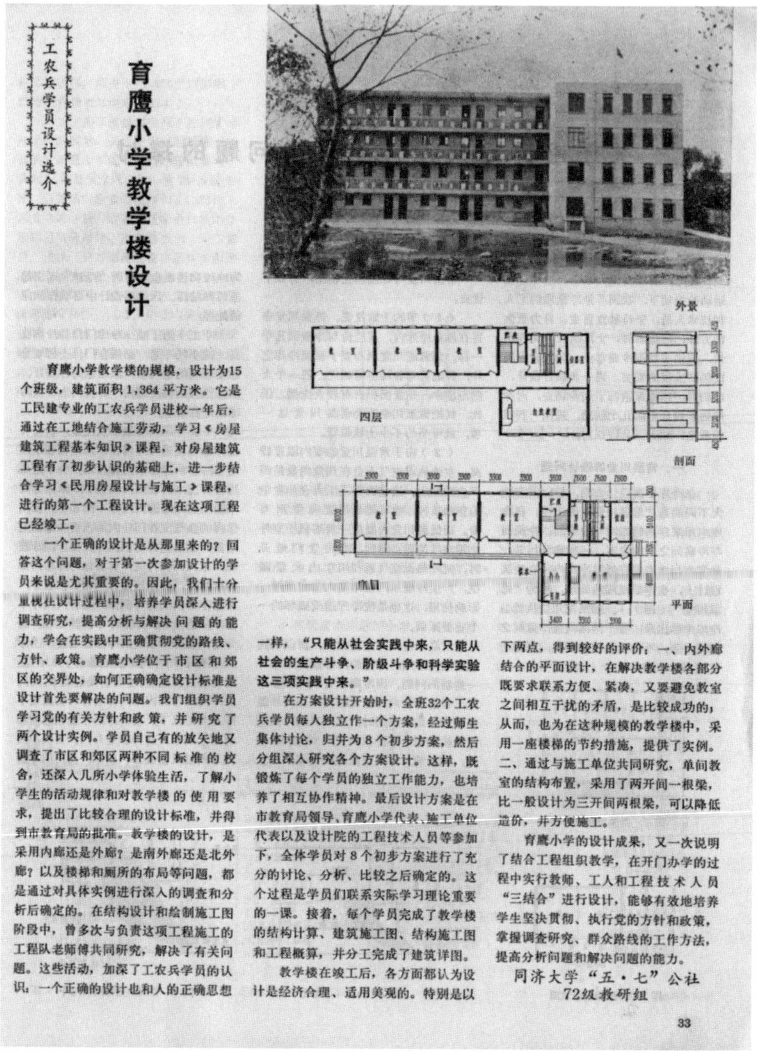

育鹰小学教学楼设计

育鹰小学教学楼的规模，设计为15个班级，建筑面积1,364平方米。它是工民建专业的工农兵学员进校一年后，通过在工地结合施工劳动，学习《房屋建筑工程基本知识》课程，对房屋建筑工程有了初步认识的基础上，进一步结合学习《民用房屋设计与施工》课程，进行的第一个工程设计。现在这项工程已经竣工。

一个正确的设计是从那里来的？回答这个问题，对于第一次参加设计的学员来说是尤其重要的。因此，我们十分重视在设计过程中，培养学员深入进行调查研究，提高分析与解决问题的能力，学会在实践中正确贯彻党的路线、方针、政策。育鹰小学位于市区和郊区的交界处，如何正确确定设计标准是设计首先要解决的问题。我们组织学员学习党的有关方针和政策，并研究了两个设计实例。学员自己有的放矢地又调查了市区和郊区两种不同标准的校舍，还深入几所小学体验生活，了解小学生的活动规律和对教学楼的使用要求，提出了比较合理的设计标准，并得到市教育局的批准。教学楼的设计，是采用内廊还是外廊？是南外廊还是北外廊？以及楼梯和厕所的布局等问题，都是通过对具体实例进行深入的调查和分析后确定的。在结构设计和绘制施工图阶段中，曾多次与负责这项工程施工的工程队老师傅共同研究，解决了有关问题。这些活动，加深了工农兵学员的认识：一个正确的设计也和人的正确思想一样，**"只能从社会实践中来，只能从社会的生产斗争、阶级斗争和科学实验这三项实践中来。"**

在方案设计开始时，全班32个工农兵学员每人独立作一个方案，经过师生集体讨论，归并为8个初步方案，然后分组深入研究各个方案设计。这样，既锻炼了每个学员的独立工作能力，也培养了相互协作精神。最后设计方案是在市教育局领导、育鹰小学代表、施工单位代表以及设计院的工程技术人员等参加下，全体学员对8个初步方案进行了充分的讨论、分析、比较之后确定的。这个过程是学员们联系实际学习理论重要的一课。接着，每个学员完成了教学楼的结构计算、建筑施工图、结构施工图和工程概算，并分工完成了建筑详图。

教学楼在竣工后，各方面都认为设计是经济合理、适用美观的。特别是以下两点，得到较好的评价：一、内外廊结合的平面设计，在解决教学楼各部分既要求联系方便、紧凑，又要避免教室之间相互干扰的矛盾，是比较成功的；从而，也为在这种规模的教学楼中，采用一座楼梯的节约措施，提供了实例。二、通过与施工单位共同研究，单间教室的结构布置，采用了两开间一根梁，比一般设计为三开间两根梁，可以降低造价，并方便施工。

育鹰小学的设计成果，又一次说明了结合工程组织教学，在开门办学的过程中实行教师、工人和工程技术人员"三结合"进行设计，能够有效地培养学生坚决贯彻、执行党的方针和政策，掌握调查研究、群众路线的工作方法，提高分析问题和解决问题的能力。

同济大学"五·七"公社
72级教研组

33

By the early 1970s, debate among party leaders over the nature of architecture's contributions to socialist China contributed to festering factionalism within the party over the country's direction. A clique of core leftists led by Mao's wife, Jiang Qing, head of the so-called Gang of Four, urged the party to continue its campaigns promoting class upheaval, while a group of slightly more moderate party members, organized around Premier Zhou Enlai, began to question the benefits of prolonged civil strife to the country's politics, economy, and international affairs. Mao occupied an ambiguous middle ground, though a rapid series of unprecedented diplomatic events in PRC history indicated a rebalancing of the party's center.

In October 1970, Canadian Prime Minister Pierre Trudeau recognized the PRC, becoming one of the first leaders of a Western democracy to do so. In April 1971, a team of U.S. table tennis players became the first U.S. delegation to visit China since 1949, prompting the relaxation of the

United States' twenty-year trade embargo with China and the lifting of U.S. passport restrictions to the PRC. That September, Mao's handpicked successor, Lin Biao, and members of his family perished in a mysterious plane crash in Mongolia—an apparent and unsuccessful (though still unconfirmed) defection attempt that further destabilized a Chinese leadership already struggling to distance itself from the violence of the Cultural Revolution and prepare for life after Mao. Just over one month later, on October 25, the PRC was admitted into the United Nations at the expense of the Republic of China. U.S. President Richard Nixon's visit to China—the first by a sitting U.S. president since 1949—followed in February 1972. Collectively, these events composed a watershed moment indicative of a consequential if provisional shift toward pragmatism within the party.

New design and construction in Beijing, Guangzhou, and elsewhere emerged in relationship to these changes, though the full catalytic impact of such work would not fully manifest within the country's ideological and physical landscape for several more years. Following the deaths of Premier Zhou Enlai and Mao and the subsequent arrest of the Gang of Four in 1976, the Cultural Revolution was officially brought to an end. Succeeding Party Chairman and Premier Hua Guofeng initiated a series of incremental changes before eventually being superseded by newly appointed Vice-Premier Deng Xiaoping, who began his reascendance to the top of the party's ranks in 1978, after being punished for his criticism of the Cultural Revolution and outmaneuvering Hua for control of the party. That year marks the conventional launching of reform in the party's official narrative; it was at the Third Plenum of the Eleventh Central Committee of the Communist Party of China, held in Beijing in December 1978, that Deng urged officials to "emancipate the mind and seek truth from facts" while consolidating the party elite's apparently unanimous support.[15]

Over the next decade, Deng worked with Zhao Ziyang, Hu Yaobang, and other reform-inclined officials to implement the goals of the Four Modernizations. Like its Mao-era predecessor, the Deng regime emphasized material development and technology as key vehicles in marking China's progress toward achieving modernization, though in doing so it promoted new forms of market-based economic experimentation, foreign investment, and international outreach. Having begun to condition China's built environment for transition during the early to mid-1970s under Mao, architecture actively contributed to the transformative if unsteady recalibration of both the party and China under Deng. Such work was seemingly brought to an abrupt and violent end following the events of June 4, 1989, though beginning in 1992, Deng and others used their remaining political capital to readjust the project of reform in ways that buoyed the country's continued economic liberalization while limiting the possibility of further social unrest.

UNDERSTANDING REFORM THROUGH ARCHITECTURE

These historical complexities and sensitivities inform *Designing Reform*, which offers an architectural history that tests many of the standard chronologies and accounts often used to understand the era. Both the Cultural Revolution and, to a lesser extent, the early reform period remain delicate topics in Chinese academia, particularly given recent vicissitudes in how the party's current leadership desires its own history to be interpreted.[16] Friction over the party's post-Mao leadership structure, doubts over the economic and social effects of more market-friendly policies, dramatic reform-era increases in party corruption, illicit economic activities, and moments of ideological inconsistency—these trials thread throughout the era's history and continue to reverberate through China's governance, making the early reform era an uncomfortable political period to reconsider even today.[17]

Within the specific disciplinary parameters of architectural history, the early reform era also occupies contested intellectual terrain. Most accounts portray the period as unduly hampered by confusion over the country's ideological direction and ultimately constitutive of little more than the tired rehashing of historical debates from earlier periods in China's architectural development, including questions concerning the role of tradition versus modernity in architectural expression.[18] The era's architectural aesthetics are often judged harshly—a pastiche of mirrored curtain walls, abstracted Chinese ornamentation, and disjointed translations of foreign architectural ideas that seem to suggest a superficiality evocative of an awkward, adolescent phase in China's development.[19]

For all of the challenges inherent to a study of reform's history, however, and despite the various stylistic shortcomings that may be evident in its architectural production, the era remains a uniquely creative and experimental period in Chinese design worthy of reconsideration. If the 1970s marked the party's initial reconsideration of more technologically sophisticated, foreign-derived forms of architectural expression, the 1980s signaled an unprecedented moment of freedom to engage with once verboten architectural ideas, images, and practices. The writer Bei Dao has described the decade of the 1980s as "a white corridor connecting two nights"—an evocative metaphor that captures both the period's uncertain liminality and the invigorating if temporary infusion of optimism that accompanied it.[20]

Reexamining the era's key architectural objects, ideas, and events is valuable because it reveals both the creative and intellectual capacity unleashed by liberalization and the spectrum of conflicted negotiations taking place within multiple spheres of China's complex and multifaceted system of governance in relation to reform. These deliberations remain unparalleled in the PRC's history and complicate accepted narratives of the Reform and Opening era as a unanimous, party-wide embrace of technocratic pragmatism launched by Deng only after Mao's death in 1976 and his reascendance in 1978, and consisting of China's seamless passage into an age of more abundant, evenly distributed economic prosperity.

The architectural history of reform illuminates similar negotiations taking place in relation to space, form, and a range of other disciplinary concerns. It presents new sets of temporal and spatial frameworks that contribute to our understanding of China's history after Mao in relation to the party's official retelling of what took place. Occasions such as the CCP Work Conference and the Third Plenum of the Eleventh Central Committee meetings held in December 1978, for example, are often used to punctuate the party's history of reform—undeniably important turning points that emphasize the party's united coalescence around Deng's vision for the country.[21]

Such events did not represent the only catalysts of change, however, nor do they fully capture the complex, multifaceted process of change itself. Less than one month prior to the CCP Work Conference and Central Committee meetings held in December 1978, for example, members of the Architectural Society of China's Standing Committee gathered in Nanning, Guangxi Province, to debate the implications of impending modernization on Chinese architecture. The group included representatives from China's most prestigious architectural educational programs and design institutes, and discussion focused on how China's designers could best contribute to the government's reinvigorated efforts at urban planning, the party's desire to improve people's lives, and the necessary strengthening of China's economy, among other issues. Cloaked in Mao-era rhetorical flourishes, the meeting nevertheless anticipated a number of ideological, procedural, aesthetic, and scalar issues at stake in reform's implementation.[22] Such evidence offers additional perspective on the era's party-approved history and, in so doing, opens up exciting new terrain in the study of post-Mao Chinese architecture and society at large.

The architectural quality of duration—the time it takes to design and build, and a completed structure's lifespan—proved consequential to China's economic liberalization and prompts important questions regarding the process and implementation of reform relative to the built environment. Buildings remain long after they are completed and involve temporalities that do not necessarily align with other time frames typically used to characterize the era, such as the country's five-year plans or the iterative nature of multiple campaign cycles, for example. Tracing interactivity between architecture's multiple ontologies—design and construction—and the party's various reform-era policy shifts dispels any notion that China's architectural or political messaging after Mao was singular, centralized, or fixed.

Designing and constructing a building are two different activities, and each possessed a certain, limited responsivity to change. Architectural drawings can be edited, erased, and begun anew; building construction generally cannot. Despite their divergent fates, however, the processes of translating ideas into drawings, and subsequently into buildings, remained entwined. Working in tandem, they rendered visible economic and social processes that could be perceived as alternatively contributing to and undermining the project of reform, depending on largely coincidental alignments of construction processes and a particular ideological climate.

This book overlays histories of design and building upon broader swings in party political-economic policy, from more "liberal" phases of reform (1979–80, 1984, 1986–87, 1988) to conservative shifts rightward against reform (1981, 1985–86, 1987, 1988–89), to reveal synchronicities and gaps between design, construction, and ideology that challenge perceptions of how China's built environment was both produced and managed after Mao.[23] Architecture, like all forms of cultural production in China, was vulnerable to these oscillations, particularly as it related to design and construction approval processes, financing, and various aesthetic, material, programmatic, and site-specific considerations.

Yet architecture also possessed certain physical and procedural qualities that defied these fluctuations, particularly as compared to other forms of cultural expression such as art, literature, or film. A number of ambitious projects were conceived during relatively liberal phases in party politics, only to be completed in a more conservative political environment. Throughout this book, the design and construction of examples such as the Chairman Mao Memorial Hall, completed by Xu Yinpei and others between 1976 and 1977, or the Fragrant Hill Hotel, completed by I. M. Pei & Partners in 1983, alternatively reinforced, contradicted, and transcended multiple political campaigns. Projects were initially championed only to be criticized upon their completion, before being officially and popularly embraced several years later. Understanding these time frames as interrelated but distinctive processes of becoming allows for a new and uniquely architectural historical reading of the era that also informs how we understand reform itself.

Interiority—a building's ability to delineate and discipline space that is largely discontinuous from its exterior—provides another uniquely architectural vantage point on the era. International expertise and investment was a crucial influence on China's economic liberalization, even as the projection of control remained a vital source of the party's power. Buildings helped to mediate between these forces by demarcating what could be seen and experienced when, and by whom. The organization and curation of late Mao-era events such as *The Exhibition of Archaeological Finds of the People's Republic of China*, which traveled to the National Gallery of Art in Washington, D.C., and other international destinations between 1974 and 1978, required the design of new interior spaces for various climatic, logistical, and ideological purposes that insulated China and its cultural production from any surrounding institutional context.

These impulses took on noticeably expanded and different forms after 1978 through the establishment of special economic zones (SEZs) such as Shenzhen and the regulated interior environments of international hotels such as the Great Wall Hotel in Beijing, completed by Becket International in 1984, among other examples. Interiors that distanced foreign visitors and investors from the sobering realities of socialist China while also shielding average Chinese residents from the incongruous extravagances taking place inside theoretically enabled smooth and uninterrupted infusions of foreign exchange into China.

These conditions and the logic behind them were specific to early reform-era China, but they also align with architectural ideas taking shape outside the PRC, and prompt a reconsideration of the relationship between capitalism, governance, and the atmospheric and sensorial effects that echoed through a number of new architectural interior environments in other parts of the world at the time, including Berlin, Los Angeles, and New York City, among other locales.[24] Mapping these and other theoretical linkages reveals the contours of new, global architectural and urban histories rooted in notions of interiorization and the various climatic, social, and political regulations that facilitated them.

Architecture's inherent physicality and public visibility offer another key disciplinary contribution to the study of the early reform era. China's economic liberalization reverberated throughout multiple forms of cultural production, and the country's artists, musicians, filmmakers, and writers actively engaged with foreign ideas, practices, and objects in the age of reform. More than perhaps any other form of cultural expression, however, reform retained a foundational relationship to architecture.[25] The Marxist cultural critic Walter Benjamin's argument for architecture as the quintessential cultural product "received in a state of distraction and through the collective" offers insight as to why.[26] Architecture had a particular use value under Mao, and it aimed to deliver on the state's promises, successfully or not, in ways the country's populace came to accept and absorb as part of their daily activities. Reform-minded officials anticipated similar effects and relied upon architecture as a vessel through which change would be projected, received, and eventually normalized over time, despite the radical new formal expressions, design methods, and financing schemes at work.

Party perceptions of technology, and how technology could be used to visualize and project economic development through the built environment, is also relevant in this regard. Concepts of technology were by no means new to socialist China, but the term took on an expanded, panacea-like meaning over the course of the 1980s in relation to the Four Modernizations. Similarly, Chinese perceptions of the West as an essential source for technology did not originate with reform, but economic liberalization was in part inspired by associations between technological advancement and internationalism produced in part by what CCP officials saw on official study tours to Hong Kong, the United States, and Japan, among other destinations.[27]

Subsequently, the party's expectations that new, market-based policies and visible displays of their effectiveness through technologically sophisticated objects and spaces would somehow solve the country's various economic, political, and social ills came to dominate economic and architectural thinking during the era.[28] As the party eagerly pursued new forms of technology to import into China, they also sought new ways of representing progress through technology—what American Studies professor Steven Lubar has described as "the marks on paper, wood, and steel that describe and abstract technology."[29] The party's search for technology and its desire to display and reveal such technology to the public—often through buildings—produced an associated semiotics that expanded architectural meaning in China. The notion of design transformed accordingly, from a form of expertise to a representational strategy to a performative kind of technological machinery in itself.[30]

In these and other respects, a reassessment of the era and its architectural production sheds light on the processes by which change was introduced into Chinese society through the built environment. Architecture's significance as both an art and a science—a form of economic production and cultural expression, with physical as well as metaphysical implications—makes it a particularly valuable source of knowledge in this respect. Recent architectural historical scholarship has pushed our understanding of architecture beyond the notion that buildings simply represent broader political, economic, social, or cultural forces in society, and toward the very real ways that architecture defines and manages human activity and how we engage with society at large.[31] At the same time, economic and political power is also often reified through buildings in ways that has prompted debate as to the discipline's ability to effect change.[32]

Approaching the early reform era as more than a sweeping, top-down, and industry-wide embrace of new, often foreign-derived architectural ideas and practices, or the simple and state-sanctioned imposition of a certain style, is therefore critical. The innumerable and singular, individual acts of design, travel, construction, exchange, and communication that composed reform must be taken into account, particularly given that architecture derives its meaning from the ideas, experiences, and beliefs that people generate. In rendering those internalities public and social, architecture helps to produce contributing citizens of societies and the social structures upon which people depend, regardless as to whether those structures are capitalist or socialist in their ideological composition.[33] These tensions prompt questions concerning architecture's agency that are particularly relevant to the study of Chinese architecture, making the role of design and building in the early reform era an important and timely issue to explore.

REFORM'S CONTRIBUTIONS TO ARCHITECTURAL HISTORY

Just as the historical study of design and construction enriches our understanding of the early reform era, so does the examination of post-Mao Chinese architecture provide insight into the limitations at work in twentieth-century architecture's historiography, particularly with respect to terminology and temporality. For example, modernism—cultural iterations of broader socioeconomic processes known as modernization—has historically been used to connote a specific temporal framework and aesthetic related to forms of industrial capitalism in Western Europe or North America beginning in the early twentieth century, though recent scholarship has convincingly argued for the existence of multiple modernisms and modernities in a range of non-Western contexts.[34] The term "postmodernism" has been similarly defined and understood, namely, as a particular, Euro-American response to perceptions of the modern movement's aesthetic and formal exhaustion, and, more generally, a crisis of meaning in architecture triggered by the postindustrial forces of late capitalism taking place in the United States and Western Europe beginning in the early 1970s.[35]

Both modernism and postmodernism pose challenges for architectural historians of China, however. During the reform era, for example, the coterminous dissemination of so-called modern and postmodern architectural aesthetics and ideals throughout China produced material manifestations that do not necessarily align with how modernism and postmodernism have been defined and understood in other parts of the world—a juxtaposition captured, for example, by the first issue of the Chinese journal *Modernization* (*Xiandaihua*, 1980), the front cover of which featured a paternal Premier Zhou gazing approvingly upon an industrialized Chinese landscape, and its back cover consisting of an image of the "postmodern" interior of John Portman & Associates' Hyatt Regency, completed in San Francisco in 1973, overlaid with the term "modernization" (figs. 4, 5).

Incorporating China into a more comprehensive and global historiography of twentieth-century architecture remains an urgent if unfinished task. To do so, architectural historians must reconsider the deployment of certain terms and images to articulate and categorize architectural styles, discourses, geographies, forms, and design practices in relation to different parts of the world. The early reform era is illuminating in this respect. China's Four Modernizations was a socioeconomic process of industrialization that signified something distinctive from any foreign equivalent—an official campaign to reinvigorate an unfinished socialist project through rapid influxes of foreign, market-derived capital with cultural manifestations that ranged in their aesthetic and discursive orientation from the so-called modern to ostensibly postmodern expressions, all of which were designed to serve the broader interests of the state.

Fig. 4 Front cover of *Modernization* (*Xiandaihua*), featuring Premier Zhou Enlai. Originally published in *Xiandaihua* 2, no. 1 (January 1980).

Fig. 5 Back cover of *Modernization* (*Xiandaihua*), featuring the interior of the Hyatt Regency, John Portman & Associates, San Francisco, 1973. Originally published in *Xiandaihua* 2, no. 1 (January 1980).

Further confusion stems from the concurrent translation of key modernist texts and postmodern discourse into Chinese during the late 1970s and 1980s, which upset their presumed chronology and denied Chinese architects the kind of contextual grounding both theories possessed in other parts of the world. The subjective experiences of party officials and architects who visited Hong Kong, Japan, the United States, and Western Europe, among other destinations, and returned home with inspiring images and memories of foreign buildings and landscapes is another influential factor to consider. Given these challenges, both "modernism" and "postmodernism" in particular are often difficult terms to define in relation to China's architectural history, even as both have received scholarly attention in relation to early reform-era Chinese art, literature, and film.[36] Some have omitted postmodernism from the recent history of Chinese architecture altogether.[37]

Despite the various problems and opacities involved in the mapping and meaning of terms such as "modernism" and "postmodernism," both remain relevant to the architectural history of reform in the PRC and global architectural historiography more generally. China may have lacked the economic and political conditions for the kinds of discursive criticality historically understood as vital to modernism, let alone postmodernism—a fact many in China's architectural establishment came to understand and critique over the course of the 1980s. Yet Chinese architects and thinkers still engaged with a range of distinctly postmodern-influenced architectural ideas that resulted in consequential entanglements of architectural expression and meaning that remain relevant to Chinese architectural thinking today.[38]

At the time, such alignments posed challenges both for Chinese architects struggling to triangulate China's own design history within such theorizations and the party's own approved development narrative, and for foreign designers working to transfer and translate architectural ideas from abroad into China. New reform-era vocabulary intertwined with Mao-era architectural discourse to produce original yet familiar ways of thinking and writing about China's architectural production—a blending of disciplinary positions that engendered different ways of conceptualizing China's architectural past, its present, and its future. Such amalgamation necessitates a reconsideration of postmodernism's meaning relative not only to China, but to the history of global architectural discourse, particularly as many of the aesthetic and material hallmarks of modernism—glass and transparency foremost among them—began to recirculate around the world in the 1990s, disrupting postmodernism's own globalization in the process.[39]

In wrestling with the implications of architectural modernism and postmodernism in post-Mao China, one must also come to terms with the broader economic and cultural consequences of neoliberalism, or free-market capitalism, as it increasingly informed monetary policy and fueled architectural production around the world over the course of the 1970s and 1980s. Reform was not an exercise in neoliberalism, nor was China an unwitting receptacle for the loose, variegated flows of capital circulating around the world at the time. Attributing China's rapid economic growth only to the opening of its market to foreign investors, for example, or privileging the mechanism of the joint venture as the only reform-era administrative apparatus of consequence, overlooks other factors specific to Chinese society, including the wealth of human capital produced by socialist investment in basic needs, public education, and health care.[40] Privileging the market as a key driver of reform ignores preexisting organizational structures within the Chinese state, including both the state and rural collective ownership of land, and the government's ability to direct foreign capital to particular places and projects through its control over the administrative instruments necessary for major financial transactions.[41] As noted by public policy expert Richard Rose and others, "The party-state did not manage the economy; it was the economy."[42] If China's leadership did embrace different, so-called neoliberal sources of capital, it did so with the assumption that its flows would remain under socialism's control.

Nevertheless, and despite such caveats, revisiting China's role within the neoliberal-influenced restructuring of economic ideology taking place around the world at the time is relevant to architectural history, in large part because China's own economic liberalization was not in itself an archetypal example of neoliberalism.[43] Even as many of the party's existing administrative mechanisms adapted and contributed to the project of reform, there still existed a need for new spaces within which unfamiliar, experimental practices like the joint venture and, by extension, alternative methods of control could be introduced, tested, and disseminated throughout the country over time. Here, architecture had specific and lasting contributions to make. Acknowledging the influence of forces specific to the PRC while also attending to the country's embrace of multiple sources of foreign capital from paradigmatic neoliberal economies such as Hong Kong and Taiwan opens up new directions for understanding the history of architecture as a mediating force in much of the socialist and post-socialist world.[44]

In doing so, this work also has the potential to advance disciplinary knowledge regarding the relationship between architecture and so-called capitalist and socialist forms of economic organization, in all of their varied institutional ontologies. A study of the early reform era provides new knowledge concerning architecture's ability to manage consequential moments of economic transition, particularly procedural and ideological ambiguities between capitalism and socialism, processes of technological exchange, and the global emergence of varied forms of economic liberalization during the late Cold War era.

The confluence of neoliberal economic ideas, postmodern architectural thinking, and intensified physical development in the PRC carried consequences relative to architectural production and meaning that echoed far beyond the country's physical boundaries. In expanding our understanding not only of China's reform, but postmodernism's global histories, particularly in relation to the socialist world, this book also contributes to emerging discourse concerning the rise of a "global China."[45] Recent Chinese construction in Africa, for example, has roots in reform-era practices and discursive formations that prompt a reappraisal of how China's international expansion is understood in relation to the study of global architectural history and globalization more generally. China's strategy to induce and represent consequential technological change domestically through greater international exposure, particularly in architecture, also informed how it designed and built architecture and infrastructure abroad.

Scholars appraising the relationship between technology and architecture may thus look toward early reform-era China to understand not only how a government attempted to reorganize society through particularly visual methods of modernization, or the ways in which a political authority aggressively deployed architecture to shape anticipated futures, but how these notions of progress, articulated through building technology, were exported and shaped national aspirations in other parts of the world. Over the course of the early reform era, it became increasingly clear to Chinese observers that architecture entailed more than simply the technical resolution of scientific problems, particularly as architectural production took on unanticipated and, at times, uncomfortable representational power in relation to broader processes of economic and social change in both China and other parts of the world.

OVERVIEW OF THE BOOK

Designing Reform is organized into three parts in an effort to both distinguish the important differences existing in China under and after Mao and fully capture the early signs of change evident in the late Mao-era architecture, the more robust and diverse range of disciplinary contributions made to the project of reform after 1978, and its international reverberations. Each section examines a series of broad thematic phases organized into chapters related to architecture's engagement with reform, which are roughly organized chronologically. Certain processes, projects, firms, discourses, and individuals appear across multiple chapters and reinforce for readers the circulations of people, ideas, and things that took place during the period in question.

Part I is titled "Anticipation," and it features three grouped chapters that explore the spatial, material, and cultural politics of architecture in late-Mao China, and the extent to which new physical forms of design and construction, new types of design expertise, and new processes of building production portended more dramatic changes to come. Chapter 1 examines China's architectural reorientation in relation to the specific spaces that accommodated the country's expanded cultural, diplomatic, and economic sphere over the course of the mid-1970s, including the Beijing Hotel, the city's diplomatic residential compound, the International Club, and the Friendship Store. Chapter 2, by contrast, focuses on design expertise by addressing the range of intellectual and professional exchanges within the discipline of architecture prior to the official advent of reform. Chapter 3 illuminates shifting material practices taking place in China's building industry prior to reform's official launch—changes in brick and concrete block and panel production that show how processes of reform began to take physical form through objects that reorganized experiences and relationships between workers, the party, and the built environment.

Part II, "Implementation," consists of three chapters devoted to architecture's participation in the official enactment of reform beginning in 1978. These contributions include the design and enactment of new financial and spatial mechanisms necessary for reform, the reinvigoration of building types such as the international hotel, and the deployment of architectural history in the party's pivot away from the physical and psychological damage inflicted upon the country by the Cultural Revolution. Chapter 4 discusses the role of architectural history and heritage in reform-era China. What did China's past mean in connection to early reform-era Chinese architecture, and how was it to be used to advance the cause of modernization? Chapter 5 introduces the joint venture and the SEZ, two essential components of economic liberalization through which China could begin to develop a more export-based economic model through the construction of new corporate relationships and industrial environments without disrupting the socialist landscape that surrounded them. It attends to the first architectural projects proposed and constructed within the special economic zone of Shenzhen—a city that has been thoroughly studied as an urban model for rapid economic development, but one that still affords new ways of understanding the realities of reform as they took shape on the ground, in relation to particular building projects. One of the early reform era's most ubiquitous building types, the international hotel, was another early site for economic and spatial experimentation, and is the subject of Chapter 6.

The book's third part is organized under the theme of "Integration," and it situates China's reform-era architectural design and production within a broader global context. Postmodernism was an influential if misunderstood theory imported into post-Mao China from abroad, and it is the focus of Chapter 7. Chapter 8 examines changes within reform-era architectural education enacted in part due to the study of foreign design pedagogies. Consequential shifts in architectural practice also took place, some of which relied upon foreign organizational models and management strategies for design labor. Chapter 9 traces reform-era exportations of Chinese architectural expression to the African continent, where the ideological polarities embedded in earlier, Mao-era rhetoric clashed with the party's newfound embrace of market-derived forms of capital. The resulting architectural forms and practices may be understood as marking the rise of a new "global China" as a unique developmental model.[46] *Designing Reform* acknowledges the events of June 4, 1989, as a defining moment in the history of China's political and architectural systems before concluding with Deng's famous 1992 "Southern Tour" of Guangdong Province, which signaled the party's recommitment to reform, even as it also marked an important shift in the government's strategy for economic liberalization moving forward. These reconfigurations triggered new questions concerning architecture's role in relation to reform that continue to reverberate through China's architectural production and discourse today.

The administrative and ideological machinations required to initiate and sustain reform continue to test China's leadership, and new historical narratives and interpretive frameworks are needed that allow us to understand the origins of these dynamics and trace the ways in which the country has adapted to its reformation over the past forty years. In privileging architecture's role in the production, reflection, and naturalization of reform, this book relies upon a range of architectural objects, practices, and ideas as a means of documenting and reassessing China's past through acts of design and construction. Primary and secondary source materials, including images, plans, photographs, firsthand recollections, and archival documents, much of which has not previously been accessed in relation to the study of post-Mao China, capture numerous, previously unheralded relationships between architecture, China, and the world. Such documentation covers many topics that are specific to architecture yet also reveal how much Chinese society has inalterably changed since Mao.

Unprecedented transformation has reconfigured how China's people live and engage with each other and their built environment. At the same time, we all live in a world still undergoing large-scale cultural and geopolitical reconfiguration in part through China's economic ascent. It is important to recognize architecture's historical contributions to this development, which informs how we understand its role today and imagine what may come next.

PART I

Anticipation

CHAPTER 1

Reception

On February 21, 1972, U.S. President Richard Nixon landed on the tarmac of the Beijing Airport aboard Air Force One. The flight, composed of a circuitous route via Honolulu, Guam, and Shanghai, underscored both the logistical difficulties of international travel at the time and the delicate geopolitics at stake. No U.S. president had ever visited the PRC, and it was unclear just what such a visit might portend. Early indications revealed an understated, tightly controlled Chinese reception. President Nixon was greeted by twelve people at the airport, including Premier Zhou Enlai, and as his motorcade made its way into central Beijing, U.S. officials saw nothing but deserted streets. The Chinese government, fearing the meeting would alienate both its populace and other socialist allies, completely cordoned residents off of the procession's main route. The only evidence of active, urban life consisted of brief glimpses of people several blocks away—an odd distancing effect that contributed to the event's surreal and unprecedented nature.[1]

The trip, long considered a turning point in the Cold War and U.S.-China relations, provided a catalyst in the party's internal efforts to reimagine Beijing's diplomatic infrastructure. Years prior to Nixon's visit, in fact, Zhou and others had already begun to pursue the design of new spaces for diplomatic exchange both at home and abroad, particularly as evidence mounted of the Cultural Revolution's catastrophic effects on China and officials began to reassess the country's uncertain prospects after Mao.[2] New forms and practices of architecture were already beginning to emerge within China that indicated broad cultural, economic, and political shifts taking place unrelated to the U.S. president's visit. Yet Nixon and Mao's meeting contributed additional urgency to the task of building new spaces within which China's relationship to other foreign countries could be better managed. Reform was by no means a foregone conclusion at this point, but party leadership understood that the country's existing economic conditions required improvement—a scenario, as this chapter argues, for which architecture was uniquely equipped.

Between 1970 and 1975, the completion of projects such as the Beijing Hotel, new diplomatic residential towers, the Friendship Store, the

International Club, and construction of Chinese and U.S. liaison offices in Washington, D.C., and Beijing aided China's search for greater reciprocity with the world at large.[3] As the number and scale of China's international engagements increased and its domestic plans for economic development began to emerge, these projects accommodated these needs. A contemporaneous series of architectural and infrastructural works designed and built by Chinese technicians in Africa, most notably the Tanzania-Zambia Railway Authority (TAZARA) Railway, underscore that China's expanded diplomatic sphere was by no means limited to Western Europe and North America, however, though the rapid blossoming of U.S.-China relations both overshadowed and dovetailed with a broader reconfiguration of China's international interests.

In coordination with the announcement of improved U.S.-China relations, for example, Mao approved a State Planning Commission proposal to spend \$4.3 billion USD in hard currency on complete sets of industrial manufacturing equipment from the West at the same time that China's financial commitment to the TAZARA Railway totaled over \$400 million USD. A dramatic increase in U.S.-China trade, from \$4.9 million USD in 1971 to \$111 million USD in 1972 and over \$900 million USD in 1973, helped to offset such costs.[4] U.S. participants understood these deals as potential steps toward China's economic liberalization, and it generated a "euphoria" that rippled through the world's business community.[5] As new forms of foreign capital began to flow into the country, however, questions also arose concerning how to best manage China's new partnerships, its continued commitment to socialist revolution, and its support of other developing countries in advancing their own nation-building projects.

The search for appropriate, party-accepted forms of architectural production and expression capable of addressing these challenges necessitated new forms of architectural making and knowledge that set in motion consequential changes concerning architecture's relationship to Mao and the Chinese state. This chapter examines that pivot, which needs be seen as more than simply an exercise in stylistic recalibration, particularly given its occurrence at a time in which the embrace of foreign ideas remained fraught with the possibility of political repercussion and the task of achieving consensus among party leaders was difficult. In fact, increasingly rancorous infighting among the party's radical and moderate factions over the country's direction forward found a certain expression in such architectural work, which official party mouthpieces framed as consistent with Chairman Mao's revolutionary objectives, despite its clear technical and aesthetic divergence from the proletarian ideological aims claimed to be at the core of the Cultural Revolution.

For a Chinese architectural workforce pummeled by accusations of bourgeois elitism, disrupted by the country's civil unrest, and largely unfamiliar with the rigors of international building standards, these projects proved difficult to realize, and as lingering Cultural Revolution–era ideology clashed with the technical realpolitik of the new construction taking place, contradictions mounted that threatened to further affect the party's ability to rule. Problems also presented themselves abroad, where Chinese designers, technicians, and diplomats alike were tasked with representing China through forms of artistic and architectural expression specific to a foreign context with which they were unfamiliar, at a time in which the trajectory of the party's domestic politics was difficult to predict. Embedded within these contradictions and problems, however, lay the conceptual designs of a basic if uncertain way forward.

DESIGN AND DIPLOMACY

In socialist China, the physical production of buildings was both an index and symbol of the party's rule. Architecture was also an important instrument through which officials orchestrated the country's foreign affairs. High-level, temporary guests of state often stayed in Diaoyutai, an exclusive party compound located in the city's center and composed of diplomatic guesthouses and residences for elite party members. Controlling the party's image was essential to its international messaging, and space offered a means by which visiting officials' impressions of the country could be shaped toward the party's objectives. Diaoyutai served these purposes well. The heavily guarded complex was under constant surveillance and was rarely if ever glimpsed by outsiders in its entirety, resulting in visitors' fragmented recollections of estimated spatial arrangements and dimensions (fig. 6).

Hotels, which were also under tight state control, provided alternative accommodations to foreign guests while also dictating where and how visitors would experience socialist China. Buildings such as Beijing's Peace Hotel, completed by Yang Tingbao in 1953, projected a certain aesthetic austerity in keeping with the capital's urban atmosphere, while its multiple secondary entrances allowed individual groups of foreign dignitaries to be discreetly funneled through the city independently of each other. Working in combination with an interlocking spiral of entertainment spaces, including a banquet hall, dining room, recreation room, and teahouse, the hotel effectively cordoned visitors off from the radical, occasionally violent reconfigurations taking place within Chinese society over the course of the 1950s and more particularly the 1960s.[6] Following time spent at the hotel as a member of the much-publicized Simone de Beauvoir and Jean-Paul Sartre–led delegation to China in 1955, Michael Croft described its spaces as "having an atmosphere of their own, for nobody is ever seen to pay a bill and, while everybody is being looked after by somebody else, nobody seems to know who anybody else is.... People talk in little groups at their own tables, are provided with their wants, retire to their rooms, disappear in government coaches and cars, but what they have been doing and where they are going are questions which nobody cares to ask."[7]

Over the course of the late 1950s and early 1960s, Beijing's foreign hotels and existing diplomatic compounds supported a small but interconnected diplomatic community consisting of forty or so representatives from both the communist and capitalist blocs. Some foreign residents lived northeast of the city center in Sanlitun, an area earmarked by the government specifically for foreign embassies; others resided in a residential compound completed in 1959 near Ritan Park along Chang'an Avenue due east of Tiananmen Square. Following Zhou's 1962 establishment of the Beijing Diplomatic Service Bureau to oversee the growing spatial demands of China's international affairs upon the nation's capital, proposals to build new diplomatic residential facilities surfaced in 1969.[8] A 20,300-square-meter site was targeted for development near the residential block built on Chang'an Avenue in 1959, though these efforts were temporarily derailed by the Cultural Revolution.[9] Belgian Sinologist Pierre Ryckmans, who wrote under the pseudonym Simon Leys, described these sites in 1972 as "ghettoes" and "joyless" facilities that resembled "part army barracks, part railway station, part hospital."[10]

Through these spaces, the government effectively limited the foreign community's access to the city at large, producing forms of diplomatic life that were by many accounts peculiar and alienating. Many restaurants did not serve foreigners, and travel outside the capital's municipal

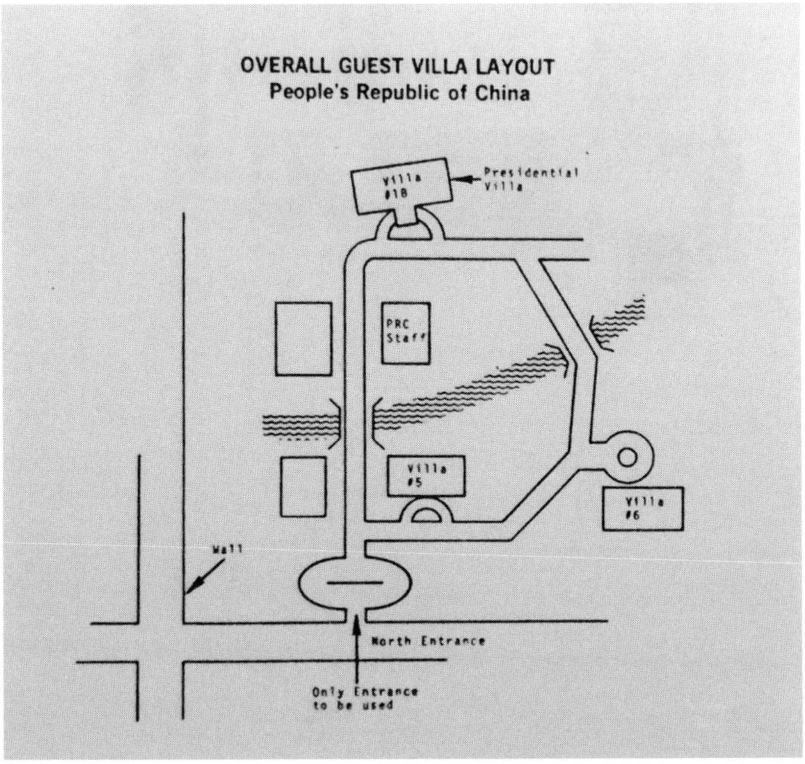

Fig. 6 Plan, Diaoyutai Compound, Beijing, ca. 1973.

limits required special permission. Contact with Chinese residents was restricted to those people who worked in these buildings, embassies, or hotels as guards, cooks, cleaners, and drivers. Diplomatic activity took place in formal reception rooms located in hotels or occasionally a public building. Most of these spaces accommodated twenty to twenty-five people and were often filled with various pieces of furniture, including couches and chairs covered with white antimacassars and oriented armrest to armrest to facilitate photography. Tables positioned in front of these seats offered room for paper and tea. Such facilities were stage sets for ceremonial activity, rather than for active, sustained, and occasionally contentious negotiations.[11] The intimate and constrained state of affairs also produced odd diplomatic bedfellows; representatives from Great Britain, for example, were known to openly socialize with their Soviet adversaries, blurring the ideological battle lines of the Cold War era.[12]

The Cultural Revolution further hampered already limited opportunities for social engagement and outreach, particularly as foreign representatives found themselves a specific target of public ire. In 1967, for example, public mobs burned the British Embassy in Beijing and attacked its employees in the streets. Despite these uncertainties, however, Beijing's diplomatic community gradually grew thanks in large part to dogged efforts on the part of Zhou and others at international outreach, particularly throughout Africa and other parts of the decolonizing world. Plans to expand the city's diplomatic housing reemerged in 1969 as China committed to the distribution of approximately $722.5 million USD in foreign aid to allies throughout the developing world—a figure that dwarfed the country's commitments in previous years.[13] Over half of this funding was earmarked for the construction of the TAZARA Railway.

Other funded projects included canal and road construction projects in Algeria, agricultural development in Senegal and the Upper Volta, and general economic and technical support to Benin, Burundi, Madagascar, Mauritius, Nigeria, Rwanda, Togo, and Tunisia, among others. As China's international promises grew, the number of foreign dignitaries traveling to and from Beijing increased. New housing on both the Jianguomen Wai and Qijiayuan sites was expected to accommodate the city's expanded diplomatic corps, though the design and construction of new diplomatic residential facilities remained a sensitive proposition, both due to intra-party controversy over the direction of China's international affairs, and to the fact that China's architectural community was still reeling from attacks of elitism as a result of the Cultural Revolution.

Responsibility for the projects fell to small working groups of young architects within the Beijing Institute of Architectural Design (BIAD) under the tutelage of a handful of older architects who had lost their jobs during the Cultural Revolution, only to be rehabilitated by the government in the hopes that their expertise in construction and city planning would hasten the projects' successful completion.[14] Party stalwarts Wan Li and

Zhao Pengfei were also assigned to these efforts to ensure that the buildings satisfied the government's vision. With little consensus between officials and architects regarding the aesthetic direction forward, however, a handful of younger, less-experienced team members such as Wu Guanzhang, Weng Rubi, Ma Guoxin, Liu Yongliang, Song Shifen, and others were given unique latitude over the work, the forms and appearance of which reflected foreign-originated, so-called modernist architectural ideas introduced into China over time both prior to and after 1949.[15] By 1972 a nine-story building had been completed on the Jianguomen Wai site; several structures on the adjacent Qijiayuan site also began to take shape over the course of 1972 and 1973.

Procedurally, however, socialist design practices remained intact. For the design of the Qijiayuan buildings, teams worked collaboratively to produce eighteen different block types before reducing the scheme to three distinctive types, including a plate column model, a tower model, and the preferred option, a composite of the two. The composite strategy led to a proposed arrangement consisting of two sixteen-story high-rises and three smaller, six-story blocks. Room layouts were determined through a similar fashion. Three distinctive options were initially proposed for the compound's two tallest towers, including a symmetrical block plan, a trident plan, and the final choice, an interlocking rectangular plan, which accommodated both one- and two-bedroom units and included kitchens, living rooms, and bathrooms (figs. 7, 8). Proposed amenities included balconies, elevators, individual water units, large plate-glass windows, and concrete latticework along the balconies—all unprecedented features in average Chinese residential architecture. Structurally, too, each building was unique and consisted of rectangular, reinforced concrete slab construction, with prestressed concrete beams and purlins used to strengthen and support the complex's two sixteen-story towers, which became the tallest buildings in Beijing upon their completion in 1973.

Collectively, these projects posed challenges to architects seeking to reengage with international design trends, accommodate the country's own technological limitations, and provide both foreign emissaries and the party with the spaces and symbols appropriately aligned to the party's diplomatic recalibrations.[16] Large prefabricated wall panels had not previously been widely used for high-rise construction in China, and though their use allowed builders to both build higher and incorporate new convection radiator heating units throughout the entire complex, they also taxed the country's building expertise.[17] The technology imbued the complex with a lightness of form relative to average Chinese construction even as it also made the building process more "troublesome" than anticipated, requiring more time and labor than what the project's coordinating engineering team had originally intended.[18] Aesthetically, the towers' horizontal bands of outdoor terracing enlivened

Fig. 7 Qijiayuan Foreign Diplomatic Compound, Weng Rubi and others, Beijing Institute of Architectural Design, Beijing, 1969–73. Originally published in *New Chinese Architecture* (*Xin Zhongguo jianzhu*, 1976).

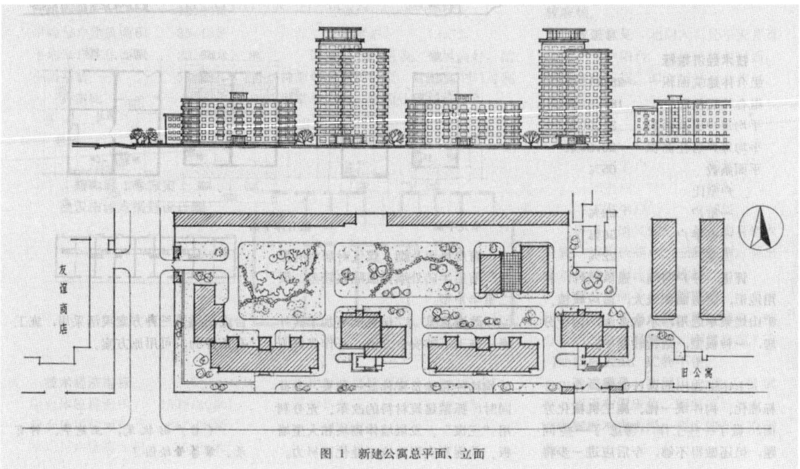

Fig. 8 Site plan and elevations, Foreign Diplomatic Compound, Beijing Institute of Architectural Design, Beijing, 1969–73. Originally published in *Architectural Journal* (*Jianzhu Xuebao*), no. 1 (1974).

their façades with a novel texture and depth as seen from the street below—a contrast to much of Beijing's urban environment, which consisted of mid-rise symmetrical residential compounds built of thick, flat, reinforced concrete walls.

In their privileging of structural and aesthetic innovation against the economic and political risks of labor wastefulness, Beijing's new diplomatic buildings gestured toward some new direction in design thinking that would reverberate throughout the country. State-run media trumpeted the boldness of the scheme, though in an effort to temper the buildings' striking departure from precedent, articles also detailed the buildings' primary significance as embodiments of collective acts of design. The design team, for example, was lauded for a layout that would "mobilize the masses" in the face of ongoing class struggle, despite the project's intended clientele.[19] Group-based compromise was an operative theme highlighted as particularly crucial to the project's composition—an asymmetrical and cost-effective arrangement of the complex's tallest residential towers and more modest apartment blocks bound together through circulation and landscaping to produce a "rich" and vital streetscape.[20] The complex's visibility, coupled with its programmatic remove from everyday life, offered its foreign residents both a limited form of access to China and freedom from China, while locals, who were otherwise prohibited from entering the facility, could do little but marvel at its monumentality from afar. The project's unprecedented technological and structural bravado was framed as emblematic of the Cultural Revolution's still smoldering, utopian spirit, but in these same exceptional qualities lay the makings of a different political project—one that would test the government's capability and willingness to accommodate difference.[21]

Beijing's new residential compounds were accompanied by the International Club, which was designed by BIAD designer Wu Guanzhang and others to serve as the social hub for the city's foreign diplomatic corps (figs. 9, 10). It was originally intended for construction beginning in 1966 to replace the city's preexisting international club, which was described in May 1972 by Joseph Kraft in the pages of the *New Yorker* as "a virtually unused white frame structure with peeling paint, landscaping gone to seed, an empty swimming pool, and a volleyball court where members used to play tennis."[22] Due to the disruption of the Cultural Revolution, the new facility was not completed until later that same year, and consisted of a low-rise compound that included several two- and three-story structures organized around a series of courtyards and exterior paths.

The presence of a vehicular roundabout via the building's main Jianguomen Wai street entrance and parking indicate visitors were expected to arrive at the club via automobile, a rare luxury in China at the time. To the lobby's north lay coat and meeting rooms, while to the south, one found barbershops for men and women and a reading room. Extending from the main lobby were separate Chinese and foreign dining rooms. The complex also featured a theater stage and auditorium, health club, billiard room, and ping-pong room, while air-conditioning and elevators contributed to the creation of a technologically sophisticated environment designed for elite comfort and play. In the club's extensive array of privileged recreational and leisure activities, however, design challenges emerged, with few, if any, of the assigned designers, let alone the majority of the country's population, having had any access or experience with these spaces. Unfamiliarity on the part of the project's designers with the labor and cost required to sustain such amenities led to budgeting woes that limited the building's performance following its completion and underscored both the design-related and political adjustments required

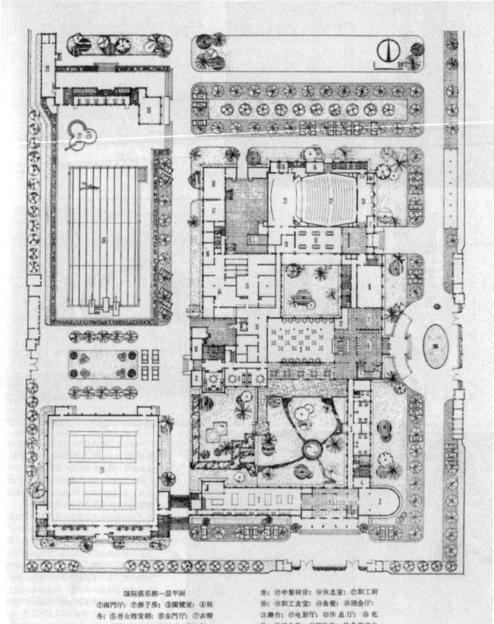

Fig. 9 International Club, Wu Guanzhang, Ma Guoxin, and others, Beijing Institute of Architectural Design, Beijing, 1971–72. Originally published in *New Chinese Architecture* (*Xin Zhongguo jianzhu*, 1976).

Fig. 10 Plan, International Club, Wu Guanzhang, Ma Guoxin, and others, Beijing Institute of Architectural Design, Beijing, 1971–72. Originally published in *Architectural Journal* (*Jianzhu Xuebao*), no. 1 (1973).

to accommodate the demands of foreign-derived consumption standards within China's planned economy.[23]

The Friendship Store, designed and constructed east of the International Club over the same period, also anticipated expatriate demands (figs. 11, 12). With the city's native Chinese and foreign populations required to use different currencies, the Friendship Store provided one

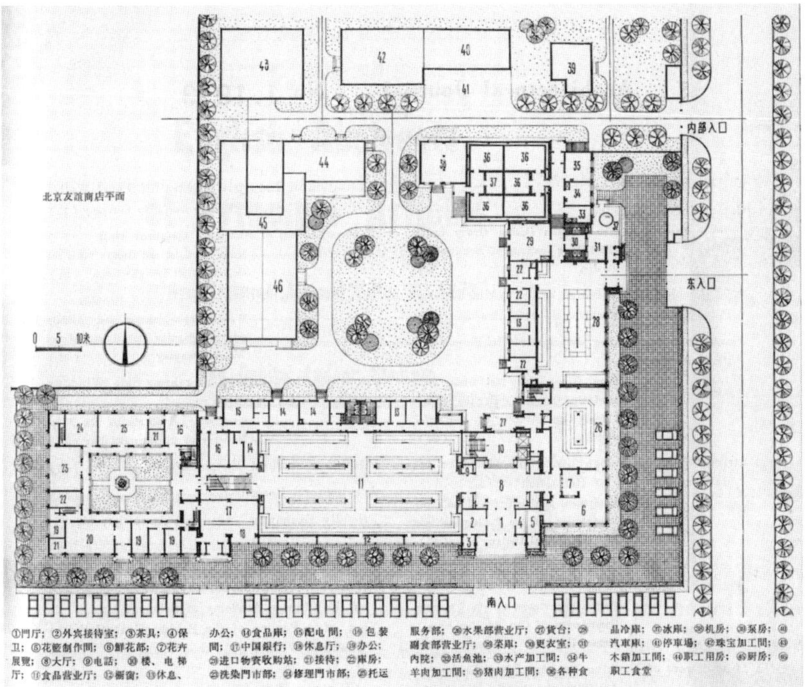

Fig. 11 Friendship Store, Wu Guanzhang and others, Beijing Institute of Architectural Design, Beijing, 1971–72. Originally published in *New Chinese Architecture* (*Xin Zhongguo jianzhu*, 1976).

Fig. 12 Plan, Friendship Store, Wu Guanzhang and others, Beijing Institute of Architectural Design, Beijing, 1971–72. Originally published in *Architectural Journal* (*Jianzhu Xuebao*), no. 1 (1973).

of the only sites where the city's foreign population could purchase anything. Items for sale included liquor, toiletries, porcelain, furs, jade, straw objects, jewelry, clothing, flowers, shrubs, fruits and vegetables, fish and meat, chocolate and sweets, nuts, sporting goods, shoes, cameras, fabric, bicycles, umbrellas, paper goods, souvenirs, and other general needs. Its array of goods underscored its central role in the lives of most of Beijing's expatriates and as a site for impromptu social encounters between various segments of the city's expansive and diverse diplomatic corps. Its form, consisting of a simple cubic volume articulated by a rigid, orthogonal concrete structure perforated by windows and several hollow block screen walls, echoed the architectural language of both the International Club and the diplomatic residential towers. Along the building's south façade, BIAD designers positioned the store's main food hall, repair shop, and consignment bureau. The east entrance provided access to additional markets for fresh produce, dry goods, meat, and live fish. A central, circular driveway provided access into the block's interior for delivery trucks while also separating the site's main grocery spaces from a series of showrooms devoted to jewelry and handicrafts, including wooden furniture.[24]

The 1974 completion of the Beijing Hotel's new east wing composed the fourth and final architectural component of Beijing's expanded international sphere following the construction of the diplomatic residential compound, the International Club, and the Friendship Store. The hotel's location in the center of Beijing, due west of these other buildings along the city's most celebrated boulevard, Chang'an Avenue, anchored the city's rejuvenated diplomatic axis. Designed in response to the existing hotel's deterioration, the east addition was expected to provide new amenities to foreign tourists, who were becoming a vital source of foreign currency to the Chinese government, as well as to growing numbers of businesspeople arriving in the city and unable to find adequate office and housing space.[25]

China's hotels became de facto offices for many corporations and organizations eager to capitalize on its rapprochement with countries such as the United States, though few of the country's existing facilities were equipped to handle the technological and logistical demands of international business activity.[26] The Beijing Hotel's east addition addressed these shortcomings by providing a new, pioneering structure with well-furnished rooms, attractive and comfortable public spaces and services, contemporary logistical operations, and advanced mechanical and electrical equipment (fig. 13). Buoyed by a relatively relaxed public atmosphere in the capital after 1972, the project's designers were encouraged to "go all out and strive for the best."[27] The final design of the Beijing Hotel emerged through a contentious and intergenerational design competition, and was eventually led by a team of young designers headed by Cheng Delan with oversight provided by Zhang Bo, a chief BIAD architect who had been disgraced during the Cultural Revolution, with additional assistance provided by Zhang Kaiji and Yuan Ershi, two other established, senior architects. The building featured a number of tightly jointed orthogonal planes efficiently arranged into several sets of spacious, ceremonial halls topped by sixteen floors of rooms, though its program, which included separate foreign and Chinese dining halls as

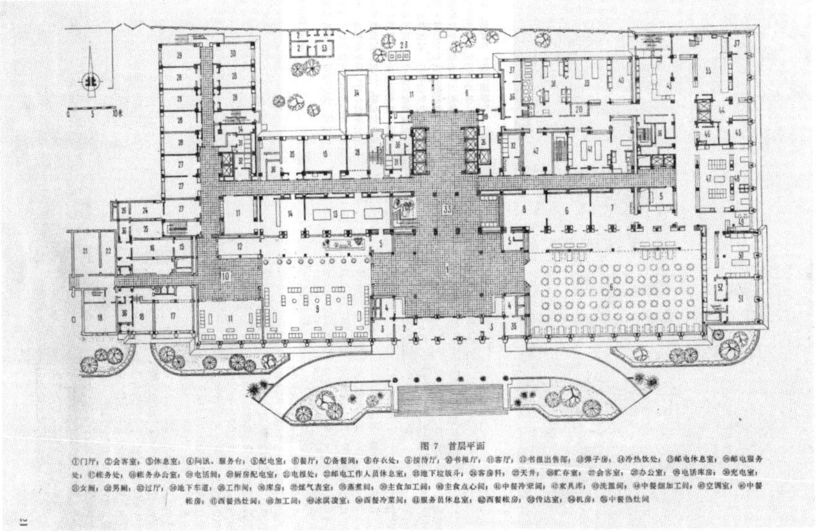

Fig. 13 Ground floor plan, Beijing Hotel, Zhang Bo, Cheng Delan, and others, Beijing Institute of Architectural Design, Beijing, 1970–74. Originally published in *Architectural Journal* (*Jianzhu Xuebao*), no. 5 (1974).

well as kitchens, coupled with the appearance of more technologically advanced utilities such as a telegram and telephone operator's office, registered the political mediations taking place and the intensified international economic interactivity they had begun to support.

Given the building's prominent location and significance relative to the country's diplomatic agenda, emphasis was placed on projecting visible evidence of China's industrial and technological sophistication. As in the city's diplomatic residences, the building's reinforced steel, in-situ-cast concrete structure was designed to support precast reinforced concrete panels, reducing the need for on-site concrete casting and allowing for a taller building. Double-loaded corridors provided ample space for circulation, elevator cores, and lobbies, while a central mechanical room allowed staff to monitor the hotel's interior temperature and ensure guests' comfort—the first building in Beijing to have such capability.[28]

Upon its 1974 completion, the eighty-meter structure was publicly promoted as a fitting monument to mark the twenty-fifth anniversary of the country's founding. To that end, everything in the building was made in China, a fact hotel staff were eager to point out to foreign visitors.[29] Privately, however, intraparty controversy had already arisen around the building's height, which provided unobstructed sight lines into both the Forbidden City and the government's headquarters and private residences in Zhongnanhai to the west, and eventually necessitated the construction of a series of new buildings blocking its view.

Moreover, and despite official rationalizations of the hotel as a testament to Mao's ongoing revolution, its design and construction also undermined the ideological and technical capabilities of the party apparatus in consequential ways. The prefabrication technology used for both the diplomatic compound and the Beijing Hotel produced a lighter massing and overall form that stood in stark contrast to existing construction standards in the city. China's building material manufacturers were not able to mass produce the thin panels necessary to properly showcase such technology, nor had each project's designers fully mastered the detailing needed to capitalize on such material advancements, resulting in façades that gestured toward a certain structural precision and spatial depth without fully achieving it. The result was an "awkward" beauty that exposed the limitations of China's labor force and fueled state investment in additional research, technology, and training necessary to realize similar projects in the future.[30]

Foreign observers could not believe the production taking place. "Construction work on Third Avenue, or elsewhere in New York, is almost noiseless compared with what assails us here," noted Beijing-based U.S. Chief Liaison Officer David Bruce in August 1973. "Pile drivers to right, bulldozers to left, cranes to the rear, volley and thunder weekdays and Sundays. The present estimate is that five diplomatic compounds are to be finished by Christmas in our immediate neighborhood."[31] *South China Morning Post* editors explained, "The pictures may look like a familiar scene from Hong Kong's building boom. But they are in fact evidence of a new wave of ultra-modern construction that is now sweeping Beijing."[32]

By 1974 these new projects effectively reoriented central Beijing's main east–west axis around the party's goals of greater international engagement, creating a constellation of spaces for international business, diplomatic, and tourist activity. Foreign diplomats, for example, could now enjoy "good housing, international shopping centers, a huge Club having every convenience except a bar, a summer resort, sponsored travel, and other amenities infinitely more luxurious than any open to Chinese bureaucrats, whose spartan life contrasts sharply with that of foreigners," wrote Bruce.[33] Other members of the press described Beijing's new diplomatic landscape and its exclusive amenities as a "little Manhattan" designed to accommodate China's opening to the world, though the metaphor also suggested the elitist, enclave-like sensibilities propelling such work forward.[34] Kitchens, closets, billiards, bowling lanes, swimming pools, tennis courts, air-conditioning, access to international goods—these and other amenities enclosed within these projects were indeed difficult to reconcile with living conditions for most Chinese residents and the weakened but still potent ideological tenets of the Cultural Revolution. Political sensitivities thus imbued the projects with the risk of ideological contradiction.

Despite the diplomatic demands underlying these new spaces and the outward-looking relationships they seemed to accommodate, each project's spatial layout was informed by an inclination toward interiority and isolation that captured these fears by limiting local access and, in turn, foreign experiences of China. Foreign diplomats could, in theory, host dinners or parties in these spaces while pursuing less formal, more spontaneous forms of entertainment and engagement, through these activities that remained difficult to organize. Guards ensured average Chinese residents could not wander into these facilities, while layers of landscaped courtyards, walkways, and tree-lined façades provided additional spatial depth and distance that further discouraged Beijing citizens from entering. Official approval was required for access, and foreign interactions with their Chinese counterparts remained fraught with the formality of performative pageantry.

As a result, and despite the new accommodations, a foreign diplomat's social life consisted of little more than "attending diplomatic receptions, Governmental banquets, trips to the airport, national day celebrations, and protocol calls on colleagues."[35] Such control remained intact over the course of the 1970s, even after Mao's passing. "All day long, one can see faces of passersby peering in through holes in the outer shrubbery to gaze at this new Socialist monument and the strange foreign guests and limousines that issue from it," observed *New Yorker* reporter-at-large Orville Schell during his stay at the Beijing Hotel as part of his first visit to China in 1977. "It is strange that almost our first contact with this proletarian nation should be opulence—a quality alien to most of China."[36]

Nevertheless, the production of these new effects and experiences aligned with certain aesthetic and recreational features to indicate some slight diplomatic and economic détente in motion, even if the direction forward remained unclear. Through such work, the dynamics of expatriate life in China and, by extension, the government's ability to manage them, began to change. As architectural expression, the diplomatic compounds, Friendship Store, International Club, and Beijing Hotel's new wing all owed aspects of their appearances to international architectural trends from the earlier twentieth century, including relatively slender structural formwork, asymmetrical formal compositions, and a striated, orthogonal planarity that can be traced back to the work of Frank Lloyd Wright and the International Style more generally. These influences originally circulated throughout architecture departments at Tsinghua and Tongji universities during the 1950s and early 1960s before being suppressed during the Cultural Revolution. The international design trends evident in such work seemed incongruous with Mao's proletarian vision, which had fueled anti-foreign attacks on embassies in Beijing and Guangzhou just several years prior. Their redeployment offered hints of the shifting aesthetic—and, by extension, political—principles at work, particularly as the limits of Mao's efforts to modernize the country through socialist revolution were becoming increasingly evident.[37]

Nor were Beijing's new monuments isolated architectural endeavors. More than 1,600 kilometers south, for example, a new exhibition hall was completed over roughly the same period in the southeastern city of Guangzhou for the city's annual trade fair, China's largest annual export commodities exposition. Planned for construction on the site of an existing China-Soviet Friendship Building, a new exhibitionary complex was conceived to promote a redirection in China's expanded trade ambitions; it consisted of a new display hall, four new hotels, and the Guangzhou Friendship Store, and coincided with the first invitation of the U.S. business community to the fair in 1972.

As in Beijing, officials scrambled to find the necessary architectural talent to realize their plans, particularly as many of Guangzhou's architects and engineers had been sent down to reeducation camps. Led by figures such as Lin Xi, She Junnan, Mo Bozhi, and Cai Dedao, these efforts materialized between 1972 and 1976 as projects such as the Guangzhou Trade Hall, which featured an approximately 180-meter-long wall composed of transparent glass—the first of its kind in China. An adjacent services building featured an air-conditioned, 750-seat cinema, offices for telegrams and long-distance telecommunications, and shipping and banking operations as part of a massive new renovation of the site. Associated projects included plans for the construction of a highway directly linking Hong Kong to Guangzhou for the first time, creating a new infrastructural corridor between the two cities that prefigured more dynamic economic interactivity to come. A two-story "VIP House" in Shenzhen, a stopover town located nearly 145 kilometers south of Guangzhou along the China–Hong Kong border, was completed in 1974, and by 1975 railway services between Hong Kong and mainland China were extended to address a predicted increase in oil, freight, and passenger through traffic. The White Cloud (Baiyun) Hotel, which became the country's tallest building upon its completion in Guangzhou in 1976, offered early evidence of Hong Kong's notable influence upon mainland China's architectural community.[38]

For foreign observers, these projects signaled cautious if inevitable plans for the country's gradual internationalization as dictated by diplomatic considerations and economic necessity. At least one U.S. business visitor to the fair, for example, perceived that these developments "can only mean that the Chinese are committed to the substantial expansion of their trade relations with the rest of the world."[39] For China's citizens, the vast majority of whom were unaware of the complex intraparty machinations or diplomatic maneuvering taking place, the physical production of buildings also offered one of the rare and unambiguous signs of change afoot. Other, more understated signs also existed; on October 1, 1973, for example, at the twenty-fourth anniversary of the country's founding, officials did not make a public appearance—a subtle but visible indication of intraparty dissension. By the end of the year, no official reports had yet been released to foreign diplomats detailing the conclusions reached at the Tenth People's Congress held earlier that August, in another sign of major disagreement existing among the party's ranking members.[40] One year later, on October 1, 1974, neither Mao nor Zhou participated in the public events celebrating the PRC's twenty-fifth anniversary. Many of the CCP's younger leaders were present, but the absence of Mao meant that no parade could be held to commemorate the important date.[41] The particular erasure of this traditional party spectacle, which party watchers perceived as evidence of a widening schism at the heart of the country's politics, further attested to uncertain semiotics and party dynamics at work. Beijing's new monuments projected some kind of transition few could deny.

THE LIAISON OFFICE

Repairing China's economy in the immediate wake of the Cultural Revolution required more than new diplomatic amenities. It also necessitated new trading partners, including committed "imperialists" such as the United States.[42] By 1971 China had lost almost one hundred international economic enterprises involving private foreign capital due to fear over the Cultural Revolution, including textile and paper mills, rubber factories, sugar refineries, and hydroelectric plants originally established in the early to mid-1950s along the southeastern coasts of Guangdong and Fujian provinces and former treaty ports such Tianjin and Shanghai.[43]

Such disruption crippled China's industrial production, dropped the country's standard of living and economic productivity to among the lowest in the world, posed logistical challenges to many large-scale construction projects, and gutted its educational system. The party's more moderate faction considered the reestablishment of these connections as vital to the country's economic future. President Nixon's February 1972 visit to Beijing was an important step in stabilizing China's diplomatic and economic footing, though it also left party leaders polarized over how to balance the effects of ongoing class warfare and greater international interactivity.

The years 1972 and 1973 marked an unprecedented moment of optimism for Sino-American relations. Former U.S. ambassador to China Arthur Hummel described "the huge flood of euphoria" with regards to U.S.-China relations following Nixon's trip, which fed an immediate and speculative spike in trade and the materialization of a range of economic and cultural exchanges.[44] Examples included intensified exchanges of delegations from the American Economic Association, the National Committee on United States-China Relations, and the National Council for United States-China Trade as well as the first multimillion dollar U.S.-Chinese business deals, including one between Pullman Kellogg Company and the Chinese government for the construction of seven nitrogen-fixation plants for synthetic urea production. One year later, in February 1973, U.S. Secretary of State Henry Kissinger traveled to Beijing and found his conversations with Mao to be "the freest and most candid, and our reception the most cordial . . . of any of my visits."[45]

It was during this trip that Kissinger and Zhou agreed to establish unofficial embassies called "liaison offices" through which U.S. and PRC officials could communicate with each other without threatening existing diplomatic relations between the United States and Taiwan. With so many unresolved economic and political issues at stake between the PRC and the United States and significant doubts as to what could be safely discussed between the two countries without the threat of geopolitical recourse, the physical construction of space for negotiation and dialogue was an important and delicate matter. Architecture created a sphere for experimentation. It proved capable of demarcating the administrative and logistical terrain for a further strengthening of relations should both parties want them to occur, while its physicality provoked discussions of the future of U.S.-China relations, in particular the necessary laws and codes of political exchange that would later enable formal normalization to occur.

Negotiations through space, form, and material contributed to the diplomatic mediations taking place. The arrival of ten members of China's first liaison delegation in Washington, D.C., in April 1973 consummated "one of the most delicate arrangements in modern diplomatic history."[46] Of foremost concern was the acquisition of space to support the endeavor. China's potential purchase of real estate in the United States, and vice versa, posed daunting legal and spatial challenges, particularly given the lack of formal relations between the two countries. Certain protocols that distinguished the PRC's presence in Washington from that of the Republic of China were also important considerations.

Some of these measures proved relatively easy to establish. For example, the group was not met at the airport by any formal diplomatic delegation. Huang Zhen, head of the People's Republic of China liaison office, was to be referred to as "chief," along with his deputy chief, Han Xu, former chief of protocol in the Foreign Ministry.[47] Other standard diplomatic immunities, including tax and customs exemption, proved more difficult to resolve, however. Property taxes posed a particularly thorny obstacle. Although any real property acquired by a foreign government for specific diplomatic purposes was typically granted a tax exemption, the exceptionality of the liaison office disqualified it from such freedoms. Rectifying this exclusion required congressional legislation authorizing the U.S. president to extend to China's liaison mission and its staff those privileges equivalent to standard diplomatic missions.[48] Moreover, extending diplomatic immunity to the PRC required that the U.S. government be granted similar rights by China—a move that was eventually completed in early 1973.

The temporal dimension of China's accommodations in Washington was also of key concern. In addition to a liaison building, housing was also needed for the delegation's chief of mission and staff. Mainland officials believed that the existing Chinese embassy, then occupied and maintained by Taiwan, was rightful PRC property, and PRC representatives were initially content seeking only a "stopgap" solution to their housing needs, with the possibility of forcibly removing Taiwanese officials from the premises not appearing to have been officially considered.[49] PRC officials visited several available properties in the Washington area with the help of U.S. assistance before focusing their attention on the purchase of a private residence off of Embassy Row for the delegation's chief of mission. The Windsor Park Hotel, an apartment and hotel complex located at 2300 Connecticut Avenue, along with the St. Albans apartment building at 2310 Connecticut Avenue, was identified as a desirable location for embassy staff housing (fig. 14).[50] The properties were eventually secured in July and November 1973 for approximately $500,000 and $5.5 million USD, respectively, at which point officials moved in and began renovations.[51] As the U.S. State Department worked to produce the legal framework necessary to allow Chinese officials to operate within the country, the liaison delegation temporarily settled into twelve rooms, each equipped with color television sets and air-conditioning, within the Mayflower Hotel.[52]

As a building type designed to accommodate transition, the Windsor Park Hotel was a logical purchase. Chinese officials determined available apartment houses to be too extravagant and expressed concern over the possibility of tenants who might prove difficult to evict.[53] A hotel, by contrast, addressed China's spatial requirements and was theoretically easier to empty. It also provided the delegation with all of the accoutrements considered necessary for the exercise of international diplomacy, including the facility's restaurant, silverware, dishes, three changes of white sheets and pillowcases, and two hundred black-and-white television sets.[54]

Renovation work proceeded over the following year and included the raising of the ceiling of the Windsor Park Hotel's lobby to accommodate the hanging of a ceremonial lamp and white-striped moiré satin

Fig. 14 Windsor Park Hotel, Washington, D.C.

wallpaper. Thirty Chinese laborers traveled to Washington to complete the process, which also involved carpet and brocade installation, the purchase of crimson velvet lounge chairs, tables inset with marble, and contemporary silk embroidery decor. Chinese liaison officials, perhaps sensitive to the extravagance of their aesthetic decisions, publicly noted that all of the renovation decisions were done collectively, and that liaison staff had also "helped a bit" with the installation work itself.[55] Nevertheless, the design and aesthetic decisions had an impact on U.S. perceptions of Chinese diplomacy and its priorities. "Not all communist states reflect the austerities of their ideology in the embassy buildings they choose," bluntly concluded one U.S. journalist in response to the showy renovations taking place.[56]

The U.S. delegation, led by Chief Liaison Officer Bruce, arrived in Beijing in May 1973 and encountered similar difficulties. That April an advance team preceded the official delegation to scour the city looking for property. They toured a site located in northwest Beijing before settling on a plot of land for the liaison office closer to the city's center, east of Tiananmen Square, near the new diplomatic compound, the International Club, and the Friendship Store. U.S. officials resided just west of the site in the Beijing Hotel as the new liaison offices and permanent U.S. residences were constructed by an estimated force of three hundred workmen and technicians working twenty-four hours a day, seven days a week. The building was officially completed on July 1, 1973.

The liaison office was itself a relatively simple construction project, and like Beijing's other recently completed diplomatic works, it featured a rigid orthogonal form composed of prefabricated panels (fig. 15). U.S. diplomat Charles W. Freeman, Jr., recalled, "I drew a building and explained that the top floor should have no windows, and that this should all be built to vault specifications and whatnot. Two hours later, they called us back and showed us a completed architectural drawing." The city's Number 1 Construction Company worked around the clock to finish the building per State Department specifications. Freeman described the construction process as "basically using workers and throwing them away when they were exhausted. They built the whole thing in sixteen days, and most beautifully. The upper story, where the communications were to be, had false windows, so it looked perfectly normal from the outside. And inside, it had beautiful walnut paneling."[57]

These initial encounters with Chinese labor reinforced positive U.S. impressions of China's seemingly inexhaustible workforce and their unerring commitment to the task at hand—selling points pushed by U.S. companies and government agencies interested in expanding into China despite the fragile and uncertain trajectory of early U.S.-China relations. The performative spectacle of Chinese labor notwithstanding, however, the project involved a complex and unprecedented construction process in the capital requiring layers of administrative responsibility that

Fig. 15 U.S. Liaison Office, Beijing, 1973.

disrupted standard procedure in Beijing, just as the establishment of a Chinese liaison office tested U.S. law. An intersecting tangle of municipal, national, and international interests engaged in the project's construction, including members of the Beijing Municipal Construction Committee, BIAD, and the city's Bureau of Construction and Engineering with involvement from the Beijing Municipal Gas Company, the Beijing Municipal Telephone Bureau, and the Bureau of Power Supply.[58]

It was in part through these early trials that Chief Liaison Officer Bruce and other U.S. officials urged caution in relation to the future of U.S.-China relations. Bruce, for one, saw the undeniable potential of China as a new market for U.S. businesses, particularly in relation to construction; just months following his arrival in Beijing, for example, he noted in his diary that "with bricklayers and carpenters available at wages of about fifty cents American a day, a foreign capitalist if permitted by the Government—but he would not be—could engage in an orgy of building."[59] Yet Bruce also read in China's deep-seated suspicions over U.S. motives and the party's insistence upon self-sufficiency in early negotiations evidence that U.S. enthusiasm regarding China's potential willingness to transform its domestic industries with U.S. trade and investment interests in mind was premature, if not entirely misguided.

By 1974, and despite the difficulties surrounding the new relationship, both missions had become important if exceptional mechanisms in facilitating diplomatic and commercial communication between China and the United States. That February, Bruce acknowledged in his personal diary that the liaison office's "inadequate office building" had become overcrowded, with a number of personnel having already spent more than one year living in a hotel.[60] Regardless, the Chinese government warned U.S. officials that no more housing would be granted until the needs of other international missions had been fulfilled. The indistinct, tentative nature of their coexistence remained, but such ambiguity was, in fact, an essential component of their shared purpose, insofar as it allowed them to function "practically as embassies (and consulates)" despite no formal basis to do so.[61] In Washington, China's liaison office ballooned to eighty staff, while in Beijing, twenty-six U.S. employees and a rotating team of U.S. Marines worked within the compound, though most lived in the nearby Friendship and Beijing hotels.

Through each office, a basic geography for diplomatic life began to materialize, including the identification of schools and housing for liaison employees and their families. Parties and receptions provided opportunities for U.S. and Chinese representatives to acquaint themselves with each other while also providing insights into the administrative frameworks and institutional hierarchies behind each edifice. Clandestine activities also emerged in relation to these spaces. Chinese officials, for example, began to collect information on the size and composition of ethnically Chinese communities in the greater Washington, D.C., area. In Beijing, fears arose among Americans over the likelihood that the liaison was bugged, and officials installed a "so-called bubble, classified conference room built of plastic inside another room," with no windows and blowing fans so that conversations could not be heard.[62] James Roderick Lilley, the CIA's first China-based station chief, successfully secured half of the liaison office's communications room for CIA purposes and installed a darkroom in the facility to share with State Department colleagues.[63]

These Cold War–era anxieties both depended upon and produced architectural conditions of a distinctive isolation from the urban environments in which they existed—rooms nested within rooms capable of operating independently of their surroundings. This deep interiority was demanded by the delicate intelligence maneuvering at work, the need for secure communications with home governments, and shared, pervasive uncertainty over how U.S.-China relations would proceed. The possibility of the mission's failure inevitably influenced the activities and the spaces that enabled them. Design and construction choices were not necessarily determined with permanence in mind; the liaison office, for example, was designed to facilitate engagement, but it could not function as a working embassy did, lest it be perceived as facilitating an active and robust diplomatic mission that could not legally exist. Perceptions of a fundamental incommensurability between U.S. and Chinese society was another factor. With neither side completely committed to lasting diplomatic and economic integration, contingency remained a dominant theme of the era and the environments it produced.

ARCHITECTURE AND THE CRITICIZE LIN BIAO, CRITICIZE CONFUCIUS CAMPAIGN, 1973–74

In October 1973, six months after the establishment of U.S. and Chinese liaison offices, drawings and photographs of the diplomatic residential block, club, and Friendship Store were published in *Architectural Journal* (*Jianzhu Xuebao*) with an accompanying editorial comment reminding readers that such work should be attributed to the ceaseless revolutionary efforts of Mao and the Chinese people in advancing the socialist cause.[64] Emphasis was placed on the anonymous labor responsible for these projects, which helped to situate these exceptional spaces within China's broader ideological domain. Nevertheless, such work aggravated oppositional factions within the party's conflicted leadership. On one hand, it enabled the new kinds of diplomatic possibilities favored by Zhou and other party moderates, even as it also courted controversy among the party's more radical, Gang of Four–affiliated members.

These frictions were further laid bare several months earlier at the Tenth Party Congress held in August 1973, when Zhou rejected calls for a revival of the Cultural Revolution and warned cadres of the "great disorder" set to reshape global relations and China's transformed standing vis-à-vis the rest of the world. Zhou quoted Lenin's evocative analysis of world contradictions—"the wind sweeping through the tower heralds a rising storm in the mountains"—and cautioned party representatives of additional turbulence to come.[65] His oratory further strained relations with Jiang and the Gang of Four, who launched the Criticize Lin Biao, Criticize Confucius campaign later that fall and declared war on any and all feudal or capitalist revisionism, in an explicit swipe at Zhou and his allies. The campaign opportunistically coincided with Zhou's hospitalization for bladder cancer and the continued deterioration of Mao's health due to Parkinson's disease, and it allowed Jiang and other Gang of Four–affiliated party members to temporarily wrest control over the country's diplomatic and cultural affairs and demote Deng from the party's upper echelons of power.

Over the course of late 1973 and early 1974, the clique railed against Zhou, the relatively moderate policies he represented, and the architectural interventions he supported. Foreign observers were generally aware of the struggle taking place; as completion neared on several of Beijing's new diplomatic projects, U.S. representatives detected a noticeable ideological shift within the party as major state-run media outlets began to publish warnings concerning China's dangerous exposure to the undue foreign influence of capitalism. The noticeable chill in relations gave way to admissions of regret on the part of U.S. officials that rapprochement had perhaps occurred too quickly, resulting in "absolutely unrealistic expectations, both on the Chinese and on the American side."[66]

Fig. 16 Wu Yinxian, Beijing Hotel, East Addition Dining Room, Beijing, 1975.

Shifting political currents also registered in publicized controversy surrounding the United States' physical presence in Beijing, where the jarring and unseemly visibility of U.S. Marines was aggravated by the opening of a Marine bar called the "Red-Ass Saloon" in the liaison office for after-hours socializing that quickly attracted expatriate residents from Beijing's diplomatic quarter and led to complaints from neighboring residents.[67] News of the construction of a new U.S. embassy in Taipei, in accordance with Nixon's decision to nominate a U.S. ambassador to Taiwan, also tested relations.

Despite these machinations, however, architecture itself proceeded apace; once initiated, the scale, time, and expense of construction made projects like the diplomatic residential compound resistant to the political controversies generated by a months-long campaign against Zhou. Rather, it was in the completion of such work that opportunities for criticism arose. By early 1974, intraparty tension flared up over the use of imperial-era Chinese artwork in the interiors of the new addition to the Beijing Hotel and diplomatic projects, and the perceptions of foreign exceptionalism intimated through such gestures (fig. 16). Zhou had originally approved the production of artwork inspired by traditional Chinese landscape as well as bird and flower paintings to be displayed in the buildings' interiors, and a number of famous, older artists were subsequently summoned from the countryside and tasked with producing traditional Chinese paintings, especially bird and flower and landscape motifs prohibited after 1966, as part of what came to be identified as the Ministry of Foreign Affairs' "Hotel School" initiative. The Gang of Four eagerly made an issue of such production, launching a reassessment of the interior decoration of all foreign-frequented architecture in Beijing, including embassies, hotels, and even restaurants. Over the winter of 1974, the Gang of Four also organized several exhibitions in Shanghai and Beijing focused on these historical, "black" painting traditions, including specific examples from Zhou's approved artworks, many of which were removed.[68]

At the core of the controversy was the synthetic aspect of a foreign visitor's experience of China, and the contradictions these extraordinary atmospheres seemed to evoke. Officials were sensitive to the ways in which these spaces could capably curate subjective, inherently artificial experiences of China, and traditional Chinese culture in particular, at a time in which the country and its cultural identity ostensibly remained firmly tethered to the party. These exceptionalities carried particular bourgeois overtones—a claim Premier Zhou attempted to refute by arguing for the work on the basis that China could begin to support forms of "facing in" as well as "facing out" art in equal measure—the former for domestic Chinese residents prohibited from entering foreign-oriented premises without prior approval, and the latter for the enjoyment of international guests. Hou Yimin, a well-known Chinese muralist involved in the project, later noted that "because hotels mainly serve overseas guests, murals that serve the purpose of educating Chinese citizens and young people about our revolutionary tradition have no place there."[69] The notion that multiple forms of art could simultaneously exist within Chinese society was antithetical to Maoist doctrine, and Zhou's initiative constituted a radical departure from the party's historical efforts to compress so-called high and low forms of cultural production into one collective expression of, and for, the people.[70]

The episode, which would later reverberate in controversies concerning hotel construction in China after 1978, illuminated the entrenched ideological constraints at work within the party and the ways in which a new architecture designed for greater international engagement exposed them. Reform-inclined officials like Zhou understood that the CCP needed to embrace a greater degree of ambassadorial courtesy if it was to be taken seriously as an international partner. To the country's more radical leaders and a Chinese populace long indoctrinated to suspect the undue influence of countries such as Japan and the United States, however, any disturbance from the normative routine threatened to produce social instability, contradiction, and damage to the party.

In 1973, for example, and soon after détente, reports surfaced of foreign visitors being stopped and arrested by a group of schoolgirls in a Beijing *hutong,* or small alley, on suspicion of spying. In Hangzhou, a public bus was apparently flagged down and ordered not to move until several foreign tourists could be transferred to an officially sanctioned hotel minibus.[71] Casting aside such paranoia proved difficult, but moderates remained committed to facilitating a more sustainable degree of international engagement through diplomacy and trade. Censoring artwork composed one strategy for maintaining control in the face of greater international exposure; ensuring architecture's adherence to such limits proved another, different challenge.

PIVOTING FROM THE "FIRST" TO THE "THIRD" WORLDS

As construction of Beijing's diplomatic residential compound and the Beijing Hotel projected China's newfound embrace of international visitors all over the world, and endeavors like the liaison offices advanced an aspirational diplomatic infrastructure with long-standing adversaries like the United States, party leaders also pursued building projects capable of signaling the party's commitment to socialist revolution and the modernization efforts of existing allies throughout the developing world. Beijing-based U.S. officials noted the "assiduous courting" by the party of so-called "Third World countries, especially those in Africa," but the party's ideological recalibration vis-à-vis capitalism prompted confusion and frustration on the part of Mao-inspired leaders such as Guinean President Sékou Touré and Malian President Moussa Traoré.[72] China's economic redirection toward the West thus represented an important hinge point in China's other international engagements that risked destabilizing existing diplomatic relationships and the delicate balance of power at the center of the CCP's leadership.

The TAZARA project embodied these complex ambitions. Initiated in 1965 and eventually completed between 1970 and 1975, the railway was designed and built with significant financial and technical assistance from the PRC. It represented the country's largest, most expensive overseas commitment, though China's support for the project came only after numerous other countries and funding agencies rejected Tanzanian and Zambian officials' requests for assistance—a point CCP leaders shrewdly capitalized upon in championing China's unwavering commitment to anti-imperialism and the benefits of collaboration among its recently decolonized, developing allies, even as it simultaneously pursued relations with a so-called imperialistic superpower such as the United States.

In an effort to underscore their consistent approach to foreign policy, Chinese officials were quick to draw distinctions between aid projects implemented by the United States, which came with risks of exploitation of natural resource or "strategic materials" extraction, and China's own limited support system, which comprised a series of simple commodity credit agreements whereby Chinese goods worth the equivalent of a particular loan could be imported into the partnered country, and the proceeds from their sale could then be used to purchase a partner's goods or to support local costs incurred by Chinese technicians. Other PRC loans took the form of long-term, no-interest bank credits to be repaid through the purchase of Chinese products and materials.[73]

Much has been written about the TAZARA project and its history, including the physical and logistical difficulties involved in its construction, the complicated cross-cultural interplay at work within the Chinese, Tanzanian, and Zambian labor teams, and the themes of mutually beneficial modernization embedded in the project's rapid realization.[74] As a physical artifact of change, however, the project remains an underexamined architectural case study of China's search for an architectural language capable of expressing its increasingly multifaceted international aspirations and the shifting objectives at work in China's own modernization efforts. It also serves as an important counterpoint to China's burgeoning relationship with the United States, which had begun to manifest itself architecturally through projects like the liaison offices.

The technological dimensions to the project also warrant attention, particularly China's decision to deploy valuable technical expertise and equipment to Africa as China simultaneously sought out new sources for advanced technical knowledge from other parts of the world, and at a time in which China was struggling to address its own poverty. Collectively, these aspects all speak to a struggle on the part of China's leaders to reconcile the evident failures of the Cultural Revolution with China's ongoing development work both at home and abroad, and its ability to help in the management of allies' nation-building efforts when its own attempts at modernization through socialism suddenly seemed uncertain.

The TAZARA Railway offered the party an opportunity to address these concerns. Publicly, party leaders celebrated the project as indicative of China's determination to realize socialist revolution around the world through the exportation of its empowered labor and technology in cooperation with socialist-inclined allies equally committed to principles of anti-imperialism. Privately, however, Zhou and others encouraged Chinese workers to ignore the project's ideological dimensions and focus on the task at hand, namely, completing the railway, training African workers, and demonstrating China's technical efficiency. In meeting the

Fig. 17 Train Station, Ministry of Railways Third Design Team, Dar es Salaam, 1974–75.

project's timeline for construction, it was argued, China's political goals would also be achieved.[75] Surveying began in 1965, following which a comprehensive design strategy was formulated. During the construction phase, which began in 1970, Chinese foremen were responsible for organizing work teams composed of local laborers, occasionally resulting in language obstacles and cultural misunderstandings.

In fact, the entire design and construction process itself was managed by thousands of Chinese engineers, with plans and drawings typically completed in Chinese and necessitating Chinese oversight on-site. Given China's lack of foreign currency to exchange, Chinese aid was also predicated on the use of Chinese products, with large gaps of time existing between China's commitment of aid and its actual disbursement. These logistical challenges delayed the project, and it was only by 1974 and early 1975 that the TAZARA's terminal station in Dar es Salaam—the anchoring monument of the massive enterprise—took physical shape (figs. 17, 18).

All of the railway's ninety-three stations were designed and completed by members of the Third Design Team under China's Ministry of Railways and Tanzanian workers. Unlike the railway's other depots, however, Dar es Salaam composed the key terminal point for the project, and the crucial interface between the infrastructure of the railway and the port of Dar es Salaam itself, from which Zambia's natural resources would in theory be shipped around the world. The terminal station consisted of two floors organized around a massive waiting hall topped by a soaring, two-story dome and bands of pivoting windows designed to allow air and daylight to permeate the space below (fig. 19). A stately, central stairway linked both floors, while a basic rectilinear arrangement of offices, lounges, and open-air waiting rooms extended along each of the building's two main wings. Sunken courtyards anchored each wing while providing light and air to the spaces framing them. Visitors approached the ground floor on foot, entering underneath a broad balcony that con-

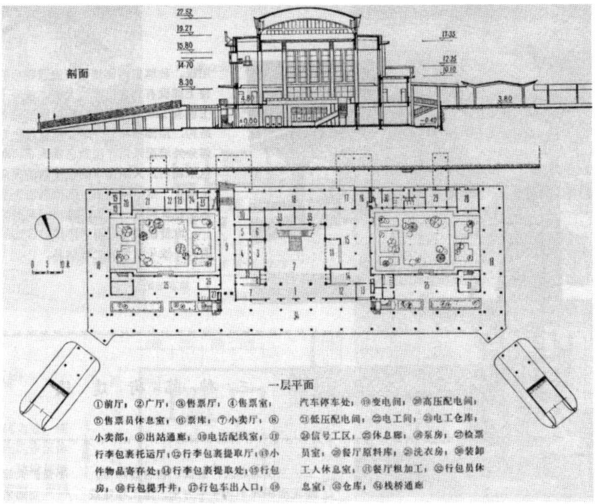

Fig. 18 Plan, Train Station, Ministry of Railways Third Design Team, Dar es Salaam, 1974–75. Originally published in *Architectural Journal* (*Jianzhu Xuebao*), no. 6 (1975).

nected to a car ramp extending from the ground up to the second floor. A series of platforms extended along the station's rail tracks.

Aesthetic and programmatic similarities between the Dar es Salaam station and domestic Chinese projects like the Beijing Hotel and diplomatic residential compound suggest a global congruity to China's efforts to identify a basic syncretic architectural expression capable of capturing its expanding if unsettled worldview. As in China's contemporaneous design work, themes of labor and efficiency figured as dominant organizational and aesthetic motifs. All of the TAZARA Railway's stations were "starkly simple in design and entirely functional," producing an overall aesthetic rooted in material and spatial expressions of China's fundamental reliability.[76]

The Dar es Salaam station was perhaps the best-known, most visible monument of the initiative, and its layout was designed in the shape of the character 工 (*gong*), or work, in accordance with the Chinese Ministry of Railways' insignia but, more generally, to represent the labor force responsible for the project. With this basic spatial organization, the Dar es Salaam station also evoked existing typological models in China, in particular the Beijing and Guangzhou train stations. Other structural and aesthetic features, including its rectangular slab construction and the simple, clean lines articulated along its façade through alternating rhythm of windows and sun-shading, resonated with Chinese domestic examples such as Beijing's International Club and diplomatic compound. Unlike those projects, however, the Dar es Salaam station was a monument to international collaboration built on foreign soil, and it required a certain localized approach. The station's two courtyards acknowledged Dar es Salaam's hot and humid climate, while its open-air waiting rooms were purportedly designed with local customs in mind.[77] Despite these efforts, however, the project was an inherently foreign object that transformed the city upon its completion and, in so doing, posed

Fig. 19 Interior, Train Station, Ministry of Railways Third Design Institute, Dar es Salaam, 1974–75.

conceptual challenges to China's renewed architectural diplomacy moving forward.

ARCHITECTURE, CHINA, AND THE WORLD

Chinese design and construction work between 1970 and 1975 was part of a larger party struggle to reposition China in a world undergoing dramatic political and economic change, though it was unclear at the time just how permanent the transformations taking place might be, and how actively China would contribute to them. That China's emergence would mean something new to the Cold War–infused geopolitics of global architectural production seemed likely, however. On October 24, 1975, the first passenger train from Zambia arrived at the station to a boisterous welcome from crowds, though in an uncomfortable evocation of colonial-era rhetoric used to rationalize Europe's civilizing mission to Africa decades prior, observers described its materialization as a "miraculous apparition which puts one in mind of the emporia of the central European spa towns of 60 years ago."[78] The station immediately became Dar es Salaam's largest single edifice upon its completion: "bigger and more splendid than any other building" in the city, with marble flooring and cream wall tiling that stood in stark contrast to existing Tanzanian architecture.[79] As an effort to reconcile the ideals and facts at the core of the CCP's ideological struggle, the project attempted to square two competing visions of China's socialist modernization but, in doing so, risked exposing its semiotic limitations.

These challenges also echo in boldly confident self-promotions of China's technological superiority vis-à-vis its African partners from the era—rhetoric that was sometimes recognized as being rather misleading but nevertheless registered the complex and conflicted geopolitical perspective of China's leadership. "Our leaders realized that China was rather backward in railway construction," one senior Chinese official was quoted as declaring following the TAZARA Railway's completion, "but we should help countries which are more backward—this is our internationalist duty."[80] Such contradictory self-promotions of China's design expertise relative to that of its allies illuminate China's own anomalous geopolitical standing, and the difficulties it faced in attempting to balance its existing relationships within the Global South with its aspirations for economic integration with a superpower such as the United States.

On one hand, China had the largest population in the world and an ample abundance of resources, with a total Gross Domestic Product (GDP) that made it the world's eighth-largest economy in 1975. A readjustment to a per capita basis, however, left China's production at just $178 USD per person, far below its "backward" partner Zambia ($530 USD).[81] Such statistical dissonance provided Chinese leaders with broad rhetorical latitude to simultaneously claim common ground with poorer and wealthier countries alike, though the increasing visibility of Chinese architectural expertise at home and abroad threatened to expose these discrepancies, resulting in buildings that aimed to concretize China's existing partnerships and secure newly formed alliances while obscuring the atrophied state of China's own modernization efforts.

Chinese officials were aware of the contradictions embedded in such work and the problematic power relations it posed, and they struggled to reconcile their newfound geopolitical standing with the United States vis-à-vis their continued commitment to a "Third World" revolution against U.S. as well as Soviet oppression.[82] In April 1974, as the Dar es Salaam train station took physical form, Vice-Premier Deng Xiaoping made the case for China's unique brand of foreign policy to the United

Nations' General Assembly as part of its sixth special session on the Non-Aligned movement. In his now-famous speech, Deng iterated China's "Three Worlds" theory in an effort to assuage both allies' and adversaries' concerns regarding the country's still ambiguous ambitions.

Deng's formulation was based upon Mao's own 1946 theorization of a geopolitical "intermediate zone" of smaller colonial and capitalist countries sandwiched between the Soviet Union and the United States, and included a "First World" of the world's two superpowers, the United States and the Soviet Union, a "Second World" consisting of intermediary European countries and Japan, and a "Third World" composed of relatively poor, decolonized countries in Asia, Africa, and Latin America. China considered itself a Third World country, but should it one day transcend such a status, Deng argued, "and everywhere subject others to her bullying, aggression, and exploitation, the people of the world should identify her as a social-imperialist, expose it, oppose it and work together with the Chinese people to overthrow it."[83]

With its pragmatic focus upon China's existing economic conditions and its aspirational gestures toward the future, Deng's speech represented the first formal articulation of China's reconfigured foreign policy. Architecture aided the government in these efforts, particularly as the party's more moderate leaders recognized the economic value of its existing international partnerships and understood that the country would need to be a more active participant in the world export market if its tentative gamble on imported technology from Japan, Western Europe, and the United States was to succeed. Reaffirming China's own technological standing vis-à-vis other socialist countries and repositioning itself as a nation capable of broader diplomatic responsibilities in the wake of the Cultural Revolution was part of this strategy, and buildings served as the first indices of how these new sensibilities would take shape on the ground.

Whether they would stabilize and illuminate the unpredictable dynamics of Chinese domestic and international affairs remained an open question, however. "The free zone for foreigners around Beijing may have been enlarged by a few miles, a few more museums, monuments, and temples may have reopened, a little more variety may have been introduced into the theaters, bookshops may display more books, and so forth. And on the whole the atmosphere may be more relaxed and pleasant," acknowledged Simon Leys in comparing his 1976 travels to Beijing with time spent there in 1972. "Yet these appearances could be quite misleading if the visitor were to take them for permanent features of the regime."[84]

Despite such skepticism, however, it was evident some type of reordering at work in the socialist modernization project was taking place. U.S. visitors to the Guangzhou Trade Fair noticed that, by 1975, a "mellowing trend" was apparent, with Chinese Trade Corporation representatives more willing to engage seriously in negotiations and answer personal questions. Ideology no longer seemed an obstacle based upon the financial investment and time evinced by the country's new construction, which also underscored the consequential nature of these shifts. "While one can only guess where the present liberalization will take the country," concluded observers, "it seems clear that China is now determined to take its place in the world as a major, independent, industrial nation."[85]

These shifts reconfigured the dynamics of international politics, boosted international trade, and prompted a reconsideration of the differences in political economy that had dictated Cold War diplomacy over the previous decade. Architectural work helped to demarcate the new physical and conceptual territory required for these changes, with an eye on advanced technology that might further allow China to integrate itself within the global capitalist economy, even as socialist economic development remained the party's priority. The buildings produced during this early yet consequential shift may have superficially borrowed from the aesthetic and formal precedents of the International Style, and certainly lacked any conceptual grounding in the historical basis for modernism itself as it was understood in Western Europe and North America.[86] In such appropriation, however, China's architectural establishment signaled its pursuit for a new architectural language and logic capable of expressing a unique moment in the country's history. If such production signaled the emergence of some new, modern Chinese architecture, it was a position that tacitly rejected the ideological zeal at the heart of Mao's socialist Chinese project in favor of some new, expanded conception of China's position relative to a world within which it had suddenly become a more active and integrated part.

CHAPTER 2

The Study Tour and the Exhibition

Over the course of 1971 and 1972, both the study tour and the exhibition —long important instruments in Mao era Chinese international relations whose frequency had waned beginning in 1968 due to the Cultural Revolution—regained favor as official vehicles for diplomatic and scholarly exchange. Tours and exhibitions were useful vehicles to promote party-approved aspects of socialist life to international audiences; many visitors from capitalist countries often left China dazzled by the performative messaging and discipline at work in the various sites and displays they were shown throughout the country. "Even their sight-seeing is a totally planned activity," marveled Henry Kissinger to U.S. officials preparing for a 1975 Congressional delegation tour of the country. "They will take you out to the Ming Tombs or the Great Wall. You can set your clock on the schedule they follow, but when you are there no one is looking at their watches; there is no sense of pressure."[1]

For dignitaries from newly decolonized countries in search of new economic and political models, these experiences were similarly convincing. For example, Zaire President Mobutu Sese Seko, a U.S. ally and anti-communist leader in the central African region, was so impressed by the choreography of his January 1973 official state tour that he returned to Zaire and appropriated China's model of self-reliance as part of his own recently launched nation-building project, which he called "Radicalization of the Revolution," to pay homage to Mao's efforts.[2]

More than art, literature, or film, among other forms of cultural production, it was architecture that effectively composed and controlled what visitors saw and how they understood Mao-era China. Schools, museums, farms, hospitals, and model factories—these spaces and the activities taking place within them were formative in shaping visitors' first impressions of life under Mao. The effects produced by these spaces projected a convincing sense of order and discipline that often extended beyond the confines of the tour to encapsulate entire villages and cities. "Beijing looks like a capital of austere revolutionary purity, the capital of a society of equals," admired Italian journalist and Communist Party member Maria Antonietta Macciocchi upon her first visit to the city in 1972.[3] Other visitors, including the French literary theorist Roland Barthes, found the experience so frustrating and specific to the distinctive, architectonic dimensions of the tour itself that he was unable to characterize it in terms that were anything but spatial, and existing entirely "behind the double-glazed window of language and the [Chinese Travel] Agency."[4]

As convincing, meticulously calibrated living simulacra of the party's desired self-image, both the study tour and the exhibition were exercises in design. Architecture's value and popularity as an early form of interchange between China and the world derived in part from its inherently visual and spatial properties, which helped to create convincingly immersive environments capable of sustaining the array of demonstrations, performances, objects, and events that comprised tours and displays. To many Chinese officials and architects, the practice of design also offered a useful form of reciprocal expertise through which professional and scholarly ideas about buildings and architectural history could be expressed and exchanged between architects in China and other parts of the world, thus establishing some degree of relativity, at least in principle.[5]

Importantly, too, architecture was also not considered as political as other forms of cultural production such as art or literature.[6] As a result, architects were some of the first study tour participants to and from China after 1970, and their observations of the built environment, in all of its tactile and phenomenological dimensions, produced insights that reverberated through the discipline of architecture, both within China and in other parts of the world. For foreign architects, particularly those from the United States, Western Europe, and Japan, China represented an opportunity to engage with an unfamiliar political, economic, and building system distinctive from those to which they were accustomed. Chinese architects and engineers selected to travel abroad at the behest of the state also returned home with new perspectives on architecture born of the unfamiliar economic practices specific to capitalism. These reflections subsequently informed design practices.

This chapter explores those experiences, simultaneously charged with excitement over the new and rife with the risks of alienation, elitism, and exoticism. A closer study of architecture's contributions to late Mao-era China's international engagement through both the tour and the exhibition reveals imbalances and artificialities that shaped the ways in which the world came to understand socialist Chinese architecture and urbanism, and the processes by which China came to terms with new architectural objects, ideas, and environments in other parts of the world. Tours and exhibitions were loaded with cross-cultural, geopolitical, and disciplinary possibility, though numerous anxieties and difficulties also arose through such exchange, which was often limited by basic language obstacles and cultural differences as well as the fundamental divergences in the nature of cultural production within China and other parts of the world. The asymmetry and incommunicability particular to these events, and to the phenomenon of travel itself, was heightened by subjectivities specific to architecture, though foreign and Chinese participants alike generally understood and accepted these challenges, and the architectural products, ideas, and practices that grew from them reflected such impediments.[7]

Such opacity proved to be a consequential force in shaping the kind of knowledge production and exchange that took place. Through these experiences emerged interpersonal relationships, institutional linkages, and forms of knowledge specific to the ideological, social, and cultural constraints of the tour and the exhibition, all of which became an important foundational basis for China's economic liberalization. Conceptualizing tours and exhibitions as performative experiences in design thus provides insight into the forms and types of architectural expression and production that emerged in part through them, particularly after 1978, and the party's architectural strategies for normalizing the complex strangeness that later composed the experience of reform itself.

STUDY TOURS TO CHINA

A handful of institutions were active generators of early pre-reform forms of engagement, including organizations such as the Society for Anglo-Chinese Understanding (SACU), established in 1965 through the work of Joseph Needham to promote British-Chinese relations. Following the lifting of restrictions on U.S. citizens' travel to China on March 15, 1971, foreign interest in traveling to China spiked. Organizations such as the Committee on Scholarly Communication with the People's Republic of China, the National Committee on United States-China Relations (NCUSCR), the National Council for United States-China Trade, and the U.S.-China Peoples Friendship Association (USCPFA), among others, sponsored some of the first exchanges between both countries, most notably the Chinese ping-pong team's visit to the United States in 1972.[8] Most worked with representatives in the Ministry of Foreign Affairs and the Chinese People's Association for Friendship with Foreign Countries in Beijing to coordinate Chinese sponsorship. The establishment of Chinese and U.S. liaison offices was also valuable in these efforts, which gave rise to new networks of institutions, agencies, corporations, and individuals across an array of levels and scales. It was through these organizational bodies that a basic conceptual and logistical framework for reform emerged at both interpersonal and institutional levels.

Within the discipline of architecture, early tour participants included French designer Charlotte Perriand, who visited China with her husband in 1970, and Chinese-American architect Henry C. K. Liu, president of Liu Urban Design Associates and a faculty member at Harvard University's

Fig. 20 I. M. Pei observing Chinese craftsmanship on the American Institute of Architects' tour of China, 1974. Originally published in *Architectural Record* 156, no. 9 (September 1974).

Graduate School of Design who was also commissioned to redesign the Mission Building of the Chinese delegation to the United Nations. The Swiss conservator Bernard Zumthor traveled to China in July 1972 and toured Tongji University's School of Architecture in Shanghai. The first substantive group tours in architecture took place in October 1973, when students and faculty in architecture and town planning at the Architectural Association (AA) in London organized a study tour to China with assistance from the SACU and the Architectural Society of China (ASC).

Other delegations of American, Canadian, Romanian, and Hong Kong designers soon followed. In October 1973, a team of Canadian architects met with a selection of Chinese representatives and visited Hangzhou, Shanghai, Beijing, and Guangzhou. A 1973 contingent of U.S. academics included the Chinese-Canadian architect Joseph T. A. Lee. A group of fifteen American Institute of Architects (AIA) members, led by outgoing AIA president Max Urbahn, I. M. Pei, and Pei's wife, Eileen, visited in April 1974, becoming the first group of U.S. professional architects to ever visit the PRC (fig. 20). Groups of Japanese and Sri Lankan engineers arrived for visits that June. The Hong Kong–based Kiu Kwong Investment Corporation also sponsored a trip that summer that included several designers from the British colony, including Ronald Poon. Teams of Japanese building technicians traveled through China in October 1974 and May and June 1976. China did not forget its longest standing socialist allies, however. A delegation of North Korean architects visited Beijing, Changsha, Guangzhou, Shanghai, and Qingdao, among other destinations, between June and July 1973.[9]

Although the professional motives and orientation of these tours differed, many of China's foreign visitors were treated to similar experiences of China—short-term, carefully choreographed introductions to life structured through rehearsed exercises and staged sets of model schools and work units designed to dazzle guests with the demonstrable advances of socialist society.[10] Of key concern to party leaders was the construction of events, processes, and environments that seemed authentic. The carefully prescribed cultural, financial, and commercial aspects of the study tour were intended to produce a certain reality through fiction, resulting in immersive atmospheres so comprehensively shaped by Mao-era pageantry and suggestive of a completely transformed social system that what was actually true no longer seemed to matter.

Participants were at least partially aware that what they were allowed to see during these trips was propagandistic in nature, though most seemed more than willing to play along with the stagecraft at work. Perriand, for example, recognized the artifice on display but, like "every friendly visitor to China," she accepted her limited access to a model farm, textile factory, and a village that included a peasant's house, a school, and a health center.[11] The medium of the tour itself conveyed the message of truth. For party leaders, the only valid source of architectural meaning was the physical construction on display itself. Any evidence of abstraction—a term long derided by Mao, and generally understood within the party to mean an expressed set of symbolic principles divorced from the content of everyday life—was considered antithetical to the state-sanctioned theoretical model, and to be avoided at all costs.[12] Following his own 1972 tour, Henry Liu reported that "the Chinese have had little time for reflection about architecture as symbolism."[13] Members of the 1974 AIA study tour to China also noted that "communication of any idea approaching the abstract" with Chinese representatives proved difficult.[14]

As the frequency of China's tours increased, however, the risks posed by greater foreign scrutiny of China also increased, as did the potential for problems associated with inappropriate foreign interpretations of the Chinese realities they were witnessing. The quality of socialist Chinese architecture and engineering was a particular concern that grew more acute in late 1973 and 1974 amid a temporary resurgence in the Gang of Four's authority over the party and its staging of the Criticize Lin Biao, Criticize Confucius campaign against Zhou and his allies.

A similar, related campaign was launched against abstraction in film—and, by extension, in architecture—through a condemnation of the Italian filmmaker Michelangelo Antonioni's film *China* (*Chine*), which the director had completed following a 1971 trip to China at the behest of Zhou, who requested that Antonioni produce a film about everyday life and people that might appeal to Western audiences and counter Western propaganda about socialist China. Following the film's completion, and over the course of early 1974, party radicals decried the unreleased film for its perceived slander of Chinese civil engineering, specifically the

Nanjing Bridge, which was completed in 1968 as a symbol of China's self-reliance following the Sino-Soviet split. Antonioni's decision to shoot the project from below to include images of men and women washing their clothes in the Yangtze River was lambasted for its malicious reduction of the structure into an embarrassing symbol of lingering Chinese backwardness through techniques of cinematic abstraction.

Antonioni later acknowledged the difficulties of capturing the complexities of Chinese socialism on film, admitting that "social and political structures are abstract entities which are not easily expressed in images." In further reflecting upon the Gang of Four's reaction to his work, Antonioni reasoned that the carefully staged environments he had been asked to document were, in fact, "not a lie.... The 'representations' are evidently the image that the Chinese want to give of themselves, and it is not an image radically different from the reality of the country."[15] Such spaces were designed, staged, and documented to create experiences that left no room for alternative interpretation.

For many foreign visitors, the tour's carefully crafted environments and their effects proved vital in generating knowledge many visitors to China were already predisposed to embrace—a disciplinary position that may be characterized as Maoist in nature, and originating from someone living "in a capitalist society but who is fed up with capitalism—a cultural critic, in other words, who wants a social order opposed to the one that is supporting her own undertaking.... What she wants is always located in the other."[16] Such images were distinctive from the multiple realities unfolding in China at the time, but efficient factories, clean and lively schools, and immaculate hospitals created by "universally cheerful and friendly" people willing to greet guests "at each airport or railroad station" proved all too tempting material caricatures of successful social revolution at work.[17]

Designers in particular were seduced by the physical products and labor processes of an alternative development model in action that neatly aligned with certain aspects of architectural work, including collaborative teamwork. For example, Joseph T. A. Lee marveled that "everyone appears to put the good of the group above individual gain—indeed, to ignore completely the possibility of individual gain. There seems to be no greed nor envy (perhaps a uniformity of living conditions helps in this, but one cannot be sure it is only this); everyone seems content to work at whatever they are assigned."[18] Henry Liu noted, "China today is far from an authoritarian society. No one aspires to be elevated or to elevate himself above the masses."[19] *Architectural Record* editor Walter Wagner marveled at people's "Puritanical" honesty, the absence of homelessness, and the unwavering devotion to Chairman Mao expressed by everyone with whom his group met.[20]

Foreign visitors eager for evidence of socialism's successes perceived in the reconfiguration of the architect's responsibilities confirmation of a transformative, Maoist revolutionary spirit at work. For the more politically active members of the AA-organized tour, for example, "the Chinese social experiment" seemed to offer an exciting contrast to what they were studying at home in Great Britain, at a time in which key institutional and economic mechanisms for land development and urban policy there appeared to be breaking down.[21] At one tour stop, the delegation interviewed a professor of architecture from Tongji University, who detailed a year of reeducation spent at a rural building site. "I came back to college to teach students, I still had some fear that it would not work," admitted seventy-three-year-old Professor Chang, who was tasked with carrying bricks to and from the building site. Chang ultimately extolled the valuable lessons of his experience to tour members, however. "As I studied and taught with the students, my fear melted into the background. . . . I do not now feel old, I feel young again!"[22]

AA tour members subsequently left China amazed by what they considered to be complex, empowering spatial and social systems on display. "Something very interesting has been happening [in China]," wrote participants in special issues of *Architectural Design* (1974) as well as *Progress in Planning* (1977) published following their return home. "The tide has turned. . . . The newly liberated countries of Asia have adopted conscious policies aimed at de-urbanization, at returning people to the land, at achieving that balance between town and country which Marx and Engels, from *Communist Manifesto* days on, urged as an alternative to mindless urban agglomeration."[23]

Architecture reinforced these impressions. In Hangzhou and Shanghai, for example, tour participants observed long-span concrete shell truss construction purportedly designed and completed by workers themselves on-site—challenging exercises only without adequate construction equipment. Visits to "old temples and ancient buildings . . . so carefully and beautifully restored that it was difficult to tell where the old ended and the new began" presented problematic examples of the erasure of Cultural Revolution–era destruction already taking place, though none of the AA participants acknowledged it.[24]

For study tour participants less enamored with Maoist utopianism, however, there also existed architectural evidence of a different kind of transition at work. As early as 1972, for example, tour participants observed the construction of a number of new and existing tourist-related facilities in response to the "large number of foreign guests and the people of all nationalities" visiting the site, including projects such as the Beijing Hotel's east addition, International Club, and Friendship Store.[25] Walter Wagner opined that several recently constructed buildings seemed to possess a "lighter and brighter and more human" dimension than those produced under Soviet tutelage.[26] Archibald C. Rogers, chairman of the international firm RTKL, president of the AIA, and a member of the 1974 AIA delegation, noted the contrast between China's urban vernacular and the new high-rise hotels and exhibition center in Guangzhou and elsewhere as evidence of economic growth, though Rogers also interpreted the continued existence of certain ceramic-making practices and the restoration and preservation of famous landmarks such as Beijing's Forbidden City as signs of "the persistence of tradition."[27]

Following their return home to the United States, members of the AIA tour characterized the workers and technicians they met as part of a "throwaway" generation committed to improving "the lot of future generations" through the feverish construction of apartments, schools, and hospitals and efforts to automate the country's industry, though panelists did express surprise at how "totally disinterested" their Chinese hosts seemed concerning environmental issues.[28] Embedded in these observations may be discerned an outlook characterized as more Dengist in its orientation—an experience shaped less by the Cultural Revolution–era performative theatrics on display, and more by the relatively mundane, individualized efforts of improving lives through a recommitment to the act of building itself.

On-site observation and conversation with Chinese counterparts in architectural design and education also yielded evidence that the disruption to the industry caused by the Cultural Revolution was unsustainable, particularly for architects, and would require reconciliation if Chinese architecture was to thrive. The collapse of so-called advanced and elementary cultural production into one privileged form of collectively made art, and the collapse of the architect's standing relative to the laborer and engineer within a work unit, was unlike anything many foreign designers had experienced as practicing architects and teachers. "My experience in the United States," admitted Liu, "has not seemed to prepare me for fully understanding these relationships."[29] Following his trip, Liu also noted, "I pointed out to my colleagues in China that the direction they have been going in architecture would not, in my opinion, lead to a satisfactory solution, and they more or less agreed."[30] Zumthor concluded, "One might argue that [China's architectural training] provides itself with good engineers but not with architects."[31]

Those designers trained in Western architectural history and modernism found it particularly difficult to imagine China's collective approach to design and construction would produce exemplary design. As Wagner noted following the AIA delegation's tour, "As in all work there is little opportunity in China for the hand of a single brilliant architect to emerge."[32] The structure of the study tour itself, with its careful staging of on-site collective action, was crucial in shaping such impressions. Talented individual architects certainly existed in socialist China, but the notion that such figures could thrive in China ran counter to Mao's revolutionary vision and seemed impossible to imagine given the immersive spectacles of collectivity on display.

Collectively, foreign impressions suggested a profession and a country on the precipice of change, though it was unclear what form or direction it would take. For many foreign and Chinese participants in late Mao-era study trips and exhibitions, perceptions of incommensurability between disparate design philosophies and planning models rooted in distinctive political and economic systems proved difficult to overcome. Many departed for home with a range of complex emotive responses related to the inherent strangeness of the encounter itself, from the deeply affecting and serendipitous to feelings of alienation and despair, and the imbalances of knowledge and expertise they produced. "It is difficult to measure in Western terms the 'value' of such an educational system," noted Zumthor following his 1972 visit. "China is certainly not training the same kind of architect as we are."[33] Wagner, upon reflecting on the AIA's 1974 tour, concluded that there was "nothing for us to learn, but nothing for the Chinese to be ashamed of."[34] Wagner's ambivalence notwithstanding, however, lessons were imparted that made lasting impressions, and as the initial strangeness of these first encounters dulled over time, new visions of future possibilities emerged.

CHINESE TOURS ABROAD

Although the term "international exchange" suggests a certain reciprocity between partners, early study trips between China and other parts of the world were inherently incommensurable experiences, with distinctive sets of expectations and objectives on the part of all participants involved. For those Chinese representatives selected to travel abroad, the study tour was a rare, government-sanctioned opportunity to meet foreign experts, observe living standards and economic processes, and learn from the architectural educational and building systems being practiced and implemented. The Cultural Revolution had isolated China from both socialist and capitalist countries, and exchange allowed Chinese experts and officials to reengage with established socialist allies and historical capitalist adversaries alike, including Romania, North Korea, Hong Kong, Singapore, Japan, the United States, France, and Italy, among others, in pursuit of knowledge.[35]

Senior Chinese architects were active members of these early engagements. Beginning in 1970, the party's core leadership requested that selected, well-established members of the ASC, many of whom had been reassigned for reeducation at the height of the Cultural Revolution, be recalled back to Beijing to work with them in reenergizing the country's major architectural research institute. Figures such as Yuan Jingshen, former head of the Beijing Industrial Design Institute, returned to work and helped reinitiate the ASC's disciplinary activities, which included foreign exchange.[36] The Ministry of Construction and the Federation of Returned Overseas Chinese also supported an early, controversial trip to Hong Kong and Macau in 1972, which allowed Zhang Bo and other members of the design team working on the Beijing Hotel's east addition to experience the amenities of high-end tourist accommodations firsthand.[37] Other early international tour participants included notable ASC-affiliated designers and academics such as Yang Tingbao, Dai Nianci, He Guangqian, and Jin Oubu (fig. 21).

Many of these re-empowered individuals had studied abroad prior to 1949 and possessed fond, lasting memories of their early international experiences, though subsequent decades spent in China limited their knowledge concerning more recent architectural and urban development taking place around the world.[38] Officially sanctioned reencounters with foreign architecture and urbanism thus posed new, often jarring experiences from what they had remembered. Buildings and cities shaped by capitalism presented one kind of unfamiliar, foreign encounter; tours to socialist countries produced equally strange if not even more alienating experiences because they were ostensibly socialist environments that looked and operated in radically different ways from the "modern" socialist cities and architecture that had materialized in post-1949 China.[39] In both cases, Chinese architects were forced to confront and reevaluate the successes and failures of design under Mao.

The political sensitivities surrounding these trips ensured limited media coverage abroad and particularly at home, but technology—its observation, documentation, and, if possible, collection—was a recurring refrain and primary motive behind these trips.[40] In January 1973, for example, a fourteen-member team from Beijing traveled to Hong Kong to visit the Connaught Centre's construction site, where they spent three hours studying the building methods and "mechanized techniques being employed."[41] Hongkong Land Company, owners of the Connaught Centre, and Gammon (HK), the building contractor, organized the tour, which aimed to improve the company's relations with mainland counterparts. That same month, a five-person delegation attended the International Union of Architects meeting in Budapest, Hungary—an opportunity that led to exchange invitations from architects in Switzerland and France.[42]

This trip was followed, in June and July 1973, by an eight-person tour

Fig. 21 Architectural Society of China's visit to Bulgaria, August 1972; participants include Dai Nianci, Yuan Jingshen, Zhao Jin, and Yang Tingbao. Originally published in *Contemporary Chinese Architects: Dai Nianci* (*Dangdai Zhongguo jianzhudashi: Dai Nianci*, 2000).

of Japan led by ASC Director Yang, with stops in Tokyo, Osaka, Kyoto, and Yokohama to visit several industrial and residential zones, subway systems, and a number of notable recently constructed architectural projects.[43] The group also met with a number of Japanese designers, politicians, professors, administrators, and technicians, including Kenzō Tange, Architectural Institute of Japan President Takamasa Yoshizaka, and business executive Aiichirō Fujiyama, among others, reaffirming "friendship and mutual understanding" between the two countries while "exchanging experiences with architectural science and technology."[44] In October 1973, a He Guangqian–led trip traveled to Italy, where members attended an industrial building exposition in Bologna, toured high-rise construction in Milan and Rome, and visited several building material and structural component manufacturing facilities. The group also traveled to France to see Paris and meet Pierre Vago, publisher of *L'Architecture d'Aujourd'hui* and honorary general secretary of the International Union of Architects.[45]

The Gang of Four's resurgence in late 1973 through 1974 curtailed international travel, and in February 1974, the ASC organized a Criticize Lin Biao, Criticize Confucius conference in demonstration of the organization's commitment to the revolutionary cause.[46] By the summer of 1975, however, six ASC representatives were again able to travel to Japan.[47] In September and October, a twelve-member ASC delegation led by He and Li Ting, vice president of ASC's Shanghai branch, visited the United States at the invitation of the AIA, in reciprocation for the organization's sponsored trip to China one year prior.[48] AIA-affiliated hosts noted their guests' deep interest in "American building technology . . . particularly in precast concrete construction and mechanical systems" as well as "expansion factors, wind bracing, noise dampening materials and the like."[49] During a 1977 month-long tour of the United States by Chinese educators, including Yang Tingbao, Chinese participants purportedly expressed concern over their country's university-level training of scientists and technical personnel. Chinese tour organizers specifically prioritized the search for engineering technology not yet available at home. During a 1978 tour of Chinese architects to Washington, D.C., Baltimore, New York, and New Haven sponsored by the NCUSCR, participants visited Bella Vista, a 1,088-unit apartment complex for senior citizens completed in 1972 in New Haven and marveled at a kitchen sink's garbage disposal unit while expressing interest in high-rise apartments, prefabrication, and "anti-earthquake" architecture.[50]

These encounters, with their emphasis on more technocratic, economically pragmatic methods of architectural production regardless of the exchange partner, complemented material experimentation already being rehearsed on the ground in China, as discussed in Chapter 3. Upon their return home, architects were expected to contribute to these efforts by transforming these technologies into viable architectural systems, though it remained unclear whether China's political system had stabilized to an extent that it could support such work. Following years of social upheaval, technology retained an aura of modernity that proved irresistible to the party's elite, and returning Chinese observers were expected to recommit to the idea of a social revolution triggered not by class warfare, but by scientific and technological invention.

Fusing that technical knowledge to China's reality upon returning home proved difficult, however. Foreign ideas remained controversial, sensitive topics, particularly as many Chinese participants realized in part through engagements with foreign people, environments, and objects just how disastrous the Cultural Revolution had been to China's physical development. Of key concern was not simply how to integrate advanced technology and different forms of capitalistic practices within China's built environment, but how to best harness the new knowledge and investment in demonstrable ways that reignited the perceived value of socialism, thereby relegitimizing the party and its plans moving forward. These goals enlivened architecture's relationship to Chinese society, even as they proved difficult to implement in the country's unsettled political climate.

OBJECTS

In the immediate wake of the Cultural Revolution, intensified focus upon the new theoretical and procedural frameworks needed to rejuvenate China's economic development triggered thinking about how architects could best synchronize and consolidate global circulations of architectural knowledge in accordance with the party's shifting principles. Study tours offered one selective form of capacity building, but raising disciplinary awareness of the discrepancies existing between building technology in China and other parts of the world required multiple modes of knowledge exchange. To that end, people were not the only conduits for interchange during the late Mao era. Objects also traveled and were vital sources for design-specific knowledge in China, particularly as tours were selective, sensitive, and expensive experiences unavailable to most foreign and Chinese residents. Traveling exhibitions offered opportunities for greater numbers of people to see and perhaps touch material things representative of a distinctive culture or social system.

In this regard, and like tours, objects were strange and potentially destabilizing, which made them distinctly political, particularly in late Mao-era China. Following the opening of the U.S. liaison office in Beijing in 1973, for example, U.S. Chief Liaison Officer and Ambassador David Bruce and his wife, Evangeline, supported plans to install several famous examples of U.S. abstract expressionism from the Museum of Modern Art in their own residence. Mrs. Bruce selected the artwork herself, which included examples from Willem de Kooning, Adolph Gottlieb, Louise

Nevelson, Mark Tobey, and Jackson Pollock. "Museum officials suggested that we have a retrospective of modern American painting because the mainland Chinese have never seen this art form before," she explained.[51] Although the Bruces were eager to see the reactions of those Chinese officials allowed access to their residence, the loan was indefinitely postponed for undisclosed reasons in April 1974, at the request of the liaison office and the State Department.[52] The incident exposed the political risks involved in seemingly innocuous acts of cultural interplay and the need for more critical, substantive assessment of material culture in China, which remained an active conduit for communication between the United States and China, despite the blunder.

A 1974–75 traveling exhibition of archaeological objects unearthed in China since 1949 proved a more fruitful if ambitious experiment in the management and presentation of material culture in relation to late Mao-era China. International interest in supporting a traveling exhibition of imperial-era Chinese art and archaeology traces back to the 1960s, but it was not until 1971, when Henry Kissinger visited Beijing and expressed interest to the Chinese government, that plans were secured for Chinese objects to travel specifically to the United States.[53] Kissinger's 1973 trip to Beijing laid further groundwork for the exhibition, which was eventually coordinated through the liaison offices in Beijing and Washington, D.C. Some 380 objects were included in the show, titled the *Exhibition of Archaeological Finds of the People's Republic of China*, which was first publicly exhibited in Beijing in the summer of 1972, before its international tour to Paris, London, Vienna, Stockholm, Toronto, Washington, D.C., Kansas City, and San Francisco beginning in 1973.

Prior to the objects' passage, a series of special treaties was required to be drafted and signed to ensure their safe and secure legal movement around the world; Chinese representatives also reminded all participating foreign institutions to refer to China as the "People's Republic of China."[54] In preparation for the Washington, D.C., show, Chinese and U.S. officials wrangled over the language dictating the standards for the objects' shipping, handling, and maintenance. Valuation for insurance purposes was a key concern. Edits proposed by the State Department's legal counsel prompted a series of strict changes on the Chinese side. An additional round of edits on the part of both parties followed, prompting U.S. observers to note that if the exhibition was going to take place, it would have to be "on Chinese terms."[55] Negotiations extended until October 1974, less than two months prior to the show's scheduled opening.

The exhibition was not in itself devoted to Chinese architecture, but it offers insight into the kinds of demands placed upon objects and design practices in mediating international relations with socialist China both at home and abroad. Chinese officials demanded that the exhibition adhere to the party's standard chronological framework, regardless of the variety of different curated forms it took along its international journey. In Washington, D.C., exhibition designers worked on the show for more than a year, and also visited the exhibition three times, in London, Paris, and Toronto, to study potential layouts. A host committee responsible for oversight included representatives from several museums, the State Department, the National Endowment for the Humanities, and the NCUSCR.

In accordance with the party's linear, chronological narrative, the National Gallery show comprised thirty-four distinct sections, each of which corresponded to the excavation sites where the objects were found. The final exhibition scheme totaled 1,579 square meters, which made it the largest installation ever attempted in Washington. The scale and complexity of the endeavor necessitated the design and construction of "a museum-within-a-museum" that transformed the National Gallery's entire ground floor into a new exhibition experience.[56] Every object had to be positioned within a "sealed environment" and completely protected through special boxes produced especially for the National Gallery. The construction team later acknowledged they had never had to build anything so precisely.[57]

The emphasis placed on interiority, in particular the nesting of spaces and objects within larger spaces, was dictated in large part by the museum's ability to display an unprecedented amount of Chinese art, and the need for climate control to support the fragile objects themselves (fig. 22). Sustaining one exhibition interior within another may also be read in reference to the distinctive curatorial and promotional procedures agreed upon by the Chinese government and the State Department, however. For example, China insisted that the exhibition include its own independent Chinese curatorial team and that the exhibition catalogue be produced in China, independently of the National Gallery's existing publication plans. More generally, National Gallery staff were instructed to pay careful attention to customs of "Non-Westernized Chinese," with internally circulated guidelines reminding employees as to how China should be referenced in conversation, how to greet Chinese visitors, and what they would prefer to eat.[58]

Despite these efforts, however, the exhibition was nearly derailed following preparations for a special press preview, which was cancelled prior to the exhibition's opening when the National Gallery could not meet the Chinese liaison office's demands that press representatives from Taiwan, South Korea, South Africa, and Israel be prohibited from attending. Further controversy arose from questions concerning the catalogue's publication in China. "The Chinese insisted upon, and were granted, the power to determine not only the intellectual content of catalogs and all public statements, but also even the books to be sold by the National Gallery Bookstore!" wrote the legal scholar Jerome Cohen in the *New York Times*.[59]

Fig. 22 *The Exhibition of Archaeological Finds of the People's Republic of China,* National Gallery of Art, Washington, D.C., December 13, 1974–March 30, 1975.

Notwithstanding China's efforts to control the exhibition's intellectual content and access to the press, the event proved to be a tremendous cultural success, attracting approximately seven hundred thousand visitors to the National Gallery of Art alone, 370,000 in Paris, and 777,300 in London. This exhibition of China's imperial-era objects was one of the most popular and best-known international art events of the decade, and proved a productive test of the difficulties involved in more substantive diplomatic engagement. Critics of U.S. policy toward China identified the perceived concessions made on the part of the U.S. government in relation to the exhibition as evidence not only that the United States was "losing all over the world," but that the U.S. spirit was "enfeebled."[60] For example, the noted conservative pundit William F. Buckley, Jr., argued that communist China was engaged in a "psywar" in which Chinese cultural artifacts and history itself represented nothing more than weaponry aimed at neutralizing any U.S. advantage.[61] In the eyes of the U.S. public, however, China was not an ally, nor was it considered an enemy. It was first and foremost a curiosity, and in the battle over the public's interest, the party's deployment of Chinese culture had proven a convincing and effective reset.

The United States was by no means alone in pursuing these opportunities, but its involvement with China was consequential to reaffirming the country's ascendance on the world stage. Importantly, too, such forms of cultural engagement established a basic scaffolding upon which numerous other countries could, in theory, establish more substantive relations with China. Indeed, over roughly the same period, several for-

Fig. 23 Brochure, *Photographs of Finnish Architecture, 1961–71* (*Fenlan jianzhu tupian zhanlan, 1961–71*), Beijing, Shanghai, and Guangzhou, 1973.

eign architectural exhibitions were also organized in China to inform the public as to processes and forms of physical development taking place elsewhere. Given the sensitivities and expenditures surrounding study tours, exhibitions were logical forums through which large numbers of residents could gaze upon curated examples of architectural production taking place in other parts of the world.

Images and ideas could also be more easily controlled through the exhibition format. In April 1973, for example, a photograph exhibition of Finnish architecture produced between 1961 and 1971 opened in Beijing before traveling to Shanghai and Guangzhou (fig. 23). Finland was one of the PRC's oldest diplomatic partners in Europe. The event was sponsored by the Chinese People's Association for Friendship with Foreign Countries in coordination with ASC, and it featured approximately forty-five images of notable Finnish architecture, including an emphasis on large-scale residential projects such as Olari, a residential district in Espoo designed by Simo Järvinen, Eero Valjakka, and Vesa Huolman (1969–72), a mass-produced modular housing unit by Kristian Gullichsen and Juhani Pallasmaa in 1969, and the Wolfsburg Cultural Center by Alvar Aalto (1958–63). Between September and October 1973, a display of recent Chinese architecture was sent to Hanoi. Collectively, these exhibitions emphasized technical craft, labor, and efficient, well-conceived design. Although they were limited in their outreach and presumed effect, they nevertheless indicated the expanded internationalism of China's study of modern architectural conditions beginning to take place prior to reform—an inspiring but incomplete form of knowledge that signaled something new.[62]

Object exchange continued through tumultuous national events, including the passing of both Zhou and Mao in April and September 1976, respectively. In November 1976, just two months following the death of Mao, an exhibition of Swedish furniture design organized by the country's Association for Friendship with Foreign Countries was held in Beijing. Sweden was the first Western country to recognize the PRC, in May 1950, and exchange between the two countries remained steady throughout the 1950s and 1960s. Although Sweden was an industrialized, capitalist economy with an expensive labor force, China's architectural media convincingly framed its design culture as the output of talented craftspeople capable of prioritizing economized material practices and work processes. Composed of sixty-three images, ninety-nine pieces of furniture, thirty examples of lighting and other material articles, the show emphasized Sweden's history of wood craftsmanship, the precise and beautiful simplicity of its object-making processes, and the refined practicality of such work.

Formal analysis of the objects themselves testified to their straightforward and efficient yet ingenious design decisions, with little if any evidence of material waste. Valuable insight was also gleaned from the furniture designers themselves, several of whom traveled to Beijing to participate in the exhibition's opening. "These experts met with our own furniture makers and engaged with each other on issues related to technical expertise, and they were impressed with the effects of the 'Three Combinations' collaborative practices that emerged from the Cultural Revolution, including workers-led management practices, technical innovations, and self-made machinery," explained Ceng Jian in the pages of *Architectural Journal* (*Jianzhu Xuebao*).[63]

Framed as an exercise in engendering more comprehensive understanding of architectural and industrial design on the part of China's designers, the exhibition also presented idealized forms of material culture to a Chinese public unfamiliar with alternatives to their own mass-produced consumables. In the show's curated effort to establish certain equivalences between Chinese and Swedish design traditions, practices, and values despite fundamentally different political, economic, and cultural orientations between the two countries, questions of taste and discrepancies in quality were bound to emerge, particularly in relation to the production methods and standards of late Mao-era China. In the display of beautiful objects otherwise unattainable to their Chinese audience, the exhibition gestured toward the emergence of long and publicly suppressed desires that threatened the visage of austerity and egalitarianism carefully crafted by those in power. It also anticipated a new, much-coveted figure in the world economy—the Chinese consumer. In the immediate wake of a new, post-Mao reality, these objects and the material culture they celebrated took on new meaning that would reverberate throughout the country.

FROM EXCHANGE TO REFORM

By the late 1970s, the increasing intensity, odd intentionality, and inclination toward misunderstanding of Sino-foreign encounters had begun to reverberate throughout multiple forms of popular culture, but they retained a certain foundational relationship to the physical environment.

Fig. 24 Tseng Kwong Chi, *New York, New York,* 1979. Gelatin silver print, 16 × 16 in. (40.6 × 40.6 cm). From the self-portrait series *East Meets West,* 1979–89. © Muna Tseng Dance Projects, Inc.

In a collection of over one hundred images alternatively known as the *East Meets West* or *Expeditionary Self-Portrait Series,* taken between 1979 and 1989, for example, the Hong Kong–born Tseng Kwong Chi dressed as an enigmatic Chinese emissary, in a gray Mao suit and sunglasses, and posed in front of numerous natural and, more famously, architectural landmarks around the world (fig. 24). The iconic images reveled in the cultural politics of Othering—an inscrutable and estranged dignitary seemingly from a dissonant foreign culture encountering but never fully engaging with odd, new built and natural worlds.[64] In reality, however, the influence of exchange in relationship to architecture produced very different effects over time. In the transition from the end of the Mao era to reform, for example, opportunities for exchange intensified to an extent that doubts concerning commensurability and what was considered possible in China began to blur despite the rigid capitalist and socialist systems theoretically in place.

Mao-era emphasis on the discipline, sacrifice, and work ethic of the Chinese people—what AIA tour participants observed in 1974 as the people's desire to "improve their society, their rate of progress, their hard work"—took on new meaning amid the professional opportunities and cheap labor suddenly available in China after 1978.[65] What seemed utterly insurmountable to members of a 1979 U.S. urban planners' delegation to China, for example—a strangeness stemming from witnessing urban development in a centralized socialist state that "no amount of briefing—not even years of study" could blunt, coupled with the apparent absence of any "local autonomy, free economy, voluntary association; no defense contractors, no real-estate developers, no highway lobby; no land market, no legislative process, no conservation movement"—nevertheless contained nuggets of familiarity, including "much central bureaucracy, much inter-agency confusion, much red tape."[66] The point was made in jest, but delegation members concluded, "These last problems, at least, are most familiar; administrators from our largest cities felt right at home." Humorous irony notwithstanding, there was evidence to suggest a search for equivalence and familiarity had begun to take hold, influencing multiple forms of architectural production and exchange, including the designation of special spaces within which foreign capital could be invested in China, Chinese reproduction of foreign-inspired architectural forms, the importation of particular discourses such as postmodernism, and certain market-oriented design practices.

At the same time, individualized methods of information transfer produced through exchange began to privilege selected groups of international intellectuals and China's intelligentsia, each composed of academics and technicians, including architects vilified during the Cultural Revolution. These figures increasingly found themselves re-empowered to make decisions as to what economic liberalization looked like, and how it operated, in architectural terms—a form of cultural capital that proved valuable to these fortunate, well-positioned individuals over time. The expertise that developed through travel abroad produced experts, or managers of architectural meaning, who became essential to the country's modernization as the very project of modernization was redefined from a pursuit rooted in Mao-era ideology into a more technocratic pursuit. The shifts taking place in relation to exchange revealed these adjustments—from an exercise in the spectacle of juxtaposition and contrast into a form of arbitration intended to reconcile difference and induce new forms of technological progress through acts of international engagement.

Much of the knowledge produced through exchange remained cursory and shallow, and ultimately, study tours offered little more than images of objects and environments untethered from the complex social, political, and economic systems that enabled them. As exercises in abstraction, however, exchange inevitably encouraged China's designers to begin to shift away from Mao-era positivism and toward the indeterminacy of the greater imagined international community of designers of which they were now a part. Wang Tan, professor of architectural theory and design and vice dean of the Department of Architecture at Tsinghua University, worked at Taliesin under Frank Lloyd Wright between 1948 and 1949, and he traveled to the United States on an official tour in 1981. Upon his return home, Wang penned a review of the work of the U.S. corporate firm Skidmore, Owings & Merrill (SOM) based upon his experiences in New York City and Chicago. "China may not proceed to build 100-story skyscrapers, and we may not like this or that kind of unadorned, casket-like architecture. However, if the economic basis for change is inevitably reflected through skyscrapers, then that remains my guideline! Large-scale collective industrialization is going to transform our aesthetic conceptions and standards as it extends its position into our lives. To me, there is much value to be gleaned from SOM's experience!"[67] Such observations—rooted in fleeting, subjective immersions in a complex alternative reality that looked and felt fundamentally modern and new—proved consequential to the architecture of reform, in particular the focus on aesthetics, internationalism, and the speed of physical development itself.

In courting these new relationships and experiences, the party also had to reckon with the awkward and uncontrollable oddness intrinsic to travel and, by extension, to reform. Ultimately, and as exemplified through processes of exchange, architecture moved different people in different ways, producing imbalances and irregularities that emerged prior to the formal launching of the Four Modernizations and quickly began to test the party's ability to control them, particularly after 1978. The possibility of the absorption of forms of knowledge on an individualized basis, and often beyond the party's influence, remained a key concern among CCP leadership throughout the 1980s. Architecture, an active conduit for new kinds of thinking relative to the liberalization taking place, would also figure as an instrument theoretically capable of controlling liberalization's undue effects.

CHAPTER 3

The Brick, the Block, and the Panel

In October 1973, a short notice in the back of *Architectural Journal* (*Jianzhu Xuebao*) announced that China's National Construction Committee was standardizing the size of architectural drawings in the country in an effort to improve design and construction quality.[1] The notification was published as construction on Beijing's diplomatic projects and the east addition of the Beijing Hotel was reaching completion, and it suggested renewed party interest in centralizing the management of architecture's representational practices around the country—a departure from the decentralization of technical knowledge that had taken place at the height of the Cultural Revolution.

Standardized architectural drawings and practices augured broader changes in how architecture was implemented on the ground and circulated through the profession, yet their reintegration into Chinese architectural practices has been overlooked in the broader narratives of architectural representation and production in late twentieth-century China. The decision to recommit to the standardization of architectural techniques and practices was an important step not only in reconfiguring the processes by which socialist Chinese architectural production occurred and design knowledge was organized and disseminated around the country, but in mediating the contested politics that had bitterly divided the party.

The news came as the Gang of Four launched the Criticize Lin Biao, Criticize Confucius campaign that fall, which represented an effort to foment the party's ideological lurch back toward radicalism while Zhou Enlai and Mao Zedong both lay temporarily sidelined from party politics due to deteriorating health. A series of pro–Gang of Four editorials published in *Architectural Journal* in early 1974, including "The Malignant Distortion of the Features of Our Great Capital Peking Will Never Be Tolerated" and "No Slander of New China's Municipal Construction Will Be Brooked," railed against the new construction taking place within the capital and the deleterious influence of capitalism it indicated.[2]

These pieces acknowledged the encounters with foreign buildings, materials, and technologies taking place through state-sanctioned study tours and exchanges while reminding readers that Beijing was not some symbolic, imperial vestige of the country's feudal past designed for sightseeing but rather comprised the vibrant socialist epicenter of a New China realized through Mao's reinvention.[3] Continuing to build the country through "thrift and hard work," rather than through foreign-introduced technologies and building procedures, was the only path toward developing an advanced, modern socialist system.[4]

A concurrent movement to promote the nationwide adoption of hollow brick, concrete block, and concrete panel prefabrication known as "wall reform"—the focus of this chapter—signaled efforts on the part of moderate leaders such as Zhou, Deng, and others to counter the Gang of Four's attacks by redoubling their own strategy to modernize the PRC through intensified technological study, importation, and innovation. Bricks and concrete blocks represented two fundamental indices of socialist Chinese architectural production as well as representation, and through their technical re-enlivenment, officials sought to rejuvenate a building industry hampered by decentralization and logistical dysfunction. Beginning in 1973 and extending through 1976, technologies ranging from more efficient hollow brick and block production to prefabricated wall technology were reintroduced into the country's building industry.

These materials and products were not all new to China; many consisted of recirculated manufacturing techniques originally introduced into the country in the 1950s to promote greater construction efficiency throughout the country. But the reemergence of these materials and practices was a tacit acknowledgment that the Cultural Revolution had not produced the socialist Chinese landscape imagined by its proponents, and that certain forms of architectural knowledge and procedures had to be reinstated for Chinese society to function. This was a sensitive admission, but it was a point upon which both moderate and more radically inclined officials could ultimately agree, even as the political rationales underlying each clique's position differed.

As a material and procedural divergence from established Cultural Revolution–era construction practices, wall reform resulted in projects, practices, and semiotics that both reinstated and challenged methods and values at the core of socialist Chinese architectural production. Changes in the material nature of bricks, blocks, and panels—from solid to hollow—through new production and construction methods necessitated technological improvements that challenged a Chinese architectural establishment struggling to come to terms with the increasingly evident failings of Mao-era governance, yet deeply uncertain of its alternatives. In bridging the ideological gulf at the heart of China's governance, these procedural changes gestured toward a political way forward. The intensified promotion of hollow material manufacturing methods aimed to improve China's limited technical knowledge in relation to construction, even as it also acknowledged the country's economic shortcomings. New production practices allowed workers to save on material costs but also required more expertise to manufacture.

The campaign's calls to improve building quality appropriated Gang of Four–inspired rhetorical flourishes of class struggle, though its embrace of technical expertise also resonated with the concerns of more moderate officials led by Zhou and Deng. These transformations affected the role of the architect in Chinese society and how the state encouraged and promoted more technically oriented forms of knowledge exchange within the building sciences and industry—key steps that ushered in the implementation of more dramatic restructuring in Chinese design and construction practices after 1978.

THE BRICK AND CONCRETE BLOCK AS SOCIALIST CHINESE BUILDING TECHNOLOGIES

Bricks and concrete blocks were early and important components of modern socialist Chinese architecture dating back to the country's founding. Neither possessed the machinic, industrialized aesthetic of a steel I-beam or the sleek transparency of glass—two definitively modern but expensive building materials that challenged the young socialist nation's production capabilities. By contrast, the brick and the block were easier and cheaper to make, and could be manufactured using local resources. Importantly, too, each also offered a more effective index of collective labor's performative productivity than steel or glass by providing a modular, quantifiable approximation of human effort as a natural resource (fig. 25).

At the same time, one of the factors at work in understanding the brick's and block's lasting representational value in socialist China was the general perception, promoted by the government beginning in the 1950s, that each was a material technology with a fundamental, material connection to the worker, and that each could be adapted and improved by laborers on-site, thereby empowering the proletariat through opportunities to acquire and demonstrate applied knowledge. Bricks and blocks thus endured as affordable, productive tools in promoting socialist China's modernization throughout the 1950s and 1960s, despite numerous political vicissitudes and shifts in party messaging taking place.

In fact, brick and concrete block production required a degree of expertise and skilled technique that upset established building practices around the world over the course of the twentieth century. As architectural historian Adrian Forty has argued in reference to postwar Europe and North America, concrete did more than "just change the economics of construction. It affected the entire composition of the building industry, shifting the balance between skilled craft labor, unskilled labor, and

Bricklaying by the Su Chang-yu method. The present record is 6,000 bricks per man-shift.

Fig. 25 Bricklaying demonstration in Beijing, 1953. Originally published in *China Reconstructs* 2, no. 2 (February 1953).

professional experts, to the advantage of the latter two groups and the disadvantages of the first."[5] Similar disruptions took place in socialist countries such as the Soviet Union, where new concrete panel production destabilized relations between manual labor and automated manufacturing practices in the name of creating new material realities.[6]

This kind of labor disturbance also presented problems in late Mao-era China, where paradoxes emerged through the party's efforts to emancipate the proletariat through the popularization of more grassroots brick and concrete as well as rammed earth production techniques during the Cultural Revolution. Officials considered these materials essential to the physical and aesthetic production of a truly socialist China because they were economical, capitalized upon local, vernacular building techniques and resources, and—perhaps most importantly—seemingly did not require skilled labor.

Another pressing and practical challenge to building material production in China concerned transportation costs. Long-distance hauling proved prohibitively expensive due to the country's size and poor transportation infrastructure, and over the course of the mid-1950s through the early 1960s, the government attempted to decentralize a significant amount of its building material production to remedy its unsatisfactory material distribution systems. Empowering work units to devise their own material production systems had both practical and ideological dimensions, and by the early 1970s, the proliferation of small-scale cement and brick production facilities throughout China could be lauded for empowering the country's rural proletariat through locally produced construction materials for projects ranging from reservoirs and power stations to barns and pigsties.

The government touted these projects as evidence of the dramatic reorganization of material processes taking place.[7] During his 1972 trip to China, for example, Chinese-American architect Henry C. K. Liu observed that much of the country's built environment was indeed composed of "a lot of brick and a lot of concrete block."[8] In 1972 alone, for example, the country built more than six hundred small cement works, bringing the total number of small-scale production facilities to 2,400, which were responsible for 48 percent of China's total cement production. In a country of 862 million, predominantly rural and impoverished inhabitants, however, such efforts were of limited effectiveness.

Moreover, as the technical knowledge subtending these materials began to atrophy, concerns emerged regarding the material quality of much of this production.[9] Pierre Ryckmans, writing as Simon Leys, observed, "To gradually foist on public acceptance the myth that illiterate workers are better than trained specialists at making technical improvements and scientific discoveries is a policy fraught with danger for the future. It generates the feeling that engineers, researchers and scholars are actually superfluous."[10]

New hierarchies were generated through such subversion, which was originally orchestrated to equalize the relationship between experts and workers. Those laborers empowered through Three-In-One on-site building practices frequently lacked blueprints, meaning "the entire building [was] in [their] heads" and ensuring their complete control over both the design and construction processes.[11] The absence of drawings was particularly consequential in this regard, as they could dictate building procedures based upon memory despite a lack of basic knowledge in geometry, trigonometry, or the calculation of stress loads. The resulting power dynamics imbued existing brick and wall production with many of the same hierarchical imbalances present in socialist Chinese construction practices prior to the Cultural Revolution, which had been identified as one of the reasons for class struggle in the first place.

THE PREFABRICATED PANEL

If the more efficient production of bricks and blocks posed one set of practical and conceptual difficulties, prefabricated large-panel construction presented imbalances of a more complex sort. Bricks and blocks were also prefabricated building components requiring individualized assembly processes involving collective labor, but large prefabricated panels were more difficult building components to manufacture in factories and then transport to building sites, where a specific form of technical knowledge was necessary to integrate them into structures to compose buildings. Due to Soviet technical assistance, prefabricated panels had been a known building technology in China since the 1950s, though by the early 1970s, China's capacity for mass-producing them remained limited. During the Cultural Revolution, a different set of material and aesthetic sensibilities derived from vernacular construction practices like rammed earth construction had been popularized and paradoxically hailed by party radicals as evidence of a truly socialist form of progress on display. Renewed interest in prefabrication—the making of objects prior to their arrival on-site—thus challenged existing, Cultural Revolution–era building practices in consequential ways.

In capitalist and socialist countries alike, prefabrication was generally understood as a universal solution to design problems that transcended national identity or cultural specificity, though localized contexts and forms of expertise were important contributing forces to the technology's successful implementation in particular places at particular times.[12] The successful incorporation of panels in work such as Beijing's diplomatic residential compound towers, for example, was in large part due to the city's prominence as the national capital, and the willingness of municipal and national leaders to support those designers responsible for the technology's use, even as it also generated political controversy. Such a visible, material display of China's technological achievements in relation to a program such as diplomatic residences was considered helpful to the burnishing of China's international reputation, particularly in the wake of the Cultural Revolution. Domestically, too, these projects theoretically offered a model by which to improve and increase the country's housing production.

Problems arose in relation to China's limited technological capacity, however, which limited the speed and quality of the panel production process. Much of the era's architecture bore evidence of improper design methods and poor structural integrity resulting from a lack of dependable production methods and design expertise. During his visit to China in 1972, for example, Henry Liu witnessed difficulties in specific relation to the production of prefabricated panels, their assemblage into architecture, and the work teams responsible for them. In chronicling the collective installation of a prefabricated panel, he noted that "architects, workers, truck drivers, representatives of the glass factory—all involved participated in solving the problem."[13] Liu also watched as the group's efforts proved unsuccessful, however; for all of the collective spirit at work, participants failed to prevent the panel's embedded glass windows from breaking during its on-site assembly.

An additional challenge concerned the physical scale of the architecture being realized through such materials. Several iconic projects had been completed with much official fanfare, including landmarks such as the Beijing Hotel's east addition and the diplomatic residential compounds. Such work remained exceptional, however, and party representatives recognized the national dissemination of more advanced and comprehensive construction practices needed to occur before similar projects could be realized around the country. The decentralized construction of small, local enterprises—what one foreign observer described as "little steel mills, fertilizer factories, cement works, small food-processing plants, agricultural implement repair shops"—evinced the limitations imposed upon China's building capacity and, by extension, its economy.[14]

A 1974 *National Housing Design Exhibition* testified to the technological limits of such an approach, particularly in relation to the economies of scale at work (fig. 26). In a published selection of some of the exhibition's most notable residential district projects, including examples from the famous model industrial city of Daqing, a fundamental technical constraint could be observed in all of the work—namely, height. Few if any of the highlighted case studies comprised buildings over seven stories. Indeed, the country's tallest housing projects were limited to large cities such as Tianjin, Beijing, and Shanghai, where the manufacturing facilities capable of producing such material were based. Lighter building materials produced in these urban centers using more economical manufacturing techniques and assembled using better construction equipment were highlighted as models for the rest of the country, but they remained impossible without the infrastructural improvements required for national distribution.[15]

Given the political uncertainties at work in late Mao-era China, the idea that buildings realized through these techniques demanded different, more standardized forms of labor, and that they would appear formally and structurally taller, lighter, and thinner than earlier socialist Chinese constructions, also posed ideological questions. Over the course of 1974, amid the Gang of Four's efforts to regain their control over the party's leadership through the Criticize Lin Biao, Criticize Confucius campaign, CCP elders wrestled with the economic effects of continued interruption of the country's building industry, which was proving increasingly damaging to any sustained physical development.

How to promote such activity remained in dispute, however. In an effort to quicken the pace of industrial development, moderate leaders orchestrated the purchase of thirty complete industrial plants from capitalist countries between 1973 and 1974 at a price tag of $2 billion USD. Capitalism remained a constant concern in need of vigilance despite and because of improving relations with the United States, however, and the party's more radical leaders opposed such acquisitions, arguing that smaller, localized enterprises were more effective at empowering the country's rural population and could be operated at a scale better suited to exploit natural resources on-site while saving on transportation costs.

In June 1974, a week-long industry-wide meeting was held in Beijing to discuss how designers should combat the creeping influence of capitalism into their profession.[16] Despite the dangers associated with the free market, moderate officials advocated the continued study and importation of advanced building technologies existing in other coun-

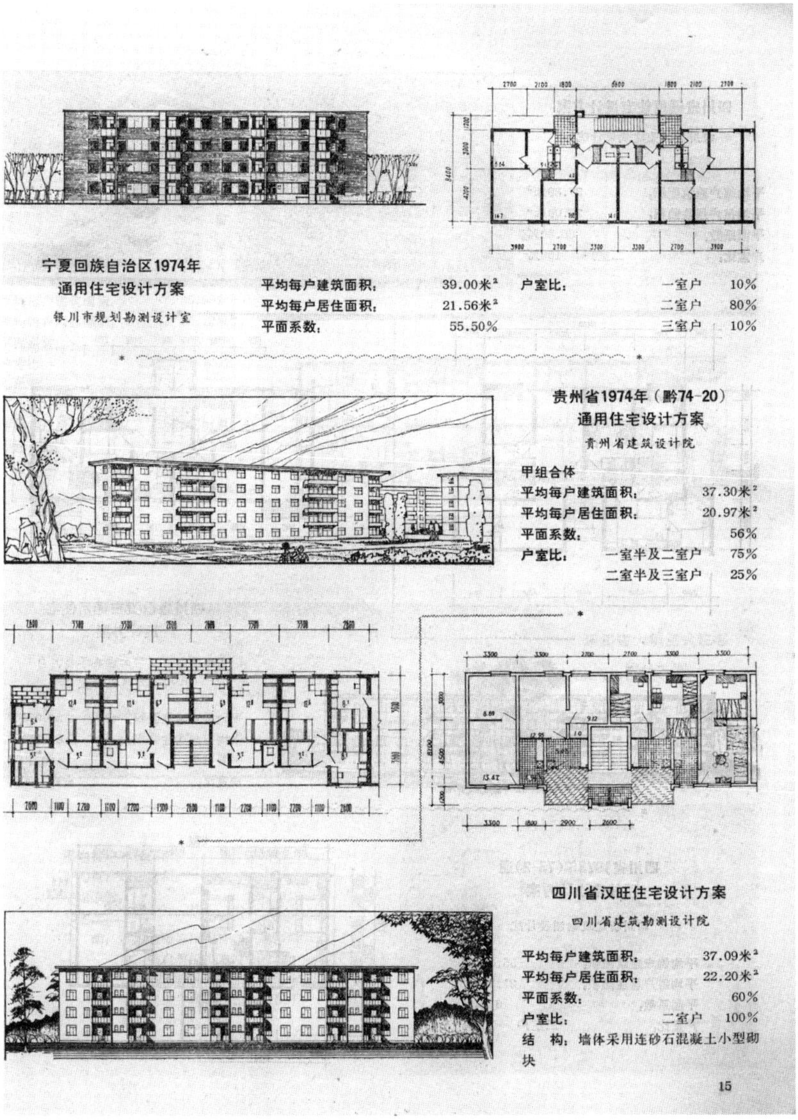

Fig. 26 *National Housing Design Exhibition*, Beijing, 1974. Originally published in *Architectural Journal* (*Jianzhu Xuebao*), no. 6 (1974).

tries as a means of improving China's own economic condition. The party's radicals, by contrast, championed continued class struggle and the intensified production of People's Communes as representing the country's only viable route toward a higher level of socialism. At the dispute's center lay important questions concerning the material quality of China's built environment and the extent to which the continued importation of foreign technology would aid in the country's modernization efforts.

In January 1975, Zhou summoned his last reserves of political clout in an effort to reposition the country on firmer economic ground. In one of his last major public appearances at the Fourth National People's Congress, Zhou revived an aborted 1964 campaign to promote China's economic growth through "Four Modernizations" in agriculture, industry, national defense, and science and technology.[17] The plan called for new state investment in these four sectors, each of which had suffered significantly during the Cultural Revolution. Zhou was supported in these efforts by Deng, a pugnacious veteran of the Long March who had been purged during the Cultural Revolution, only to be reinstated by Zhou and made deputy premier in 1973. In 1975 Deng subsequently became vice-chairman of the party's Central Committee, a member of its Political Bureau (Politburo), and chief of the general staff—powerful positions from which he could combat the Gang of Four's continued attacks upon Zhou and the technical pragmatism he championed.

With the Gang of Four entrenched as a potent obstacle to any large-scale, systematic restructuring of the country's economy, Zhou's patronage of Deng gave hope to those officials committed to supporting technological investment and expertise through greater international exchange. That same year, for example, Deng spearheaded the publication of several new party positions on technological innovation, including "On Some Problems Concerning the Work of Science and Technology," "On the General Program of Work for the Whole Party and the Country," and "Some Problems in Accelerating Industrial Development." Deng was given concurrent posts of vice-chairman of the party's Military Affairs Commission and vice-premier of the State Council, and he sought to implement a new state development strategy and introduce comprehensive structural reforms in scientific research and industrial management.[18] All of these efforts were challenged by the Gang of Four, who famously dismissed the documents as "three poisonous weeds" intended to derail the country's revolutionary progress. Nevertheless, they helped to reinforce perceptions among party elite that only through investment in technology would the country achieve the kind of economic growth it desperately needed.

Architecturally, Zhou's and Deng's redoubled efforts took shape through the rejuvenation of a series of older, established party objectives organized around notions of technical advancement that privileged standardized, economical building components like hollow bricks and blocks and prefabricated wall panels. Given the deteriorated quality of building expertise within the country, however, reinitiating the technical procedures required to produce and install prefabricated panels, from the creation of measured drawings and diagrams needed for their design to the machinery and knowledge required for precise manufacturing methods, proved problematic. Many of the country's design institutes remained understaffed if not closed altogether, and the professional status of both architects and engineers remained in flux.

The existing semiotics at work in promoting China's building production was also an issue. An active construction site bustling with workers and materials carried a particular social agency, whereas technological diagrams were generally more abstract in nature, and produced different forms of meaning (fig. 27). Those who could produce and read

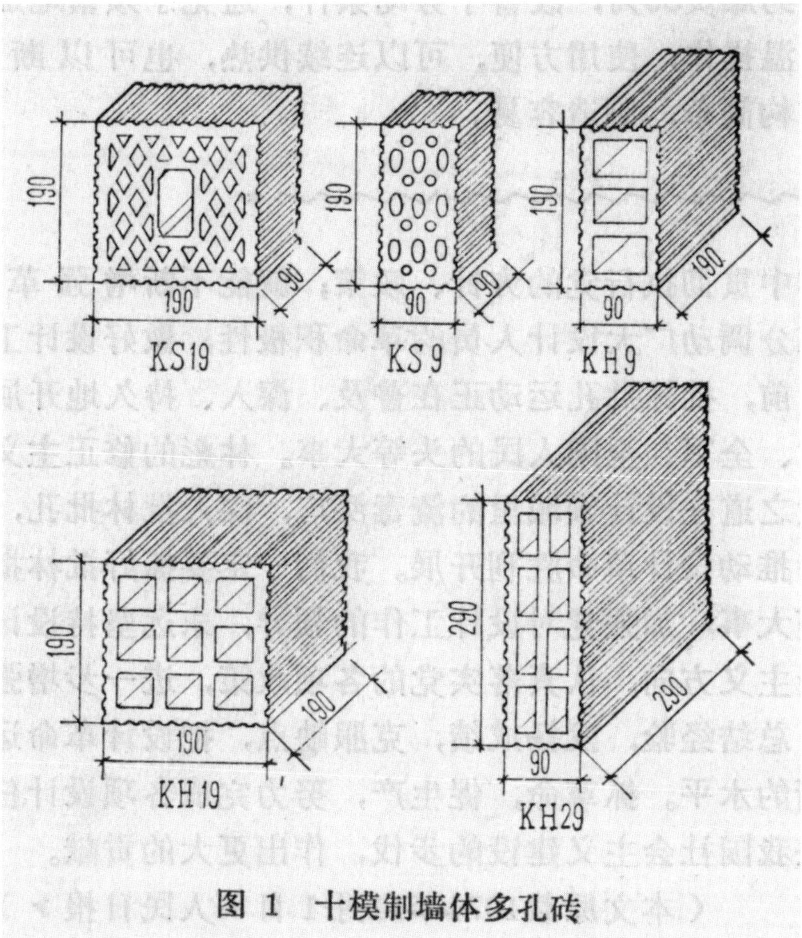

Fig. 27 Perforated brick and block construction, Xingning Brick and Tile Factory, Nanjing, 1974. Originally published in *Architectural Journal* (*Jianzhu Xuebao*), no. 6 (1974).

such drawings possessed an expertise that made them valuable to the assembly tasks at hand while depriving the Cultural Revolution's foot soldiers—mid-level workers and students—of their ideologically charged intermediary role on-site. No longer would collective groups of workers, students, cadres, architects, material manufacturers, and truck drivers necessarily need to deliberate over the benefits of one particular construction method over another. Rather, technical expertise would increasingly dictate how bricks, blocks, and panels were designed, cast, transported, and assembled into architecture.

In abandoning the sense of equitable collectivity on display in these on-site practices, the party risked losing the construction site as a key performative space for revolution. Avoiding this loss and, more generally, ensuring construction bureaus around the country had access to these new techniques, was key. A series of open forums were organized throughout the country in 1975 in which representatives from municipal and provincial design institutes and construction bureaus in Shanghai, Zhejiang, Jiaozuo, Henan, Harbin, and Fujian discussed their experiences with different kinds of building blocks, aeroconcrete and formwork, and

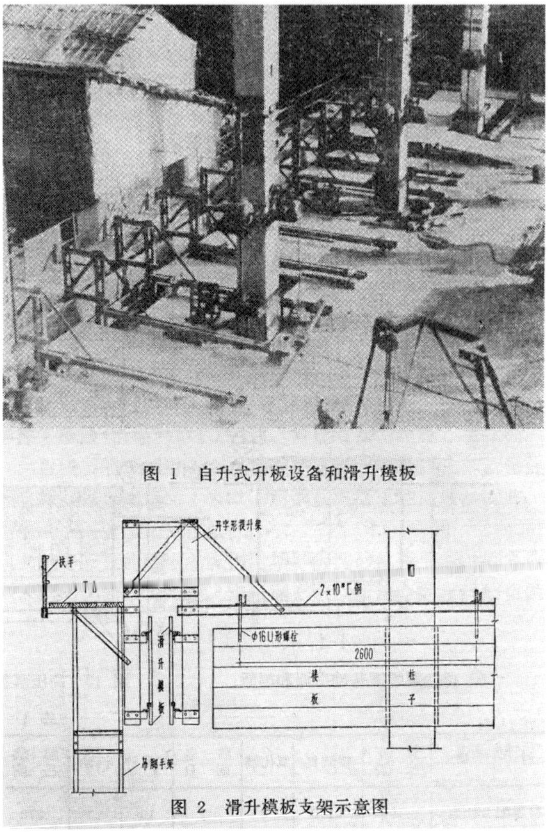

Fig. 28 Hydraulic mechanism for lifting floors and sliding formwork, Shanghai Fifth Engineering Company. Originally published in *Architectural Journal* (*Jianzhu Xuebao*), no. 3 (1975).

cast-situ concrete. These materials were introduced and discussed in relation to "proletarian theory."[19] Discipline-specific media outlets such as *Architectural Journal* promoted the labors of individual work units such as the Shanghai Fifth Engineering Company, members of which invented a hydraulic lift system that solved the problem of lifting and positioning prefabricated materials onto multistory buildings (fig. 28). The work evinced on-site initiative by laborers who had refuted the "blind worship of everything foreign" and instead imagined the potential technology themselves.[20] Nevertheless, the emphasis placed on technical proficiency began to push architecture's representational agency in new and unsettling directions. The circulation of images of these new technologies and the objects that accompanied them suggested a process of uniform application around the country that did not in fact exist. In each photo, individual workers figured as crucial domesticating agents of these new practices who helped to localize the practices, regardless of where they may have originated. However, imbalance was already embedded within these practices and the efforts to promote them. By highlighting the ingenuity of a select number of work teams, the party's leftist faction could not help but contradict its message of proletarian equitability. The promotion of model workers and model units was standard policy propaganda procedure, but through these efforts—the appearance that some work teams were better than others—an inherent inequality was embedded within these more technologically advanced construction practices.

FROM WALL REFORM TO ECONOMIC REFORM

The term "wall reform" first appeared as the title of a 1976 pamphlet published by the National Building Research Institute chronicling recent advancements made throughout the country in relationship to brick, concrete block, and prefabricated wall panel production (fig. 29). Less a campaign than a summary of the country's recent achievements in building technology, the pamphlet drew attention to the efforts undertaken around the country to implement and improve brick, block, and wall panel production techniques and the extent to which these materials possessed the capacity to transform the nature of socialist Chinese building standards and practices.[21]

The publication highlighted a number of built examples extending back to the mid-1960s through 1976, with obvious gaps occurring between 1967 and 1970, the height of the Cultural Revolution. In doing so, it imbued more sophisticated brick, block, and panel technology with a degree of political and economic urgency specific to the reconstruction of the nation, though embedded in the pamphlet's messaging also lay a determined effort not to stoke the flames of class conflict. It did not reject the ideological fervor of grassroots building and production procedures of the era so much as it redefined them as sets of localized practices dependent upon new infusions of knowledge and new opportunities for experimentation still considered revisionist among some party leaders. In promoting certain forms of expertise, the text did not abandon what were still considered to be the CCP's key if fluctuating ideological tenets.

To that end, wall reform seemed geared toward reconciling the ideological gulf dividing CCP leadership through the material practices of architectural production. Importantly, the campaign promoted prefabrication methods that already existed in China, having been first introduced beginning in the 1950s via the Soviet Union and subsequently marginalized during the Cultural Revolution amid the party's ideological shift away from foreign technology and toward class struggle. The recirculation of these technologies was vital to the movement's potential success, and in official propaganda for the campaign, new production techniques were artfully framed as reengagements with the broader historical arc of Mao's revolution, and a necessary innovation in the country's seemingly ceaseless war against class oppression. The campaign's 1976 pamphlet, for example, traced the movement back to practices initiated by workers in the early 1960s in accordance with Chairman Mao's exhortation to "Destroy Foreign Conventions, Pursue the Path of National Industrial Development" and the 1964 Mass Design Revolution movement.[22]

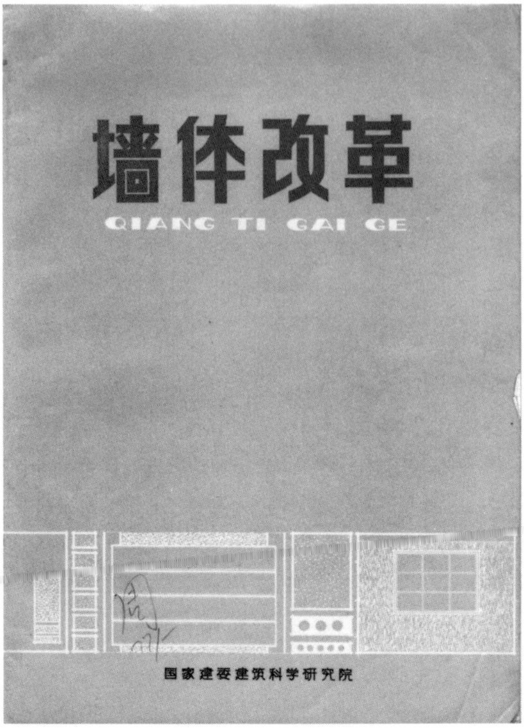

Fig. 29 Cover, *Wall Reform* (*Qiangti Gaige*, 1976).

The ongoing and anticipated technological transformation was thus understood as both a reengagement with socialist Chinese building practices and a localized, grassroots initiative—a fusion of past and present with an eye on realizing a new socialist future. Evoking earlier monuments and eras in socialist Chinese history validated the campaign and reminded readers that although the implementation of more efficient manufacturing methods had proven slow and cumbersome, a jolt of revolutionary rejuvenation would enable their true transformative potential. Localities all over the country were encouraged to embrace "new building materials, new architecture, new experiences," thereby allowing "a hundred flowers to contend in beauty"—an allusion to an earlier and controversial party campaign in which intellectuals were encouraged to independently voice their opinions of the party, only to be punished for their outspokenness.[23]

Municipal-, county-, and provincial-level leaders inspired by Beijing pushed the campaign forward. Distinctive varieties of brick and concrete from different parts of the country were highlighted to convey the spectrum of innovative new practices taking place, including examples such as coal cinder building blocks, concrete hollow blocks, sandstone bricks, and aerocrete production. "Our work is still not enough, and implementation and understanding has only just begun," exhorted members of the Zhejiang Provincial Architectural Design Bureau within *Architectural Journal* in 1974. "We remain determined to follow the spirit of the 'Ten Great [Buildings],' empower ourselves through the criticisms of Lin Biao and Confucius, embrace revolution, promote production, fulfill the goals of wall reform, and from today forward, continue to improve hollow concrete block production in service to socialist construction."[24] The process of design itself was likened to an ideological battlefront where workers were devoted to "defeating the blind and slavish imitation of all things foreign," and only through the maintenance of China's independence through the "hard struggle" of revolution would the socialist achievements inscribed into the country's landscape be preserved.[25] Through these and other strategies, the party attempted to infuse hollow bricks and concrete blocks with a tangible symbolism capable of enabling a clean pivot toward a new technologically oriented direction without abandoning its proletarian spirit.

On one hand, the promotion of once and future prefabrication techniques was an opportunity to bring the country's revolutionaries and building experts together, thereby achieving a long-desired party goal at the heart of the Cultural Revolution and its Down to the Countryside movement. Several related articles from the era lauded the architectural achievements of China's "worker-peasant-soldier student" Red Guards, and "Three-Combinations" procedures were celebrated as tangible, lasting proof of the Cultural Revolution's success, even as the new material practices being introduced portended their obsolescence.[26] National construction committee members in Changshu, Luoyang, Shanghai, and Xi'an, among others, were hailed as model workers and inspiring voices behind new wall and roofing materials, technological innovation, and brick and panel architectural production, and were tasked with leading sharing sessions all over the country in an effort to convey the bottom-up nature of the change. Leaders from Xi'an, Jiaozuo, and Nanning, among others, were highlighted as particularly active proponents of the new technologies.[27]

Despite efforts to integrate the campaign within the broader history of socialist Chinese construction, hollow brick and prefabricated concrete walls were still new technologies to the vast majority of the country. Approximately 98 percent of China's bricks were still made by traditional, self-pressed processes, and brick and concrete labor costs accounted for 50 percent of an average Chinese construction project. These economic and procedural realities affected how bricks, blocks, and panels were understood as material objects and signifiers of socialist Chinese construction by the population at large.

A new accompanying representational logic was thus necessary to justify thinner, lighter architecture and counter perceptions that the robust materiality emblematic of socialist Chinese buildings or the labor supporting it was somehow in decline. The 1976 *Wall Reform* (*Qiangti Gaige)* pamphlet helpfully informed readers that the Cultural Revolution had reinvigorated brick and concrete production by starving it, resulting in a sinewy ideological zeal in stark contrast to the "fat beams, plump columns, heavy roofs, and deep foundations" of past precedent.[28] The emphasis placed on the corporeal-like excesses of a building was striking, given the depravity inflicted upon human bodies in the name of the party just years prior, but marrying the aesthetic and the economic helped to normalize lighter, thinner, and more efficient architecture. Concrete's unique material and representational agency—its ability to appear both thin and thick—proved valuable in this regard, insofar as it remained a material constant for the procedural and structural modifications already taking place.

Even as wall reform promised to unshackle all workers involved in China's building processes, however, the rejuvenation of hollow brick and concrete wall construction reintroduced sophisticated methods of building material production that risked privileging certain segments of the workforce at the expense of others. Hollow manufacturing methods used less material than standard brick and wall production; they were cheaper but also more difficult to realize. As a result, they demanded more technological expertise than other practices, which made them politically contentious in a nation caught in an ideological struggle over the country's future, and in which building was itself still understood to be a revolutionary act.

TOWARD A NEW MATERIAL REALITY

Official debate over material innovations such as hollow brick, block, and prefabricated panel construction spanned a range of practical, technical, aesthetic, and ideological considerations that affirm their significance to the state. Bricks, blocks, and panels were the connective tissue linking the party's goals of socialist modernization to the built environments that made these goals tangible and real to the country's population. It was at the scale of the brick, the block, and the panel that the party's control over a citizen's life was ultimately made material and palpable; it was also through these specific objects that the deep deficiencies in the country's governance became tangible.

On July 28, 1976, the various abstractions at work in reforming China's building material standards and culture were rendered tragically real when a massive earthquake centered around the city of Tangshan in Hebei Province, located approximately 180 kilometers east of Beijing, killed an estimated three hundred thousand people. The specifics of the tragedy, including an accurate death toll, remain politically sensitive and make it difficult to determine the role, if any, particular construction techniques may have played in the devastation. However, it is estimated 95 percent of the city's buildings were destroyed, including thousands of two- and three-story brick masonry structures, many of which were of dubious structural quality. Over nine hundred thousand people were displaced by the tragedy, prompting efforts to recycle the city's bricks and blocks to build new, temporary housing. Although building standards were issued for these units, on-site crews were ultimately responsible for making most of the construction and design decisions due to time constraints, building material shortages, and a lack of design expertise.[29] The sheer scale of devastation, and the government's ongoing refusal to release information concerning the disaster, indicated fatal flaws in Mao-era Chinese construction standards and building procedures, which many took as evidence of the party's own deterioration.

Four months later, on November 15, Beijing residents were warned of an impending aftershock. In preparation for the predicted tremor, many of the city's residents fled their existing apartment buildings to build makeshift shelters on the street out of concern for the structural integrity of their own homes, and despite the chill of early winter. Beverley Hooper, an Australian student living in Beijing at the time, observed that foreigners were not allowed to sleep on the second or third floors of their dormitories due to the risk of collapse. She also saw Chinese citizens "feverishly" building temporary structures that paradoxically remained occupied through the end of the month. "Using picks and shovels, people dug five or six feet into the rock-hard earth before commencing work on their half-buried houses," noted Hooper. "They built walls from old bricks or made new mud bricks on the site. Most building still seemed to be done on an individual family basis. Later, some larger shelters which would hold a number of families were built and a few prefabricated wooden structures appeared on the scene, making the earlier efforts look like children's playhouses. But even the playhouses were organized." Hooper herself sought shelter from a friend living in Beijing's recently completed diplomatic residential compound.[30]

Both events and their respective, anxious aftermaths offered devastating reminders of the structural weaknesses in socialist Chinese architecture and, more generally, socialist Chinese governance, and following the tragedy, designers and officials pursued nationally standardized building regulations to ensure a degree of material and procedural consistency in relation to the country's architectural production.[31] In this respect, wall reform, like China's architectural diplomacy and its contemporaneous efforts at international exchange through tours and objects, was an early admission that Chinese society required change if the founding goals of a modern, socialist China were to be achieved.

Enhancing the country's material reality through improved building systems was a political project as much as it was an architectural endeavor, particularly given the lingering effects of building Mao's "dreamworld and catastrophe."[32] If diplomatic edifices designed and built in the name of greater international interconnectivity marked one of the party's first visible shifts away from the Cultural Revolution's ascetic fervor, and the study tour conveyed the CCP's desire for more advanced technical proficiency, brick and wall reform expressed official acknowledgment that China's physical environment—and the various forms of knowledge and technical procedures undergirding that environment—also needed to change. The initial inscription of these changes upon China's buildings through bricks, blocks, and panels also revealed that party dissension had real, material consequences—a lesson that also confirmed architecture's value in the changes to come.

Hollow brick, block, and panel production was able to briefly but consequentially disrupt the ideological triangulation between architecture, labor, and party rule, in part because it acknowledged a need for technical proficiency beyond the capacity of most of China's material manufacturers, without dismissing the aesthetic and ideological power of the construction site itself. Ultimately, however, the procedural and technical complexities of material production necessitated localized technological leaps—acts of design—that privileged forms of specialization over which the government did not necessarily have firm control, thus hastening the transition away from *hong,* or Red, toward *zhuan,* or expert, that took place within the official government lexicon after 1976.[33]

This realization took place as thousands of architects, engineers, and scholars of design returned to their homes and livelihoods from reeducation camps and were tasked with conceiving of a post-Mao Chinese architecture capable of contributing to the economic, political, and social changes deemed necessary to complete socialist China's modernization. Collective, on-site acts of design and construction lost their ideological charge as new techniques emerged that challenged how architecture was produced and, by extension, understood in relationship to Chinese society at large. Although architecture remained a political act, the ideological foundation for those politics had begun to crack in part from the pressures produced from the country's material reality, presenting China's designers with new challenges and an uncertain way forward.

Of foremost concern to officials and architects alike was the identification of a convincing and effective architectural vision for China's future after Mao. Rendering the party's policy shifts visible to the broader Chinese public required new, more variegated forms of architectural expression, and officials determined that reinvigorating China's architectural production necessitated a more substantial importation of new architectural ideas from abroad. However, it was difficult to encourage architects to pursue innovation when, just years prior, people had been punished for taking such initiative.

Over the course of 1978 and 1979, the party's previous attempts at reconciling ideology and technology within the country's building industry gave way to more concerted, official efforts to induce greater technical innovation through appeals to test truth through practice. Many designers eager to restart their professional careers recommitted themselves to a new, technological revolution designed to modernize

China anew, despite questions concerning the discipline's new truths. It was evident that the architecture produced during the Cultural Revolution had not facilitated the kind of socialist modernity envisioned by Mao. What came next remained an open question, however.

PART II

Implementation

CHAPTER 4

Architectural History and Heritage

On January 8, 1976, Zhou Enlai passed away from a long bout with bladder cancer. That April, and in accordance with a traditional Chinese tomb sweeping holiday, thousands of mourners gathered at the Martyrs' Memorial on Tiananmen Square to lay wreaths and hold posters and images aloft extolling Zhou's contributions to the country. The spontaneous event surprised party leaders with its somber yet striking rebuttal to Mao Zedong and his more radical followers. It also fanned the Gang of Four's anger against Deng Xiaoping, who days later was dismissed from the party a second time at Mao's behest and forced into hiding until early 1977. These two events were followed, on September 9, 1976, by the death of Mao. If Zhou's death left the party without its most pragmatic statesman, Mao's demise denied the government its key ideological referent, resulting in a crisis of faith among the country's citizens that necessitated the party's attention.

The loss of both men prompted a reevaluation of China's international standing vis-à-vis the world at large while dimming the prospects of continued class conflict. In early October, less than one month following Mao's death, Jiang Qing and the other members of the Gang of Four were arrested on charges of attempted usurpation of the party during the Cultural Revolution, a verdict that blamed them for the brutal campaign while essentially clearing Mao's name. Hua Guofeng, Mao's chosen successor, was named chairman of the CCP, chairman of the Central Military Commission, and premier of the PRC—the top offices of the country's government, its dominant political party, and its military. The passing of both Zhou and Mao, followed in rapid succession by Hua's ascendance and the arrest of the Gang of Four, transformed the composition and ideological orientation of the country's leadership.

Fearing the prospects of political instability, the CCP turned to the past—a strategy previously employed by officials in times of crisis, and often involving the party's selective erasure of historical moments to reinvent a new official narrative. "In Maoist China it is the past which is unpredictable," remarked the Chinese-French journalist Bao Ruowang, also known as Jean Pasqualini.[1] Architectural editorials and images were deployed to aid in the party's efforts to pivot to the new era by instrumentalizing recent history. A 1977 issue of *Architectural Journal* (*Jianzhu Xuebao*), for example, informed readers that recently discovered structural deficiencies in the Shanghai Indoor Stadium—one of the few large-scale public engineering projects completed during the previous ten years—originated not with the project's designers or builders, but in the self-aggrandizing exploits of Wang Hongwen and other members of the Shanghai-originated Gang of Four. Officials also purportedly discovered in each Gang of Four leader's private home an array of illegal technologies and excessive decor, which served as additional evidence of the clique's degenerate, counterrevolutionary decadence. Jiang Qing purportedly insisted on living in two buildings within the New Summer Palace (Yiheyuan), while Wang's "villa," located west of Beijing, included a television room, movie theater, and swimming pool.

Such scandalous, unsubstantiated claims underscored the speed with which the party's re-empowered moderate faction sought to discredit their radical adversaries by turning their own ideological weaponry against them. "Through their residences, one can easily see the deception at work in the Gang of Four's criticism of others' bourgeois habits," charged the editors. "They are bloodsuckers who will stop at no evil."[2] The party's instrumentalization of the built environment and its history against those blamed for the Cultural Revolution illuminated shifting power dynamics at work not only in the country's politics, but in the architectural production and meaning undergirding them.

China's architectural history had long presented challenges and opportunities to party ideology. A State Bureau of Cultural Relics (SBCR) was established soon after the country's founding in 1949, and over the course of the 1950s and 1960s, imperial-era sites, palaces, and temples were opened to the public and maintained as parks to educate people regarding the role of the masses in the literal construction of imperial China. Most of these sites were closed during the Cultural Revolution but were gradually reopened beginning in the early 1970s amid the moderates' turn back toward history and the protection of China's rich cultural legacy. Beginning in 1973, and under Zhou's leadership, the SBCR was renamed the State Cultural Relics Enterprises Management Bureau (SCREMB) and put directly under the supervision of the State Council to provide more comprehensive oversight over the country's embattled cultural heritage. At the same time, international events such as the traveling *Exhibition of Archaeological Finds of the People's Republic of China* shrewdly capitalized upon the diplomatic value of imperial-era China's material culture.

Reopening, repairing, and, in some cases, rebuilding architectural vestiges of China's past took on additional if ambiguous import after

1976 amid the government's desire to rally socialist China's national spirit around Hua and the Four Modernizations. Chinese citizens were asked to aid the government's attempts to revitalize the "historical continuity and spiritual contour" of the Chinese nation just years after being encouraged to rise up against the country's feudal past.[3] Saving physical remnants of China's traditions achieved these ends but also raised thorny ideological questions concerning how to now utilize China's architectural history to the party's advantage, and in accordance with the government's new, forward-looking agenda.

Architectural heritage—the process by which historical architectural production is reorganized and assessed using distinctive criteria determinant of a culture's perceived value—offered a means by which these contradictions could be resolved, and through which the country's architectural past might contribute to the nation-building efforts taking place. The act of architectural reconstruction is an opportunity perhaps unique among the arts—a chance to design an idealized past for the present—and it offered party leaders a tool to fix socialist China's national and cultural identity around new sets of ideological parameters.[4] The study of architectural history reemerged as an active field of scholarly inquiry in the years following Mao's passing, but it was architectural heritage—a far more limited interpretation of the past that is more susceptible to shifting political, cultural, and social influences, and thus more likely to be deployed to enforce national narratives and legitimize particular identities—that presented architects and officials with a praxis capable of overcoming the physical and psychological damage wrought upon China's cultural traditions and reconfiguring the value of historical buildings and sites to the state's goals.[5]

Prior to the completion of special economic zones (SEZs), international hotels, office buildings, and exhibition halls that so neatly embodied China's opening to the world, it was the notion of architectural heritage that triggered a reconceptualization of China's architectural landscape from a revolutionary tool into a form of capital to be distributed, adapted, and consumed in accordance with reform. Buildings were present and tangible components of everyday life in China, and acts of repair and rehabilitation seemed to offer constructive responses to a dark moment in China's recent past. At the level of national policy, too, salvaging the country's architectural past served specific economic objectives. In 1978, for example, one hundred thousand foreigners and six hundred thousand overseas ethnic Chinese visited China; by 1980 China's tourism industry was generating $607.2 million USD.[6] Travelers, both foreign and Chinese, needed sites to visit.

Over the course of the late 1970s and early 1980s, architects, working in conjunction with the state, embarked upon a process of selective cultural reconstruction that transformed China's architectural history into heritage. Their efforts to redesign objects, memorials, sites, exhibitions, and urban districts helped to stabilize the party's image by reimagining how China's architectural heritage was understood, utilized, theorized, and circulated both within the country and internationally.

Heritage could be a difficult topic to address in post-Mao China, particularly coming after a period in which the country's preexisting architectural fabric and traditions had come under the state's direct, physical attack. In some respects, the state's curation of certain historical themes and narratives through reform-era conservation design mimicked the controlled, carefully prescribed dynamics of the Mao-era study tour and the exhibition. Such work also diverged from earlier, Mao-era engagements with China's architectural past in several important ways, however. For one, architects had relatively more freedom to engage in a broader and deeper range of historical sites and spaces than what had been allowed under Mao. Greater access to international knowledge fueled these efforts, and Chinese designers and scholars studied, published, and discussed international histories of architecture in relationship to China's architectural past in a more comprehensive fashion than perhaps at any point in the country's history since 1949.

The conservation work undertaken during the early reform era itself was also uniquely international in its scope and impact, with numerous foreign agents and organizations involved in Chinese architectural heritage consultation and design projects. Their presence complicates the narrative that these efforts were particular to China, singularly driven by the state, or somehow incidental to the country's broader economic reform. Foreign experts and ideas were influential to the party's conservation efforts after Mao, and China's architectural past was essential to modernization itself—a consolidation of time and public memory in the name of refurbishing the party's legacy both at home and abroad before it could proceed with building socialist China's future anew.[7]

PRESERVING THE PARTY

Ironically, the first act of conservation following Mao's death was Mao himself. On October 8, 1976, two days following the Gang of Four's arrest, party officials led by Hua Guofeng determined a memorial hall should be built to commemorate Mao's service to the People's Republic, within which the chairman's embalmed body would be interred. Preliminary design work on the project actually began several weeks prior to his death, when designers, artists, and laborers from around China traveled to Beijing to begin deliberations. Following debate over possible locations, it was decided to build the project on Tiananmen Square, and construction began in early 1977. The building was completed and publicly commemorated on September 9, 1977, one year following Mao's death, and despite his insistence that his body be cremated after death (fig. 30).[8]

Fig. 30 Mao Zedong Mausoleum, Beijing Institute of Architectural Design, Beijing, 1976–77. Originally published in *Architectural Journal* (*Jianzhu Xuebao*), no. 4 (1977).

Documentation and analysis of the building's design and construction has highlighted the internal politics involved in its siting, its awkward aesthetic engagement with both imperial-era Chinese and U.S. memorial architecture, and the calculus of legitimacy behind its construction.[9] Officials studied a number of tombs and memorials around the world, including both Lenin's mausoleum and the Lincoln Memorial, before settling on the final scheme—a brick and concrete structure clad in red marble and composed of a monumental terraced platform, severe colonnade, and overhanging eaves reminiscent of earlier capital construction such as the Beijing Hotel, foreign diplomatic compound, and the Friendship Store. Built to consolidate Hua's control over the party, the project represented a hasty exercise to relegitimize Mao's authority and thus stabilize Hua's position as his political heir—a process that extended well into the first years of the reform era. Indeed, if the building's initial construction embodied Hua's determination to maintain power as Mao's preferred successor, the subsequent revision of several of the hall's aesthetic and spatial details, including the 1983 addition of memorial rooms devoted to Zhou, Liu Shaoqi, and Zhu De, reflected Deng's more measured assessment of Mao and more critical reappraisal of the party's legacy.[10]

In the immediate aftermath of Mao's passing, and amid the design and construction of his mausoleum, officials also undertook several refurbishments of sites associated with both recently deceased lead-

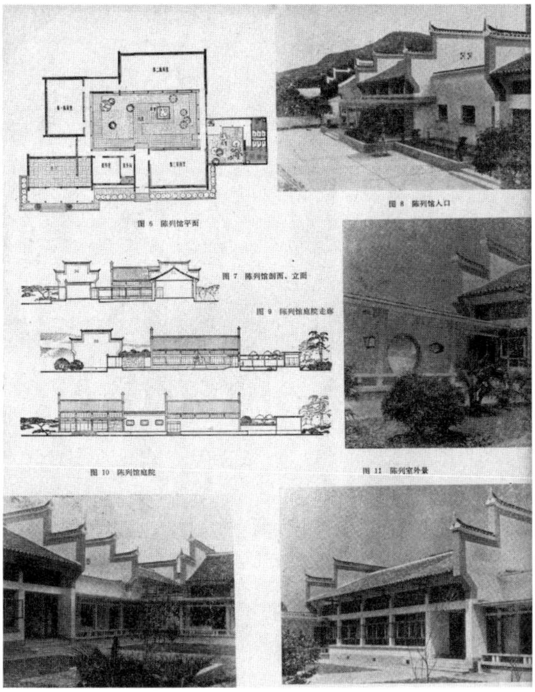

Fig. 31 Memorial, 1927 Autumn Harvest Uprising, Hunan, 1978. Originally published in *Architectural Journal* (*Jianzhu Xuebao*), no. 2 (1978).

ers and the party's history. A renovation of Zhou's childhood library in Shenyang, Liaoning Province, was completed in 1977. In April 1977, officials in Hunan Province decided to construct an exhibition hall on the site of the 1927 Autumn Harvest Uprising, a Mao-led revolt that led to the creation of the Communist Army (fig. 31). The new, 10,002 square-meter exhibition space was organized into three new display rooms and a lecture hall asymmetrically organized around a central courtyard. The composition of large and small structures, and the balance between solid and void, aimed to evoke the surrounding environment; it also intensified the sense of enclosure and "solemnity" associated with the site.[11] Careful consideration was given to the old site's original form, and the architectural details of Hunan's vernacular style, including simple post-and-beam construction, small black roofing tiles, horse-head gabling, window screens, and whitewashed walls.

In addition to these acts of architectural reconstruction, a series of articles appeared extolling the historical import of key revolutionary sites throughout China, including Mao's childhood home at Shaoshan, and Zunyi, site of the January 1935 meeting that cemented Mao's leadership over the party.[12] These articles did not specify whether renovations were taking place, but they provided readers with overviews of each site's historical significance and the process by which these locations were selected as heritage sites in anticipation of increased tourism. Accompanying drawings, maps, and diagrams detailed the spatial and topographic nature of each site.

None of these projects offered radically new curations of figures and

Fig. 32 August 1 Memorial with detail of Hua Guofeng's calligraphy, Nanchang, 1979. Originally published in *Architectural Journal* (*Jianzhu Xuebao*), no. 3 (1979).

moments already etched into the collective conscious of the nation. Nevertheless, their physical improvement fulfilled two major party objectives under Hua, namely, to mitigate lingering intraparty as well as public antipathy toward the Mao era by redirecting established national narratives and geographies around the party's new leader, and, more generally, around the needs of international and domestic tourists.[13] Instrumentalizing these sites through acts of repair and expansion were important steps in cementing Hua's grip over the party and countering fears of the country's destabilization, but they were not without controversy, nor did they guarantee that Hua or the government would be able to reconcile the party's damaged standing to its new modernizing mission.

These tensions became literally inscribed upon at least one example of design work from the era. On January 8, 1979, the August 1 Memorial was completed in Nanchang (fig. 32). Designed to commemorate the first battle between the Communist and Nationalist armies in China's protracted civil war, the forty-two-meter, steel-reinforced stone stele adhered to standard socialist Chinese precedent, with long, horizontal bas-relief carvings of the communist soldiers embedded along the north and south sides of its base. Several carved inscriptions memorializing the event by Hua himself ran vertically along the stele's shaft, along with standard party insignia. The sculpture was crowned by an abstracted Chinese flag carved of stone and depicted as waving from the similarly abstracted shaft of a rifle. Per past precedent, *Architectural Journal* provided a comprehensive review of the monument's design and selection process, including alternative schemes and detailed descriptions of the monument's measurements, graphic detailing, and material composition in its May 1979 issue.[14]

Eight months later, however, in January 1980, the journal countered its own coverage by publishing a critical reassessment of the memorial written by Zhu Yuqing. In the essay, Zhu called the completed project a weak and frail monument lacking in vigor, and lamented its tired embrace of China's memorial precedent.[15] In its place, Zhu argued in favor of a rejected alternative flag scheme, in which both the flag and the rifle composed the monument's mass (fig. 33). "The author [of the original article] argues that 'the inscriptions are not well-positioned on this rejected version,' but the privileged position given to Hua's calligraphy threatens to overshadow the event itself. Hua is the successor to our great Chairman Mao," reasoned Zhu, "and a prudent and virtuous man of the people who would not agree with this decision. Privileging the calligraphy in this way (and it may not have been the designer's choice) is inappropriate." In his advocacy of bold, more solidly iconographic architectural work, Zhu urged architects to consider that "from today forward, building revolutionary commemorative architecture must not continue to use old customs."[16] His architectural critique also served

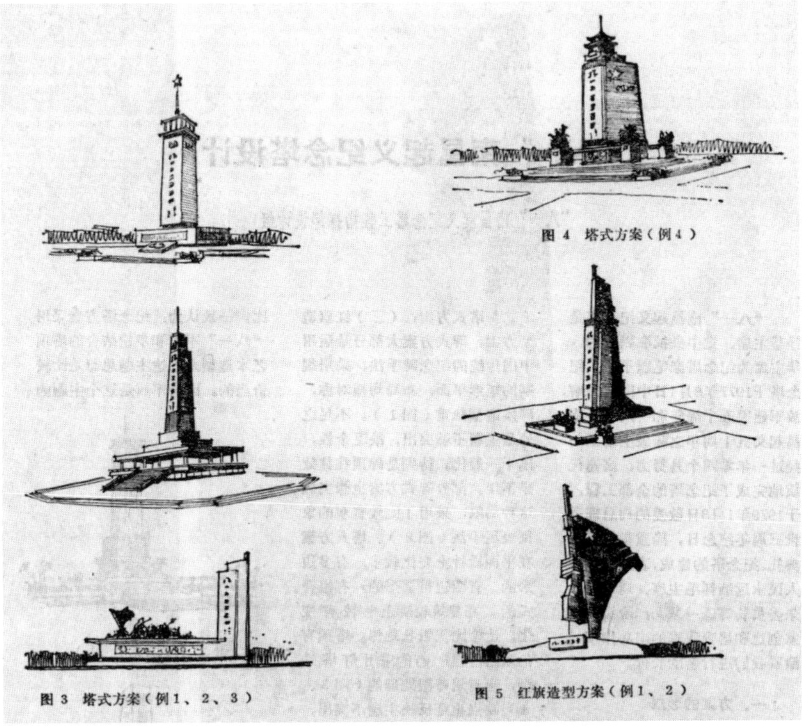

Fig. 33 Alternative "pagoda" and "red flag"-style proposals, August 1 Memorial, Nanchang, 1977. Originally published in *Architectural Journal* (*Jianzhu Xuebao*), no. 3 (1979).

political ends, however, and contributed to Hua's diminishment within the party's ranks.

Hua's standing within the party was ultimately and permanently destroyed by another unusual and similarly public set of architectural challenges that took place in February 1979, following the introduction of Deng's new reform policy to party leaders, and at a time in which Hua was still technically in charge of the country. Earlier that winter, in late 1978, a big poster movement was launched to further criticize the already disgraced Gang of Four and, by extension, diminish Hua's authority, thereby ensuring Deng's eventual control over the CCP. Over the course of December and January, however, the movement quickly gained public attention and transformed into the Democracy Wall movement, an unsanctioned and spontaneous series of public protests calling for party action concerning China's broader political and social ills. Architectural signs of excess were again weaponized against certain party members; for example, Wang Dongxing, a former bodyguard to Mao, was accused of building a private palace in the Zhongnanhai government compound.[17]

A more subversive attack on Mao and his legacy took shape through wall posters calling for the construction of a memorial hall and statue in honor of Zhou Enlai. One anonymously produced image from the era depicted the placement of such an edifice between Mao's Memorial Hall and the preexisting Monument to the People's Heroes (fig. 34). The proposed memorial adhered to formal socialist Chinese memorial precedent, but its siting severed the visual and spatial axis linking Mao's hall to Tiananmen Gate and the Forbidden City, thereby elevating Zhou to a symbolic position above that of Mao.[18] More than a simple gesture to honor Zhou, the radical intervention challenged Mao's unquestioned grip on the country's time and space, thereby undermining Hua and promoting Deng in the process.

The search for new expressions of remembrance and their political undercurrents echoed other contemporaneous forms of cultural production arising in the wake of the Cultural Revolution, including artistic examples such as Luo Zhongli's *Father* (1980) and so-called postrevolutionary "scar" literature.[19] In their specific engagement with the unbuilt, however, both Zhu's essay and the proposed Zhou memorial were specific architectural efforts to counter Mao-era demagoguery and the trauma it had produced with the more pragmatic, technologically oriented ambitions offered by Zhou and Deng. Neither proposal mounted an open criticism against the party per se, but through their speculative use of form and site, each attempted to make physical and conceptual space for past suffering and the grave political mistakes made. Testing the ideological boundaries of the "unreal" in post-Mao China was an idealistic project to which architecture was uniquely well-suited, and these projects aimed to capitalize upon the revolutionary spirit at the heart of Mao's utopian vision and

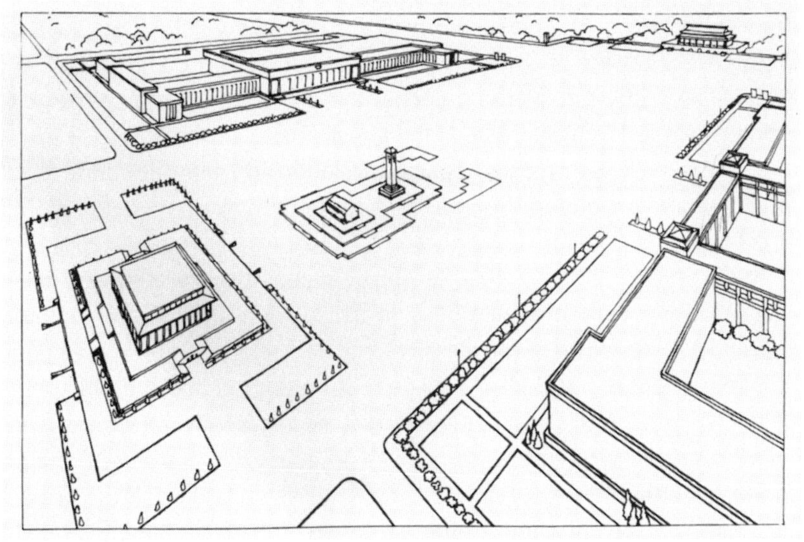

Fig. 34 Beijing wall poster showing the Mao Memorial Hall with projected Zhou Enlai Mausoleum next to the Monument to the People's Heroes, February 1979. Originally published in Ellen Johnston Laing, *The Winking Owl* (1988).

redirect it into alternative, imagined forms and spaces within which a new China might yet take shape. Early conservation efforts were designed to similar effect, though not before the study of architectural history itself was revived, expanded, and called back into action by the state.

FROM HISTORY TO HERITAGE

With various architectural commemorations to the party's history underway, architects and officials focused their attention upon reintroducing broader swaths of the country's architectural past into the present as acceptable topics of study. It was important to capitalize upon China's building traditions to revalidate the party as a protector of the country's cultural heritage and bridge its self-imposed isolation from architectural ideas circulating through other parts of the world. What kinds of histories could be safely discussed within the discipline, and how particular topics should be framed relative to the ideological shifts beginning to take place remained unclear, however. The specific contributions to be made by history and heritage to the country's economy and the Four Modernizations was another pressing concern.

Although the physical redesign of China's recent politics helped to steady both the party and its influence over the country, such work required parallel efforts on the part of historians to rebuild the country's architectural historical narrative, which aided in the party's pivot away from the ideological excesses of the late Mao era toward a broader range of more discipline-specific concerns. Organizations such as the Architectural Society of China (ASC), which facilitated China's reengagement with international architectural ideas through study tours organized prior to 1978, helped to shape these early discussions. In October 1978, for example, the ASC sponsored a conference devoted to defining architectural modernization for the early reform era.[20] Disciplinary stalwarts such as Zhang Bo, architect of the Beijing Hotel's east addition, Zhang Kaiji, Lin Keming, and others delivered speeches that aimed to rationalize the government's need to modernize China anew. The event helped to resuscitate terms such as form and space in relation to Chinese architectural discourse and promoted the need for competitions and the rejuvenation of theory.

It did little to clarify the relationship between history and design, however. Between 1978 and 1980, several articles published in *Architectural Journal* each aimed to reconcile architecture's relationship to the country's recent politics and how architects should approach such history.[21] Of these, Wang Zhili's 1980 essay "A History Lesson: Recollections from Two Phases of Architectural Work" was notable for its particularly harsh condemnation of the discipline's ideological corruption after 1966.[22] Early, previously criticized trends in the country's architectural past, including the abstraction of imperial-era Chinese architectural motifs that took place during the mid- to late 1950s, were reevaluated on the basis of new assessment criteria, including aesthetic beauty and perceptions of cultural integrity and identity.

The public resuscitation of key scholarly figures and their long-neglected work on China's architectural history also contributed to the initial post-Mao enlargement of China's architectural historical field. In 1977 Tong Jun, a University of Pennsylvania alumnus and faculty member at the Nanjing Institute of Technology, began work on *New Architecture and Styles* (*Xin jianzhu yu liupai*), an early and influential synopsis of late nineteenth- and twentieth-century Western architectural history and theory that signaled the new boundaries of acceptable intellectual engagement within the discipline relative to international, European, and U.S. architectural development.[23] This volume, eventually published in 1980, was followed by the publication of the complete, multivolume works of the architectural historians Liang Sicheng and Liu Dunzhen in 1982.

In 1984 Liang's *A Pictorial History of Chinese Architecture* was published by MIT Press under the guiding editorial hand of Wilma Fairbank, wife of U.S. historian John Fairbank and a noted scholar of Chinese art and architecture in her own right. Both Liang and Liu had been severely criticized during the Cultural Revolution for their experiences as students abroad in the United States and Japan, respectively, and for their relatively erudite approach to architectural history—abuse that may have contributed to their relatively early deaths.[24] Salvaging the reputations of these figures and enlightening a generation of Chinese designers untrained in the specifics of imperial Chinese architectural history served several important purposes, however. Collections of each author's writings and studies of China's built environment provided a foundation upon which China could rebuild itself and its historical landscapes.[25] More generally, it signaled that imperial-era Chinese architectural history was an acceptable topic of study. Such history also offered the government a means by which the aesthetic and formal palate of acceptable architectural expression in China could be expanded following years of standardized, monotonous socialist building production.

A range of preexisting and new publishing outlets was also influential in enhancing the study of China's architectural history. Beginning in 1979, published references to several canonical Western architectural texts reappeared in the pages of *Architectural Journal*—an important indicator of the party's liberalizing position on imported architectural and planning concepts.[26] New titles such as *The Architect* (*Jianzhushi*), *World Architecture* (*Shijie Jianzhu*), *New Architecture* (*Xin Jianzhu*), and *Time and Architecture* (*Shidai Jianzhu*), each established between 1979 and 1985, stretched the scope of China's architectural discourse beyond the strict parameters of Mao-era ideology into earlier, historically marginalized aspects of the country's architectural production. Collectively, these publications offered new perspectives on the conceptual, programmatic, aesthetic, material, and economic value of Chinese architecture; they also provided forums for design scholars to test the acceptable theoretical and temporal boundaries of China's architectural past. An additional stratum was composed of underground student journals, including titles like *Spatial Culture* (*Kongjian Wenhua*), which was published by students at Southeast University in Nanjing.

These publications introduced new, often foreign-imported theory and discourse such as postmodernism—a topic addressed in Chapter 7. The discussion of architectural trends in other parts of the world such as Hong Kong, Taiwan, and Singapore helped to broaden the standard geographical scope of Chinese architectural discourse from the strict geopolitical borders of mainland China toward a more inclusive acknowledgment of historical architectural activity taking place within China's diasporic communities.[27] These journals translated and disseminated the work of seminal European and U.S. modernist designers, historians, and critics, including Bruno Zevi, Sigfried Giedion, Le Corbusier, Frank Lloyd Wright, and others, in China for the first time without major comment or critique.[28] Japan suddenly figured as a welcome influence on contemporary Chinese cultural production following years in which state propaganda portrayed the country as an unwitting pawn of the United States.[29] Such publications also offered theoretical space for critiques of the ways in which architecture had previously been utilized and abused in China to serve the ideological interests of the state.

Exhibitions also helped to redefine the parameters of acceptable architectural subject matter, which ranged from China's own architectural past to contemporary architectural production then taking place in parts of the world from which China believed it had something to learn. In August 1980, a display of imperial-era and post-1949 Chinese architectural drawings was organized in Beijing. The show, sponsored by the Beijing Civil Engineering Society and held at the Soviet Friendship Palace, featured over three hundred objects from the Beijing Institute of Architectural Design and the China Building Technology Institute, among others, including representations of Lama pagodas and historical projects forbidden from public view during the Cultural Revolution.

This event was followed, in June 1982, by the opening of an exhibition of more than eight hundred pieces of work by Hong Kong architects in Beijing. The collection consisted entirely of photographs and drawings of notable postwar Hong Kong residential, commercial, and civic projects from twenty-two professional firms, Hong Kong's Housing Authority, and the School of Architecture at the University of Hong Kong, and included examples such as the City Hall, completed by Alan Fitch and Ron Phillips in 1962, the Peak Tram's Upper Terminal by Chung Wah Nan (1972), and the Jockey Club Sha Tin racecourse, completed in 1978. The exhibition traveled from Beijing to Zhengzhou, Shanghai, Chengdu, Kunming, Nanjing, and Guangzhou; in Beijing, it was estimated thirty thousand people visited the exhibition daily. A reciprocal exhibition of historical Chinese architectural objects, including 112 panels of cities, palaces, temples, residential architecture, and gardens, opened in Hong Kong in August. These first, early reform-era exhibitions shared a curatorial inclination toward inclusivity that suggests their primary function was to introduce the public to an array of acceptable architectural ideas and objects beyond China's borders or its own history. Collectively, such production resulted in an expanded historical sphere of knowledge from which new architectural expressions would, in theory, emerge.[30]

One dominant narrative to surface over the course of the early reform era was a recapitulated polemic from the 1950s concerning the articulation of a definitively Chinese architectural modernism. During that earlier period, Chinese designers, then working under the influence of Soviet socialist realism, experimented with imperial-era motifs such as overhanging-eaved roof structures in the search for a distinctly national yet universally socialistic architecture produced through some ideal ratio of "traditional" and "modern" elements. The revival of this pursuit began with the construction of projects like Beijing's diplomatic residential towers and, particularly after 1978, the reemergence of terms such as "national form," "pluralism," and "symbolism," all of which conveniently evoked an earlier period of economic productivity in socialist Chinese architecture while obscuring the violence that had rocked the country in the late 1960s. The recirculation of these topics was accompanied by the rise of other new influences, however, particularly from abroad. It was within China's architectural journalism, for example, that postmodernism—discussed in Chapter 7—and its related dichotomous arguments (that is, "genuine versus fake," "less versus more," and "new versus old") took on additional, distinctive meaning in relationship to the new economic forces wrought by reform.[31]

Another important, international influence concerned networks of preservation specialists, multilateral funding organizations, and governing agencies eager to help resituate China's architectural history as heritage through the application of broader sets of international practices and standards, not all of which aligned with the party's own conservation objectives. China's rediscovery of architectural history—both its own and numerous other historical narratives originating from abroad—may have been framed as a national effort driven by the government's desire to reposition itself as a protector of the country's cultural heritage, but such work was conceived and produced through a range of distinctly international links and interests. Foreign experts and organizations with access to capital and sophisticated conservation techniques and technologies that far exceeded China's existing capacity were considered attractive partners and helped to introduce heritage discourses and procedures to Chinese architectural historians, thinkers, and designers, resulting in the discovery of overlooked, controversial, and other previously marginalized aspects of China's architectural past and the histories of other parts of the world.

As architects began to reengage and experiment with China's architectural history and the history of architectural ideas from other parts of the world, the party struggled to delineate the acceptable, political limits of such inquiry. The re-entanglement of China's past and present through the early reform-era study of architectural history and, even more importantly, through the design of architectural heritage, complicated socialist China's cultural identity in relation to the built environment. Nationalism offered a means of aligning the party's seemingly contradictory commitments to rapid, large-scale industrialization and the preservation of historical monuments. Architects were encouraged to put the excesses of the Cultural Revolution behind them and reminded that just as "old things serve the new," so did "foreign things serve China," in reference to previous architectural campaigns launched decades prior.[32] Just as the country's history could be put to use in developing the country's present and its future, so would foreigners assist the state in these efforts.

Reconciling the renewal of China's historical building traditions to the country's broader liberalizing agenda prompted suspicion among those within the party's ranks concerned with the potential romanticizing of China's imperial history. The prospects of relying upon outside expertise in such work proved equally rankling. In mid-December 1980, party conservatives mounted their most aggressive response against reform to date—doubts triggered, in part, by Poland's turbulent experimentation with economic and political reforms over the previous summer. A campaign to "Oppose Bourgeois Individualism" was also launched by the party's more conservative faction to counter reform and the new histories it had begun to produce. At the same time, the participation of reform-inclined officials such as Central Committee Secretariat Wan Li and Vice-Premier Gu Mu in the ASC's 1980 annual meeting suggested architectural design as well as theory's entwinement within the reformist agenda.[33] These tensions informed not only the study of architectural history in China, but the reimagining of history as heritage through acts of design, and the acceptable sets of political and cultural values to be derived from it.

REDESIGNING CHINA'S PAST

Broadening the scope of China's architectural history through scholarship, journalism, and exhibitions provided a conceptual scaffolding within which the physical reimagining of China's architectural heritage—and design more generally—began to develop. One of the initial major obstacles to such work was the government itself, however. Conservation laws passed in 1950, 1951, and 1961 placed value on maintaining a site's original appearance, though urgencies associated with economic development often led to lax enforcement. At the same time, responsibility for preserving and maintaining historical sites often fell to provincial governments and communes, making nationwide coordination difficult. The Cultural Revolution further hampered conservation work, though a handful of individualized efforts to preserve key architectural monuments materialized during the mid-1970s. Beginning in 1973, for example, ASC members Yang Tingbao, accompanied by Tao Yizhong, began to conduct surveys of historic architecture in Shanxi, China, one of the country's most celebrated areas for existing imperial-era landmarks, in an effort to establish benchmarks for heritage evaluation and intervention. Such work was followed in 1977 by an unprecedented, nationwide campaign to reinvigorate the documentation, monitoring, and preservation of built heritage—efforts also intended to buoy the national sentiment of an exhausted and distressed citizenry.[34]

Developing a robust architectural conservation strategy in early reform-era China was a difficult proposition in part because it comprised complicated machinations involving collective memory, political reconciliation, material science, international diplomacy, and economic speculation. As Deng and others pursued the implementation of early reform-era economic policy, architects argued that a firmer, more empirical basis was necessary for the practice of architectural conservation. "The conservation of historical architecture is a science," wrote Qi Kang, a well-known professor of architectural design at Nanjing Institute of Technology (later Southeast University) in 1980.[35] Such arguments attempted to build for conservation a standard system of practice supported by quantifiable data and expertise, and thus in accordance with the technologically oriented goals of the Four Modernizations. Conservation was also an ideology and industry, however, and as architects and officials sorted through China's reemergent histories, they also sought to assign new value to China's architectural heritage relative to both the ideological needs of the state and, equally importantly, its economic output.

The country's burgeoning international tourism industry offered the most direct means by which China's architectural past could be turned into profit. Numerous imperial-era monuments and sites, perceived as popular among international tourists and long since neglected or damaged during the Cultural Revolution, were targeted for improvement. Architects proved important agents in these initial labors, which took physical form as a series of small-scale endeavors that attempted to balance the needs and desires of growing numbers of international tourists with equally subjective impressions of each site's authenticity.

In 1980, for example, debate concerning the construction of an overhead scenic cableway at Tai Mountain (Tai Shan) in Shandong offered an early flashpoint in these determinations. The proposed cable car first emerged in designs completed in June 1978 by the Beijing-based Ministry of Metallurgy's Architectural Design Institute for the Party Committee of Shandong, and it aimed to provide tourists with easier access to the mountain and views of the landscape below. Following the selection of a proposed route directly across the mountain's main views and over its main temples, however, several architects from around the country lodged their objection to the proposal on the grounds that it damaged the historical integrity of the site. A conference attended by over forty participants was held in Tai'an, Shandong, in 1980, and following input from a number of the country's most prominent designers, it was decided to redirect the cable car away from the site's main tourist route.[36]

A larger, more ambitious and ideologically charged conservation project, also initiated in 1980, took place on the grounds of the old imperial summer palace Yuanming Yuan. Located eight kilometers northwest of Beijing's center, the site was best known for a series of extravagant, European-inspired baroque palaces designed by Jesuit advisers in service to the Qianlong emperor during the mid-eighteenth century. The complex and its grounds were subsequently ransacked and burned by hundreds of French and British troops in 1860 as part of the Second Opium War, with tens of thousands of priceless artworks, furniture, textiles, and objects pilfered from the site by foreign troops and local looters. Transformed by such violence into ruins and an enduring symbol of China's oppression at the hands of foreign aggressors, the grounds fell further into disrepair over the course of the twentieth century; during the Cultural Revolution, for example, many of its existing trees were cut and its land tilled by members of the fifteen work units living on the site. Beginning in 1977, however, steps were taken to reassess the site's historical significance, and a Yuanming Yuan organizational committee was established by academics with expertise in history, architecture, and garden design. Over the course of 1979 and 1980, the palace grounds also became an unofficial source of literary and artistic inspiration, in part because the site's ruined state seemed to evince China's multiple deaths—first at the hands of foreign invaders, and second as a result of the torturous Cultural Revolution.[37] It was architects, however, who were vital to the popularization and commodification of Yuanming Yuan by reinventing it as a "famous historical site" worthy of inclusion within the nation's heritage portfolio.

In August 1980, an ASC-organized conference gathered nearly one hundred architects, landscape designers, and historians to discuss possible strategies for rebuilding the palace and its grounds. Another, larger event was held that October as part of the 120th anniversary of the site's destruction, and a petition supporting the project was circulated and endorsed by over 1,500 people, with funding raised in anticipation of restoration work. Wang Zhili, a designer, scholar of traditional Chinese architecture, and author of an *Architectural Journal* essay criticizing the Cultural Revolution's effects on architecture and its history, spearheaded the project's initial organization. In another published piece for *Architectural Journal,* Wang argued that Yuanming Yuan's value derived not simply from its status as an infamous symbol of China's past humiliations, but in the promotion of the "nationalist education" and socialist culture and ethics that might result from its preservation and commemoration as a park. Wang outlined a strategy to restore the site and channel its symbolism as a space of national shame toward the further promotion of Chinese patriotism. Importantly, too, he rationalized the preservation of imperial-era architecture such as Yuanming Yuan as having potential meaning to the country's modernization efforts, particularly its ability to attract domestic and international visitors and foreign capital.[38]

By early 1981, a tentative conservation strategy was outlined and published in *Architectural Journal* by members of Tsinghua University's Architecture Department and Urban Planning Research Unit. In 1982 the Beijing municipal government approved plans for the design and reconstruction of the park, pending funding. Lacking archival resources, financing, and expertise, however, Chinese participants struggled to complete the work necessary for conservation, and CCP officials subsequently approached France's Ministry of Foreign Affairs and requested the services of French experts in Chinese and baroque art, architecture, and landscape to assist with the project. The French team worked in coordination with Chinese partners to complete surveys, measured drawings, and models of the site. France had been formative in the early intellectual development of several party leaders, most notably Deng Xiaoping. That it reemerged as an important partner in an early attempt to nurture and preserve the country's cultural history imbued the project with an additional significance and complexity, particularly given that French troops were involved in the site's original destruction. Nevertheless, France was seen by many Chinese officials as a vital force in cultural patrimony and had become an influential site for official Chinese tours abroad, particularly after 1978. It seemed to offer a model for the research, design, and curation of heritage that CCP leaders were eager to emulate.[39]

Despite official approval and international involvement, plans for the project were slow to materialize, however. Yuanming Yuan's charged historical and geopolitical nature complicated the arduous decision-making process, which involved input from central and Beijing municipal officials, the SCREMB, scholars, and designers in determining the site's fate. Potential reconstruction proposals ranged from a complete restoration to leaving the site intact; the possible construction of a hotel on-site was also discussed. Eventually, two specific sites were targeted for reconstruction, including Fuhai Lake and the Xiyang Lou, the European-style imperial structures most commonly associated with the complex. The restoration of Fuhai Lake was completed in 1984, but the Xiyang Lou was delayed over additional deliberations concerning its aesthetic and political contributions to the nation.

The involvement of foreign experts, an interest group who approached the site with their own professional, economic, and national interests in mind, further complicated negotiations concerning the degree of restoration. With research still being completed in coordination with the French team, for example, Chinese representatives began to implement their own plans for the site.[40] Debate regarding the palace's reconstruction involved practical discussions involving the financing, expertise, and time required for such an endeavor. Equally importantly, however, such an effort also presented an ideological test. Restoration meant the erasure of physical evidence of China's historical oppression by Western powers, and some voiced concern that any effort to preserve a site so emblematic of imperial-era decadence was itself an inconsistency in need of reassessment. Leaving the site in ruins, by contrast, presented an alternative and enduring commemoration to China's past—a memorial to injustices suffered by the Qing Empire but, more generally, a state-supported testament to the country's cultural resilience and its subsequent liberation and rise under socialism.

Ultimately, Yuanming Yuan was redesigned as a relics park organized around pieces of the site's original structures, which were collected, cleaned, and artfully reassembled into a series of sculptural objects to prompt introspection and reflection on the part of visitors (fig. 35). Portions of the original grounds were rebuilt; for example, the site's labyrinth was reimagined in stone and its circulation paths and plantings repaired and expanded. A number of other complexities continued to swirl around Yuanming Yuan following the completion of the first stage of its restoration, including doubts regarding what was originally on-site, the rights of residents who lived on the site and were forced to leave, and

Fig. 35 Yuanming Yuan, 1984.

China's efforts to reclaim the looted objects from art collections around the world.[41] Nevertheless, the work undertaken at Yuanming Yuan during the early reform era provided an official position on architectural destruction, heritage, and its commodification. The site was never an exercise in conservation. Its historical integrity was certainly discussed but never constituted the driving impulse behind the project, which composed a reimagining of history intended to accommodate visitors, trigger retrospection, and, in doing so, perform a national service. As such, Yuanming Yuan offered a model of how one might approach spaces born of sensitive periods in China's past and the narratives they could tell in the interests of the state.

The involvement of French partners is important in this regard. Using the project to reinforce an anti-foreign narrative while simultaneously relying upon foreign experts for scholarly and technical support underscored the party's lingering commitment to the utopian idealism of China's Mao-era past, namely, the belief that China could proceed along its self-determined path of economic progress on its own terms, with assistance but not interference from foreign forces. Sites like Yuanming Yuan were essential to the preservation of these ideals. Debate concerning the politics and financing of Yuanming Yuan's restoration, meanwhile, helped to influence the central government's recognition that a more robust set of laws concerning the conservation of historical sites and objects was necessary. In November 1982, officials passed the Law on the Protection of Cultural Relics, along with its first list of national heritage sites, at the Twenty-Fifth Meeting of the Standing Committee of the Fifth National People's Congress. The SCREMB was given a 10 million RMB budget for restoration work, with two project categories established, including national-level and provincial-level ranking.[42] It was an important step in the government's efforts to comprehensively and systematically survey, catalogue, and measure projects on a national scale, and it helped to cement the importance of the past to reform.

REDESIGNING CHINA'S PRESENT

The reinvention of Yuanming Yuan offered one specific kind of architectural intervention in China's past—an iconic if obsolete monument that proved eminently capable of projecting a narrative consonant with the party's own desired message. A series of proposed conservation and development schemes brokered between the Aga Khan Foundation and the Chinese government over the course of the early 1980s evinced different sets of problems arising through early reform-era heritage projects, particularly those sites that remained actively used by segments of China's population and did not necessarily align as neatly with the party's self-interest but were considered to be of international significance. These projects suddenly embodied a kind of global presentness that proved architecturally and politically challenging in ways that went beyond the theoretical and logistical difficulties inherent to conservation work.

The Aga Khan, a title held by the imām of the Nizari Ismāʿīli Shias, was an early participant in the exploration of China's architectural heritage through his subsidiary organizations, including the Aga Khan Architecture Award and the Aga Khan Foundation. In 1981 the foundation helped to coordinate "The Changing Rural Habitat," the first international conference on architecture held in China following the Cultural Revolution. Following the event, the Aga Khan and other foundation representatives expressed interest in partnering with Chinese authorities on a series of development projects within the Aga Khan's specified areas of interest, including conservation, tourism, and medical assistance. The Aga Khan was particularly interested in supporting economic initiatives within rural, predominantly Muslim-inhabited parts of the country such as Xinjiang—a sensitive site and topic for CCP officials following years of Han-directed oppression of the autonomous region's Muslim Uyghur population. During the Cultural Revolution, for example, the relocation of five thousand to six thousand Han Chinese youths to Xinjiang was followed by the desecration of mosques—a number of which were closed and converted into factories, schools, and even pigpens—and discrimination against the local population. The party eventually acknowledged its mistakes in 1979 and began to work to repair Han-Uyghur relations through an emphasis on rebuilding cultural and physical heritage. In 1980 the Xinjiang Islamic Association was reestablished. Mosques were restored and reopened; new facilities were built. The party also made it easier for the area's predominantly Muslim community to travel to other Islamic countries.[43] Nevertheless, tensions remained.

In the autumn of 1981, representatives for the Aga Khan and members of the Bureau of Public Health of Xinjiang, ASC, and central party leadership, including Gu Mu, discussed the financial and spatial parameters of a potential cooperative venture. The Aga Khan expressed a desire to undertake a project only if it would aid in China's economic development; in response, Gu communicated the government's desire for large-scale capital investment in both light and heavy industry. The possibility of constructing a hospital was discussed, as was the potential training of Chinese architects in the design of medical institutions, though collective interest eventually focused on a hotel scheme in Kashgar that would adhere to the country's National Plan for tourism development without clashing with the area's social and cultural heritage. Aga Khan officials pledged $51,000 USD for preliminary investigation into an architectural restoration project that might merge each party's economic interests, and hurried to organize a team visit in April 1982 to tour active heritage sites in order to identify an appropriate design and conservation strategy for their own project.[44]

Aga Khan representatives were eager to see China's standard conservation practices at work in several important and active Islamic religious sites such as the Great Mosque in Xi'an and the Afāq Khoja Mausoleum and Edka Mosque in Kashgar. The trip proved enlightening. Participants were surprised by the lack of centralized control over conservation programs throughout the country, particularly one under socialist governance. They also noted the poor overall quality of most of the restoration work taking place, which they attributed to the decentralized nature of conservation in China and an ineffective administrative structure. At the Lama Temple in Beijing, for example, they witnessed numerous unnecessary repairs and the restoration of painting work that bore little resemblance to its original nature. Exceptions existed; Paul Collard, an administrator with the Aga Khan Architecture Award, noted that in the renovation of Xi'an's Small Wild Goose Pagoda, the SCREMB had decided to retain the pagoda's original exterior, which included visible evidence of damaged brickwork, even as they gutted the monument's interior structure and replaced it with concrete beams. In general, however, China's conservation work remained a fragmented endeavor born of a lack of central coordination and oversight. Aga Khan representatives worked with the SCREMB to craft a strategy for an architectural conservation and restoration initiative that would suit both parties' interests.

Through these discussions, it was decided that the Aga Khan would be allowed to help conserve the Xi'an Great Mosque. Xi'an, one of imperial-era China's ancient capitals and the departure point for the Silk Road, was an important urban center of Muslim activity in the country, and the Great Mosque, originally built in the eighth century, lay at the spiritual heart of the city's Hui quarter, an unofficial district occupied predominantly by Chinese Muslims. The mosque possessed the essential spatial qualities required by Islamic worship, but aesthetically, it resembled a

Chinese temple—a syncretic aesthetic that began to create political difficulties during the reform era. By the mid-1980s, pressure to develop and "modernize" in accordance with the government's vision for reform was acute, particularly in relation to popular tourist destinations. Many of the district's mosques were targeted for reconstruction and rehabilitation following destruction and misuse during the Cultural Revolution and were still in the process of being reopened and assimilated to Chinese society.

The Great Mosque, which had been designated a national historic site in 1961, had not been subjected to such treatment, but a preservation strategy was needed. At the same time, however, the central government did not want foreign assistance in the restoration of these spaces due to lingering, Cultural Revolution–era sensitivities. Questions concerning the appropriate style for mosque preservation—older, "traditional" aesthetics versus new, more "Arabic" motifs—were also active, unresolved concerns within the local Muslim community and its relationship to the Chinese state. These issues spoke directly to the ambiguities of China's modernization project. Arabic, distinctly Islamic architectural styles were becoming more popular within the neighborhood amid greater international engagement between Chinese Muslims and the Middle East, and thus seemed more emblematic of reform, even as they conflicted with the more authentic, hybrid nature of Hui mosque architecture emblematized by the Great Mosque.[45] Although both the local Hui population and the party were eager to engage international audiences through architectural heritage, the nature and origins of such heritage emerged as contested ideological terrain. Debate over the conservation of mosques as an act of modernization thus revealed complex and at times contradictory aspirations specific to the state's objectives, and born of entwined local, national, and international faith-based identities and the loyalties believed to exist therein.

These issues were particularly relevant to the government's negotiations with the Aga Khan, a wealthy, charismatic international Muslim leader seeking to engage with China's Islamic community through targeted acts of conservation and development. By June 1985, a three-year development program and budget draft covering the Great Mosque's conservation totaling $504,045 USD was produced for final approval. Momentum quickly shifted yet again, however, as mosque representatives demanded that they maintain all local control of the funding—a stipulation that prompted the Aga Khan's representatives to renounce the project and restart discussions. Eventually, the two groups failed to agree on a collaborative venture, and the Great Mosque's conservation was completed by local officials working in accordance with the central government's existing provisions for heritage sites. Nevertheless, the protracted, frustrating negotiation process provided Aga Khan officials with insight into a national conservation strategy still taking form.

Preserving and preparing these sites for international tourists was paramount, and publicly, the Chinese government expressed a willingness to adhere to international standards for architectural conservation. In 1985, for example, party representatives attended the annual meeting of the International Council on Monuments and Sites; that same year, the government also announced plans to identify twenty-four Chinese cities as "historically and culturally famous" and thus prioritize their protection. As became clear to the Aga Khan advisors, however, Chinese officials courted foreign expertise for assistance with implementing and financing architectural conservation projects only until such work proved too politically sensitive for international collaboration. The potential intervention in these sites by the Aga Khan carried numerous perceived risks to the party, in particular, the prospects of a foreigner becoming "part of the political hierarchy of the country."[46] Recognition that such a figure could have an effect on sites, spaces, and, more importantly, the people who regularly used them potentially posed problems in governance. Heritage in China was first and foremost a political project in modernization, and one that aimed to achieve specific economic aims even as it appeared shrouded in a determined sensitivity to protecting the past. Foreign assistance was thus helpful only insofar as it could be used to advance the interests of the state; rebuilding edifices and sites that conflicted with the party's narrative threatened the state-directed project of modernization itself.

Another international effort to reimagine China's architectural present proved more successful in part because it was neither a site nor was it physically located in China at all. The exhibition *Everyday Life in China* (*Environnement quotidien en Chine*), which was held at the Pompidou Centre in Paris from May 19 to September 20, 1982, was designed to introduce but not necessarily enlighten a foreign public as to the realities of life in early reform-era China. Its origins derived from a trip to France in March 1979 by then-ASC chairman Zhang Kaiji, who traveled to Paris with the intention of discussing the organization of an exhibition there focused on some aspect of the living environment of a Chinese village, and general "life in China." Zhang's trip was in part enabled through the efforts of Xavier Luccioni, a French architect who lived in China between January 1974 and September 1976, and Chinese designer Léon Hua Lanhong, who had first moved to Paris in 1936, returned to China in 1952 to contribute to the country's reconstruction efforts before being persecuted during the Hundred Flowers campaign, only to return to France following the Cultural Revolution. Zhang, Luccioni, and Hua, all of whom were practicing architects, became important channels between French and Chinese teams and integral participants in the design of the exhibition's physical and temporal parameters, the preliminary design of which was completed by early 1981 and slated for installation in the Galerie du CCI (fig. 36).[47]

The exhibition's initial layout consisted of an octagonal installation divided into "rural" and "urban" sections, along with an informational grid detailing various aspects of Chinese urban and rural life such as work, school, health, and hobbies. Visitors entered the space through a replica of an imperial-era Chinese gate before proceeding to a series of mounted boards featuring statistics and photographs depicting China's countryside and cities. At the installation's center, a slide show of images projected onto three large screens. A model of a Suzhou garden extended from one side of the display, sandwiched between a projected newsreel of pre-1949 events in Chinese society and a series of drawings, photographs, and objects depicting life and the built environment of five selected Chinese cities, including Beijing, Shanghai, Guangzhou, Shaoxing, and Tangshan, as well as images of several old and recently constructed rural homes. Other selected objects included scale models, drawings, architectural and urban plans, life-size mock-ups, furniture, maps, everyday objects, photographs, and videos detailing various aspects of rural and urban environments in China. A brief history of famous Chinese people in France was also included to convey the intellectual linkages between the two countries.

Everyday Life in China, which ran from May 19 to September 20, 1982, produced images, objects, and an environment that expanded upon the party's prescribed narrative of China's modernization. Content was organized into the party's standard historical chronology; visitors were first informed about the deterioration of Chinese society under the Qing

Fig. 36 Exhibition opening, *Everyday Life in China* (*Environnement quotidien en Chine*), Pompidou Centre, Paris, 1982.

Fig. 37 Urban housing interior installation, *Everyday Life in China* (*Environnement quotidien en Chine*), Pompidou Centre, Paris, 1982.

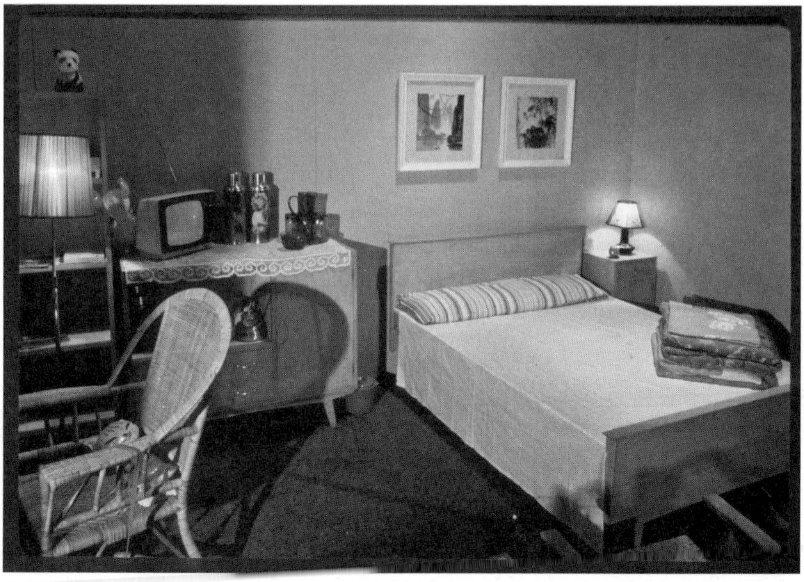

Dynasty, the trauma of the Opium War, and China's drift toward social chaos prior to 1949. Maps and data from China's urban and rural areas contextualized the exhibition, and were accompanied by architectural drawings, models, and photographs showing new construction taking place. Very little of the material displayed had been previously seen outside of China, including plans of low-rise and high-rise apartment blocks and city maps, recently built rural courtyard constructions, details of decorative motifs, and various interior arrangements of people's homes. Photographs of street activity, daily labor, public exercise, and people ranging from children to elderly subjects all helped to reconstruct a well-balanced social milieu. The inclusion of manufactured objects, including thermoses, fans, and enamel plates, provided visitors with a sense of China's recent manufacturing trends, while diagrams of social structure re-created the bureaucratic systems at work in the country.

Importantly, the exhibition included none of the experimental, more controversial architectural vehicles for liberalization such as the international hotel or the SEZ, which were still in various processes of design and construction. The monolithic scale of China's cities, contrasted with the textured, vernacular fabric of its countryside, composed the spectrum of acceptable physical realities with which the exhibition's French audience could engage. In eschewing these more radical, reform-era architectural and urban experiments, the party instead produced a narrative of modernization in which all economic processes remained firmly under its own control and in line with its own ideological arc. State-manufactured objects were particularly helpful in this respect. Each physical thing on display served as a vessel for engagement that accommodated the party's ideological constraints while still satisfying the expectations of an international audience eager to experience

Fig. 38 Rural housing interior installation, *Everyday Life in China* (*Environnement quotidien en Chine*), Pompidou Centre, Paris, 1982.

a simulacrum of material China, albeit removed from the country's political, economic, and social realities. For example, little information was revealed regarding the human labor behind the design or production of such work, prompting French curators to muse on the anonymity of China's creative producers in the exhibition's catalogue.[48]

Of key concern to Chinese organizers was reinforcing the narrative that China's own everyday modernity was of its own volition, and in keeping with Mao-era precedent. To that end, the exhibition also explicitly challenged the assumption that change was only taking place in China's cities. Visitors were made aware of the physical development also occurring in China's countryside, which was, in fact, one of the first environments where economic reforms were introduced, if not necessarily where the first physical effects of reform began to materialize. Nevertheless, a series of models and visual depictions of new architectural spaces in the countryside suggested a comprehensive evenness to reform's physical results (figs. 37, 38). The architect was an important figure in this process as well. In both the city and the countryside, the architect was depicted as a key public servant operating within urban bureaus and design institutes around the country for the betterment of Chinese society, and as a vector of information and innovation flow between urban and rural China, and the government and its people.

The exhibition was devoted to contemporary Chinese architecture and urbanism, but it may also be understood as an exercise in preservation. In its return to a pre–Cultural Revolution narrative of forward-thinking progress, the exhibition counteracted the themes of social revolt and physical destruction still associated with China in France and other parts of the world. The objects on display thus helped to stabilize, or restore, China's image abroad. As an act of restoration, the exhibition also represented an act of renewal, with a respectful treatment of historical Chinese customs, iconography, and spaces that obscured the extent of what had been lost in the recent past and redirected attention to China's future. *Everyday Life in China* was not the only architecture exhibition co-organized between China and a foreign government, nor was it the only China-themed exhibition organized at the Pompidou.[49] However, its emphasis on ordinary objects and spaces in Chinese life was unique and offered a relatively unheroic representation of the country—a projection of China's everyday reality abroad that was ironically in itself an extraordinary mission charged with paradox and spectacle.

Organizers understood the fictions at work; in the exhibition catalogue, the French curator Hélène Larroche acknowledged that the effort to represent the "reality" of China's rural and urban complexities in 3.6 square meters of space was an impossibility, given both the physical challenges of curation and the inclination of Chinese and French representatives to privilege certain narratives over others. Even as the show sought to project the achievements produced by socialist China, it also relied upon a certain exoticized architectural image of China. From a Chinese perspective, however, the exhibition was successful insofar as it helped to demarcate the acceptable parameters for the international study of socialist Chinese architecture and urbanism following years in which little was known outside China with respect to its built environment. For the event's French organizers, the exhibition indicated that China's buildings and cities could be resituated within a certain capitalistic culture and world order, regardless of party intentions to do so. As Larroche argued, the exhibition revealed that "there was conceptual room within the habits, daily practices, and graphic standards of an industrialized country for China."[50] As an exercise in cultural and geopolitical mediation, the exhibition shrewdly used Chinese objects and environments to produce a discursive foundation capable of ameliorating Cold War–era tensions between the West and China and upon which some new reality could be built.

PRESERVING CHINA'S FUTURE

Although many techniques of architectural conservation in early reform-era China were themselves vestiges of curatorial and design practices from earlier periods in socialist Chinese history, the 1980s signaled consequential changes in China's relationship to its architectural past. By the end of the decade, heritage had begun to take on the contours of an industry, with standards for evaluation and interpretation designed to ensure a certain degree of quality in the hopes of attracting tourists and the central government's financial support. Heritage fulfilled a number of national goals, and architects contributed to its invention as part of China's modernization, and a component of China's modernity more generally, just as they did in other modernizing cities around the world over the course of the twentieth century. Within the context of reform, however, heritage carried particular value as a form of cultural, political, and economic production in early reform-era China that could be deployed to assuage fears that the country was opening up too quickly and that modernization was proceeding at the expense of China's identity, which was, in fact, very much in flux.[51]

This paradox was perhaps most visibly apparent in the physical environments undergoing the most dramatic transformations in China. For example, in Shenzhen—one of China's first four SEZs, and the subject of the next chapter—officials and architects initiated a proposal to preserve Shenzhen's original town center just eight years after the launching of special economic activities there, which were themselves intended to unleash new forms of creative destruction upon the site. Rather than attempting to preserve Shenzhen's "nondescript old town," however, which was composed of several one-hundred-fifty- to two-hundred-year-old farmhouses, gun towers, and one- to two-story traditional brick, rammed earth, and concrete block constructions, the proposal suggested building a simulacrum of the original site designed to give tourists more of what they "want to see."[52] By 1988 a more comprehensive Old Shenzhen rehabilitation proposal emerged that sought to reproduce physical and intangible aspects of the city supposedly lost in the flurry of speculative construction, including several selected settlements in and close to the SEZ (fig. 39). Emphasis was placed on the re-creation of each neighborhood's street life, the rejuvenation of traditional shopping and food markets, and small, self-managed shops and restaurants, which would "ensure a lively environment from early morning to late evening." The project's proponents explained, "Whilst much is lacking in individual quality, the area has a coherence that is absent from many of the more recent development areas elsewhere in the SEZ." More than a reinvention designed for tourists, the proposal was also framed as a socioeconomic strategy that would ease the transition of rural workers moving into the SEZ by providing them with more appropriate and familiar forms of housing that provided basic service amenities, while also reflecting sympathy for "established living patterns of migrants."[53] Such "restoration" work would, in fact, compensate for the poor urban quality of reform itself—the deployment of an imagined past to compensate for a haphazardly designed future.

The project was never implemented, but its objectives illuminate the ways in which heritage both contributed to and compensated for the shortcomings evident in the state's reform agenda. More than simply protecting the past and generating revenue for local municipalities, heritage was put forward as a means by which jarring physical change could be rendered normative, progressive, and acceptable to China's population. Efforts to preserve Shenzhen's Old Town in the face of swift physical

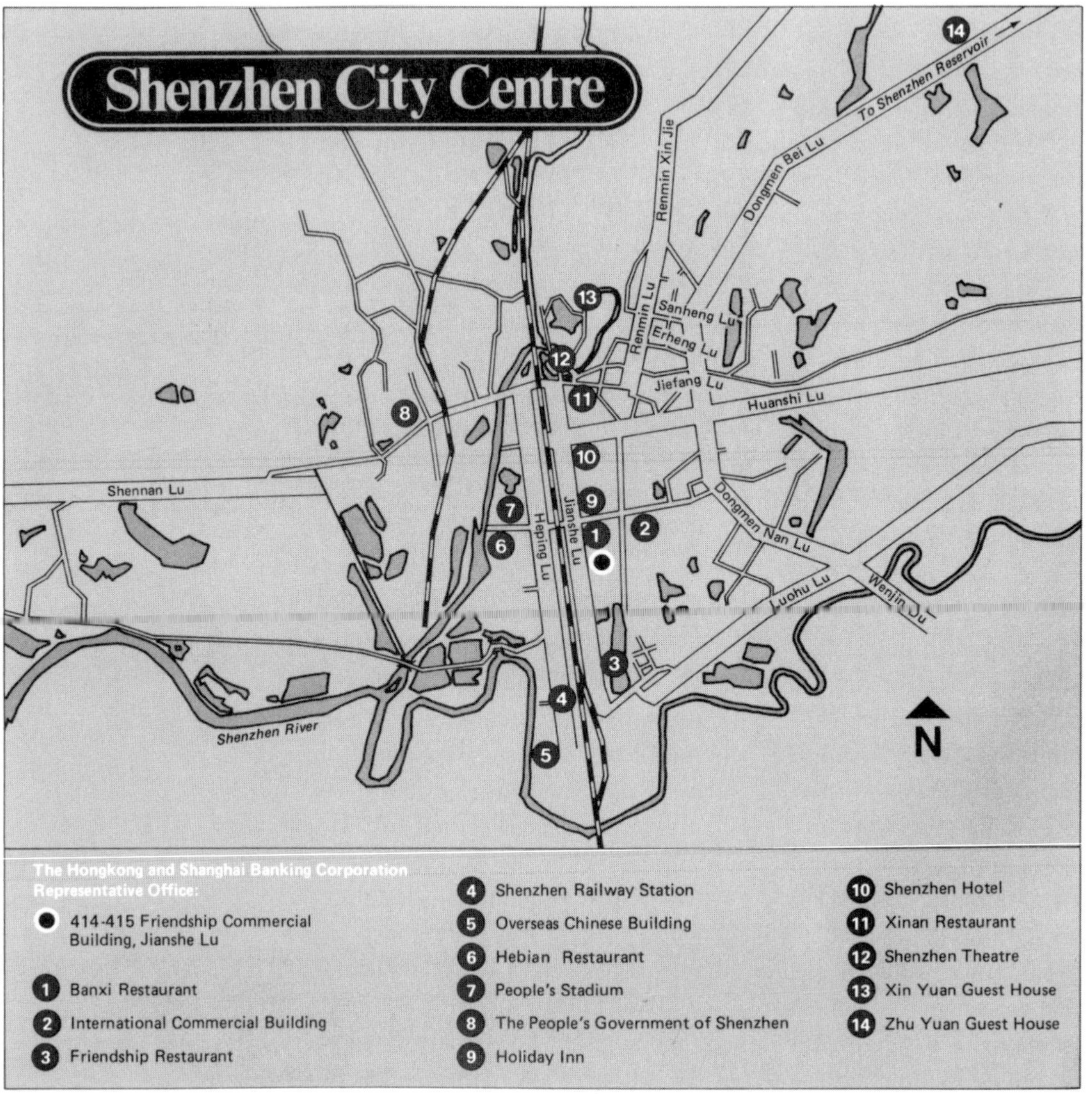

Fig. 39 Map, Shenzhen City Center, 1982.

development demonstrates that heritage was by no means a discourse restricted to China's oldest monuments and built environments, nor was it even limited to the past. Rather, it was a new and special economic activity driven by a multitude of motives, and one that affected the entirety of China's physical landscape. As both a discourse and an object, heritage's value lay in the ways it enabled a distinction between physical change and progress. The difference between the two was relevant throughout the country, but its urgency became particularly apparent in rapidly, radically transforming environments like the Shenzhen SEZ, where it became a useful selling point of reform itself.

Rejuvenating China's cultural identity through architecture and the country's building traditions in particular was important to the government's efforts to derive new authority and revenue from Chinese culture. As this chapter has argued, China's architectural heritage and the complex, multilateral aggregations of Chinese and foreign officials, designers, and preservation experts involved in its production reveal architectural history's early and influential role in the country's pursuit of economic progress. Developing and promoting a national architectural heritage allowed the party to reinvent itself, both at home and abroad, in part because it accommodated change and somehow signaled its reversal—an ideological sleight of hand intended to satisfy economic, political, and social ends.

CHAPTER 5

The Joint Venture and the SEZ

A foundational condition to reform was the design of spatial and legal mechanisms capable of enacting it. Party leaders understood the promises and problems of exchange, and the ways in which buildings and environments could help in developing and sustaining new forms of international engagement, even if the many complexities associated with more robust contact with the world had not yet fully materialized in China. Official opportunities to travel rapidly expanded in the years just prior to and following 1978; at least thirty official CCP trips abroad to at least forty countries helped to provide decision-makers with formative glimpses of spaces, objects, and systems that key CCP representatives would subsequently propose as vital to the country's economic liberalization.

These experiences also proved influential in the state's efforts to reconfigure the relationship between capitalism and China, through Chinese design systems and forms of foreign-derived corporate activity that challenged existing Chinese perceptions of architecture and the underlying economic and political forces responsible for its production. In 1978, for example, Vice-Premier Gu Mu, a major supporter of Deng's economic reform policies during the 1980s, participated in a tour of France, Germany, Switzerland, Denmark, and Belgium, where he observed numerous and visible trappings of industrialized landscapes, from heavy industrial machinery to advanced technological devices to basic physical superstructure emblematized by factories, textile production facilities, city and port infrastructure, schools, research institutes, and housing projects. It was Gu's first trip abroad, and he returned home confident that China could achieve anything if it could acquire more foreign currency. That aspiration, however, was dependent upon the development of particular spaces that would allow investors to safely invest in the country's future without having to struggle against the daunting bureaucratic and ideological obstacles present within the country.

Following his return home, Gu submitted an official report to the Central Committee and State Council encouraging the party to establish industrial processing zones "closed off from surrounding areas, where foreign businesses could invest and establish factories under a tax-free regime, and directly exporting production."[1] Over the course of 1978 and 1979, government representatives debated the strategy of "build[ing] nests to attract birds"—the design and construction of a physical and legal framework to lure international capital for free economic exchange within the socialist country.[2] On July 1, 1979, China passed its first joint venture law, which institutionalized new forms of economic collaboration by allowing state-run institutes to partner with foreign corporate entities for the first time. While the new law created an operational channel through which foreign direct investment would be allowed to flow into China, physical spaces were designated with beneficial tax rates and low import levies to provide the ground where such investment could concentrate.

Shanghai, Tianjin, and Beijing were initially prioritized as potential sites for foreign partnerships, and officials in these places were allowed to sign agreements directly with foreign counterparts for contracts and projects valued under $3 million USD. These cities posed challenges for rapid investment and industrial development, however, in large part because of the fixed political, social, and spatial systems in place. A simultaneous series of more localized economic experiments taking place in Fujian and Guangdong provinces proved more successful, and eventually attracted attention from the central government. Importantly, these areas were less developed, marginal locations adjacent to the colonies of Macau and Hong Kong as well as Taiwan, existing on the periphery of Beijing's control. It was within these spaces that the new speculative realities of China's liberalization first took distinct, physical form.[3] Eventually accorded certain legal and spatial privileges as special economic zones, or SEZs, these spaces included Zhuhai, a small city north of Macau, Xiamen and Shantou, two cities located on the Taiwan or Formosa Strait across from Taiwan, and Shenzhen, a border town located on the China–Hong Kong border. Of these zones, Shenzhen grew to become the largest and most economically profitable, largely due to its proximity to Hong Kong and the closely knit familial connections linking both sides of the border.

Much has been written about the history of the SEZ in the PRC, particularly in relationship to Shenzhen. Much of this scholarship, in turn, is rooted to the notion of the master plan. The master plan remains an essential mechanism to understanding the history of these cities. It was at the scale of the plan, for example, that the SEZ's developmental potential was first imagined and subsequently assessed by teams of officials, economists, academics, and businesspeople, and through acts of top-down planning, both as a spatial and procedural exercise, that the party's respective and competing visions for the SEZ were conceived and subsequently implemented. Macro-scale, urban-level planning remains the dominant spatial and procedural paradigm through which scholars have generally historicized and understood SEZs, particularly Shenzhen, and their impact on China's built environment, from trade and investment to labor and migration, among other issues, though recent scholarship has convincingly argued for the importance of studying the consequential participation of individual actors and bottom-up, grassroots participation in these processes.[4]

This chapter builds upon that work to examine the first buildings that preceded the plan, and the organizational systems, financing, and expertise that produced them—a shift in focus to the scale of individual, architectural objects designed and constructed in the Shenzhen SEZ in an effort to understand both the abstract and concrete dimensions of capital as it first materialized on the ground in early reform-era China. Understanding architecture's role in reform necessitates a closer look not simply at the Chinese state's relationship to physical form and space or the economics and politics at work in design and building itself, but at how both first entwined through processes of initiation, negotiation, and testing into new material environments produced through economically speculative activity.

In particular, the Shenzhen experience illuminates the importance of the new architecture produced through these convergences—structures designed not as testaments to socialism's virtues, per se, but as spatial and corporate speculations oriented toward hypothetical transactions between the cadre and the investor, the developer and the architect, the market and the party, and China and the world. A focus on several early speculative projects, including the Bamboo Garden Hotel (1980), two residential estate projects, the East Lake and Green Bamboo housing estates (constructed in 1981), and the Shenzhen International Trade Center (completed in 1985), offers insight into the experimental aggregations of "hyperbuilding" composed of market-based speculation, state-oriented planning policies and behaviors, and projected revenue estimates designed to support the necessary conditions for reform while protecting the country's socialist system from the deleterious effects of foreign capital.[5]

It was through architecture, and at the scale of the building, that the political and ideological stakes of economic experimentation were tested and first coalesced as physical form to a public otherwise unmindful of the changes taking place. The production of socialist China's first "investment climate[s]"—immersive and interiorized spheres like SEZs created by and for economic speculation—required "efficient buildings in which to conduct [foreign investment joint venture] operations."[6] Architectural production was an early and important realm for foreign direct investment, and professional architectural firms were some of the first corporate entities to practice in reform-era China in coordination with their joint venture partners and state-run design institute counterparts. Buildings themselves composed the first efforts to extract capital from China's land through market-based proclivities. These projects were new building types demonstrative of a chaotic rush for land and capital that reified existing connections between China and other parts of the world, particularly Hong Kong, and fulfilled the SEZ's role as an anticipated threshold for international exchange.[7]

THE SEZ

The conceptual roots of the SEZ trace back to historical models found in capitalist and socialist societies dating back to the sixteenth century. They initially emerged as global phenomena following World War II in the form of export processing zones, or EPZs, and achieved particular, oft-cited success in Taiwan beginning in 1966, where they were used to transform imported raw materials and semifinished manufactured goods into completed duty-free products for export. Collectively, these spaces, of which the Gaoxiong EPZ was the first and arguably best-known example, served as a kind of Cold War–era ideological showcase for the efficacy of free-market Chinese development in contrast to the communist mainland. Importantly, Taiwan's EPZs also facilitated technology transfer via the training of Taiwanese workers abroad or through on-the-job training under the oversight of foreign specialists. These two aspects garnered particular attention from Chinese officials, for whom security and knowledge transfer were critical to reform's success.[8]

The implementation of China's SEZs was distinctive from the EPZ model, but the EPZ model served as a catalyst for China's desired ends, particularly in the ways these spaces reduced cumbersome top-down economic planning models into one flexible yet controlled system of "loose" parameters for management and production that could be implemented, tested, and adjusted over time as necessary.[9] Politically, too, control remained a delicate concern in China, and the physical delineation of EPZs from their surrounding contexts proved appealing if largely impossible to enforce. Mao had long derided traditional technology transfers on the basis that these types of transfers evoked the exploitation on display in China's treaty port system, and his ideological legacy continued to weigh heavily on substantial swaths of the party's ranks. However, reform-inclined officials led by figures such as Gu argued that China had little choice but to seek out such opportunities, particularly in light of the country's limited reservoir of technological know-how. Identifying sites where rapid knowledge exchange and investment flow could take place was key.

In a border town like Shenzhen, tangles of interpersonal, commercial, governmental, and organizational threads extending to and from Hong Kong were already present and active on both sides of the border, and they offered useful interpersonal and infrastructural connections upon which special forms of economic activity could be built. For all of the party's concerns over the destabilizing risks of the SEZ as a new spatial and economic model for reform, there existed broad, largely invisible linkages of manufactured goods, food, and resources between Hong Kong and Shenzhen that extended back decades. As early as 1933, for example, enterprising Hong Kong capitalists had plans to transform Shenzhen into "an entirely new town on up-to-date lines, within a stone's throw of British territory on the other side of the Sumchun [*sic*] River."[10] During the 1950s and 1960s, troupes of mainland artists, dancers, and actors, invited to attend as special guests, traveled to Shenzhen to perform to audiences of Hong Kong residents. Mainland Chinese water was piped to Hong Kong via the Dongjiang amid unprecedented drought conditions in the British colony during the late 1950s and early 1960s. By 1967 mainland China was providing Hong Kong with 30 percent of its rice, 85 percent of its pork, 65 percent of its beef, and 60 percent of its vegetables. China, in turn, had long used Hong Kong as a market for its manufactured goods, a site for investment opportunities, a source for information, and a link to a world economy within which it sought to participate more actively.[11]

These connections expanded considerably in anticipation of reform. Beginning in 1971, the Guangzhou Trade Fair's reemergence from the Cultural Revolution, capped by the construction of a new exhibition hall completed in 1974, sought to lure international businesspeople to mainland China via Hong Kong. The event's expansion over the course of the early 1970s prompted the construction of additional hotels, roads, and the improvement of the existing railway line linking Guangzhou to Hong Kong. Over roughly the same period, groups of mainland engineers, architects, and other industry representatives traveled to Hong Kong to study its industries, infrastructure, and technology. By 1976 it was reported that the PRC was selling food, water, consumer goods, and petroleum worth $1.4 billion USD a year to the British colony while maintaining a broad portfolio of Hong Kong–based investment properties, including one splashy $130 million HKD investment in three floors of the newly constructed Causeway Centre in Wan Chai.[12]

Restrictions on foreign travel began to be lifted in China over the course of 1977, when it was estimated approximately fifty mainland Chinese cities would be opened up to foreign visitors, and Hong Kong residents were some of the first overseas travelers to take advantage of these new policies. By the end of 1977, Hong Kong Chinese entrepreneurs were allowed to cross into the Luohu district of Shenzhen without a visa. In 1979 it was estimated that China was collecting 500 million GBP in annual rental dividends and income from property investments in Hong Kong. The economic interconnectivity between the two prompted Sir Lawrence Kadoorie, a fixture of Hong Kong society and vocal proponent of greater Hong Kong–China engagement, to describe the colony as the "Free Zone of China, under British management" in 1977.[13]

The first zone-like conditions to materialize in reform-era China depended upon these linkages. Shekou, a small harbor town located on the Pearl River Delta west of Shenzhen and north of Hong Kong, became

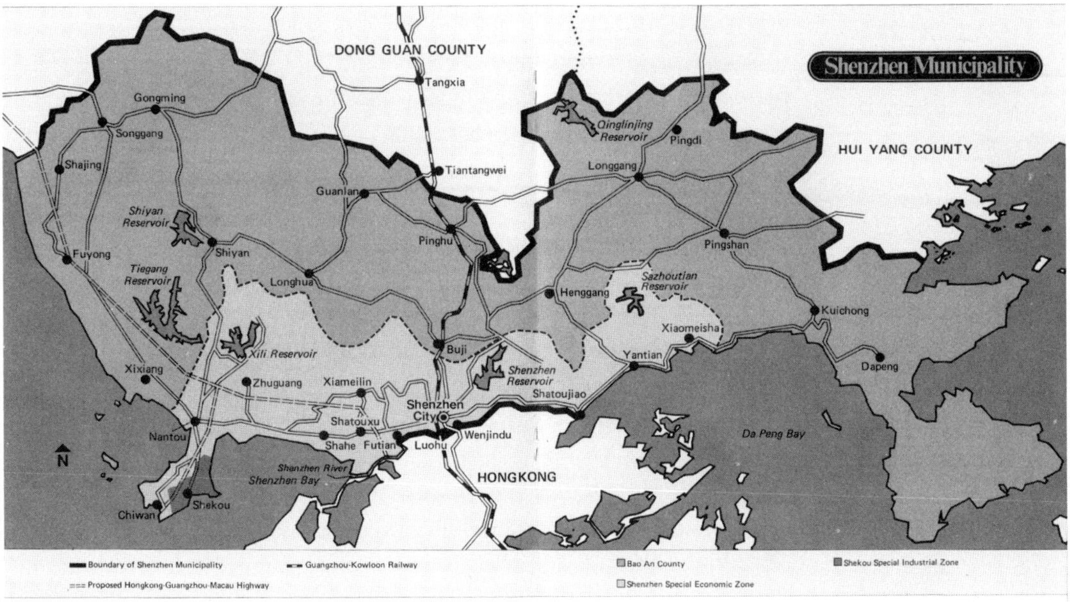

Fig. 40 Map, Shenzhen, 1982.

the first site targeted for experimental economic activity in November 1978. Initiated by local officials and the Hong Kong–based China Merchants Group, Shekou was independent and distinct from the SEZ system that would be subsequently implemented, and it was placed under the direct control of the State Council, in a sign of its political and economic significance and sensitivity. Shekou was approved in December 1978 as a first step in the design of a larger coastal development plan based on the premise that rapid and relatively informal physical growth along the country's coast would help connect China to the world economy and, in so doing, power the country's physical transformation.[14]

These steps preceded the formal administrative and legal organization of the SEZ system, which first took form as a comprehensive urban plan for Shenzhen announced in May 1980 (fig. 40). A twenty-six-article set of regulations adopted at the Fifteenth Session of the Standing Committee of the Fifth National People's Congress in August 1980 established an additional layer of control for managing and coordinating economic activity to ensure that national laws would remain applicable to the zones. By the end of 1980, new administrative committees had been created in both Fujian and Guangdong provinces to oversee the four established SEZs.[15]

These organizational devices, each regulatory and procedural in nature, collectively composed a framework for governance—a plan—designed to delineate, accommodate, and encourage the speculative economic activity set to take place. Anticipated infrastructural construction included the improvement of communication linkages, extensive land leveling, the provision of reliable electricity and water supplies, and the construction of roads and sea connections. All were considered essential to the urban futures of the SEZs but were not yet in place, and took years and billions of dollars in financing to realize. Even as local and national officials began to promote the ambitious physical efforts necessary to support the SEZ program, it became clear that the zones would encounter severe financial difficulties if quick returns on initial development schemes did not materialize. A frenzied rush of business deals between Shenzhen-based authorities, Chinese provincial governments, and state-owned enterprises, and joint venture proposals between mainland China and foreign partners, all quickly materialized in relation to an economic climate far more liberal than anywhere else in China.

DESIGN AND THE JOINT VENTURE

In Shenzhen, buildings emerged as the first physical embodiments of capital and change. Much of the economics and politics at work in socialist Chinese design and building were first tested in Shenzhen, and many of the first reform-era processes of initiation, negotiation, and experimentation took place there, adjacent to the Hong Kong border. It was also there that China's first joint ventures in architecture were formed through agreements formally reached in 1979 between China-affiliated offices, bureaus, and design institutes and Hong Kong–based parties to establish a company or work unit.

According to China's pioneering joint venture law, these agreements were allowed to take one of two forms, including joint equity ventures and cooperative ventures. Joint equity ventures were composed of shared foreign and Chinese ownership, with foreign capital accounting for at least 25 percent but typically less than 50 percent, to ensure the Chinese government's control over the enterprise. In cooperative ventures, by contrast, Chinese partners provided land, buildings, and labor, while foreign parties were responsible for capital, materials, and equipment. Profit and risk were shared equally, with each partner operating as an independent legal entity. Both types constituted lease agreements involving the transfer of ownership to the Chinese side after a certain period of time. A third, less common type of venture was also devised for enterprises with foreign investment only. These came with multiple disadvantages, however. Wholly owned ventures would be treated as local offices of foreign companies, and thus subject to higher taxes. Moreover, Chinese partners were crucial to navigate China's bureaucracy.[16]

Design and construction were vital to the joint venture. Buildings of a certain international standard were needed to support international business ventures, and the involvement of foreign architects in joint ventures first arose in direct relation to questions of quality and design-specific expertise—that is, identifying forms of architectural knowledge considered necessary by all involved parties for an enterprise's successful realization. Such experience was particularly important for projects such as hotels and other tourist-related facilities, which demanded a specific kind of visibility, technical bravado, and spatial quality. In theory, these partnerships ensured that China was benefiting from the highest levels of foreign design and building proficiency available, while enabling foreign designers to capitalize on new business opportunities in China with the help of local partners. Chinese representatives provided the knowledge necessary to navigate the bureaucracy of design in post-Mao China. They understood the language and building culture of China and the complex planning and design approval processes necessary to realize these projects, and were familiar with local building regulations. They were aware of specific site conditions and access to utilities such as gas, water, and electricity, and had contacts with government officials that proved useful. Foreign designers channeled new architectural ideas into China, but only Chinese architects understood the level of design detail required by the state-run construction companies and the availability of local materials.[17]

The nature of these partnerships created difficulties specific to the uncertainties of the early reform era, particularly in a SEZ like Shenzhen, where desired project outcomes were unclear or not shared by all partners, and prescribed processes of collaboration were often tentative, lest the government decide to reconsider a particular approach or outcome and take a different tack. Initial project negotiations between Chinese and foreign partners often revolved around identifying the necessary forms of expertise for a project and then securing their services from a range of international consortia of experts within and outside China. "The user could be, for example, a Japanese hotel corporation or bank," explained a study manual of land, property, and construction practices in the PRC funded by Levett & Bailey Chartered Quantity Surveyors in Hong Kong. "The design team may comprise a Chinese design institute, with an American architectural firm, a British structural engineer and a Hong Kong mechanical and electrical engineer. The contractor will more than likely be Chinese, but the specialist trade contractors and the product manufacturers will come from various overseas countries."[18]

The unpredictable dynamics of cross-national interaction, language difficulties, and ideological differences stemming from these complex, international aggregations often produced frustration. Problems emerged in relationship to expectations over a particular design's performative or aesthetic components, questions of design and construction quality, and overall management. Design approval processes in China, and SEZs in particular, lacked standardization, meaning that a variety of different design phases considered roughly equivalent to feasibility studies and conceptual, preliminary, and detailed design stages existed around the country. China lacked comprehensive and nationally approved standards for construction work specifications, which slowed coordination and decision-making.

The various administrative lapses and obstacles evident in early reform-era design collaborations underscored the need for relatively modest projects resulting from basic, more nimble forms of architectural practice, though even this type of work required adjustments on the part of China's existing labor system and management standards. Such difficulties attested to the daunting, broader impediments to reform, which aimed to reinvent an entire administrative culture comprised of millions of cadres, officials, and workers. Enacting such change required flexible spaces and systems. Joint venture relationships, for example, were managed by an internal joint venture board given the authority to revise agreements if it was determined that, for instance, a partnering entity lacked the necessary design, management, and construction experience for the venture, and another company needed to be appointed to manage the project on its behalf, including additional foreign partners such as project management companies, construction firms, or design practices. The language used to articulate the joint venture law was also deliberately left vague to provide flexibility in case of the need for further revision, change, or annulment. Such flexibility allowed for the emergence of a range of distinctive management structures in China relative to the specific circumstances surrounding a project, including a special construction process or building type, among other factors. It also led to questions concerning the expected duration of these deals, the specific legal and financing mechanisms involved in ownership transfer, and the potential risks posed by foreign exposure to Chinese legislation, among others.[19]

Another concern was project financing. In contrast to Mao-era design work, which depended upon the limited resources of one single source—that is, the state—the passage of the joint venture law ensured that foreign capital investment in China would be allowed. Foreign investors still had to grapple with the market limitations of China's own currency, however, which, like those of most other socialist countries, was not freely convertible on the international market. Exchange rates were based on accounting units rather than real prices, meaning that a potential investment's total costs over time were unpredictable. This made major financial dealings in foreign and Chinese capital difficult. Moreover, the Chinese government's desire to collect hard, foreign currency meant that the Bank of China would not guarantee the repayment of hard currency for every project financed through the government's central lending agency, which discouraged potential foreign investors from pursuing the necessary financing for China-based endeavors.

Following the law's passage in July 1979, the State Council approved of the creation of a series of institutional mechanisms through which Sino-foreign corporate partnerships could be more efficiently initiated and managed. These included the Hong Kong and Macau Affairs Office, the Foreign Investment Commission, the Import-Export Commission, and the state-owned China International Trust and Investment Corporation (CITIC). Each operated under the oversight of the State Council, and it was through them that the party would partake in specific business transactions and investments while controlling their impact upon China's economy and the country at large. A handful of trusted officials were put in charge of these offices based upon their expertise in relationship to market-based economic exchange; many also had particular socioeconomic backgrounds and family connections that suited the international nature of the economic experiments upon which they were about to embark.[20] These corporate entities helped to ease China's transition from a single investment source to a greater pool of international capital, which transformed the nature of architectural production in China. Redistributing the financial risks associated with construction in China encouraged Chinese institutional partners to take chances on new aesthetic experimentations, unfamiliar construction practices, and different processes of architectural production. This, in turn, enabled new architectural forms, materials, and scales to take hold.

ARCHITECTURE IN THE SHENZHEN SEZ, 1978–82

The first major architectural projects to emerge in and around the SEZ included factories, trade exhibition halls, and hotels born of joint venture partnerships between mainland Chinese design and research institutes, Shenzhen municipal authorities, and Hong Kong–based investment companies. In April 1978, amid early intraparty negotiations over reform, and six months prior to Shekou's official founding, plans were announced for a new trading center to be built along the Shenzhen–Hong Kong border that would allow visitors "to see what China has to offer without traveling too far."[21] A series of industrial plants catering to thirty new manufacturing enterprises in China, including shoes and handbags, knitwear, garments, gloves, and electronic products, and targeted for construction in Shekou, Luohu, and Shangbu, were completed over roughly the same period. In Shekou, construction began in July 1979 on a residential district featuring one- and two-story bungalows along the beach to be sold to Hong Kong residents. By 1980 officials could account for 490 established joint ventures, with 70 percent already in production and 30 percent to be built. Of these, 329 were factory operations in knitwear, garment, toy, plastic and silk flower, and building material production. Two hundred involved housing, restaurant, and hotel development. Approximately 310 enterprises were located within the special economic zone proper, while at least 180 were based in communes or brigade-run production facilities in other parts of the city, and even outside its limits. One early study of Hong Kong–derived foreign investment conducted in 1981 by colonial British officials suggested at least seventy housing estate and hotel investment and construction projects registered through Hong Kong–

based corporate entities in fifteen cities throughout mainland China.[22]

Such uncontrolled flows of foreign currency underscored the numerous financial, linguistic, managerial, political, and cultural challenges to regulating joint venture partnerships and the networks of existing personal and physical connections already existing between mainland China and Hong Kong. At the same time, both the Hong Kong and mainland Chinese governments anticipated such exchange; as early as 1975, for example, Hong Kong officials established ferry service to outlying islands within the colony's boundaries in anticipation of Mirs Bay's development into a tourist destination.[23] In September 1978, eight tourist spots were identified around the city and targeted for physical development, including the Shenzhen Reservoir, the Xili Reservoir, Yinhu Silver Lake, Xichong Beach, Yulu Hot Springs, Longfeng Recreation Centre, Meisha Beach, and Chiwan Beach. A number of associated joint venture agreements were confirmed between mainland Chinese design institutes and Hong Kong–based investors in relation to this work, and design plans rapidly took shape, but the scale and complexity of these projects slowed their physical construction. For example, Nanhai Hotel, an ambitious hotel scheme designed by Chen Shimin and proposed for Chiwan Beach, emerged through Shenzhen's first architectural joint venture, Huasen Architectural & Engineering Designing Consultants. Cofounded by Hong Kong Senyang International and the Ministry of Construction's design institute, this joint venture was created specifically for Shenzhen-based work, and it provided a conduit through which Beijing-based designers could take advantage of the more experimental opportunities already emerging in Shenzhen.[24] The hotel itself, organized into a massive, wave-like form composed of terraced rooms around a series of voluminous atria that borrowed heavily from the work of figures like John Portman, was completed in 1986.

Fig. 41 Bamboo Garden Hotel, Shenzhen Housing Authority, Shenzhen, 1980. Originally published in *China Reconstructs* 33, no. 9 (September 1984).

Prior to these efforts, however, it was the materialization of several earlier and smaller projects within the city that first catalyzed an architectural culture of intense speculation shaped by new and untested forms of economic collaboration. In October 1980, just five months following the party's official announcement of the SEZ initiative, construction was completed on the Bamboo Garden Hotel, which represented Shenzhen's first official Sino-foreign joint venture, and the first such venture completed and opened for business in reform-era China (fig. 41). Inaugurated by the Shenzhen Catering Service Company and Alan Lau, CEO of the Hong Kong–based company Millie's Group and owner of Hong Kong's *Tin Tin Daily News* (*Tin Tin Yat Pao*), the hotel was part of a larger initiative brokered earlier that January between Lau and the Shenzhen Housing Authority. The government agreed to provide land and labor for the project, while Lau contributed capital totaling $15 million HKD.

Located on Dadou Hill along the eastern edge of Shenzhen's original town center, the simple, 165-room project was designed by Shenzhen Housing Authority architects. Unremarkable in aesthetic and structural terms, its architectural value lay in the sources of knowledge and financing it concretized, and in the active flows of people and design ideas it enabled. The hotel was designed less as a traditional architectural object than as a speculative form of infrastructure, or what Lau termed a "bridge for later investors"—one that preceded many of the basic municipal services necessary for such a commercial architectural operation.[25] Indeed, inadequate communications equipment and unreliable water and electricity supplies plagued the hotel throughout its construction. The fundamental social systems necessary to manage such projects were also lacking. Yet the absence of these structures ultimately proved vital to Shenzhen's architectural production—and, by extension, to its economic success.

Struggles to open and operate the hotel in an efficient manner demonstrated the need to reconcile conflicting political and economic practices at work. Mainland hotel staff, for example, insisted upon cleaning the rooms no more than once a week to conserve water and resources, in keeping with standard communist regulations. Young female employees also purportedly refused management's requests that they wear makeup and bow and smile to customers. The Bamboo Garden Hotel's first vice general manager was purportedly fired after reports surfaced of his insistence that local Shenzhen staff remain separated from their Hong Kong counterparts. Shenzhen and Hong Kong employees also preferred to communicate among themselves, however, creating an impossible degree of fragmentation among hotel staff.[26] Economic dysfunction was another obstacle. Hong Kong and Shenzhen workers were each accustomed to different wage systems, which necessitated the creation of a new salary distribution method whereby staff received half of their salaries at the standard, party-controlled fixed rate and half at a floating rate based in part on that employee's performance. Lau proposed that both management and employees also be allowed to end work contracts with a one-month notice. The very provision of individual workers' contracts made the hotel the first work unit in post-1978 China to do so.

As Bamboo Garden Hotel management wrestled with the various difficulties resulting from discordant political viewpoints or economic behaviors, they found such obstacles could be quickly rationalized and overcome through ideological flourishes that couched these tensions in an appropriately collective tone—one that was subsequently applied to the challenges of Shenzhen's large-scale, urban development and the future of China–Hong Kong relations. "We may come from two different social systems and have different educations and life habits," explained Wen Fu, the hotel's new manager, "but we have a common goal—to run this hotel well."[27] Such on-site trial and error preceded the mechanisms designed to reconcile it—indeed, the improvised, almost accidental production methods and management structures were not incidental, but central to the hotel's mission, and they proved consequential to the hotel's legacy, labor relations in Shenzhen, and, over time, China at large. Shenzhen Special Economic Zone Real Estate and Properties Group Company was established in 1980, but it was only in 1981, following the completion of the hotel, that the Shenzhen Special Economic Zone Development Corporation and the Shenzhen Special Economic Zone Construction Company were established by the city to manage such design and construction activity. A tender system for all joint venture construction projects was subsequently established in July 1981. In 1982 the local government announced that all construction projects in the city would adhere to an open tender process. Injecting competition into the construction bidding process and centralizing responsibility for all land acquisition and use, planning, design, construction, and financing activity was designed not only to improve design or construction quality, but to avoid the bureaucratic delay caused by gaps in the preexisting system, in which construction projects were assigned to specific work units pending the support of multiple work units and agencies. Improving communication and efficiency also ensured that "construction [could] proceed more quickly."[28]

Amid the experimentation taking place in the Bamboo Garden Hotel, work began on the first phase of the East Lake Garden Estate, the first speculative residential housing venture in Shenzhen, and, by extension, China. It formed part of Lau's original agreement with the city's housing authority, and was composed of three types of housing blocks, each designed by the city's housing authority. Type C blocks in stage one consisted of fifty-five-square-meter apartments distributed nine to each floor in eight six-story buildings. Comparatively larger Type A and B blocks were planned for later phases, along with single-family residences. The entire venture covered an area of approximately 92,903 square meters

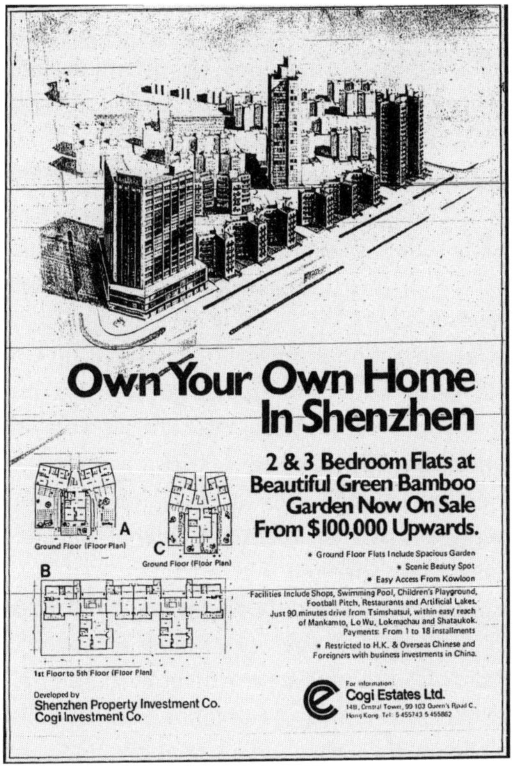

Fig. 42 Green Bamboo Garden Estate, Cogi Estates and Shenzhen Special Economic Zone Real Estate Company, Shenzhen, 1981. Originally published in the *South China Morning Post*, December 4, 1980.

and was followed five months later by announced plans for the Green Bamboo Garden Estate, a joint venture between Cogi Estates of Hong Kong and the Shenzhen Special Economic Zone Real Estate Company (fig. 42). The 139,354-square-meter, forty-block estate featured low, one- to five-story buildings and seventeen-story towers, each with sixty-five to seventy-five square-meter flats priced beginning at $120,000 HKD. The entire complex was designed to accommodate a total of ten thousand overseas Chinese and local residents. Located approximately three kilometers from Man Kam To in Hong Kong, its self-contained residential blocks featured an array of ancillary spatial features and programs, including shops, a children's playground, football grounds, restaurants, and an artificial lake.[29]

The speculative success of both projects established a new parameter for architectural quality in mainland China, with aesthetic cues rooted in efficiency and standardization that borrowed from both Hong Kong's public and private housing estates and socialist housing models. In both projects, however, the financing and promotional systems devised to sell units were of greater concern than the establishment of any particular spatial or aesthetic quality, making marketing a new architectural consideration in China. The promotional campaign was directed specifically toward Hong Kong residents who could purchase the flats for themselves or for relatives in China. In accordance with the party's demands, reasonable rental levels were established to encourage purchasing, with a fifty- to sixty-square-meter East Lake apartment listed for $136,500 to $163,800 HKD. At less than half the price of an average apartment in Hong Kong, Lau and Luo were able to sell all of their units to Hong Kong residents within the initial public offering's first three days. A second phase of the project, brokered between the Shenzhen Housing Authority and Alan Lau and announced in 1981, was also successfully presold to several classes of buyers, including retired Hong Kong residents, Hong Kong businesspeople with enterprises in Shenzhen, and overseas residents buying homes for their relatives in China.[30]

The rapid architectural materialization of foreign capital had proven financially lucrative to both investors and the Shenzhen government, but it raised questions regarding the long-term social impact of such wealth upon the city's residents. "The social effects of the sale of private dwellings to overseas Chinese are unclear, but the visibility of wealthy residents will probably cause envy," argued Australian academic Kevin B. Bucknall in 1981. However, Bucknall also acknowledged that such practices "may to a small extent act as an incentive to work hard and accumulate in order to achieve the good life, reinforcing the use of price mechanism and material incentives."[31] Reconciling the disparate incentivization systems at work between a capitalist economy like Hong Kong and socialist China would, in fact, prove challenging, particularly in relationship to the process of design itself. "[The government] is asking people to design things that they know nothing about," explained Leo Zee, a Hong Kong–based architect working in China who began to teach classes on new building planning and techniques in Shenzhen to mainland architects and urban designers from twenty-four provinces.[32] "Imagine trying to design a modern hotel, for instance, if you have never been a tourist," argued Zee. "You can't. Impossible. It's the same with coffee shops. They have seen illustrations and plans in professional Western magazines, but they do not know what they are for. They asked me if a coffee shop was where a person went to make his own coffee. Some asked if you danced in a coffee shop."

More than singular acts of design or individual buildings, these projects demonstrated that buildings in China could exist as goods or commodities to be traded and exchanged in relation to the market, even if the market itself did not technically reside in China. Their presence composed a new architectural type shaped by speculative practices and spatial logics that transformed what it meant to design and build in China. Through them, new, previously inaccessible worlds of goods and experiences appeared that would not be found in Beijing, Shanghai, or elsewhere until years later due to the overarching political control present in those cities. Following the opening of the East Lake residential complex, for example, onlookers were treated to glimpses of a spectrum of new household products, many of which were being brought in from Hong Kong free of duty and had not previously been seen in China before. They included air-conditioners, refrigerators, washing machines, and other electrical appliances; a video tape recorder, believed to be the first in Shenzhen, was also observed.[33] These objects contributed to the expanding scope of the architecture that housed them—buildings shaped by financial, procedural, and managerial experimentation that preceded and eventually morphed into the urban conglomeration of Shenzhen itself.

THE RISKS AND REWARDS OF EXPERIMENTATION, 1982–85

As Shenzhen's urban environment began to densify and expand in accordance with its rapid architectural development, CCP officials found themselves confronted with a reality that did not necessarily suit their imagined visions for reform. In February 1982, Deng Xiaoping disappeared from the world's view for thirty-seven days to travel to Guangzhou, purportedly to evaluate the progress of the SEZ enterprises and assess evidence of official corruption taking place in and around zone-related economic activity. Among Deng's team was the deputy director of the Party Propaganda Department, Zhou Yang, who personally visited Shenzhen and Shekou and lavished praise on the activities taking place. Others were not as supportive, however, and doubts had begun to emerge among more conservative officials as to the unusual economic practices and urban environments taking shape. One party member, for example, purportedly expressed skepticism as to why buildings over forty stories were being constructed in Shenzhen when the city possessed so much land elsewhere. In an effort to anticipate future growth, officials announced a twenty-year plan for the Shenzhen SEZ in October 1982. Essential and comprehensive infrastructural services, including modern sewage treatment, would not emerge until 1983.[34] Officials were also disappointed that many of the zone's joint ventures did not involve industrial technology as expected, but rather property development. Such assessments expressed both surprise and regret over the speed with which such architecture was monumentalizing the economic hustle taking place, some of which was illegal. Architectural speculation had overtaken the city's ability to control it.

Shenzhen was not unique in this regard. Throughout the country, architecture had quickly emerged to become a common, easily detected index of official graft during the reform era. By 1982, and in coordination with Deng's southern trip, the party launched a campaign against economic crimes and other examples of "Anti-Spiritual Pollution." It was a short-lived campaign intended to counter what officials considered to be mounting evidence of reform's ill effects triggered by the publication of a report by the Central Commission for Discipline Inspection titled "On the Work of Striking at Serious Crimes in the Economic Field," in which official statistics cited at least 192,000 known cases of bribery, corruption, and accounting malfeasance, perpetrated by seventy-one thousand CCP

Fig. 43 International Commercial Building, Shenzhen, 1981. Originally published in *Building Journal Hong Kong* (November 1980).

members as well as others between January 1, 1982, and April 30, 1983.[35]

Shenzhen was not considered to be immune from the party's criticism, but it was afforded a degree of leniency in relation to activities that would have been considered highly suspect elsewhere in China. As unintended forms of financialization began to manifest themselves in Shenzhen's physical fabric, for example, calls emerged not necessarily for more disciplined policing of the law, but for the establishment of additional sets of borders within the SEZs to ensure foreign capital did not "[move] about everywhere without restriction and run rampant." By late 1983, construction was completed on a ninety-kilometer, $520 million HKD boundary fence intended to control smuggling and "tax differences between the 327-square-kilometer zone and other parts of China."[36] How a physical wall would limit tax discrepancies remained unclear, however.

As the effects of foreign capital began to reverberate beyond the zone's intended parameters almost immediately, existing spatial logics rooted in the hierarchies of party rule began to be disrupted, reverberating around the city, the region, and throughout the country. "True, it is not Beijing, it is not Shanghai, it is not even Guangzhou," explained 1981 advertisements printed in Hong Kong's *South China Morning Post* for Shenzhen's then-unfinished International Commercial Building, near the Luohu border crossing (fig. 43). "But it will be the meeting point of the east and west in all important business activities." Located within walking distance from the Luohu border crossing, the tower was jointly developed by the Chung Fat Development Company and Shenzhen District Property Company. It was designed to offer retail, banking and dining, and office space for investors in an effort to attract capital away from established business centers like Hong Kong or Guangzhou and, in so doing, upend established geographies of center and periphery and the various hierarchies they suggested. "The Central will be Shenzhen. In Shenzhen, the Central will be Shenzhen International Commercial Building," declared promotions for the new twenty-story edifice, which was eventually completed across the street from the city's more ambitious,

Fig. 44 International Trade Center, Central-South Architectural Design Institute, Shenzhen, 1985. Originally published in *High-Rise Architecture* (*Gaoceng jianzhu*, 1988).

160-meter-tall, fifty-three floor International Trade Center—an iconic, unabashed monument to the SEZ's unbridled architectural and economic ambitions.[37]

If projects such as the Bamboo Garden Hotel disrupted hospitality standards in socialist China, and the East Lake and Green Bamboo estates upset architectural parameters to allow for variations of real estate speculation to take hold, Shenzhen's International Trade Center, which was announced to the public in 1981 at the Bamboo Garden Hotel, and completed in 1985, aimed to reconfigure the economies of time at work in socialist Chinese architecture (fig. 44). The high-rise was expected to provide office space to various provinces and municipalities around China so that they could partake in the SEZ-specific speculations taking place. It became China's tallest building following its construction and projected an aesthetic and procedural brashness over Shenzhen that could be traced back to numerous precedents set in Hong Kong, particularly the

Hopewell Centre, which was also crowned by a rotating restaurant and observational deck.

Several key aspects distinguished the project as a unique and important architecture specific to Shenzhen, however. One concerned the financing mechanism that enabled its construction. Shenzhen officials lacked the financing to realize the massive scheme, and they invited various provincial and municipal governments throughout China to contribute capital for the building's realization in exchange for thirty-year leases. The innovative funding partnership ensured that Shenzhen maintained relationships with officials—and emerging domestic markets—around the country. Additional funds were raised through the construction of a housing project on land provided by the municipal government, with individual units sold to eager local and Hong Kong investors. The property was traded for steel that was then sold on the market to pay for the tower's construction—a questionable series of transactions modeled on similarly complex arrangements at work in the East Lake and Green Bamboo estate projects. In fact, by 1984 Goodyear Estates and Millie's Group, the two investors involved in those initiatives, had declared bankruptcy.[38]

To many observers, the news indicated the excesses at work in Shenzhen's development, which suffered from an overdevelopment of hotels, restaurants, commercial centers, and office buildings that pushed occupancy rates "below breakeven points." Beijing officials criticized the city's leaders for putting up too many buildings and too few factories—a reminder that for many members of the party elite, Mao-era architectural aesthetics of physical production and particular, familiar forms of labor still held valuable semiotic sway.[39] In both physical and conceptual terms, however, Shenzhen already posed a consequential challenge to these precepts. Following Shenzhen's promising lead, special economic status was bestowed upon Shashi, Hubei Province, in July 1981, followed by Changzhou, Jiangsu Province, in March 1982, two relatively insignificant Chinese cities that indicated the expansive influence of the SEZ model. In November 1981, Premier Zhao Ziyang expressed the possibility of expanding special economic activity into Shanghai, Tianjin, Guangzhou, Dalian, Qingdao, Fuzhou, Chongqing, Wuhan, Nanjing, Shenyang, Mudanjiang, Xi'an, Harbin, and Ningbo. In a November 1983 article titled "Concerning the Inquiry into Reforming Our Country's Urban Structure," architect Zong Bize challenged the value of the work unit as the core spatial, social, and economic unit of China's urbanization itself.[40] These challenges, once considered anathema to the party system, now figured as viable policies.

By the winter of 1984–85, amid nationwide fears of economic overheating, skyrocketing bank loans, and the disappearance of China's foreign exchange reserves, party leaders considered another anti-corruption correction to address the emergence of a new class of urban entrepreneurs and increasingly risky forms of economic profiteering around the country. But such behavior remained tolerated in Shenzhen in ways that were exceptional relative to other parts of China. Shenzhen's more liberal economic climate both encouraged forms of financial and design-related risk-taking and led to new systems capable of mitigating such risk. To promote the rapid completion of the city's International Trade Center, for example, an architectural bidding system was introduced in relation to the project whereby all contracts for design and construction could be assigned to the work unit with the most competitive offer, theoretically increasing architectural quality through economic efficiency.

Zhu Zhenhui, an architect from the Wuhan-based Central-South Architectural Design Institute, was tasked with the building's design, and the state-owned enterprise Shenzhen Properties and Resources Development was responsible for its construction. Another key element of the International Trade Center's legacy—one that would be used to promote the uniquely speculative culture of the Shenzhen SEZ as a whole—concerned the unprecedented speed of the building's construction and the new labor processes involved in its production. Given the project's limited budget and symbolic importance, construction speed and efficiency were prioritized, which necessitated the importation of rapid construction techniques from Hong Kong. These included continuous poured concrete practices known as slip-form construction and climbing formwork that would be adjusted as the tower took shape. Neither technology had been previously used in mainland China, but following a series of mishaps and the purchasing of additional equipment, the project's construction team was able to successfully complete one floor every three days—an extraordinary feat. "Because of technical reform and improved management," explained *China Reconstructs,* "it will take only two years to complete. Each floor takes only three days to go up, a rate faster than that in Hong Kong."[41]

Celebrated as an index of "Shenzhen speed" upon its completion in 1985, amid the party's second anti-corruption drive, the International Trade Center's novel financing and form—it was the country's tallest curtain wall construction at the time—contributed to a new architectural culture born of an ambitious workforce, economic opportunism, lax oversight, loose capital, and inspiration caused by proximity to one of the densest, most dynamic urban environments in the world. Innovation is often considered a technological phenomenon, but at the center of the Shenzhen International Trade Center's rise were innovative experiments that need also be seen as organizational in their conceptual and procedural basis.

Shenzhen itself was a chaotic and unpredictable but consequential experiment in organizational innovation—a conceptualizing and realizing of new kinds of architectural production and expression designed to domesticate the abstractions of corporate finance within socialist China. Organizational experimentation proved discomfiting to the party's conservative ranks, but the economic risks and questions embodied by the tower—an architectural tribute to the SEZ itself—received Deng's support during a second visit to southeastern China in 1984. The tower would subsequently feature in a number of Shenzhen-themed magazines and promotional materials produced and distributed around the country in recognition of the city's unique "architectural art."[42] It embodied an exercise in space-time compression that married Hong Kong–derived capital and expertise with a seemingly limitless reservoir of socialist labor, resulting not simply in a model for design, but in a new architectural type that combined capitalistic means with socialist ends.[43]

FROM EXCEPTION TO MODEL TO TYPE

Scholars continue to focus on Shenzhen's distinctive urban qualities and its rapid rise from an exceptional space into what has been characterized as China's "Model City" and a global paradigm for successful development.[44] Nevertheless, it is through the study of Shenzhen's unique architectural merits, particularly economic liberalization's early on-site effects in relation to specific buildings, that the city's lasting contributions to new, early reform-era architecture become clear, particularly in relation to the concept of type in architecture. More than its perceived virtues and limitations as some fixed, replicable model, Shenzhen enabled an atmosphere of architectural relativity to take hold that helped to reshape design practices and built objects throughout China and, over time, the world at large. The design and construction of architecture in early reform-era Shenzhen came to embody a certain set of similar formal, procedural, and operational qualities, producing new architectural types shaped by the various impulses of access and control at work in the city, which were themselves derivative of the new practices, behaviors, and experiences taking place. New semantic and syntactical logics emerged through these buildings as well. Officials, designers, and workers studied and participated in such phenomena, and from them learned to navigate the uncertain interplay between the built environment, market-derived capital, and the state in relation to design.

Over time, distinctly public architectural work emerged around Shenzhen that contributed to its transformation into a stable civic entity. This included large-scale projects demonstrative of a particularly visible civic-mindedness such as Shenzhen University, designed by Luo Shengqi; the Shenzhen Public Library, constructed between 1983 and 1986 by the Guangdong Institute of Architectural Design in coordination with the contractor Sichuan Huaxi Enterprise Company; the Shenzhen Museum (1984–87); Shenzhen's Science Museum (1984–87); the Shenzhen Gymnasium (1984–85); the Shenzhen Theatre (1984–89); and Shenzhen's News and Culture Centre (1987), among others. These projects remain important public institutions that stabilized Shenzhen's rapidly growing population as a citizenry in ways that proved beneficial to the city's sustained development. However, their materialization and subsequent celebration as key monuments of a model city represent a distinctive chapter in the maturation of the city's architectural culture over time that obscures the individual architectural experiments that preceded them and were honed during Shenzhen's early years as an SEZ.

The value of the SEZ as an organizational and procedural framework for architecture lay in the early and individualized architectural experiments it enabled—experiments that produced typicalities particular to early reform-era China that were by no means limited to the spatial delineations of the SEZ itself. By 1986 SEZ pilot projects of one scale or another were underway in seventy-two cities, collectively offering a spectrum of spatial deregulation that still left much of the country lacking the same institutional environment for sustained free-market production, exchange, and distribution.[45] Nevertheless, the circulation of SEZ-produced architecture through new, popular forms of media, state-driven accounts of their success, the movement of workers in and out of the city, and the work of design and construction institutes responsible for projects in and outside SEZs collectively spread its influence beyond the confines of the SEZ context itself.

As profits and wages from processing, compensation trade, tourism, commerce, and real estate circulated throughout the country, they took shape as buildings and ideas about buildings, even as party leaders such as Deng oscillated in their public pronouncements as to whether the SEZ system itself was successful or not. Shenzhen's first, frenzied years of operation as a SEZ had proven that architecture did not necessarily require a stable physical or regulatory environment to materialize, and in cities such as Beijing, Shanghai, and Nanjing, where existing party infrastructures inhibited the introduction of more liberal, market-friendly practices, building-scale interventions were already occurring with similar, if more intensified, effects.

CHAPTER 6

The International Hotel

In May 1978, a national conference on hotel design in China was held in Guangzhou. The topic of tourists' accommodations had been of primary concern for the discipline for several years, and though the government had prioritized an increase in domestic hotel construction in cities such as Guangzhou, Shanghai, and Beijing beginning in 1971, bed and room shortages remained a chronic problem. Over the following year, additional articles on various issues and potential solutions related to hotel design circulated through the discipline. In May 1979, for example, the Architectural Society of China and the National Architecture and Design Research Group published a full-color pictorial book on Chinese hotels titled *Hotel Architecture* (*Lüguan jianzhu,* fig. 45). Featuring an unprecedented array of photographs, plans, elevations, and sectional drawings of forty-two recent Chinese hotel designs throughout the country, the publication attempted to collate the information produced through the conference and accompanying research and disseminate it, along with sets of design standards, plans, elevations, and photographs, to architects around the country. Clear distinctions were made between local and foreign tourist facilities, and readers were reminded of China's preexisting hotel classification system, which included five- to eight-story travelers' hotels known as *lüguan,* which catered to provincial and regional-level cadre activity, as well as larger *binguan* or *fandian,* known as international guesthouses or hotels and designed with overseas clientele in mind. "With people from all over the world set to visit China, we must hasten the country's tourism industry's rapid development," reminded the volume's editors. "Quickly improving the speed of hotel construction and improving hotel design quality is a crucial question."[1]

With its detachment from the perceived particularities of place, the hotel has long constituted a popular trope employed by scholars in indexing capitalism's global expansion over the course of the twentieth century. Over the course of the 1970s, the international hotel's emergence in China, and its entwining with the introduction of market-friendly economic policies there, coincided with a fundamental turning point in architecture's intensified relationship to capital—a watershed

Fig. 45 Yongjiang Hotel, Guangxi Architectural Design Institute, Nanning, Guangxi Province, 1973. Originally published in *Hotel Architecture* (*Lüguan jianzhu*, 1979).

some observers identified in the intensified focus on hotel design and interior space in other parts of the world, particularly the United States. In China, a consequential basis of the hotel's agency lay in its ability to separate China's "inner" and "outer" worlds—a spatial quality present in several of the pre-1978 diplomatic projects highlighted in Chapter 1 that would become more pronounced after 1978.

Imbued with new political agency during the reform era, the hotel quickly became an essential component of China's own modernizing agenda, and international hotel construction quickly emerged to dominate Chinese architectural design and discourse over the course of the 1980s. Hotels served as portals for foreign investment and Chinese architectural exchange—spaces through which foreign currency and other economic modifications could be tested and made visible without any obvious signs of political duress. Hotels also offered the party a valuable building type through which to project a sense of progress and improvement without actually lessening the party's overall position of power. In this respect, they represented crucial nexuses through which officials and architects attempted to ameliorate, if not completely resolve, the contradictions arising from the destabilizing process of economic liberalization.

Although tremendous factionalism existed within the party at the time over the nature, method, and speed of reform, China's developmental model remained grounded in a singular modernist vision that aimed to improve people's lives as quickly as possible without delegitimizing the CCP or endangering its grip on power. Realizing this objective required a dual politics of detachment and visibility capable of communicating both progress and control. Working both within and beyond the confines of governmental control in the visualization of a new, rehabilitated regime still beholden to the legacy of its predecessor required legal and spatial mechanisms such as the joint venture and SEZ; it also necessitated the aesthetics and technology of international hotel design. The typology's ability to sustain new inner worlds within a quotidian external one appealed to the CCP's more economically and politically moderate officials seeking to re-graft China's economy to the world market while gradually jettisoning the material and cultural infrastructure of Mao-era socialism. Yet the trappings of international tourism also directly challenged the ideological missives and mechanisms hard-liners considered essential to the government's right to rule. With reform, the international hotel operated as a politically sensitive but economically significant experimental typology within which officials began to test systems of international engagement above and beyond what the party as a whole necessarily considered acceptable for average Chinese residents or the country at large.

THE HOTEL AS INTERFACE

Tourism was the first economic sector opened to foreign direct investment in China, and it served as an important mode in acquiring foreign capital. Hotels, in turn, were crucial laboratories of transactional economic activity in which entrepreneurs, officials, and architects worked at improving China's economic condition without fundamentally upsetting the socialist-manufactured urban landscapes that surrounded them. Politically, tourism was considered a relatively safe ideological arena for experimentation because it did not yet constitute a fundamental component of the country's centrally planned economy. Hotels required relatively little investment and carried potential for quick rewards and high profits at a time when China's isolationism made transnational monetary exchange difficult. Hotels also offered a means by which the international service sector, an increasingly important component of the world economy at the time, could be studied and assessed within the context of China's own commodity-driven, state-directed economic system.[2] In this respect, the hotel served as a valuable microeconomic model of the mechanisms and practices increasingly at work across global capitalism.

Sensitivities related to foreign interactivity remained an issue in early reform-era China, however, and over the course of the late 1970s, the government struggled to capture the appropriate language necessary to justify the hotel development beginning to take place in relationship to increased business and tourist activity, even as it began to profit handsomely from such demand. Chinese-language articles explaining to the

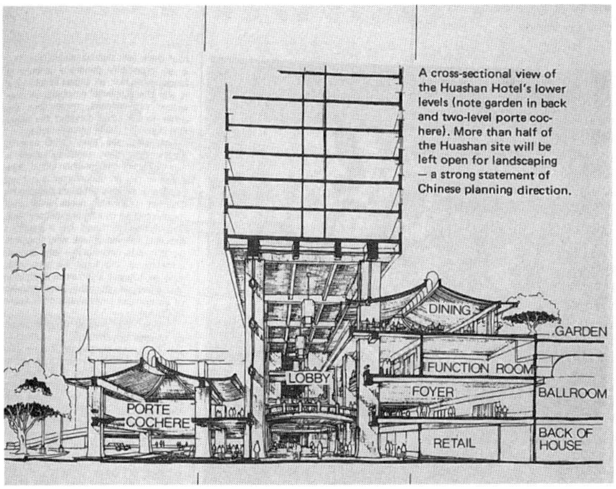

Fig. 46 Huashan Hotel (proposed), Wimberly, Whisenand, Allison, Tong, and Goo, Shanghai, 1979. Originally published in *Asian Architect and Builder* (August 1979).

Chinese public the need for hotels did so to underscore that China's socialist revolution was proceeding apace, as the numbers of workers, peasants, and soldiers needing to take business trips was "increasing daily." In reality, foreign demand was a more pressing, albeit unspoken concern; by 1981, for example, companies such as the French pharmaceutical firm Rhône-Poulenc were paying $1,300 USD for a two-room suite at the Beijing Hotel, which was approximate to room charges in Tokyo.[3] Translating these issues into the fixed, neutral terms of architectural dimensions helped to alleviate official anxiety as to the undue effects of greater numbers of foreign visitors. Early reform-era articles on hotel design argued that rooms with only one or two beds were not adequately addressing the economics of supply and demand, while rooms with six or more beds created significant inconvenience for hotel management teams. Avoiding the design and construction of single hotel towers, which proved taxing to service and utility systems and disruptive to the surrounding urban environment, was paramount.

Despite efforts to control tourism-related growth through domestic hotel construction, foreign business and tourism continued to climb, and in late 1978, news was leaked of a Chinese government-led "crash program" to build fifty thousand new, international-quality hotel rooms as quickly as possible with the help of U.S.-, Hong Kong–, and Singapore-based designers and investors. Gregory Mun Biu Tong, vice president and corporate treasurer of the Honolulu-based architectural firm Wimberly, Whisenand, Allison, Tong, and Goo, was one participant in the program. Following an official tour of China, in which he helped the government identify sites for potential hotel projects, Tong's firm was given the commissions for two hotels, including Huashan Hotel to be built in Shanghai and a resort property located in Guilin. Negotiations were difficult and shrouded in secrecy, as China and the United States did not have diplomatic relations until January 1979. The Huashan proposal was composed of a 1,250-room, thirty-eight-story high-rise tower to be built on a nearly 29,340 square-meter site along the Bund (fig. 46). Amenities were to include a two-level porte cochere, six-story lobby, two-thousand-seat ballroom, cocktail lounge, coffee shop, swimming pool, barber and beauty shop, and rooftop and main dining rooms. The Guilin project included a twelve-story hillside hotel on 242,811 square meters outside Guilin. Both projects were to be built and operated by the Chinese government, with technical and managerial expertise provided by Kuok Travel Service.[4]

Neither project was completed—a testament to the political obstacles of designing in early reform-era China beyond the more experimental confines of a SEZ like Shenzhen. Nevertheless, details of project negotiations reveal the government's early concerns regarding the impact of such new architecture on the country's existing socioeconomic systems. Providing adequate services for staff was key. For example, the Huashan design was expected to provide parking for four hundred bicycles and living quarters for three hundred staff members. "In a typical Western hotel, on-site housing is often provided for such upper-level personnel as the general manager, assistant manager, executive chef, and director of housekeeping," reasoned Tong. "In China, quite the reverse is true: on-site housing is provided for unmarried busboys, waitresses, and so forth." Tong was informed that the project would need to provide housing to accommodate a typical city-based family of four with a one-bedroom apartment, in which the children slept in the living room. "The severe housing shortage is one reason so much space has been allocated for staff members' living quarters," he explained.[5] Another reason was early morning shifts, which dictated that staff members sleep on the premises. Other unique design requirements included dining rooms capable of serving all of a hotel's guests at a single serving to accommodate organized tours, and extensive kitchen space to provide adequate room for the "painstaking" preparation of Chinese cuisine and the large number of staff required.

Another aspect of the hotel's value to China derived from its service as a teaching laboratory in design, construction, and operation for contractors, technicians, and other workers. On one hand, tourism was a simple but effective means of replenishing China's foreign exchange reserves. The travel industry was also a labor-intensive industry at a time in which China was searching for job opportunities for youth returning home after years in the countryside during the Cultural Revolution. Hotels often required approximately one employee to service each room, making them valuable employment resources for a young, postrevolutionary workforce seeking exposure to international people, experiences, and ideas. In addition, with reform, China suddenly found itself in need of many more international guests than it could reasonably accommodate. In 1978 alone, for example, over one million tourists visited China; by 1979 this figure had jumped to over four million. Of these, just 163,000 were non-Chinese, with the rest made up of overseas Chinese from Hong

Kong, Macau, and the rest of the world.[6] These considerations made the hotel a vital instrument, not only in the accumulation of foreign capital, but in the reformation and stabilization of a Chinese workforce desperate for new skills and experience.

THE JIANGUO HOTEL

As selected foreign designers pondered the challenges of designing in China, the country's leadership continued its push for relevant foreign development models. In January 1979, Deng embarked upon his celebrated trip to the United States to normalize relations. The tour may not have featured any shopping malls or private homes, but it did include time spent in the Peachtree Plaza Hotel in Atlanta, designed by John Portman, Houston's Hyatt Regency Hotel, and the Washington Plaza Hotel in Seattle, completed by John Graham Associates in 1969. These spaces exposed China's leadership to a uniquely American urban paradigm of enterprise districts anchored by high-end international hotels such as Atlanta's own Peachtree Plaza and Atlanta Mart (now AmericasMart) that would reverberate through China's own urban ambitions. Certain time-tested spatial strategies for limiting the problems posed by undue foreign influence remained in place, however. The country's preexisting high-end hotels employed unmarked guards who stood outside hotels to question any Chinese trying to enter, while elevator operators recorded every visitor entering and leaving guests' rooms. As the country barreled toward the physical reality of reform, questions remained as to whether these measures would be enough to deter illicit behavior. As early as fall 1979, for example, the Peace Café, a small restaurant serving beer and soda near the Beijing Hotel, became an active hub for young Chinese social activity before it was closed down following rumors of a prostitution ring.[7]

Despite these hazards, reformers pushed forward. Two of the first three official joint venture agreements supported by the Chinese government comprised hotel development projects, including Clement Chen's Jianguo Hotel and the U.S.-based E-S Pacific Development and Construction Company's one-thousand-room, $75-million USD Great Wall Hotel.[8] China International Travel Service (CITS) Deputy Director Zhuang Yanlin oversaw China's interest in both projects, including contract negotiations and construction management. The Jianguo Hotel was formally approved on October 20, 1979, and completed in Beijing in 1982 (fig. 47). It sought to reshape the anxiety generated by reform among certain segments of the party into productive, physical form. The building was initially proposed in 1979 by the Chinese-American architect Clement Chen, Jr., with the logistical support of CITS and the financial backing of the Hong Kong and Shanghai Bank, which had just begun to explore investment in tourist-related infrastructural projects in China.

Fig. 47 Jianguo Hotel, Clement Chen and Associates, Beijing, 1981–82. Originally published in *Architectural Journal* (*Jianzhu Xuebao*), no. 9 (1982).

Chen was a distant cousin of Liao Chengzhi, head of the newly established Hong Kong and Macau Affairs and Overseas Chinese Affairs Offices, a connection that likely played a role in the awarding of the project. Born in Shanghai and having studied at Rensselaer Polytechnic Institute in Troy, New York, before working as an architect for Wurster, Bernardi & Emmons in San Francisco, Chen's professional career was highlighted by a series of collaborative development projects he embarked upon with the hotel management company Holiday Inn, including a 566-room hotel in San Francisco's Chinatown, constructed in 1971, and the Palo Alto Holiday Inn, which was finished in 1973. Over the course of the 1970s, the Palo Alto hotel became a particularly popular destination for mainland Chinese delegations, in part because Chen's wife served Chinese food at the hotel, and it served as the physical and operational prototype for the Jianguo Hotel.

Doubts over the viability of reform reverberated in negotiations over the Jianguo Hotel's economic potential and the possibility of political repercussions. In securing 49 percent ownership over the hotel for ten years before total ownership would revert to the party, for example, Chen also obtained a guarantee from the government that his portion of the project's debt would be covered in the event of any political tumult. The initial absence of a governing agency capable of assessing the project's potential necessitated that the hotel be approved by all twelve vice-premiers and some vice-chairmen of the Standing Committee of the National People's Congress. The 480-room, $22.6-million USD project eventually opened along Beijing's East Chang'an Avenue after being completed by the Beijing Number One Construction Company in accordance with standard PRC construction and material practices. Programmatically, however, the Beijing project hewed to its Palo Alto antecedent, with a central lobby containing all of the facility's main dining and recreational options; these included Justine's, Beijing's first French restaurant since 1949. On either side of the lobby lay two carefully landscaped courtyards with pools, shielded from public view. Two blocks of guest rooms lay to the hotel's north and east, distinctively arranged into a disaggregated series that at least one Chinese critique favorably compared to the "elastic" and "lively" compositions of interior courtyards and assorted roofing types characteristic of traditional Chinese architecture.[9] A roundabout driveway provided easy automobile access, despite the relative absence of cars on the capital's streets at the time.

Access to the hotel was limited to foreign guests; with the exception of trusted cadres, guest acquaintances, and the hotel's staff, all of whom were trained by the Hong Kong–based Peninsula Hotel management group, average Chinese residents were strictly prohibited from entering the building. Chen voiced the problems that too much pedestrian traffic would engender from the perspective of international service standards: "Thousands of them [Beijing residents] arriving for a cup of tea, and then spending the rest of the day sitting around enjoying the air-conditioning. I knew that it would be impossible to run a first-class hotel that way." The building's recessed entrance ensured that no Chinese citizens would actually gain entry, while a glass façade projected tantalizing views of unimaginable comfort to startled passersby. *New York Times* contributor Orville Schell, having observed Beijing residents' fascination with the Beijing Hotel's east addition in 1977, described similarly hypnotic effects of the Jianguo on gathered crowds in 1983, which created "a silent phalanx of common people, staring transfixed through the plate-glass windows at the activity inside the brightly lit hotel lobby."[10]

The public's reaction to the Jianguo Hotel, and the odd sense of remove generated by its siting and design, echoed earlier responses to late Mao-era antecedents such as the Beijing Hotel and the foreign diplomatic projects. Both moments in architectural production represented uncertain engagements with foreign ideas and objects that resulted in paradoxical situations in which such architecture needed to both present and withhold the benefits of change. In all of the edifices, visibility proved crucial to the politics at work, as moderate-inclined officials hoped that the average Chinese citizen would gaze upon these buildings and recognize the progressive aims its physical presence portended without directly engaging with the ideological compromises that their production may have embodied. Urbanistically, too, the two generations of work aligned with each other along Beijing's preeminent east–west axis extending from Tiananmen Square in Beijing's center along Chang'an Avenue to Jianguomen Road out to the Third Ring Road then under construction.

Despite such resonance, however, the Jianguo Hotel also departed from these earlier works in important ways. Projects like the Beijing diplomatic compounds were exercises in a form of socialist Chinese modernism—an aesthetic specific both to the early twentieth century and the architectural production of early socialist China redeployed in the wake of the Cultural Revolution to reorient the country and its built environment around themes of functionalism, economy, and technical competence. The Jianguo, by contrast, was a more complex architectural expression born of a mixture of modern and postmodern ideas imported from abroad and China's own desire for sophisticated technology. Such technology, imported and managed by the project's foreign designer, was aggressively inscribed into the hotel's façade, resulting in a more confident and playful aesthetic than its older, late Mao-era precedents. For all of the realpolitik behind the Chinese government's shift toward market-based reforms, officials remained wary of expressions of modernity that did not fundamentally reinforce the government's own authority. As a result, the Jianguo Hotel's variegated spatial configuration, extravagant collection of neon lighting and technological amenities, and "California style" decor all signaled the government's commitment to a foreign-imported "techno-optimism" capable of propelling the country toward an imagined future shaped by the party yet distinctive from earlier transformative work such as the Beijing Hotel.[11]

Internally, the Jianguo also featured a number of cutting-edge technological fittings designed to convince international tourists of China's rapid development, including bright, fluorescent lighting, centralized air-conditioning, and a comprehensive telephone wiring system. The inclusion of a color television and touch-tone telephone in each room, rare items at the time, ensured the building's status as China's first international class hotel. In other projects, incidents arose in which foreign representatives attempted to convince Chinese negotiators of the benefit of less sophisticated, but more appropriate, technology than the Chinese originally had envisioned. In negotiations over the Jianguo Hotel's design and construction, however, Chinese officials demanded that any imported technology be both reliable and up-to-date by international standards. These elements obscured the project's reinforced concrete substructure and brick infill, which evinced the socialist-era techniques still at work in Chinese architectural production, as well as the addition of an underground air raid shelter—a stark reminder of the lingering Cold War–era impulse of Chinese officials.[12]

The various electronic trappings on display, and the ways in which they masked the simple construction methods of the building itself, encapsulated the idealism at work in China's efforts to overcome years of industrial decline through rapid technological importation. Such detailing signaled a striking departure from the more rudimentary, unadorned nature of China's earlier, Mao-era diplomatic architecture. Despite the evident physical deterioration of these earlier works, however, some insisted that they retained a certain "neutrality" that made them useful spaces for exchange; in May 1986, for example, the vice minister of China's State Economic Commission, Zhu Rongji, hosted a group of U.S. executives for a meeting at Beijing's International Club, which somehow remained a viable option for international events. "Not nearly as Western as Beijing's artificially elegant new hotels," wrote U.S. journalist Jim Mann, "yet not nearly as Chinese as the formal reception rooms of

Beijing's state enterprises," the building still offered a certain remove from its context that proved desirable to foreign and Chinese representatives alike.[13] The Jianguo, by contrast, demarcated new physical and conceptual territory that spoke directly to the more aggressive display of a new, more intensified kind of international interactivity driven by rapid infusions of foreign currency and technology.

The prospect of China's swift, uncontrolled integration within a global economy promised to buoy the country's financial prospects, but it also posed risks to party power by exposing the Chinese public to the influence of foreign culture and, more generally, to the contradictions at the heart of the reform project. Efforts were made to rationalize such work within some existing Chinese architectural paradigm, though the project's remove from any theoretical precedent in China generated similar shock waves within the realm of architectural discourse. Chinese architectural critic Wang Mingxian later identified the Jianguo as both the first "glass-walled building" in China and an inaccessible "enclave of the (capitalist) outside world" that nevertheless "provoked much excitement and debate among Chinese architects," reminding them of the conceptual challenges posed by this newly demarcated yet publicly undefined space of economic openness.

An officially sponsored symposium organized by the *Architectural Journal* (*Jianzhu Xuebao*) editorial committee and BIAD just two months after the building's completion aimed at consolidating professional architectural opinion through a comparative analysis of the Jianguo in relation to another recently completed, state-designed hotel known as the Huadu. Critics weighed the merits of both buildings. The Huadu, for instance, was praised for the space it dedicated to hotel staff but criticized for the unimaginative quality of those spaces and the lack of any liberalized "design thought" in its composition—all characteristics of socialist-era building practices (fig. 48). In contrast, the Jianguo's novel spatial composition, well-appointed guest rooms, and technological sophistication drew praise, though participants noted the lack of attention paid to its workers' accommodations. In establishing a set of discursive parameters with which China's architectural community could

Fig. 48 Huadu Hotel, Beijing Institute of Architectural Design, Beijing, 1981. Originally published in *Architectural Journal* (*Jianzhu Xuebao*), no. 9 (September 1982).

CHINA DAILY

Jianguo Hotel Supplement

Jianguo Hotel an embodiment of China's open-door policy

Beijing's Jianguo Hotel— a harmonious joint venture

Fig. 49 "Jianguo Hotel an Embodiment of China's Open-Door Policy." Originally published in *China Daily*, April 28, 1982.

begin to critically position their own work vis-à-vis a joint venture project, the debate provided a template by which domestic architectural production could begin to challenge and hypothetically supersede foreign architectural activity in China over time.[14]

What allowed such a powerful, if isolated, emblem of international capitalism to resonate within the Chinese capital was the Jianguo Hotel's relative simplicity as an architectural and financial model, coupled with its status as the joint product of a Chinese-American architect and a Hong Kong–based developer (fig. 49). Financially, the Jianguo was an immediate success. It remained 95 percent occupied more than a year after its opening, with net profit reaching $1.5 million USD in its first year, followed by an annual doubling each year between 1982 and 1986.[15] Its first floor of guest rooms become known within expatriate circles as "Wall Street" for the prevalence of banking representatives housed there. In 1984 the State Council championed the hotel's foreign management model through a nationwide "Learning from Jianguo" campaign aimed at promoting international standards of service quality throughout China. Chen himself would go on to build a Jianguo replica in Xi'an.

The involvement of Chinese architects, real estate developers, hotel operators, and financiers like Chen was also understood as a factor in the hotel's success, insofar as their involvement also helped to both mask and legitimize the gradual dissolution of what Zhang Xudong has described as "the ideological totality of Mao's China" in favor of a more diverse, inclusive, and global Chinese community. Their participation proved critical in reconfiguring the conflicted political imperatives behind China's economic liberalization, displacing the public's focus onto broader culturalist notions of Chinese diasporic cooperation and unity. These figures, many of whom could boast of familial and collegiate connections with the mainland that predated the country's 1949 founding, offered conduits for architectural knowledge, industry know-how, and financial expertise that were easily construed as patriotic acts of selflessness intended to help the country move beyond the convoluted politics of its immediate past toward a more prosperous future.[16]

Overseas Chinese involvement in hotel projects like the Jianguo also helped to naturalize the cold logic of foreign capital at a consequential moment of geopolitical reconsolidation in China's history. Formal negotiations between China, Great Britain, and Portugal over the return of Hong Kong and Macau to China began in earnest in September 1982 and June 1986, respectively, and the party needed to convince both countries as well as the overseas Chinese business community of China's newfound openness to investment of global capital. The SEZ offered one kind of tax-exempt, deregulated environment for investment that became emblematic of the economic and political doctrine of exceptionality announced by Deng's "One Country, Two Systems." The Jianguo offered a similar economic and social enclave, and it demonstrated the ease with which Jamesonian tropes of displacement and fragmentation, subsequently recharacterized in urban terms by Keller Easterling as "the space of uneven developments, fences, and stratification, or the space of friction and logical fallout between segregated regimes," could become empowered by Chinese political expediency.[17]

ALTERNATIVE VISIONS

Based upon the Jianguo Hotel's success, some within the party encouraged the government to "proceed from reality" through the construction of more "ordinary, serviceable" hotels that would allow the government to do more with less money while still receiving an ample number of tourists and their foreign exchange. Official efforts to manage the visibility of reform using the relatively modest physical and operational blueprint provided by the Jianguo Hotel were quickly outpaced by a number of larger, more ambitious international hotel ventures already negotiated and in the process of being designed and built, however. Each proposed an alternative image of economic liberalization and a unique spatial organization and experience that quickly challenged what officials and the public understood to be the ideal architectural embodiment of reform.

I. M. Pei's Fragrant Hill Hotel, completed six months following the Jianguo's opening and located well beyond the municipal limits of Beijing, was one such alternative (fig. 50). The building was part of a more ambitious, three-hotel project involving the Hong Kong–based company YTT Tourism, the U.S.-based Turner Construction Company, Hyatt

Fig. 50 Fragrant Hill Hotel, I. M. Pei and Partners, outside Beijing, 1979–82.

International Corporation, and Pei, arguably the most famous overseas Chinese person in the world at the time. Pei had lived and worked outside China for over forty years. Like Chen's, Pei's work around the world seemed to exemplify the kind of international corporatism that Chinese reformers were eager to emulate.[18] Many of Pei's aesthetic demands for the project were fundamentally incompatible with the bureaucracy expected to accommodate them, however, necessitating the spontaneous creation of new sources and systems capable of satisfying his own vision for the project. Although the building is now heralded as an icon of Chinese revivalism, with Pei often championed as a visionary of a distinctly Chinese modern architectural lexicon, the hotel's extravagant detail and perceived insensitivity to the political context of socialist China—namely, the financial constraints and environmental conditions prevalent within the country—caused significant political consternation and sparked serious criticism upon its completion.[19]

Despite his interest in the project's potential as a model for China's architectural modernization, the architect defied his client's expectations from the beginning. Upon being invited to design a series of high-rise hotels around the country, one of which was prominently positioned in the center of Beijing, Pei famously declined to build within the city for fear of compromising its historic urban integrity. Instead, the architect selected a location some thirty kilometers outside the city at the foothills of an imperial-cum-party retreat known as Fragrant Hill. A presentation given by the architect in New York to a visiting delegation from

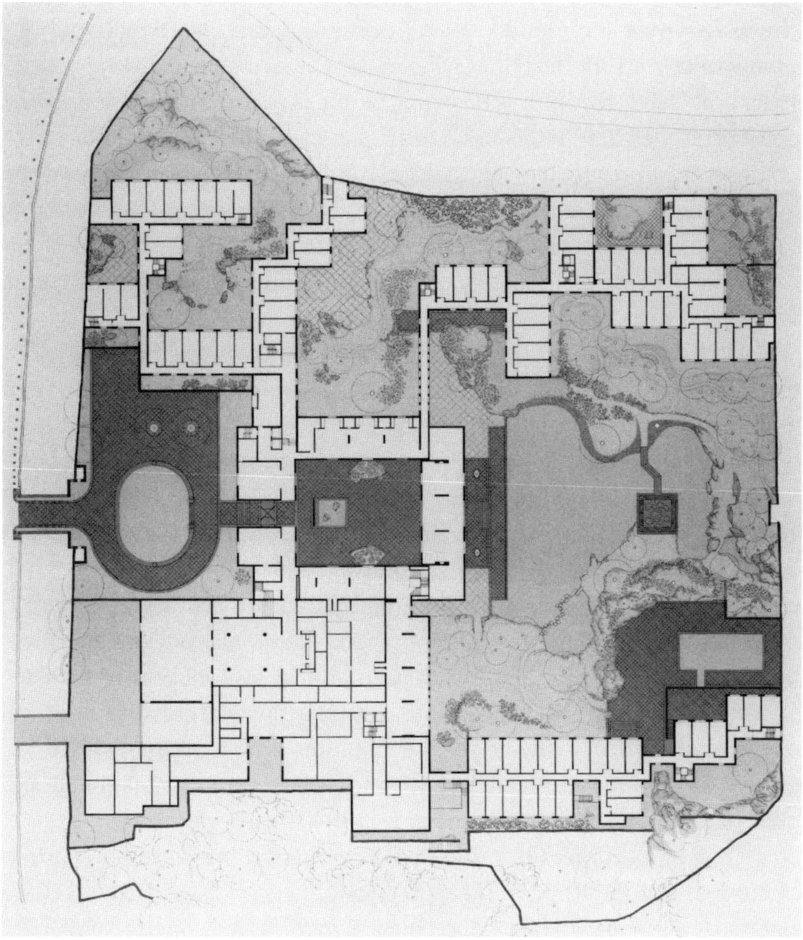

Fig. 51 Fragrant Hill Hotel, I. M. Pei and Partners, outside Beijing, 1979–82.

Tsinghua University in 1980 provides some clues as to how Pei may have convinced the government to allow him to build outside the city on his preferred site. The presentation, titled "Concerning Beijing's Urban Plan and the Nationalization of China's Architectural Arts," consisted of a series of black and white drawings identifying unique spatial and scalar features of Chinese architecture and urbanism, which Pei argued represented sources of the country's unique cultural and national identity. He contrasted these examples with projects such as the Soviet-designed and -funded Palace of Sino-Soviet Friendship and his own designs for the OCBC Centre in Singapore, which he saw as inappropriate insertions into Beijing's existing urban fabric.[20]

In accordance with this reasoning, and in keeping with his childhood memories of growing up in the southern Chinese city of Suzhou, Pei proposed a more temperate approach to his architectural and garden aesthetic: several wings of guest rooms that actively engaged with the centuries-old cedar, cypress, spruce, and pine trees existing on the premises spidered from a large courtyard (fig. 51). Because of the limited expertise of its builders, the building was a simple reinforced-concrete structure whose foundation was purportedly dug by hand by two thousand workers. Its modest, low-lying mass was embellished with Suzhou-style gray tiles, ash-gray brickwork, white-washed stucco, and small, polished stones that helped lend the project a genteel, uniquely southern Chinese charm while denying the climatic and geographic realities of the northeastern Chinese context within which the project was situated.[21] In so doing, the architect defied the government's own vision of progress to partake in a utopian fantasy of his own—a China born of recollection, untouched by communism.

In decoupling his project from the city, Pei envisioned his own pastoral imaginary of how the hotel might facilitate China's development in contrast to the party's urban-based strategy. Vividly captured by a promotional collage depicting an axonometric representation of the hotel set within the work of late Ming painter Zheng Zhong (active ca. 1612–48), Pei's hotel created an aura of cultural tradition in order to maximize its economic success (fig. 52). Unlike the Jianguo Hotel, which made certain nods to the country's architectural past, including a "Chinese" courtyard and garden arrangement placed within a structural envelope, the Fragrant Hill Hotel immersed international visitors within a pastoral landscape that was carved into a preexisting nature reserve in an extravagant effort to buy and sell encounters with a uniquely historical China—a convenient dovetailing with the party's efforts to rebuild and promote the nation's heritage as part of the Four Modernizations.

At the same time, Pei's work did not visibly remediate perceptions of the vast economic incommensurability between Western architectural standards and those of post-Mao China so much as it seemed to pull them further apart. For example, the production of five of Pei's desired bricks purportedly cost more than 50 RMB (roughly the equivalent of an average Chinese worker's monthly salary at the time), while the tiles and stones necessary for the project's decor had to be independently procured from local residents rather than through the Beijing Number Six Construction Team assigned to the project.[22] Pei's demands for these objects—and his team's willingness to pay the necessary costs—subverted established value systems in favor of new acts of commodity exchange.

Fig. 52 Axonometric drawing, Fragrant Hill Hotel, Calvin Tsao, outside Beijing, 1982.

Like Chen's work, the Fragrant Hill Hotel created a new type of economic as well as discursive terrain in China, though its contours were less certain than those defined by the Jianguo's flashy, proto-modern veneer. Inferior service standards on the part of its managing authority, CITS, led to Fragrant Hill's rapid physical deterioration just months following its completion, while evincing lingering official ambivalence with the project as an economic endeavor. Only after its completion was its conceptual value appreciated, in a number of articles published in the country's major architectural journals urging architects to look beyond the more techno-utopian paradigm embodied by works like the Jianguo. Several early and well-known foreign visitors, including Andy Warhol and Charlotte Perriand, helped draw additional international attention to the project; Perriand was particularly struck by Pei's efforts to "illustrate harmony between the old and the new."[23] The government eventually embraced the Fragrant Hill Hotel's attempted renewal of China's cultural traditions as an effort in what Pei himself termed a process of "nationalization"—that is, the renewal of historical Chinese architectural aesthetics and forms by the Chinese nation-state.

Yet even the building's most public supporters felt compelled to acknowledge the project's shortcomings. Foremost among these were the artistic liberties taken with the project. Pei's work urged the viewer to rethink what could be interpreted as old or new, real or unreal, or, alternatively, "modern" or "Chinese" in architectural design, implicitly challenging a government long used to determining for its people what constituted the truth. With such controversy came deeper questions concerning the productive forces increasingly at work in the country and how these forces should be represented in architectural terms. These issues were explored in another government-sponsored symposium organized in December 1982.

Meeting at the Fragrant Hill Hotel, over thirty attendees from China's architectural elite debated the project's merit. Liu Kaiji, deputy architect of BIAD, found the project to be a reasonable success despite its unspeakable commercialization of an imperial garden and the extent to which Pei's "superstar" status may have contributed to its "wasteful" and "extravagant" nature. By contrast, Wu Guanzhang, BIAD's chief architect, lauded both the Fragrant Hill and the Jianguo hotels for their "shocking" effects on Beijing's built environment—namely, the ways in which both buildings threw into stark relief the city's rigid, restrictive aesthetic, and the lack of any contemporary architectural variety. Other comments noted the hotel's unfortunate distance from Beijing, its underwhelming monumentality, and its insensitive engagement with southern garden design, as well as the project's imaginative decorative detail and its unapologetic embrace of Chinese architectural history.[24]

As Chinese commentators attempted to rationalize these new buildings within the broader project of reform, the relative aesthetic and formal indulgences at work in them suggested economic and moral deviations already taking place in other segments of Chinese society. In making the international hotel a testing site in debates over both the nature and aesthetics of reform, however, Chinese officials knowingly courted these instabilities and the potential for psychological and social rupture they posed. Officials were aware that the hotel would facilitate the importation of illicit goods and activities into China; a well-publicized 1981 educational campaign launched within Beijing's Friendship Hotel, for example, taught Chinese staff how to build up their "immunity" to "pornographic" magazines and other foreign goods left in guest rooms.[25] Still, the international hotel remained a major source of foreign capital. One foreign substance, it seemed, could not be absorbed without the other, necessitating the search for some new architectural language that could better compartmentalize these value conflicts.

SCALING UP: THE JINLING AND THE GREAT WALL HOTELS

China's international hotels were devised to accommodate the development of one economic system within another. The promises of reform were emblematized by the physical objects themselves, while the conflicted politics involved in this transition would remain ensconced behind their impenetrable façades. In celebrating the image of reform while concealing the compromises compelled by reform, however, the party merely aggravated the incongruities these compromises presented. By 1983 Chinese residents could not help but notice the jarring physical and social changes taking place around them, and many grew increasingly frustrated over their inability to access the new sites. Increasingly large hotels materialized that further destabilized China's urban landscapes. The Jinling Hotel, designed and built in Nanjing, represented the tallest building in the country upon its construction in 1983 (fig. 53). The project was completed through an international partnership between the Singapore-based Shing Kwan Group, the Hong Kong–based architectural firm P&T Group (formerly Palmer and Turner), the architectural design and graduate programs at Southeast University in Nanjing, and the Nanjing municipal government. Proposed for construction on a prominent corner in Xinjiekou, one of Nanjing's busiest areas, the site was imagined as a new catalyst for urban development in the city's center.

Jim Kinoshita, P&T Group's project architect on the Jinling Hotel in Nanjing, recalled the joint involvement of six architects from the School of Architecture at Southeast University, formerly the Nanjing Institute of Technology, as well as four architects from Beijing in the project's design phase. Although the Beijing faction's role was never explained to Kinoshita, he interpreted their presence as evidence of ongoing negotiations between the central government and Jiangsu provincial leaders over the realization of a high-rise hotel in a regional city that might over-

Fig. 53 Jinling Hotel, P&T Group, Nanjing, 1983.

shadow the capital's own ambitious design plans. The Jinling Hotel was eventually completed amid vociferous protests over the building's height at both the design and review stages by Beijing-based participants, and realized in part thanks to the intervention of Jiangsu Province's governor, Gu Xiulian. Following its opening on October 1, 1983, the 110-meter-high, eight-hundred-room Jinling Hotel included a range of international amenities, including a comfortable two-story central lobby, Chinese and foreign restaurants, conference facilities, a Suzhou-inspired garden, swimming pool, and a three-thousand-square-meter shopping center. Externally, the hundreds of houses and shops suddenly displaced by the thirty-seven-story building's construction, the disquieting transparency of the hotel's iron gates, mounting evidence of apathetic management by Chinese staff, and even the strange, foreign luxury of leisure travel itself all seemed to offer foreboding symptoms of a dangerously imbalanced society.[26]

Along with the Jianguo, the Great Wall Hotel, completed along Beijing's uncompleted Third Ring Road in early 1984, was one of the first joint venture agreements approved by the Chinese government, though its monumental scale and structural complexity made it a more difficult and time-consuming project (fig. 54). Like the Jianguo, it, too, was based on a U.S. prototype—in this case, the Dallas Hyatt, designed and completed by Welton Becket and Associates in 1978, visited by an official party retinue in 1980, and internationally recognizable thanks to its appearance in the opening credits of *Dallas,* then the world's most popular television show. Its Beijing iteration, designed by the firm's international entity, Becket International, with financing and operational support provided by CITS,

Fig. 54 The Great Wall Hotel, Becket International Corporation, Beijing, 1981–83.

the U.S.-based development and construction company E-S Pacific, and Unison Corporation, dwarfed any other hotel project in the capital.

Clad in Beijing's first mirrored glass curtain wall, the hotel's reflective surface was unlike anything yet seen or experienced in reform-era China, befitting its position along a new transportation corridor taking shape between downtown Beijing and the city's recently completed international airport. The unprecedented nature of the collaborative venture originally prompted C. B. Sung, CEO of Unison Corporation, to reach out to the Cyrus Eaton Group of Companies, a sprawling international conglomerate with over twenty years of experience in developing luxury hotel projects in socialist countries, including Hungary, Yugoslavia, Romania, the Soviet Union, and Cuba. The company had not previously worked in China but had successfully overcome the obstacles of socialist, non-market economies in other parts of the world. "It's difficult to determine where decisions are being made," admitted John Eaton, treasurer of E-S Pacific Corporation and executive vice-president and general manager of E-S Pacific Development and Construction Company, in reference to commercial work within the socialist world. "You are confronted with vertical compartmentalization. . . . The left hand does not know what the right hand is doing."[27]

In search of architects with similar international expertise, Eaton subsequently brought MacDonald (Don) Becket onto the team. Becket was an architect and president of the Becket Group, a large U.S. development firm that included the U.S.-based practice Welton Becket and Associates,

Becket Investments, and the firm's global operations, Becket International. Eaton and Becket had worked together on several Hyatt hotels in the United States, and Becket International possessed extensive experience designing hotel and corporate headquarters projects around the world.[28] In late 1978, Becket traveled to China to meet with government representatives; this trip was followed by a U.S. tour for CITS representatives to visit Welton Becket and Associates hotel projects, including the Hyatt Regency Hotel in Dallas, which left a particularly strong impression. Becket International assumed complete control over the design process, including all architecture, mechanical, structural, and construction management, and the services needed to realize the hotel. Drawings were promised for completion in one month—a source of astonishment and misunderstanding on the part of the project's Chinese partners, who initially insisted upon detailed drawings of each room on each floor, rather than one drawing of each room type. Drawings were eventually completed in March 1980.

The completed design featured 1,007 rooms organized into three fin-like wings projecting from a central, seven-story atrium. Stretching twenty-two stories tall and capped by an octagonal rooftop restaurant, the hotel's other anticipated amenities included an indoor pool, Beijing's first disco club, and a twenty-four-hour coffee shop. The building's physical form composed a single tower that, according to Eaton, rejected standard "twin-tower" financial and architectural models at the time, in which two identical edifices were built and independently run by local and foreign partners. "If they are actually managing the towers separately," reasoned Eaton, "who benefits from the management experience of the other?" Eaton later went so far as to suggest that their project had provided the inspiration for the joint venture system itself—an unsubstantiated claim that denied the party's preexisting studies of a range of joint venture precedents, from Taiwan to Eastern European nations, including Yugoslavia, to the historical writings of Sun Yatsen.[29] Nevertheless, the Great Wall scheme proposed by Becket International offered a management model that catalyzed procedural and structural reorganization and reified the results into a single tower of glass, steel, and concrete. The building would perform as a physical projection of its own management strategy—architecture as both object and operation.

Difficulties emerged almost immediately, and ranged from acrimonious wrangling over the specifics of the hotel's size, class, site, preferred communication method between partners, the division of profits and losses, the period of joint operation, and the proposed process for resolving disputes between the partners. Despite all of the collaborative initiative at the project's conceptual and physical core, "the Chinese basically want to have fine hotels, at least comfortable hotels, that are owned and run by the Chinese," explained Eaton. "Their long-term goals do not include continuing foreign participation."[30] Paradoxically, however, foreign participation was essential to China's ability to realize that goal, and once construction began, tensions flared over discrepancies in each partner's level of expertise.

U.S. partners quickly realized the Beijing Number Six Construction Company assigned to the project lacked the basic mechanistic and technical expertise to complete complex, high-rise construction projects, necessitating the importation of equipment from Singapore, Hong Kong, and Japan, as well as the United States. Multiple problems arose over different construction practices, including concrete casting methods.[31] As construction problems mounted, U.S. representatives struggled to adjust their expectations and oblige their Chinese partners, who recognized their own limitations but worked to accommodate the project's demands to the best of their ability. "The Chinese are not up to date in terms of computerized scheduling of procedures and manpower," explained Becket during the construction process. "They are substantially behind and can't adjust to the modern system." In July 1982, following several months of construction, Becket turned the job completely over to Chinese partners due to the "inconsistencies between U.S. and Chinese methods of construction."[32]

The hotel's reflective glass curtain wall effectively masked these inconsistencies while providing Beijing with a new, visibly modern landmark. Having considered an opaque surface as "too dominant for its environment," Welton Becket rationalized the building's mirrored exterior on the grounds that it would help dissolve the building's hulking mass by "reflect[ing] images of the surrounding landscape and traditional Chinese architecture." However, given the building's location along the city's uncompleted Third Ring Road, in proximity to both the city center and its newly expanded airport, "traditional Chinese architecture" took the form of a "Chinese" garden constructed around the project's base (fig. 55). These interventions were designed to render the city's tourist infrastructure more legible and overtly "Chinese" for foreign visitors. Other ostensibly Chinese features, including a small pavilion, were also arranged around the hotel's chrome-highlighted lobby as an artificial environment, Orchid Pavilion Court, within which foreign travelers and businesspeople could safely dictate their own level of engagement with China.[33]

While foreigners contented themselves with distorted reflections of a constructed Chinese "Other" emblematized by the hotel's garden and pavilion, Chinese officials and observers alike were compelled by the unique physical properties of the mirrored glass itself, which for many succinctly captured the successful harmonization of the United States' economic prowess and China's economic aspirations. Famously, Fredric Jameson traced this technology's apogee to John Portman's Bonaventure Hotel, completed in Los Angeles between 1974 and 1976, which he described as a kind of "postmodern hyperspace . . . [that] transcends the

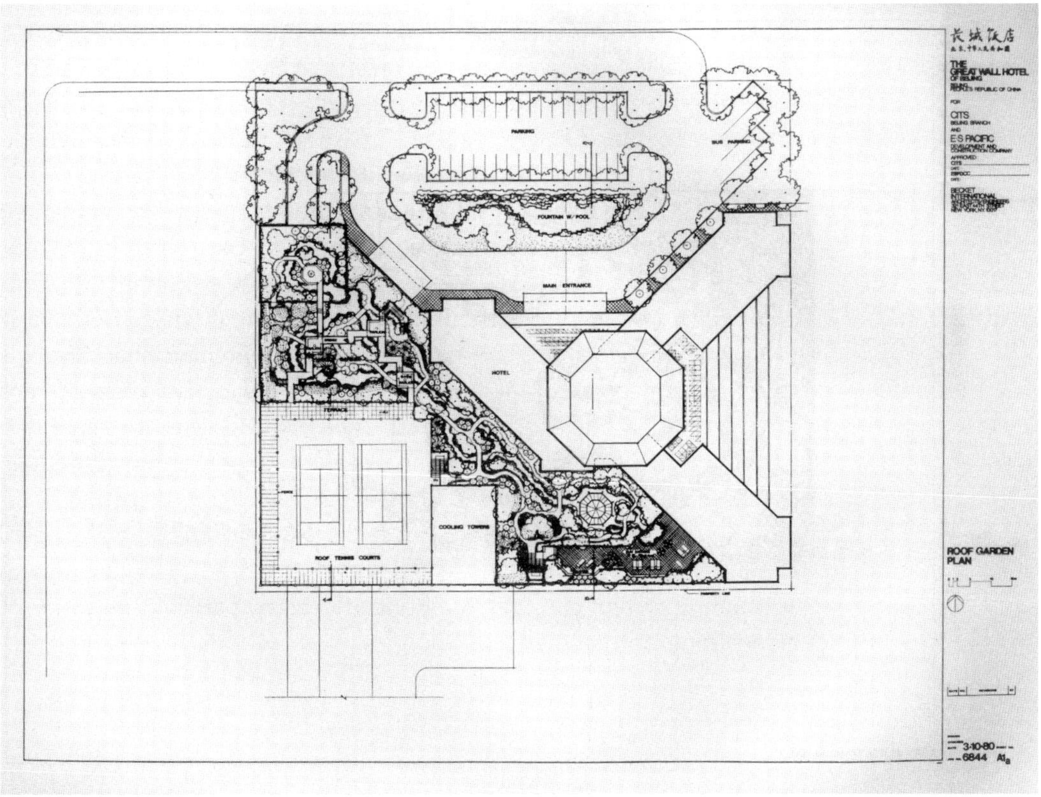

Fig. 55 Site plan, The Great Wall Hotel, Becket International Corporation, Beijing, 1981–83.

capacities of the individual human body to locate itself, to organize its immediate surroundings perceptually, and cognitively to map its position in a mappable external world."[34] The Los Angeles hotel functioned for Jameson, in other words, as an architectural "allegory" for postmodernity. However, in positioning the Los Angeles hotel as symptomatic of a distinctly American strain of postmodernity, which was in turn incapable of effecting a "proto-political Utopian transformation," Jameson's allegory dismissed the politically productive potential of the hotel (along with postmodernism) altogether, disregarding the variety of rapid, elastic economic and political mutations being simultaneously engendered by the hotel typology in other parts of the world at the time.

In China, the hotel fed on a very different cultural logic from Jameson's theorizations, namely, one fashioned by the comingling of pre-capitalist, capitalist, late capitalist, and socialist conditions in the production of space propelled by a distinct political mandate. The Great Wall's thin, shimmering membrane was less an aggressive rejection of its surrounding context—a point evocatively noted by Jameson with respect to the Bonaventure Hotel's relationship to Los Angeles—than an attempt to mediate the substantial financial risks and political anxieties posed by transnational corporate engagement with Beijing. In this way, the hotel's mirrored visage helped to negotiate between two vastly different political economic systems while camouflaging the cynical intertwining of capitalist and communist sensibilities taking place within the building. Coincidentally, Jameson spent a semester at Beijing University in 1985 soon after the hotel's construction, though he did not pay particular attention to the building's unique spectral qualities.[35] Other foreign observers did, however; Orville Schell, for example, described the experience of crossing the hotel's threshold as stumbling over "an unmarked international border into another country."[36] Like customs agents, Chinese doormen barred Chinese residents from exploring the complex, which supported one thousand staff purportedly culled from many of Beijing's most established families, including Premier Zhao Ziyang's daughter, a graduate of the University of Hawaii's tourism management program. Employees were recruited, styled, and dressed to serve and network with a distinctly international clientele hoping to gain economic purchase in China. An array of technological innovations helped to facilitate this process, including an in-house professional theater, high-speed, computer-controlled elevators, and a computerized reservations and accounting system considered advanced in many parts of the world, let alone China, at the time.[37]

MIXED USE

The ballooning scale and operational complexity on display in projects such as the Jianguo, the Fragrant Hill Hotel, and the Great Wall Hotel underscored the challenges increasingly faced by architects as well as officials in both mediating and representing capitalism's surge into China. While foreign representatives wrestled with the procedural and physical aspects of implementing the design to their client's wishes, mainland Chinese partners struggled to navigate the shifting power structures occurring at the central, provincial, and municipal levels of Chinese governance. Desire on the part of some officials for architectural models of modernization occasionally clashed with colleagues' and foreign expectations concerning what might be appropriate for China, exacerbating linguistic and logistical obstacles and a changeable political environment. Foreign executives often complained that Chinese officials seemed to be inventing building regulations as they went along. In fact, party representatives were hurriedly establishing and revising legal and tax systems to replace the obsolete Mao-era policies of its past and accommodate the country's lurch toward modernization.

A reform-era class of mediators emerged to ensure joint venture projects were completed as efficiently as possible. They included figures such as Zhuang Yanlin, deputy director of CITS, who participated in several joint venture hotel projects, including the Great Wall, and was responsible for convincing more conservative party members of China's need for international-standard hotels and their importance to China's economic future. Despite the efforts of Zhuang and other mediating agents, however, the decision-making process at all levels was not always fast enough. "When you are building a hotel in the U.S., for instance, you have got to be able to make instant decisions," admitted Eaton. "Someone has to take responsibility on a minute-to-minute basis and has to be willing to make these decisions promptly."[38]

In fact, the speed of change had begun to present both logistical and political problems for the party. Beginning in 1985, party leaders condemned the "unhealthy tendencies" within the tourism industry and launched a second "Spiritual Civilization" campaign to mitigate what were seen as the undue cultural effects of reform. In September and again in November, university students in Beijing held unauthorized rallies against Japanese militarism and the possibility of Japanese economic domination—signs that China's populace had begun to disassociate the fundamental premise of economic liberalization with its consequences. A special conference on ideology was subsequently organized by the party's Propaganda Department in Chengdu. There, a number of cadres supported the reestablishment of Marxist ideology in justifying Deng's own, unique brand of socialism. Despite these growing pressures, however, hotel construction continued apace and began to diversify in response to new market demands. Between 1984 and 1988, the number of hotel rooms in China ballooned from 76,900 to over 220,000. By the end of 1989, 409 joint ventures had been created with contracts amounting to $3.88 billion USD. By 1990 the country had 1,987 foreign hotels being run by more than 430 government entities in addition to numerous foreign partners.[39]

The Shanghai Centre, designed in Shanghai by John Portman & Associates beginning in 1985 and completed in April 1990, attempted to contain the dynamism of international corporate activity through a new typological fashion (fig. 56). Costing over $100 million USD at the time of its completion, it constituted the largest single foreign investment project up to that time in Chinese real estate and eventually included a seven-hundred-room hotel, 1,500-seat theater, 472 premium serviced apartments, thirty thousand square meters of prime office space, a three-level retail plaza, and an exhibition atrium. Anchoring the complex was a series of covered retail and exhibition spaces intended for trade fairs within which goods could be advertised to Chinese counterparts. The layering of mixed-use programs, and the unpredictable channels of capital flowing in and out of the country they seem to suggest, were masked from the street by the theater and only revealed through interior section drawings (fig. 57).[40]

As in China's other hotel schemes at the time, officials demanded that the hotel maintain a degree of physical delimitation from its surroundings in an effort to prevent the interference of Chinese residents. Two archways were subsequently constructed at each of the center's entrances to effectively deter pedestrians from entering without

Fig. 56 Shanghai Centre, John Portman & Associates, Shanghai, 1985–90.

sacrificing the integrity of Portman's design. Portman recognized his scheme's potency as a proxy for international business activity, and he argued that the project was "obviously" inspired by Chinese architecture, "with separate buildings organized symmetrically about a north-south axis." Internal correspondence and international marketing material, however, conveyed the complex's Janus-faced changeability as an "economic focal point for Shanghai," a "catalyst for future growth," and "a city within a city." More importantly, the inclusion of short-term luxury apartment rentals—the first of their kind in China—allowed foreign families to reside comfortably in the city for extended periods of time, while amenities such as a sports club, health clinic, and grocery store ensured safety as well as segregation from the local populace. The party did not anticipate foreign interest in these types of spaces, and Portman was able to retain financial control over the complex's apartments for the entire duration of the project's initial joint venture contract.[41]

Ultimately, the Shanghai Centre's disquieting physical and operational

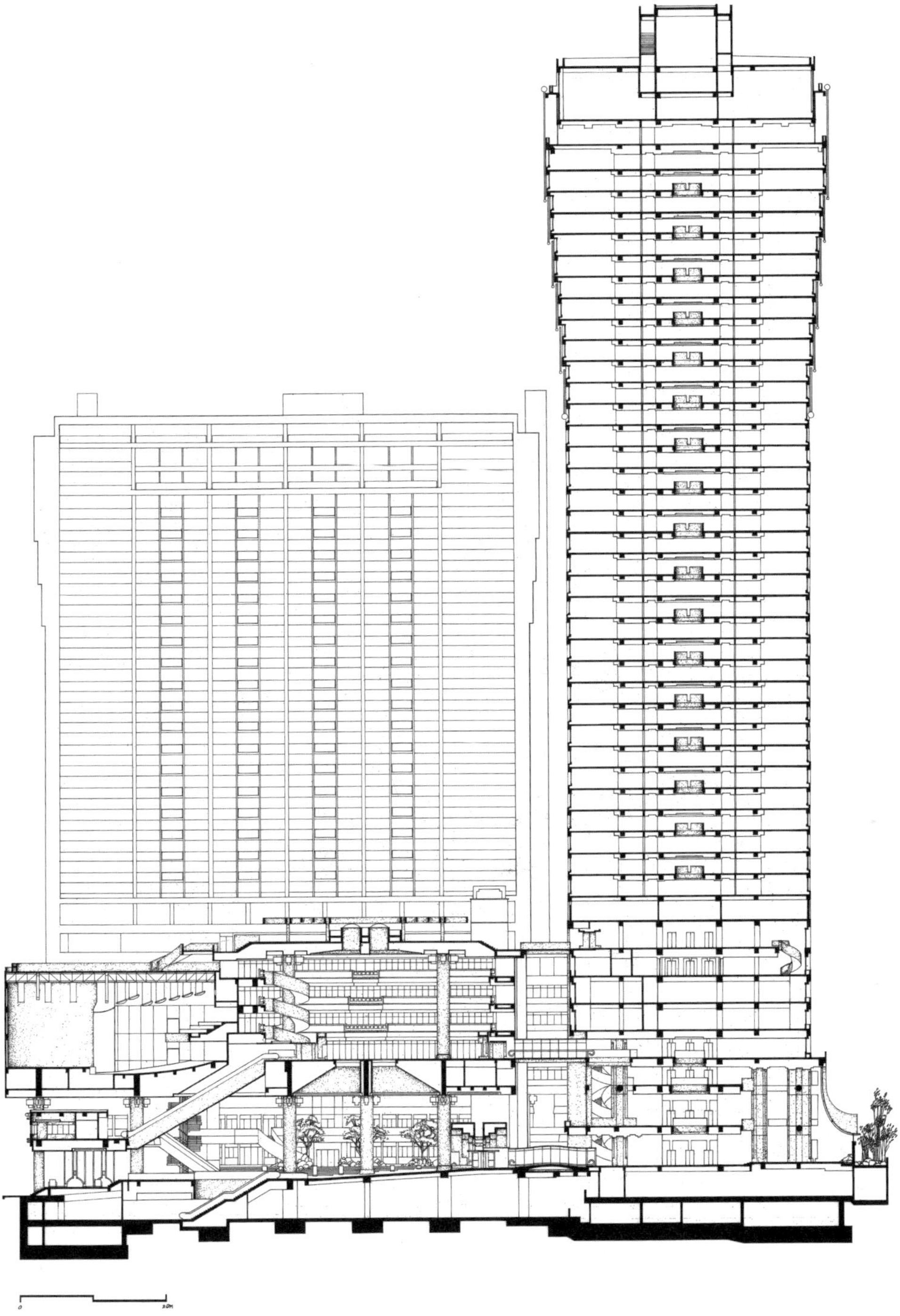

Fig. 57 Section, Shanghai Centre, John Portman & Associates, Shanghai, 1985–90.

autonomy seemed to overpower the city. As the largest single consumer of power in its urban district, the project necessitated the construction of a new 35-kV substation supervised by Kajima in coordination with the Shanghai Power Supply Bureau, while 40 percent of its generated output was engineered to be siphoned off to other urban districts around the city. A state-of-the-art BellSouth telecommunications system elided the Chinese government's antiquated infrastructure altogether by providing a satellite network through which all communication could be connected directly to "international gateways."[42] At once global and local, the Shanghai Centre offered a new form of residence within China, yet not of China. Ultimately completed in 1990 after being delayed by the events of Tiananmen, its interiorization of an entirely new urban environment seemed to satisfy Chinese government officials and international business clients alike.

Beijing's China World Trade Centre (CWTC), designed by Robert Sobel/Emery Roth & Sons, in association with Nikken Sekkei, was also completed in 1990 (fig. 58). The complex was the collaborative effort of Chinese and foreign experts—a joint investment by China's Ministry of Economic Relations and Trade and the Hong Kong–based Kerry Industrial Company. Taking its scalar and programmatic cues from the new tower construction taking place in Shenzhen, and by extension Hong Kong, the complex redefined the nature of corporate space in the nation's capital. "Hong Kong has long been known for its 'big is beautiful' mentality. Well, the territory's big brother on the mainland has caught on," trumpeted the *Asian Architect and Contractor* magazine in its review of the CWTC construction published in January 1989. The project consisted of one thirty-eight-story tower with sixty-three thousand square meters of office space; 448 apartment suites; the five-star, 743-room China World Hotel; a smaller, three-hundred-room business hotel, Traders; seventy-three thousand square meters of exhibition space; a convention center; an eleven-thousand-square-meter shopping mall; and over three thousand

Fig. 58 China World Trade Centre (CWTC), Robert Sobel/Emery Roth & Sons, associate architect Nikken Sekkei, Beijing, 1985–90. Originally published in *Architectural Journal* (*Jianzhu Xuebao*), no. 1 (1988).

parking spaces. Other amenities included a three-hundred-seat cinema, swimming pools, a gymnasium, bowling alleys, billiard rooms, squash courts, tennis courts, a children's playground, and twenty-four thousand square meters of "Chinese-style" landscape.

The project was the largest multipurpose development yet proposed for China, and the culmination of an architectural trajectory launched years prior through projects like the Jianguo. "When CWTC is fully operational it will position China as a fully-fledged member of the international business network and will feature prominently in the international network of 140 world trade centers," explained Chris Thrift, director of the property's marketing agency, Richard Ellis—the first international property consultant to be appointed in China. Like architectural antecedents such as the Great Wall Hotel or Shanghai Centre, the CWTC was imagined for a specifically foreign clientele with families willing to spend significant time in China. Approximately three hundred international and Sino-foreign joint ventures were expected to use the facility as both their business headquarters and recreational hub. "It will provide accommodation and office space for a third of Beijing's expatriate community," explained Thrift. "With its full range of shopping, dining, recreational and health facilities, the development will mark a dramatic step forward in improving the quality of life in the Chinese capital for foreign residents."[43] Chinese access was presumed, but it remained an open-ended question.

BUILDING RESENTMENT

As physical, often inaccessible indices of wealth and privilege, new international hotels produced a visual and spatial remove that fueled public perceptions not merely of official malfeasance, but deeper, ideological contradiction. The jarring materialization of the reform project into the structures and surfaces of the international hotel exceeded not only the government's ability to control their social effects, but the willingness of average Chinese residents to tolerate the contradictions they exposed. In a 1986 essay entitled "Thirty-Seven Stories of China," Liu Binyan, a well-known Chinese journalist, detailed the profound disruptions effected by Nanjing's Jinling Hotel, and the demonstrable social inequities at work in the hulking, inaccessible edifice. In its focus on the building's height and the quantity of materials, hours, and laborers required for its construction, Liu's critique shrewdly deployed the government's obsession with quantifiable national production and output to illuminate the absurd extravagances on display in such work. He also reflected upon the dizzying changes that had taken place around the country over the past ten years through the telling of a story relayed to him from a government representative concerning a U.S. tour group's 1977 visit to Nanjing, and one participant's disgust at what they perceived to be a dirty bathroom. Upon inspecting the facilities and noting its leaky faucet and stained ceramic sink, the official noted to himself, "What a tidy bathroom, damn the bourgeoisie!" Liu concluded his piece by describing the Jinling as both an exclamation point and a colon. Such work testified to both the nature and speed of China's ambitions to the world; it also communicated a society's values to the population at large.[44]

National protests in 1986, 1987, and 1989 signaled the public's reception of these values. Widespread frustration over government corruption and the unequal opportunities provided by reform in cities ranging from Beijing to Xi'an to Chengdu targeted foreigners-only hotels, with public resentment aimed not only at the foreign visitors dwelling there, but the Chinese officials who imagined and condoned such segregation. Demonstrators could not understand how certain professions, particularly those related to the tourism industry, had become so much more lucrative than others: why, for example, taxi drivers made more money than engineers, or teenagers working in joint-venture hotels more than senior professors.[45] The visibility of economic disparity, now inscribed into the skylines of China's major urban centers, was unavoidable, presenting architects with difficult questions of equal access in relationship to their work and its impact upon China's economic development.

Many struggled to rationalize their visions for their projects with the imbalances they created. Concerning questions as to whether his hotel was merely a "stockade" imposed upon average Chinese residents, for example, John Portman argued, "I don't necessarily agree with this view, but to a certain extent hotels are stockades all over the world. However, they are primarily meeting places—I have always said that hotels are people places.... Hotels will play a vital role in fostering contacts between locals and visitors not only for business but for the basic purpose of learning about each other."[46] That most Chinese residents were prohibited from entering these spaces went unacknowledged—an indication of the scant foreign professional attention paid to the multiple, finely grained effects their physical recalibrations of China's social and economic structures were producing in relation to ground conditions. Chinese architectural assessment of these projects also remained muted, particularly as Chinese design institutes were active partners in these endeavors.

Architecture may have been just one vehicle for change in early reform-era China; in fields like computer science, for example, rapid infusions of technological expertise and equipment also produced imbalances and privileges that altered Chinese society. Yet buildings monumentalized the growing disparities and inequalities in Chinese society in ways few objects could match. Handbills found at Tiananmen Square in the spring of 1989, for example, declared that "these people's public servants have used the blood and sweat of the people to build palatial retreats all over China . . . to buy foreign luxury vehicles, and go abroad on pleasure trips with their children, and even with the children's nannies!"[47] The operational and representational shifts taking place in China's architectural internationalism embodied deeper systemic changes taking place that had begun to undermine the party's grip on Chinese society and, more generally, the state of the socialist world order. Channeling public opinion into reengagements with China's architectural history and new, foreign-derived architectural ideas regarding context and communication offered one potential means through which the party might neutralize the discipline's contested semiotics and the extent to which they had both symbolized and indexed the party's capitulation to the market.

琼华饭店

PART III

Integration

CHAPTER 7

Postmodernism

In January 1980, the term "postmodernism" appeared in a Chinese architectural journal for the first time (fig. 59). Imported from abroad as the country's architectural elite grappled with reform's implications for design, the neologism arrived as an assemblage of aesthetic theories and images compiled from a variety of sources in the United States, Western Europe, and Japan that initially held appeal on the presumptive basis that it was a foreign idea with inherent, if as yet unknown, value for China. In particular, the historical and cultural disjunctions at work in postmodern theory—its perceived theoretical "break" from modernism and critical reengagement with precedent—was initially understood by Chinese architects to be of some relevance to China. Postmodernism seemed to offer a conceptual lens through which Chinese architects could simultaneously reengage with a Chinese architectural past nearly erased by the Cultural Revolution and shrink the profound discursive gap between China's architectural community and the rest of the world, thereby contributing to the country's modernization efforts and reaffirming the party's authority in the process.[1]

Despite initial Chinese interest in the term, reconciling postmodernism to China's specific socioeconomic context proved challenging. The term originated in the architectural study of postindustrial U.S. and Western European cities during the mid- to late 1960s, and presented an array of alternative design methods capable of reintroducing elements of contradiction, context, irony, specificity, and depth—human subjectivity—into architectural expression at a time in which architectural modernism increasingly seemed a failure, and unable to address the messy complexities of the lived experience. Reengaging architecture's own history, and the semiotics embedded within self-reference, was also important to the postmodern project, which offered much-needed levity to the discipline's dogmatic coupling of a building's form to its function. Emblematized through the work of figures such as Robert Venturi and Denise Scott Brown, Charles Moore, Charles Jencks, and others, the notion of an architecture after modernism gestured toward these possibilities, though for some, including the Marxist theorist Fredric Jameson, postmodernism

由西方现代建筑新思潮引起的联想

中国建筑科学研究院 杨芸

Fig. 59 Yang Yun, "Some Ideas Connected with New Trends in Western Contemporary Architecture," *Architectural Journal* (*Jianzhu Xuebao*), no. 1 (1980).

represented a more confused, cynical cultural condition demonstrative of late capitalism itself. Jameson considered architecture a particularly effective vessel for postmodernism because buildings, more than any other form of cultural production, captured the disorienting abstractions of capital, from project financing to the speculative real estate practices that subtended their physical presence.[2]

Over the course of the 1980s, Chinese architects struggled to translate these issues into terms applicable to China and grapple more substantively with postmodernism's playful, often ironic flirtations with historical precedent, abstraction, and the market. Some continued to advocate for its relevance to post-Mao China, while others began to recognize the discourse's risks to Chinese socialism, in which buildings served as a key medium of representational and practical value to the state, architects performed as public servants beholden to the needs of the people, and abstraction of any kind remained troublesome to party politics. As a result, postmodernism was rejected by numerous Chinese architects and historians. Nevertheless, and as this chapter argues, its role in early reform-era China deserves reexamination.

In many respects, postmodernism's confused relationship to history presented advantages in China, where the party's own recent past remained an ideological minefield of verboten names, dates, and events. Often framed as an incoherent appropriation of mistranslated historical pastiche, China's experimentation with postmodern ideas composed a consequential liberative moment for architects as they navigated the chronological and ideological dissonance at work in modern China's own afflicted architectural history.[3] The term's pliancy also presented distinctive political benefits, particularly given the country's new economic agenda and the demands for as-yet unidentified architectural expressions capable of satisfying reform-inclined officials, comforting their more conservative counterparts, and absorbing potentially sudden shifts in party doctrine.[4]

Equally importantly, postmodernism fueled discussions, debates, and exchanges that opened new discursive space in China. Questions regarding postmodernism's relevance to China fueled the rise of architectural judgments among architects and segments of the public over time that helped to reestablish the value of individual taste and discernment, both forbidden considerations under Mao. The cultivation of architectural opinions beyond those necessarily promoted by the party contributed to broader public deliberations on topics such as comfort, technology, and representation.[5] Through the emergence of these concerns, new forms of intellectual and social life in China took shape.

POSTREVOLUTIONARY ARCHITECTURAL DISCOURSE

China's curiosity concerning postmodernism began as the country's leaders sought new language capable of conveying the extraordinary scale of national economic development still to be achieved throughout the country without discounting Mao or the fundamental socialist objectives at the CCP's core. Over the course of 1977 and 1978, consequential intraparty debate took place concerning what China's intensified pursuit of modernity meant for the country at large and how quickly it would be achieved. Proper terminology was needed to describe post-Mao China's uncertain historical condition. In a January 1979 party conference on socialist theory, reform-inclined leaders introduced the term "undeveloped socialism" into the post-Mao Chinese lexicon.[6] The term was intended to rationalize the economic experimentations being implemented, but it also contradicted Mao-era claims that China had achieved the kind of "developed socialist" state originally imagined by Marx and Lenin. It generated active debate before being accepted by party stalwarts, which necessitated the addition of two new epochs within the country's preexisting and Marxist-inspired historical periodization—the first extending from the initial victory of the proletariat to the socialist transformation of the ownership of the means of production, and a second extending from that point to the moment when full socialism is reached.[7]

Over the course of 1978 and 1979, producers of socialist Chinese culture began the work necessary to accommodate these shifts in China's socioeconomic standing, which required a new cultural grammar capable of supporting the economic rationalizations for liberalization without challenging the political motives undergirding them. China's dalliance with postmodernism was a search for such a grammar—a concerted and official move beyond Maoist notions of modernization through class struggle in favor of some new, state-sanctioned economy of technical pragmatism and cultural consumption. Artists were encouraged to pursue more diverse methods and styles of artistic expression while remaining true to the "needs of the people," though some did pursue forms of realism that acknowledged the excesses of Mao-era governance.[8] Within the field of literature, writers began to challenge the correlation between modernization and modernism, though many eagerly experimented with visual expressions derived from so-called modern, Western forms of artistic expression such as minimalism or abstraction after years in which doing so was forbidden.[9]

For architects, too, the notion of an "undeveloped socialism," with its emphasis on the liminal, unfinished nature of socioeconomic progress, presented opportunities for creative retrospection after years in which such activity had been stifled. Undeveloped socialism suggested an openness not only to alternative systems of economic development, but to methods of governance such as democracy, which had been considered obsolete under previous, state-sanctioned methods of socialist Chinese periodization.[10] At its core, China's unfinished modernization presented architects with a fundamental question, namely, how could physical objects best convey in aesthetic and formal terms a social revolution still in process, potentially adaptable to multiple forms of economic production and governance, and not yet achieved?

As architects absorbed the party's reconfigured logic, they also confronted their eroded position in socialist Chinese society. The party's strident ideological emphasis on egalitarianism and the erasure of class distinctions between laborers and members of China's intellectual class had severely deteriorated both the quality and quantity of rigorous intellectual activity in China, including architecture. Even in the Cultural Revolution's immediate aftermath, mental labor was still considered inferior to physical labor. Restoring the perceived value of such production was difficult. "Both in the towns and the countryside egalitarianism became widespread and there was no difference in income, no matter how much work people did, how well they worked, or even whether they worked at all," explained pro-reform economist Xiang Qiyuan, associate research fellow at the Institute of Economics of the Chinese Academy of Social Sciences.[11] Early reform-era efforts to restore salary bonuses to workers in forms of material production, for example, were not matched by equivalent actions in the fields of education, science, art, and health, leading to aggravated income disparities between intellectuals and workers.[12]

On one hand, architecture's ability to index and delineate stages of socioeconomic progress through questions of scale, function, and materiality, among other methods, made it a potentially powerful instrument in steadying the party's tentative moves toward economic liberalization. Officials also recognized that restoring architecture's value—and the value of the architect—to Chinese society required new, more diverse methods and styles of architectural expression. As discussed in previous chapters, conserving the country's architectural past was one important step. New Sino-foreign partnerships also provided important opportunities for knowledge exchange that, in theory, benefited both the discipline and the state. Foreign-derived architectural theories offered yet another resource. Amid the shifting physical and metaphysical parameters of the country's so-called modern condition, designers set their sights on architectural ideas circulating through other parts of the world to better understand how they might begin redefining the architectural criteria by which socialist China was identified and understood.

POSTMODERNISM, ARCHITECTURE, AND CHINA

Existing histories of postmodernism's arrival in China and the "misunderstandings" that subsequently took place in relation to architecture tend to give an impression of postmodernism as a fixed and stable concept prior to transferal, but postmodernism was already a contested and imprecise term upon its arrival in post-Mao China. Over the course of the late 1970s and 1980s, figures such as the *New York Times* architectural critic Paul Goldberger, architectural theorist, historian, and designer Charles Jencks, and U.S. architect and designer Robert A. M. Stern, among others, worked to define and distinguish postmodernism in relation to stylistic alternatives such as late modernism, ultramodernism, antimodernism, even pop art, among others. Stern, writing in the second edition of his *New Directions in American Architecture* (1977), argued that the unique theoretical perspective of designers like Venturi and Moore necessitated a recategorization of their work from some late stage of modernism to "post-modern." The temporal dimensions of the term were also fluid; Jencks, whose writings were the most often associated with the term, initially dated the death of modernism—and postmodernism's subsequent rise—to the demolition of the Pruitt-Igoe housing complex in St. Louis in 1972, only to retroactively attribute its demise to the 1961 publication of Jane Jacobs's *Death and Life of Great American Cities.*[13]

Such abstruseness was consequently reflected in the first Chinese-language essay to employ the term, which began with an apparent mistranslation of "postmodernism," or *houxiandai zhuyi,* as "neomodernism," or *xinxiandai zhuyi.* The malapropism seemed to underscore the challenges posed by the rapid influx of unfamiliar, foreign architectural theories into a country unprepared to contextualize them but, in fact, reflected both grammatical obstacles specific to Chinese-language translations of the term and, more generally, a conceptual opacity endemic to the discursive origins of postmodernism itself. "Assessing the state of Western architecture is incredibly complex," admitted Yang Yun, the China Academy of Building Research (CABR) member who introduced postmodernism to Chinese designers through the pages of *Architectural Journal* (*Jianzhu Xuebao*). Yang did not consider the phenomenon to be directly relevant to China but nevertheless asked readers to consider two potential lessons.

First, Yang noted the emphasis placed by Western architectural discourse on formalism over what he considered to be the "substance" of function in socialist Chinese architectural production. Formalism, in Yang's assessment, constituted a luxury China's development could not afford, though he also acknowledged the value of architectural form in inspiring people and serving vital social and cultural functions. "The objective benefits of technology constitute the foundation of architectural production," the author reminded readers, even as he also acknowledged that technological determinism posed its own risks.[14] Second, Yang suggested the possibility for greater expressionism in Chinese design. In an effort to trace an emergent, formal architectural language in Chinese design, he highlighted several recent projects, including the Sirimavo Bandaranaike Memorial International Conference Hall in Colombo, Sri Lanka (1963–73), by the CABR under the supervision of Yang and Dai Nianci, and a CABR-designed athletic complex then under construction in Islamabad, Pakistan. These projects were juxtaposed with a range of foreign architectural examples ranging from the Parthenon to the work of Team X to postwar Japanese design, which he applauded for its shrewd domestication of foreign technology into internationally recognized form through projects such as Kenzō Tange's Yoyogi National Gymnasium (1964) or Sachio Otani's International Conference Center in Kyoto (1964).

Yang's call for a new, technological semiotics and an expanded aesthetic field was an important step in the delineation of new discursive parameters within which a post-Mao architectural culture could materialize. His essay sought to map and redefine postmodernism on China's own terms, and in ways that aimed to benefit its own architects—and, by extension, the party. The jumble of Yang's examples, each pulled from different temporal and geopolitical contexts and intertwined with recent Chinese design, attempted to craft a narrative out of the once-forbidden world of foreign discourse that might, in turn, inspire new ways of working through China's own nascent architectural condition. In positioning Japan as a potential template for China's own architectural advancement, for example, Yang acknowledged that China's architectural condition derived from a different kind of political system and ideological orientation. Rather than demonizing foreign architecture, however, Yang urged designers not to simply dismiss foreign architecture as "strange objects" or "poisonous weeds"—an allusion to pre-1978 efforts by the now-discredited Gang of Four to demonize foreign influence. "Don't we ultimately deepen our own knowledge by learning from the lessons of the West?" he reasoned.[15]

Though Yang's efforts may have failed to convey the nuances of context, irony, or ambiguity typically associated with postmodernism, his work nevertheless represents an early effort to close the conceptual gap that had long separated China from other, more capitalistically inclined parts of the world. In doing so, it sought to situate China within a new global architectural narrative—a daunting theoretical proposition following years of isolation from the capitalist world, yet one made conceptually possible, in part, through the dissonant nature of postmodernism itself. These new relativities, coming years after state-supported absolutism forbidding contact with nonsocialist swaths of the world, seemed to signal an exciting new era of simultaneity and proximity for China's architectural elite.

Postmodernism's initial appeal to established scholars like Yang stemmed in part from the lessons it seemed to offer regarding liberation from a specific modernism in search of some new "vitality," or *jingshen,* through history. Despite the vagaries involved, it was in part through discussions over postmodern discourse that several new intellectual positions within socialist Chinese architectural discourse began to take shape. These perspectives represented viewpoints that were both specific to China's condition yet also influenced by correlative overlap between China's emergent internationalism and economic and cultural uncertainty in other parts of the world. Organized into several distinctive categories, these positions include support for an unadorned, architecturally modern style to mark China's uninterrupted industrial progress; calls to reinvigorate China's imperial-era heritage through a contemporary reengagement with traditional architectural forms and aesthetics; and support for a more flexible, adapted postmodernism capable of overcoming both the perceived homogeneity of "International Style" modern architecture and the undue constraints of China's architectural past.[16] Collectively, these positions illuminate the delicate search for methods and discourses capable of redressing the country's incomplete socialist condition without unnecessarily criticizing the incompleteness itself.

EXPANDING REFORM, EXPANDING DISCOURSE, 1981–82

Even as postmodernism appeared to open new intellectual horizons for China's architectural community, its nebulous array of cultural meanings and discourse formations across multiple disciplines of academic study also produced confusion in China almost immediately. In early 1981, Zhang Qin, member of the design subcommittee of the State Ministry of Construction's Central Committee, published the first detailed acknowledgment of postmodernism's various and convoluted translations into Chinese in the editorial pages of *World Architecture* (*Shijie Jianzhu*) in an effort to "avoid unnecessary misreadings" of the term.[17] The announcement was published as the complexities of controlling these emerging discursive positions were already reverberating through architectural thinking and production.

That same year, for example, the Japanese architect Yoshinobu Ashihara was shocked to learn of Chinese audience members' interest in postmodernism during his public lecture at Tianjin University's Architecture Department.[18] Charles Jencks, too, expressed surprise at the speed with which he was presented with unauthorized translations of his own book, *The Language of Post-Modern Architecture,* during several early reform-era visits to China. By 1982 China was flooded with numerous foreign practitioners, theorists, and historians from Japan, Europe, the Middle East, and North America. Many visitors noted the accelerated nature of change in China, though few fully comprehended the depth of the country's intellectual thirst for foreign architectural knowledge, or the outsized effects of such knowledge on China's nascent reform-era architectural discourse.[19]

In fact, coincidental overlaps with other economic and political realities were prompting new ways of conceptualizing China's own architectural history and development, regardless of the party's efforts to dictate the appropriate terms of such thinking. Renewed emphasis on China's architectural identity through historical aesthetics, the rise of a kind of technological expressionism, and calls for increased contextual sensitivity—each of these themes resonated in reform-era China, though with different ideological intentions and results. New construction projects such as I. M. Pei's Fragrant Hill Hotel, with its self-referential curation of China's imperial-era building traditions in the name of recreational luxury, contributed to the disorienting intellectual atmosphere by suggesting a complete closure of the gap between architectural trends in China and other parts of the world. In 1984, for example, John Bryant, head of the School of Architecture at Oklahoma State, noted the "impact" Pei's hotel was having on Chinese schools of architecture in a letter he wrote to the architect informing him "that hotel by itself is causing quite a lot of debate about what is proper for the future of Chinese architecture."[20] These initial, largely accidental synchronicities were not specific to postmodernism, but they took place in relation to the increasingly international circulation of postmodern ideas and suggested the possibility for some new theoretical configurations to take shape within China beyond those dictated by Mao-era rhetoric, and in parallel with what was happening abroad.

As Chinese designers struggled to absorb the dizzying array of theoretical influences and domesticate them in relation to the specificities of China, a new and discipline-specific politics of language formed within the pages of journals such as *Architectural Journal, The Architect* (*Jianzhushi*), *New Architecture* (*Xin Jianzhu*), *World Architecture,* and *Southern Architecture* (*Nanfang Jianzhu*), among others, that both rehearsed yet was distinctive from previous theoretical debates in China, in large part due to the new subjectivities and international influences increasingly at work in China's architectural production. Numerous articles from the era introduced notions such as semiotics, context, and precedent to readers eager to understand and debate their meaning and relevance to China. Similarly, architecture's relationship to other forms of cultural production such as music, literature, and film was expanded in ways that challenged prior, Cultural Revolution–era restrictions. One example questioned whether the role of artifice in architecture could be considered akin to that of a stage production such as *Liu Hulan,* an iconic socialist opera about the life of a female spy during the Chinese Civil War, insofar as the stage set contributed to the production's revolutionary message. Another author wondered whether technological innovation, considered a genuine and substantive component of China's economic reinvention, could be considered economically productive and "true" in relation to acts of physical labor and architectural making. Another translated essay from abroad suggested that architects seek out opportunities for humor in their designs.[21]

Debate spilled out into the public sphere, and as officials and architects wrestled with how to best close the country's industrial and technological gap relative to both its past and other parts of the world, new social formations were already taking shape around architecture's role in a rapidly changing society. In 1982, for example, the Fifth National People's Congress passed a new constitution declaring that citizens had the right to "personal dignity," with clauses inserted to exclude cases involving state security, criminal investigation, or the freedoms and rights of other citizens. The ruling contributed to a period of relative tolerance toward the country's intellectual public sphere that emboldened general citizens to test the boundaries of state censorship, angering party conservatives and contributing to an increasingly charged set of cultural dynamics between the party and its people.[22]

These dynamics resonated through the discipline of architecture. In January 1983, for example, a public event devoted to the relationship between architecture, governance, and technology convened at the Great Hall of the People underscored the challenges of concealing the country's recent past through the production of a new architectural present. Co-organized by the ASC and the China Association for Science and Technology, the symposium was designed to clarify the role of the architect in post-Mao China, particularly the designer's responsibility in the harnessing of technological innovation to the broader interests of the state. Chen Zhanxiang, also known as Charles Chen, a University of Liverpool graduate, former assistant to Sir Patrick Abercrombie, and member of China's Urban Planning Bureau, argued for greater autonomy to produce quality work and avoid the homogeneity rampant in socialist Chinese architectural production. Discussion also included broader questions concerning the ideological role of architectural production in a reforming China. Xiao Tong, vice minister of the Ministry of Urban and

Rural Construction and Environmental Protection, asked, "What do we call the new socialist style? . . . What, exactly, we call a socialist style affects what we call a capitalist style, meaning that these can easily be confused." Dai Nianci, one of China's most prolific architects, and a member of an early exchange trip abroad under Mao, rephrased the same, fundamental query: "When we say a 'city modernized through socialism with Chinese characteristics,' what kinds of conditions does this exactly describe?"[23]

The event was followed that same month by visits by both Milton Friedman and Alvin Toffler to China. Friedman, perhaps the world's best-known proponent of free market economic principles, was invited to speak at the Chinese Academy of Social Sciences in September 1983. Sponsored by China's Future Society, Toffler's visit was intended to introduce Chinese readers to his books *Future Shock* and *The Third Wave,* in which he famously theorized the impact of a new, information-based industrial revolution and the unsettling cultural effects of rapid, global technological change. Reform-minded party elite, particularly Zhao Ziyang, were captivated by the possibility that China could skip specific stages of development through an engagement with more liberal, technologically driven economic policies—that, for example, and in accordance with Toffler's theory, a country could possess elements of preindustrial and postindustrial development at the same time. Toffler's visit prompted strenuous objection by conservatives to any talk of a postindustrial society, however, which they felt challenged core party orthodoxy regarding the belief that China's proletarian socialist revolution represented the final act of its own political and economic history.[24]

The temporal and etymological elasticity on display in these arguments was unprecedented in China—engagements justified by the urgency of reform, but also in part enabled by postmodernism's hermeneutic variability: what the architectural historian Reinhold Martin has identified as postmodernism's "untimeliness" and "asynchronicity."[25] The conceptual spectrum for a new, reform-inspired architectural discourse had been pushed in new and unpredictable directions, leading not merely to public acknowledgments of China's undeveloped socialism in material terms, but various theoretical proposals to address it. These shifts prompted changes in the meaning of postmodernism as well.

POSTMODERNISM, THE ANTI-SPIRITUAL POLLUTION CAMPAIGN, AND ITS AFTERMATH, 1983–85

Following China's initial infatuation with postmodernism, and as the political implications of reform began to vacillate in response to increasing intraparty conflict, the tone and tenor of architectural discourse shifted accordingly. In October 1983, party leftists launched a campaign against "spiritual pollution," or so-called Western-influenced principles believed to have infiltrated the communist Chinese psyche. Party hard-liners, appalled by Deng's calls for faster economic reform amid the perceived infestation of "Western" ideas around the country, attempted to ban certain books, films, music, pornography, dancing, and even lipstick and filter-tipped cigarettes from the country. Curtailed and eventually discontinued by January 1984, the reactive burst of authoritarianism exposed a disquieting degree of cognitive dissonance among party leaders over the speed, extent, and consequences of China's capitalization and commodification.[26] Publicly, officials continued to work to obscure the strict, structural distinctions between a capitalist economy and a commodity economy and the ideological questions such penetrations prompted. Privately, however, advocates of reform understood that if liberalization was to succeed, the personal interests of designers and other well-positioned figures in society needed validation and support. As Deng Xiaoping assured top CCP leaders, there was no need to fear "a little capitalist stuff."[27]

The campaign did not specifically target postmodernism, but it did focus attention on the broader social impact of the country's architectural discourse and production. At the Second Plenum of the Twelfth Party Congress, held October 11–12, 1983, it was made clear that Beijing was growing increasingly agitated by "gloomy and pessimistic" forms of cultural production that did not venerate the CCP's revolutionary history. At a ceremony commemorating the thirtieth anniversary of the ASC in Nanjing on November 19–22, 1983, both Vice Chairmen Chen Zhi and Wang Huapin encouraged attendees to root out any "spiritual pollution" and improve the ideological qualities of their architectural work. Attendees acknowledged that regrettable influences had begun to infiltrate the industry, and they cited reports of architects seeking unnecessary financial profit from projects as evidence of the negative impacts of "liberalization" with respect to standard disciplinary policy concerning service to the state. Architects were urged to raise and broaden the "political caliber" of their thinking as a result.[28]

A series of events was subsequently organized to recalibrate the discipline's line of thinking with respect to reform. In March 1984, Zeng Zhaofen, editor of *World Architecture* and professor of architecture at Tsinghua University, sponsored a public forum organized around contemporary theory and modern Chinese architecture. The event, which was also supported by members of a younger generation of designers trained just prior to the Cultural Revolution, including Wang Tianxi, who had worked for I. M. Pei on the Fragrant Hill Hotel and was subsequently allowed to establish one of China's first experimental architectural practices, which is discussed in Chapter 8, in late 1984. Following the forum, a series of principles was drafted concerning the proper theorization of contemporary Chinese design. The document attempted to reframe questions regarding a suitable architecture for post-Mao China around the collective search for a balance between functionalism and formalism—in other words, a socialist Chinese neomodernism. If functionalism was driven by the necessary "logic," or *li,* of socialist Chinese society, form provided a degree of *jing,* or cultural essence, that could prove both flexible and attractive, assuming the two forces could find conceptual stasis relative to each other.

That April, a contemporary architectural initiative known as the Research Group for the Creation of Modern Chinese Architecture was launched in Kunming by several of the forum's organizers, including Wang and Zeng, and others to develop a more rigorous architectural discourse in China. Working in conjunction with the larger and more established ASC, the group offered a smaller, more intensive setting for discussion on a range of issues, including how to best foster a contemporary architectural spirit in China, the role of tradition in contemporary architectural production, the effects of overseas Chinese cultural production on mainland China, and the applicability of postmodern theory to a modernizing China.[29] Collectively, these debates circled around the same basic question: How could Chinese architects conceivably revive the utopian aims of socialist China in post-Mao China?

Such debates occurred amid the rapid materialization of hundreds of new hotels, museums, cultural centers, government offices, and schools launched prior to, or during, the Anti-Spiritual Pollution campaign, thereby complicating the party's efforts to clarify its architectural messaging. In the Xinjiang Autonomous Region's Standing Congress Headquarters, for example, designed and constructed in Urumqi between 1983 and 1985 by Sun Guocheng, Gao Qinglin, and Yang Jun of the Xinjiang Institute of Architectural Design and Research, vernacular traditions were deployed to reintegrate parts of the country devastated by the Cultural Revolution and renew the state's political commitment to the region (fig. 60).

The building consisted of a rectilinear arrangement of offices as well as a polygonal, three-hundred-seat meeting hall for legislative sessions.

Fig. 60 Standing Congress Headquarters, Sun Guocheng, Gao Qinglin, and Yang Jun, Xinjiang Institute of Architectural Design and Research, Urumqi, Xinjiang Autonomous Region, 1985. Originally published in *Chinese Architecture since 1980: Selected Works of Well-Known Contemporary Architects (Bashi niandai yilai Zhongguo jianzhu: Zhongguo dangdai zhuming Jianzhushi zuopin xuan,* 1998).

Fig. 61 Shaanxi History Museum, Zhang Jinqiu, Northwest Institute of Architectural Design and Research, Xi'an, 1985–91. Originally published in *Chinese Architecture since 1980: Selected Works of Well-Known Contemporary Architects* (*Bashi niandai yilai Zhongguo jianzhu: Zhongguo dangdai zhuming Jianzhushi zuopin xuan*, 1998).

Pointed arches, abstracted crenellation, minaret-like towers, and a crowning dome sought to localize what was otherwise a solid mass, ninety-five meters wide by fifty meters tall, positioned along the main axis of the city's People's Square.[30] In an article titled "Entrusting Tradition to the Flavor of the Times," the project's architects, Sun and Gao, situated the project within a series of regional as well as international contexts. They acknowledged the project's position within a Muslim-populated area of China and the obvious Islamic-inspired motifs dotting its edifice. At the same time, they tied the dome's symbolism as a marker of authority to several international monuments, including the U.S. Capitol Building and Brazil's National Congress Building.[31]

The Shaanxi History Museum, completed in Xi'an between 1985 and 1991 by Zhang Jinqiu of the Northwest Institute of Architectural Design and Research, was hailed as evidence of the country's recommitment to its own past following the destructive anti-historicist dogma of the Mao era, and the violence such doctrine had incited upon the country's architectural heritage and, more generally, its people (fig. 61). Xi'an lies on the site of the Tang Dynasty capital of Chang'an, a prominent place in imperial Chinese history. The 45,800-square-meter project comprised a massive central gallery along with several smaller pavilion-like spaces designed for administrative and service use, each topped by a Tang-era inspired roof. A secondary series of smaller galleries wrapped around courtyards links the complex together. Its low-lying forms and understated monochromatic aesthetic sought to project a certain imperialistic gravitas worthy of a cultural edifice devoted to imperial Chinese culture and history. Yet Zhang Jinqiu was also sensitive to the era's technophilia, and in published accounts of the project, she emphasized the building's historical sensitivity as well as its structural and material sophistication.[32] Hailed by critics at the time, the building earnestly recycled imperial-era spatial organizational systems in the name of archaeological accuracy and political correctness.

At the heart of efforts to both discern quality and ascribe meaning to such work was a discipline—and by extension, a party—caught between its own ideological fatigue and the search for some new identity. As Zhang Ping reminded *Architectural Journal* readers, "The 'putting on the shoes, wearing the hat' style of pseudo-classical architecture currently in favor in China is not postmodern architecture, but rather a compromise between old and new." Zhang's critique concerned the cloaking of otherwise mediocre architecture in imperial-era aesthetics to underscore its contributions to the party's emergent ethno-nationalism. In particular, "wearing the hat" concerned the phenomenon of crowning otherwise contemporary buildings with traditional Chinese-style roofs to localize them in China's architectural traditions. Much of this work was of a poor architectural quality, but it contributed to the party's efforts to substitute Maoist notions of modernization through class struggle with some new, state-sanctioned identity politics buttressed by a reconfigured economy of culture.[33]

The variety of aesthetic, discursive, and programmatic influences circulating through the country evinced the results of a loose and expanded Chinese architectural field that made consistent messaging difficult, however. Controversy surrounding a 1984 competition for a new shopping complex in Beijing's Xidan commercial district laid bare the fruitless search for a post-Mao architectural language, and the struggles of China's architectural establishment to come to terms with the fact that the restructuring taking place within Chinese society—a process with which they were actively involved—was not a continuation or recapitulation of Mao's original vision, but something new and less familiar.

The project brief called for an eleven-story, mall-like structure, with three additional floors of subterranean space, designed to accommodate retail space for the purchasing of traditional food products, a cafeteria, a four-hundred-person movie theater, a bookstore, study rooms, and landscaping. Among the various submissions was a joint proposal by a group of young Tsinghua architecture professors, Guan Zhaoye, Fu Kecheng, Liu Xiaodu, Han Baoshan, and Wang Yu, featuring a unique integration of Chinese, foreign, and Tibetan architectural motifs into a single, massive urban block (figs. 62, 63). The proposed building's first six stories were wrapped around three sides of a sky-lit atrium, which was itself topped by an open-air void, or courtyard, ringed by a pavilion-like structure inspired by China's architectural past. The building's ground floor featured a relatively loose, heterogenous arrangement of commercial, food, and pedestrian areas designed to mimic traditional Chinese shopping streets, while the second to sixth floors were organized into an array of retail, storage, and circulation space to accommodate the purchasing of larger-scale, wholesale foodstuffs and foreign goods. Each floor featured a series of increasingly narrow double-load corridors, creating winding interior spaces reminiscent of open-air Chinese food markets.

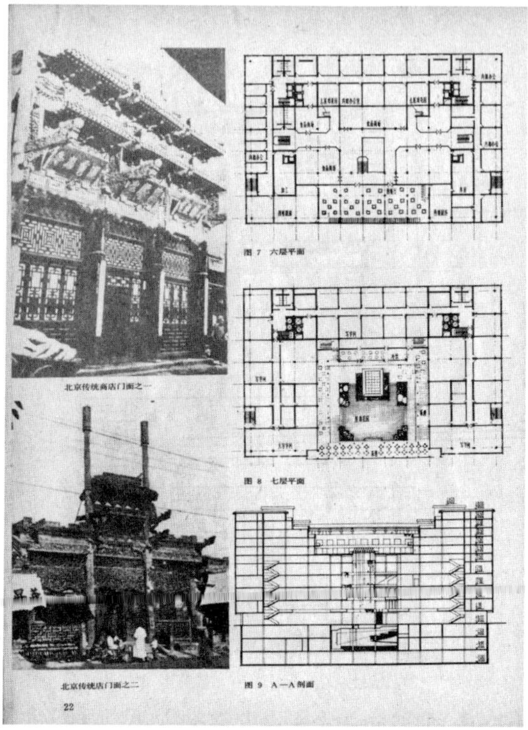

Fig. 62 Composite Commercial Tower (proposed), Guan Zhaoye, Fu Kecheng, Liu Xiaodu, Han Baoshan, and Wang Yu, Xidan, Beijing, 1985. Originally published in *Architectural Journal* (*Jianzhu Xuebao*), no. 7 (1985).

Fig. 63 Floor plans, section, and precedent references, Composite Commercial Tower (proposed), Guan Zhaoye, Fu Kecheng, Liu Xiaodu, Han Baoshan, and Wang Yu, Xidan, Beijing, 1985. Originally published in *Architectural Journal* (*Jianzhu Xuebao*), no. 7 (1985).

In an essay titled "The Path of Design Should Be Broad—A Discussion of the Winning Design for the Xidan Commercial Building Complex, Beijing," Fu justified the building's wide-ranging mixture of historical influences, from imperial-era Chinese philosophy to the country's vernacular traditions, combined with the project's compressed stacking structure, as an effort to produce a specific, disorienting effect born of heterogenous, historicized abstraction. "The roof garden on the eleventh floor offers an odd, unsuitable counterpoint to the roof of the sixth-floor skylight, producing a pulse of historical precedents worthy of deeper consideration. Through our engagement with these references, we've produced a single edifice composed of different uses that gestures toward the concavity often present in a traditional Chinese building's contour," he explained. The team's bold, collage-like approach was rewarded with first prize, though in the end, a more standard, corporate building model produced by the state-run design behemoth BIAD was selected.

Despite its failure, however, the proposal submitted by Guan and his team made an immediate impact upon Chinese architectural design and discourse. Its unabashed embrace of Western-inspired architectural theory, particularly the work of celebrated U.S. designers such as Robert Venturi, struck a nerve. "It is certainly the most influential unbuilt building in China," noted an anonymous Tsinghua colleague in 1988.[34] Critics found the proposed building lacking substance in relation to the modernizing aims of reform, however. For example, Tsinghua University professor and *World Architecture* editor Zeng Zhaofen acknowledged that there was no theoretical reason why a market or office tower couldn't take formal inspiration from a Lamaist temple. Nevertheless, Zeng feared an overabundance of pastiche could ultimately subvert the era's progressive objectives. "In ten or twenty years, if we architects are still relying on vaulted domes and pointed arches to distinguish our work, no one will consider us a progressive or creative generation of designers," he warned.[35]

Postmodernism was emblematic of that realization—an idea that seemed to offer a theoretical way forward through its engagement with the past, but one that simply reproduced images of the past for its own ends. Despite initial optimism regarding its potential contributions to China's economic progress, postmodern discourse and architectural production seemed increasingly incapable of sustaining the Mao-era utopianism still lingering among the country's architectural establishment and, more importantly, its government. Instead, postmodernism risked exposing an emptiness of meaning at the heart of post-Mao Chinese architectural production that could quickly reverberate more generally through the country's political sphere, and to the public at large. Anxiety over this conceptual cul-de-sac was perhaps most acutely perceived in Beijing, where proximity to the party's center rendered architectural discourse and production particularly fraught with ideological implications, and there existed an architectural elite divided over how to best express the post-Mao, socialist Chinese condition in aesthetic and formal terms.

A POSTMODERN ARCHITECTURE AND ITS PUBLIC, 1985–88

Beginning in 1985, a general thaw in the conservatives' ideological rectification efforts fueled a sixteen-month burst of active public debate over humanism, the limits of socialism, and the relevance of Marxist economy theory to contemporary China.[36] Postmodernism remained an active and popular topic of debate across multiple disciplines and forms of Chinese cultural production, and a testament to the perplexing interplay taking place in relation to the active importation of foreign ideas and their impact on Chinese cultural discourse. That fall, for example, Fredric Jameson spent a semester at Beijing University, where his own theorizations of postmodernism captivated a generation of students of comparative literature, who began to theorize postmodernism as representing a new kind of leap forward capable of channeling new forms of capital into the existing state apparatus. The Chinese translation of Jameson's book is notable for the removal of the term "late capitalism," making the title read as *Postmodernism and the Logic of Culture,* effectively allowing China's intelligentsia to interpret and promote mass culture as a new realm for individual liberty.[37]

Importantly, neither Jameson nor his students ever incorporated

China's ongoing architectural experimentations into their theorizations, even though Jameson's initial text placed specific emphasis on architecture as the crucial vessel through which the postmodern condition materialized. Instead, Jameson famously allegorized China in this work as "an unfinished social experiment" exhibiting "the freshness of a whole new object world produced by human beings in some new control over their collective destiny." Architecturally, it remained unclear who was in control of China's new object world, which had begun to borrow indiscriminately from the past in an effort to validate its uncertain future, regardless of any representational consequences. Although Jameson's work was enormously influential within the field of comparative literature, it had a limited impact on Chinese architectural discourse. In fact, Jameson had little to no contact with architects during his time in Beijing, though he did visit Shenzhen and had some idea of the transformative economic changes taking place there, even as physical changes and new architectural approaches had begun to manifest throughout the country.[38]

Officials recognized the risks involved in such experimentation and the potential empowerment of individual expression, particularly amid intensifying public interest in the topic of socialism's future. In January 1987, for example, General Secretary Hu Yaobang, a vocal proponent of reform and one of Deng's most trusted allies, was forced to submit his resignation following two weeks of student protests calling for greater individual freedoms. Hu's dismissal was followed by plans to mount a public campaign against bourgeois liberalization—an effort designed to limit expression, shore up CCP leadership, and purge disobedient intellectuals. Calls for unity rippled through architectural discourse. "Advocates of postmodernism may pursue their own intellectual agendas," reasoned Xu Shangzhi, a Chongqing University architecture professor and active member of the Sichuan Province's leadership, in 1984. Xu questioned the motives of those Chinese architects willing to embrace foreign ideas considered selfish and counterproductive to the broader interests of the state, however. "Protecting national culture and the identity of place is a goal that everyone can embrace."[39] Tsinghua architecture professor Zhou Buyi, who in previous writings had cited Deng Xiaoping's 1979 trip to Japan as evidence that China was at least fifty years behind other major industrial powers, argued in 1987 that blind embraces of any and all architectural lessons from abroad posed substantial ideological questions in need of further assessment. "Contemporary American architecture is lively, it broadens one's horizons, and offers insight," wrote Zhou. "But its origins and our country's socialist system are completely different, and we cannot gobble down such information without digesting it, or simply absorb wholesale Westernization."[40]

By the end of 1987, however, the government had recommitted to economic liberalization. At the party's Thirteenth Congress held that

October, for example, the Four Modernizations campaign was officially replaced by Reform and Opening Up. Efforts were also launched to identify new landmarks for a post-Mao China capable of projecting the state's enduring power in the face of change, and around which the public could rally. In late 1987, *Beijing Daily* (*Beijing Ribao*) Deputy Editor Liu Tingzhao announced the newspaper's plans to organize a public architectural competition to identify the ten new public buildings built in the nation's capital during the 1980s that best represented the unwavering national spirit at the core of reform. "We need monuments to openness and reform," explained Liu. Readers would be invited to submit ballots published in a special edition of the newspaper, which would be tallied and announced at a public ceremony.[41]

On April 3, 1988, the paper printed one million ballots and asked readers to choose from thirty projects built in Beijing during the reform era, including the Great Wall Sheraton Hotel, the Fragrant Hill Hotel, the Xiyuan Hotel, the Bank of China Tower, the Beijing International Exhibition Center, the National Library, the China International Trust and Investment Corporation Tower, and the Grand View Garden (figs. 64, 65). Within a month, approximately 224,500 ballots were returned to the paper—evidence of a "democratic selection process," stated Liu, though one subject to the ultimate judgment of a panel of experts "in case the masses make an inappropriate choice." At an awards ceremony featuring party leaders Hu Qili, Gu Mu, and Li Ximing and Beijing Mayor Chen Xitong held on April 28, the "ten most outstanding buildings of the 1980s" were unveiled, with the city's National Library declared the winner.[42]

Fig. 64 "A Public Appraisal of 'Beijing's Ten Great Buildings of the 1980s,'" *Beijing Daily* (*Beijing Ribao*), April 3, 1988.

Fig. 65 "A Public Appraisal of 'Beijing's Ten Great Buildings of the 1980s,'" *Beijing Daily* (*Beijing Ribao*), April 3, 1988.

请评选您喜爱的"北京八十年代十大建筑"
启事
北京一三六中学电子技术职业高中应聘启事
三环石棉瓦 用户皆称佳
宝花牌
天鹅牌
麦森太平洋牌
青云牌
上海日化工业供销公司 上海市美加净日化联销公司 北京市一商局批发市场 联合举办

北京市太平桥冷冻机修造厂举办制冷设备展销会
欢迎选购北京建材交易市场建材产品
关于汽车维修经营有关事项的联合通知
山东省威海市赴京举行首届商品展销大会

Fig. 66 Beijing National Library, Ministry of Construction Architectural Design Institute and the Northeast Institute of Architectural Design and Research, Beijing, 1987. Originally published in *Selected Architectural Drawings* (*Jianzhu hua xuan*, 1979).

The competition was the first public event in China to engage in a quasi-democratic process through architecture. Over 220,000 valid ballots were submitted; 173,046 preferred the library over the city's International Exhibition Center (149,000 votes), the Central TV Broadcasting Station (148,817), and the Capital Airport (140,219), among others. The process reflected intensifying interest on the part of Chinese citizens in such activities and acknowledged the subjectivities of taste and style that had begun to swirl not only through the country's architectural community but through the public at large. Senior party leaders had approved the novel, unprecedented engagement with public opinion in part because they saw resonances with Mao's earlier Ten Great Buildings campaign of 1959, though Liu himself framed the competition as a departure from the past. "Beijing's Ten Great Buildings were monuments to a previous era that no longer resonated with the population at large," reasoned Liu.[43] By contrast, the results of the *Beijing Daily*'s poll would reveal the legitimate architectural icons of reform identified by the people as worthy of greater public attention.

Designed by the Ministry of Construction's Architectural Design Institute in coordination with the Northeast Institute of Architectural Design and Research, the National Library represented a twelve-year effort to design and build an appropriately monumental edifice to protect and honor the country's largest collection of printed material (fig. 66). The project was first approved by Zhou Enlai in 1975 but was not ultimately completed until 1987. It involved a design process that included a number of Beijing's most established senior designers, including Dai Nianci, Wu Liangyong, Yang Tingbao, and Zhang Bo, chief architect of the Beijing Hotel's east addition, among other notable projects. Programmatically, the complex included a series of reading rooms, administrative offices, cataloguing facilities, and archives organized as a series of interconnected three- to five-story buildings clustered around two eighteen-story towers within which the bookstacks were located. The project also borrowed heavily from imperial-era Chinese precedent as evinced by its south-facing entrance, courtyard-like spatial arrangement, notable symmetry, and imperial-era ornament, which included a system of abstracted, green-tiled roofs. Collectively, these elements demonstrated the design teams' major intent to revive systems of traditional spatial orientation and aesthetics for a postrevolutionary China.[44] At the same time, however, the bureaucratic inertia evinced by the slowness of its materialization, coupled with its budgetary bloat—completed for 200 million RMB, the project was the most expensive structure to be built in the nation's capital since 1978—gestured toward a ballooning crisis of meaning.

It remains unknown how influential the poll's expert panel may have been in determining its final results. Nevertheless, and despite apparent and widespread public and official appeal, the library was not necessarily as universally loved within the city as its accolade suggested. In a critical assessment of China's architectural field published by the *South China Morning Post* in December 1988, for example, several interviewees dismissed the building and the process behind its recognition. One anonymous member of Tsinghua University's Department of Architecture admitted that the building was "so bad that none of the dozens of architects who took part in the project will take any credit for it." Guan Zhaoye, one of the designers behind the failed Xidan commercial building proposal, lamented that the library was "afflicted with an architectural sickness.... We have been trying to combine national character and modernism since well before 1949. But we have yet to succeed."[45] Whether postmodernism offered a direction forward remained unclear, but the discourse and the architecture it helped to inspire had triggered something party leaders had not necessarily anticipated—namely, dissent.

Despite the obvious ironies at work in the government's efforts to celebrate vernacular traditions following years in which China's history was savaged by politics, the public's preference for the overt and selective engagement with precedent on display in work like the National Library underscored the political importance of postmodernism to China, even if the library was not in itself a deliberate exercise in postmodern design. Historical revivalism dominated much of China's architectural production during the 1980s in large part because it both captured the wide range of sources, experiences, and atmospheres at work in the era and suggested China could somehow regain its sense of cultural specificity through these new conditions. In this respect, the history of postmodernism's embrace and pursuit by many within the country's architectural establishment shares more similarities to the theory's origins in other parts of the world than one might presume. Anchored in realizations of an unfulfilled modernization, and compelled by art's shifting relationship to society, architecture's reinterpretation of its own history seemed to open up new, exciting possibilities in relation to meaning, even as it also compressed and distorted time to its own shallow and ultimately self-defeating ends.[46] Postmodernism helped give form to China's yearning romanticism toward the past, but it could not ultimately rejuvenate what had come before.

THE END OF POSTMODERNISM

Postmodernism was not something foisted upon China, but an idea imported by its architectural leaders, and one that took on alternative and distinctive meanings in relationship to the early reform-era Chinese context. Its ironic and, at times, lavish ornamentalism was designed as a riposte to the utopianism of modern architecture, not a continuation, particularly following years in which the semiotic value of the country's architectural production derived from on-site, proletarian building techniques. Postmodernism initially seemed to offer the government an aesthetic and formal complement to its liberalizing agenda by allowing China's architects to frame liberalization as part of some broader, international architectural zeitgeist, even as it masked the ideological contortions upon which it was premised—a search for legitimacy through simultaneity that ultimately went unfulfilled. The prevalence of precedent in many of the era's political edifices derived not from some ironic engagement with the past, but from a calculated grasp at context and identity in relation to governance.

This is not to say more critical engagements with postmodern theory did not occur in China. Indeed, one of the legacies of postmodernism as it emerged in China over the course of the 1980s was its influence upon a young and talented generation of designers who came of age amid the public debates and experimentation taking place. Pritzker Prize–winning architect Wang Shu is one famous case in point; by the late 1980s, the emergence of work such as his Youth Recreation Center (1989–91) indicated an awareness on the part of Chinese designers of figures such as Aldo Rossi and Peter Eisenman, two prominent and active architects whose work challenged standard notions of form and function in architectural design and discourse in Europe and the United States (fig. 67). Although the work of Rossi and Eisenman was not as widely known in China as the writing of Jencks, for example, they did inspire members of China's first post-Mao generation of architects to engage questions of autonomy, abstraction, and process in relation to architectural form and function—experiments that would figure as foundational projects in China's so-called experimental architecture period during the 1990s.[47] Such examples remained exceptions, however, particularly as postmodernism found itself increasingly attacked for its international origins—ironically, a major reason for its initial appeal.

Recognizing postmodernism's influence on early reform-era Chinese architectural discourse broadens our understanding of the theory's mutability, not simply in relation to noncapitalist, non-Western con-

texts, but the extent to which it could be understood as both a cultural and political phenomenon with a representational force that extended well beyond the late capitalist, postindustrial landscape. The term's history in China sheds light on the connections and impulses that fueled its importation there and, more generally, the expansion of its meaning and application throughout the socialist world. In China, postmodernism prompted a disciplinary reconsideration of the semiotic systems at work in the country's architecture, and Chinese society more generally. It helped to rationalize the country's efforts to reanimate an architectural past devastated by the Cultural Revolution and shrink the developmental and discursive gap existing between China's architectural community and other parts of the world. Yet its introduction and dissemination through China's architectural discourse also contributed to a cleaving among the discipline's intelligentsia concerning appropriate sources and interpretations of architectural meaning—a debate that remains unresolved today.

Fig. 67 Youth Recreation Center, Wang Shu, Zhejiang Academy of Arts, Haining, Zhejiang Province, 1989–91.

For conservative party stalwarts, architecture served the state. This required that the country's architectural establishment recommit itself to modernizing the country through principles of efficiency and functionalism—goals that postmodernism did not seem to fulfill. For those members of the architectural community more amenable to postmodern theory yet equally committed to party principles, its value relative to the state lay in its ability to expand the range of representational possibilities afforded to architectural objects. The spirit of such debate sprung in part from confusion over the party's own master narrative, and it channeled broader anxiety within the discipline over its role in reinforcing the separation of governance and economic enterprise promoted by the era's more reform-minded leaders. The country's architecture system, like its economic performance, increasingly seemed to lack an ideological center, resulting in a disjointed array of discourses, practices, and styles seemingly untethered to the central authority of the state. Rather than bending "reality to theory," as China's leaders had done in the past, the country had developed a new economic theory to fit its own unprecedented reality.[48]

Postmodernism may have illuminated the representational possibilities available to the country's designers in charting the party's changeable economic and political agenda over time, but its presence in China also posed challenges to the state's ability to control meaning. By the late 1980s, its existence was used to justify the need for more reliable forms of thought management in relation to architecture. Within the context of the reform era, we can thus consider postmodernism less of a condition or discursive position than a strategy deployed by architects, officials, and well-established state-run journals to reassess and encourage previously verboten methods of architectural appropriation, allusion, and exchange with capitalist countries, particularly the United States. Ultimately, it exposed a frailty of architectural thinking at the core of Chinese design by drawing attention to perceived systemic weaknesses and growing incoherence in the state's ability to discern and produce architectural quality.

At the core of these issues were questions not only of meaning, but of authority and authorship. "Architects are free to do everything—discuss ideas, make designs, travel abroad—except build buildings," argued a young, anonymous Chinese architect on his way to the United States for work at the time. "We have no power."[49] The state-run design institute, China's main mechanism for architectural production, was not equipped to handle the increased and largely unprocessed flows of ideas and information from within and outside China. New institutional instruments were required in order to deal more effectively, in architectural terms, with a changing China and its relationship to the world.

CHAPTER 8

Architectural Education and the Profession

In 1977 the government resumed its entrance examination system for university admissions for the first time in nearly ten years. After nearly one decade of class struggle, architectural education across the country had been reduced to a combination of Cultural Revolution–era on-site training exercises and the lingering influence of the Beaux-Arts, and changes were quickly introduced into design pedagogy to better equip young designers with the references, tools, and skills needed to reimagine the country's built environment.[1] New studio topics were formulated that introduced students to topics such as architectural heritage. New types of academic exchange enabled teachers and students to absorb architectural ideas circulating through other parts of the world. Many of the country's top-ranked architectural programs hired foreign teachers to teach English and contemporary architectural theories like postmodernism. New methods of designing, drawing, and defining architectural work, particularly in relation to questions of authorship and collaboration, also appeared.

By the mid-1980s, however, evidence of widespread national progress relative to the country's architectural education system, and architecture as a professional service more generally, was difficult to find. The exceptional forms of design and construction taking place in Shenzhen had upset China's "Iron Rice Bowl" system of guaranteed job security and stable, state-supported benefits, indicating that China's architectural industry and culture could change if given an opportunity to do so. In cities such as Beijing, Shanghai, Nanjing, and Guangzhou, individual projects including the Jianguo, Great Wall, and Jinling hotels, among others, had introduced new spatial logics, material practices, and design and construction methods to China. Imported architectural theories such as postmodernism had triggered active discussion within the country over the new types of visual languages demanded of architecture by reform. In general, however, economic reform had not yet triggered the desired changes in relationship to Chinese architectural practices. Reform-minded party leaders recognized the value of the architect to China's internationalization but struggled to empower designers to undertake the kinds of creative risks expected of them by economic liberalization.

In February 1984, for example, Michael L. Joroff, director of the MIT Laboratory of Architecture and Planning, wrote to his colleague, Professor Emeritus Kevin Lynch, in anticipation of Lynch's plans to spend several months in Beijing delivering a series of lectures at Tsinghua University. Joroff had recently returned from a trip to Beijing, and he offered Lynch several ideas regarding potential themes for his visiting lectures, including an overview of Lynch's scholarship and architectural and urban conservation and heritage, which remained popular throughout the country. A third and "most difficult" subject in Joroff's estimation was prompted by a dinner conversation between Joroff and Beijing's mayor, Chen Xitong. It concerned the role of the architect in reform-era China. Chen had referred to the city's designers as "timid—like birds who have been in the cage for too long." The metaphor troubled Joroff. "How does one begin to innovate, to change, to challenge established policies in a difficult political environment? How does one pose alternatives in a situation like that? A tough subject."[2]

One particularly challenging constraint was the main mechanism for design practice in the PRC itself—the design institute. New curricular models and foreign-derived practices aided in the development of new, internationally informed design methods and the production of young designers capable of appreciating global trends. The efficacy of such adjustments was limited by the professional opportunities available to graduates to apply this new knowledge to China's architectural production, however. As the dominant organizational paradigm for architectural production in socialist China, most if not all of the country's architectural graduates depended upon these massive state-run conglomerates for employment.

China's design institutes composed some of the largest public or private architectural management structures in the world, with staff numbering in the hundreds and even thousands, and they operated at a range of municipal, provincial, and national levels. Many were multispeciality in nature, with tasks assigned to work units within each institute based upon particular industrial categories and the specific type of design work required, from mechanical to electrical to structural design (fig. 68). Work itself was collaborative and nonhierarchical yet rooted in seniority and expertise—a balance subverted by the persecution of many established designers as elites during the Cultural Revolution who were then restored after 1978. Such steps helped to stabilize the discipline and reinstate political and social value to architectural proficiency, though over time, reform-inclined officials feared that the reversion to standard industry practices had begun to slow the profession's modernization by

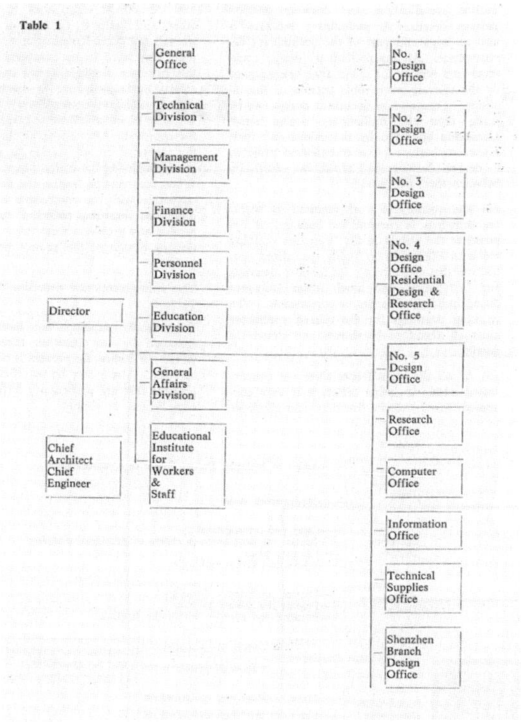

Fig. 68 Institutional structure, Beijing Institute of Architectural Design, undated. Originally published in *Building in China* 1, no. 2 (1988).

inhibiting new ways of architectural thinking and practices from taking hold.

This chapter studies a range of reform-era adjustments in architectural pedagogy and practice in post-Mao China, including shifts in design curriculum, the influence of international exchange in relationship to design education, and the introduction of several new management structures capable of capitalizing upon the reformation taking place. If architectural history and heritage, SEZs, architectural objects, and new forms of discourse each constituted distinctive media through which design contributed to China's reconfigured political economy, early reform-era modifications in architectural education and the profession signaled change of another sort—a reordering of training and management systems that upended the lives of tens of thousands of people dependent upon the state's architectural enterprises for employment.

The injection of new degrees of competition, expertise, and transactional exchange into the organizational structures responsible for architecture in China catalyzed changes that altered the act of design in the country. It necessitated institutional and psychological adjustments on the part of China's design-affiliated workforce that transformed how and why people studied, designed, and built architecture.[3] Understanding the era's legacy in these terms—as a series of diffusions of new design methods around the country, rather than simply the production of new objects, spaces, or theories—is important to appreciating reform as more than a result, but a process that reshaped organizational techniques and notions of architectural labor. These adjustments consequently changed what it meant to design in socialist China.

REAPPRAISING THE ARCHITECT

With the education of a generation of Chinese architects affected by the chaos of the Cultural Revolution, officials and administrators scrambled to steady architecture departments and schools following the official advent of reform. Officials prioritized enrollment at the country's eight most reputable architecture and civil engineering departments, with double cohorts of students admitted in 1978. These institutions reported directly to the Ministry of Education, and it was primarily within their curricula that the first pedagogical changes in relationship to reform were made. A look at the 1978 curriculum of Tsinghua University's Architecture and Civil Engineering Department, arguably the country's most prominent architectural program, reveals a course structure organized into several disciplinary subdivisions, including architecture, structural design, heating and ventilation, and water supply and industrial waste management. Core areas of study within architecture included architectural design, urban design and architectural history, design research, and architectural physics, or building science. Students were expected to complete four and a half years of full-time study (nine semesters), which included curricular requirements in studio, mathematics, history, structural design, material study, physics, and English or an equivalent foreign language.[4]

Core studio design training was complemented by surveys of Western classical, traditional Chinese, and modern Western and Chinese architectural history and representational methods courses including freehand sketching, ink line and pencil drawing, and watercolor painting—all vestiges of China's Beaux-Arts–influenced pedagogy. Cultural Revolution–era influences were also present, with students expected to complete a five-week field study on a building site (third semester), two weeks' training in the countryside developing watercolor painting techniques (fourth semester), five weeks learning one or two building trades (sixth semester), and eight weeks of office practice and travel to other cities in China (eighth semester). Studio assignments focused on the study of prevalent building types around the country, with design exercises generally organized around standardized sets of design practices devoted to "the people" and their governance.[5]

Students also completed a thesis studio in their final semester, which involved working with real sites and addressing real problems with faculty members. Housing was one particular concern; the 1978 Tsinghua University thesis studio, for example, began with a study of public policy and sets of standard "economic limitations" imposed upon housing by the government.[6] From there, students were asked to take into account standardized sets of family structures and data on existing demand for particular types and sizes of units—an important consideration at a time when China's family planning policy was undergoing official reassessment.[7] In addition to taking political policy into account, architecture students were also expected to be able to observe people's everyday living practices and desires and ultimately complete the project with a holistic assessment of all available information and construction, material, and structural technologies. Through this process students learned "step by step the whole process of design work" and the role of a qualified architect in China.[8]

Shifts in the nature of design pedagogy reflected awareness on the part of school administrators and officials that the architect's role in China was changing. Their opinions concerning the state of the field were captured in a 1978 survey of ASC members and faculty from several of China's preeminent architecture programs conducted by the Australian architect Gavin Walkley, chairman of the Architectural Panel for Australia's Committee on Overseas Professional Qualifications and past president of the Architects' Accreditation Council of Australia. His survey—the first international professional appraisal of the discipline in China since 1949—captured a profession in flux as its members attempted to recover from the abuses of the Cultural Revolution and began to reorganize themselves around the nascent ideological tenets of the early reform era. In his report, Walkley noted that the country lacked professional registration or a post-practical experience examination, and that following graduation, all architects were assigned to design institutes, which ranged in terms of size, expertise, and supervising ministry.[9]

Walkley also catalogued the various tasks required by architects at the time, including feasibility studies, the determination of certain project requirements, schematic design, design development, contract documentation, contract administration, on-site construction inspections, and contract fulfillment, and the arbitrary, often subjective hierarchies that emerged through subdivisions of the design process into subcategories and specific tasks. Use of the title "architect," for example, was technically restricted to those designers who were deemed competent by senior members of their work units, meaning there was no standard mechanism for determining or regulating practical experience or overall architectural competence. He also observed vestiges of Cultural Revolution–era thinking still inscribed in the profession; several interview subjects, for example, requested that he clarify in his report that a Chinese architect's responsibility be described not as "overseeing the construction and finishing of buildings," but as "collaborating with workers."[10] Such semantics endured as factors to consider in the enhancement of China's architectural education's potential moving forward.

Members of the ASC and the country's architectural design council recognized the challenges posed by reform to the discipline itself, and in October 1978, they met with Song Yangchu, deputy director of the National Construction Committee, to discuss the difficulties facing Chinese designers, including the need to modernize in adherence to international trends, serve the people, and identify an appropriate "national style" in keeping with socialism and China's rich cultural traditions. Many of these topics echoed debates begun in the years prior to the Cultural Revolution and, in fact, their recirculation reflected the influence of media such as *Architectural Journal* (*Jianzhu Xuebao*), which had begun to publish articles on these subjects. They also spoke to the unrealized goals of disciplinary elders and the rise of newfound optimism that resolutions could be found through a more comprehensive and deliberate study of international architecture. Foreign ideas were again acceptable, noted participant Zhang Bo, provided that they served China.[11]

Following the national conference for China's building industry held in August 1979, a series of editorials published in *Architectural Journal* made the ideological case for the selective embrace of the foreign to spur new creative directions in socialist Chinese architectural design. Provocatively titled "Break up the Old and Establish the New to Further Raise the Design Level," "Emancipate the Mind, Endeavor to Do the Design Work Still Better," and "Crush the Mental Fetters and Raise the Design Level," these essays identified the major obstacles impeding Chinese architects from fully realizing their potential as designers. Among the challenges was China's extended isolation from the rest of the world, and the speed with which architects would have to work to improve the country's design quality relative to other parts of the world.[12]

China's architectural programs subsequently began to pursue opportunities for international exchange in an effort to improve upon nearly "non-existent" interactivity between Chinese designers and practitioners from other parts of the world, a suggestion also offered by Walkley in his report. Many of these new initiatives were built upon preexisting pre-1978 networks of designers and architectural educators, and they helped to inspire changes "with the future of the next generation in mind." Between May and October 1978 alone, China received several architectural experts from abroad, including Alfred A. Lee, a Chinese-American structural engineer based in Honolulu; a ten-member group of architects from Brazil; three Japanese delegations, including teams of material engineers, city planners, and designers of public buildings; a twenty-person delegation of U.S. architects interested in technological exchange; and Walkley himself.[13]

Despite an increase in exchange opportunities, however, they remained sensitive affairs. Early exchanges involving foreign architecture students did not involve the act of design itself, but rather were organized around sets of ancillary courses such as China's architectural history. Others lacked a specific scholarly remit or objective altogether and consisted of several introductory courses in Chinese culture and history followed by carefully prescribed study tours of the country's major architectural landmarks. Short-term, reciprocal visits by Chinese experts abroad were also arranged to allow students and faculty more time to experience and learn from foreign environments, though these were also politically delicate.[14]

LEARNING FROM THE DESIGN STUDIO

Despite increasing circulations of foreign and Chinese architectural ideas and educational approaches, the design studio itself remained a challenging realm for international experimentation. One major obstacle to rigorous design studio exchange was language. In theory, drawing offered a visual language capable of overcoming communication difficulties, though the more fundamental obstacles presented themselves in relation to the process of design itself. The studio was an intimate, informal setting in which students and instructors spent long hours engaging each other in collective, iterative, and occasionally frustrating acts of creativity. Determining and pursuing shared sets of design goals in such a charged, cross-cultural setting carried with it the potential for awkward, often trying negotiations involving incompatible expectations and disappointing results. The political nature of architectural and urban design in China posed additional risks of misunderstanding and hostility.

The first Sino-foreign joint studio was coordinated between Tsinghua University and MIT in 1985 and focused on issues of conservation and urban design. The eight-week studio developed out of preexisting relationships established by Kevin Lynch and Tunney Lee, both of whom participated in a 1980 professional tour of China. In preparing for the studio, both Tsinghua and MIT faculty expressed interest in using the experience to engage questions of conservation in relationship to urban development. Over the course of the two-month program, however, it became clear to student participants and faculty organizers that different modes of thinking complicated these goals. Even prior to the start of the studio, imbalances emerged. Due to the limited time available for the studio, for example, Tsinghua University professors selected the two studio sites—Shichahai and Haidian districts in Beijing—without consulting their MIT counterparts. MIT representatives later learned that those Tsinghua students selected for the program were the school's most talented and had spent the entire previous semester completing base maps and data for the studio.[15]

Other difficulties emerged during the process of design itself. For example, Chinese students tended to tackle the problem in the abstract, only later applying specific solutions to a particular case. U.S. participants generally began by looking specifically at the site, and then deriving potential solutions from observational context. Both sides had reasonable critiques of the other's approach. U.S. students did not always understand why their Chinese counterparts began with weighty conceptual questions to address, while Chinese students wondered how their U.S. partners could develop a reasonable understanding of a site with which they had little to no sustained experience. The divergent perspectives of Chinese and foreign students concerning what constituted appropriate levels of intervention in a studio devoted to the city were never publicly articulated, debated, or resolved.[16]

Daniel B. Abramson, a participant in the 1992 MIT-Tsinghua studio, framed the limitations of the experience in relationship to the process of design itself and the broader political and economic vicissitudes taking place at the time. On one hand, the graphic and visual nature of architectural communication helped to transcend both the inherent awkwardness of these interpersonal, cross-cultural encounters while allowing participants to elude the more politically sensitive exchange of socioeconomic data. Yet discussion was frequently compromised by linguistic obstacles, disconnect as to the role of design and planning in society, and the urgency imposed upon China's architects and planners to solve the country's various ills. He observed an inductive and "tentative" nature to MIT students' design reasoning in contrast to the Tsinghua participants' deductive assessments of particular sites in relationship to other sites, and their willingness to categorize, generalize, and ultimately apply an appropriate response based upon a survey of existing methods. The shared process of design was ultimately both limited and directly informed by these divergent approaches to design thinking, giving rise to a very specific disciplinary mode rooted in the asymmetry of exchange and focused on physical design over other potential aspects of the design process, including analysis, policy-making, and advocacy.[17]

Other exchange participants expressed similar observations. Acts of design often consisted of the close reproduction of plans provided by state-produced architectural yearbooks featuring sets of programmatic prototypes, including housing complexes, hotels, and sports stadiums, recalled Anthony Vacchione, who visited China in 1982 as an architecture student at Columbia University and subsequently taught at Tianjin University in 1984–85.[18] Slight modifications helped to adapt the project to a specific program and site, though students spent more time doing watercolor renderings of the buildings they had designed. Chinese architecture students were trained to hand their drawings over to engineers and builders immediately after completion; as a result, they possessed little to no incentive to engage with the building systems of their projects. The students' architectural designs seemed to consist of little more than the aesthetic arrangement of façades and surfaces.[19]

Another significant factor in Chinese students' design methods was their job prospects. "Students were concerned about how the project could affect their long-term success or failure in society," observed Vacchione. "[Students] had to succeed in the right way in order to get into the right design institute."[20] Students were aware of and curious about the transformative shifts taking place around the country and how they might participate. Many were simply anxious about how best to integrate their skills into this new environment. In the spring of 1985, for example, Vacchione's students selected Zhuhai, one of China's recently opened SEZs located in southern Guangdong Province along China's border with Macau, as the destination for their annual department-sponsored field trip. Students wanted to see the economic experimentations taking place there and their effects on architectural design, even as it remained unclear how such changes would affect the rest of the country, and for how long. Vacchione also took his students to Beijing to see new projects like the Jianguo Hotel, which remained a sensitive site off-limits to average Chinese residents.

These and other international experiences helped to broaden the intellectual and professional horizons of elite, young Chinese designers. Cui Kai, honorary president and chief architect of the China Architecture Design & Research Group, graduated from Tianjin University with a master's degree in 1984 before moving to Beijing and eventually Shenzhen. There, he joined Shenzhen's first architectural joint venture, Huasen Architectural & Engineering Designing Consultants, and worked on the design for the Nanhai Hotel, discussed in Chapter 5.[21] In general, however, it remained unclear just how any lessons imparted were applicable to China's uncertain, rapidly shifting conditions, raising questions as to how such knowledge would inform and ultimately influence China's architectural direction moving forward.

FROM THE DESIGN STUDIO TO THE PRACTICE OF DESIGN

Shortcomings in China's architectural education also revealed themselves through early Sino-foreign joint venture experiments, particularly those based outside the exceptional zone conditions of a site like Shenzhen, where there existed less government oversight and greater willingness to experiment. A failed hotel joint venture proposed for Beijing between the Qiong Hua International Tourist Corporation, the U.S. architectural firm John Carl Warnecke & Associates, and the 2,500-person state-run BIAD, for example, offers insight into the complicated financial, organizational, and interpersonal dynamics of enacting reform in relationship to socialist Chinese architectural practice itself.

Warnecke & Associates was the largest design firm in the United States at the time, and its founding director, John Carl Warnecke, had first visited China as a member of the 1974 AIA-sponsored tour. In July 1980, Qiong Hua, Warnecke & Associates, and BIAD agreed upon the logistical and financial details for a twenty-four-story, one-thousand-room project known as the Metropolitan Hotel (fig. 69). The massive structure was intended to be built in northeast Beijing alongside the Great Wall Hotel as

Fig. 69 Metropolitan Hotel (proposal), Warnecke/Dolinsky and Beijing Institute of Architectural Design, Beijing, 1980. Originally published in *Architecture California* (October/November 1981).

part of a new "city wall" initiative composed of international hotels built along the city's airport, and adjacent to a proposed Third Ring Road then under construction. The collaboration was to be the first international architectural project in China to be financed by the Bank of China, and the tallest project to be proposed for construction in Beijing up to that point in time, surpassing the Beijing Hotel by six stories. It thus carried significant national meaning, a fact not lost on members of the Warnecke office or BIAD, who were cognizant of the partnership's importance and committed themselves to genuine and substantive collaboration through design.[22]

The design process itself began with the decision to send ten BIAD designers to the United States, where they traveled to several cities to visit notable hotels before settling temporarily in Los Angeles. There, they spent ten weeks working in both the Warnecke office and with the project's structural consultant, Martin & Huang International. Only one of the Chinese architects was able to speak English, making substantive communication difficult, and prompting Warnecke to assign several Chinese-speaking employees to the project simply to facilitate conversational exchange, including Roger Hong, then director of design for the firm's Los Angeles and San Francisco offices. Ultimately, team members developed methods of interaction based upon what one participant identified as the "the language of architecture," in particular, visual and graphic forms of communication. Throughout the project's conception and design phase, however, the U.S. design team continually struggled to adapt the required building type and form—a high-rise hotel tower already defined by the Chinese partners—to their own preconceptions of what constituted an appropriate architectural scale in urban China. Within the U.S. team, well-positioned individuals played specific and consequential roles in various design and decision-making processes, while the project's Chinese partners relied upon consensus-building practices to make decisions. "The major cultural differences are most evident in comparing the practice of architecture within private enterprise to that within the confines of a government bureaucracy," noted Hong.[23]

Project team members eventually settled on a modular design approach, and a proposed serpentine-shaped tower composed of a series of equilateral triangles took shape. Public amenities, including an atrium, tea lounge, and Chinese garden, were clustered around the building's southern façade. A series of collaboratively produced structural, mechanical, and electrical drawings in both Chinese and English, bilingual presentation boards, brochures, and a detailed building model were shipped to Beijing, where the venture's representatives introduced their vision to officials in November 1980. Following several days of intense meetings, including a large presentation to 250 people, the design team was asked to incorporate a range of suggested revisions, from the size of a kitchen to the height of a rooftop restaurant to the addition of extra parking. BIAD representatives insisted upon making the necessary adjustments themselves, and the project's U.S. partners returned home to await further word as to the hotel's progress. Over the course of the following months, U.S. representatives received a series of disheartening reports, including speculation that the project would not be built and that their fees would need to be renegotiated. Moreover, U.S.-based representatives never received any drawings detailing the project's proposed modifications. A high-rise structure known as the Kunlun Hotel, bearing a number of striking formal and structural similarities to the Metropolitan Hotel scheme but unattributed to any U.S. partners, was eventually completed in Beijing in 1985 (fig. 70).[24]

In a revealing account of the project's failure published in 1981, Hong attributed the endeavor's difficulties to the untested hybrid nature of the private-state design collaboration, though other factors included the challenges of dealing with the state as a client in a fickle political climate. U.S. designers accustomed to dealing with a hierarchical division of responsibilities struggled to adapt to the collective nature of the socialist Chinese model, though intragovernmental competition may have also played a role in the project's delayed construction. For example, Hong surmised that other agencies and departments may have criticized Qiong Hua representatives for their overreliance upon foreign partners in the design of the hotel's form—a suspicion reinforced by positive Chinese-language reviews of the nearly identical Kunlun Hotel's distinctive "Chinese" and "nationalistic" spatial qualities.[25] Ultimately, the project's failure testified to the vague and ill-defined objectives of reform itself, and the unpredictable interpersonal and organizational

Fig. 70 Kunlun Hotel, Xiong Ming, Liu Li, and Geng Zhangfu, Beijing Institute of Architectural Design, Beijing, 1985. Originally published in *Architectural Journal* (*Jianzhu Xuebao*), no. 9 (1985).

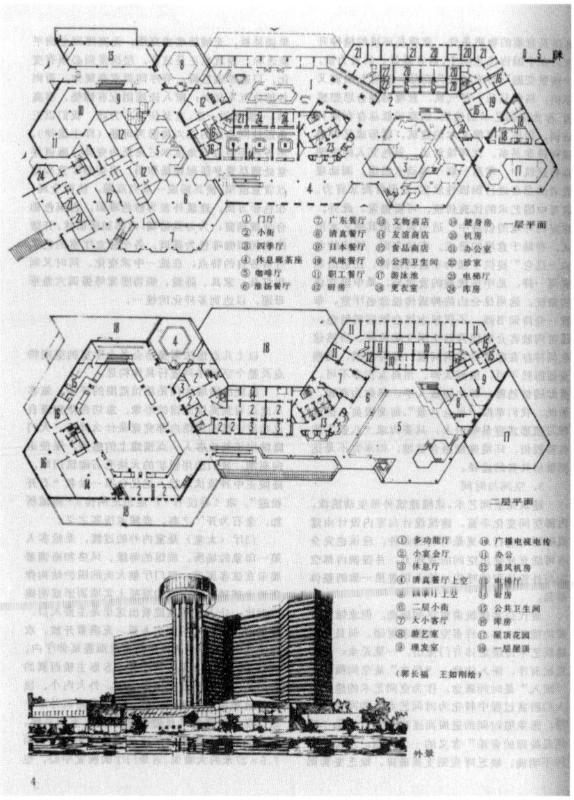

machinations taking place within the party as it sought an effective developmental model to enrich China's architectural production through professional exchange. The government's conflicted desire to project the guise of a strong and autonomous nation through collaborative, international design work exposed sets of Chinese design practices and management techniques that proved resistant to liberalization's effects. New organizational paradigms were needed to capably absorb the international lessons and expertise beginning to circulate through the country.

Official focus on the role of the design institute occurred as additional questions emerged regarding the architect's ability to address the broad, complex range of needs in China's built environment. At the first international architectural conference organized in post-Mao China, held in October 1981, for example, participants from China and around the world met to assess the state of China's rural communities and how the country's architects might best address problems associated with rural development.[26] Over fifty thousand Chinese villages, having been reorganized into People's Communes prior to 1978, were slated for redevelopment as market towns designed to support various kinds of light industrial processing for agriculture and household products. Many conference participants considered China's rural areas, particularly Xinjiang, to be exciting terrain for small-scale, localized architectural experimentation, and the conference's presentations, which ranged in subjects from rural housing in Java to self-help construction techniques in rural Senegal to a history of New Nubia to socialist villages in Algeria, attempted to draw connections between China and localized design practices taking place in other parts of the world. The role of the architect in fomenting social change, aggressive redevelopment in Beijing, and Alvin Toffler's *The Third Wave* were other, informal subjects of conversation.[27]

Through these discussions, the conference produced a moment of unprecedented international debate over the role of the architect in early reform-era China, with issues raised that probed historical notions of the architect and his/her work, both in China and abroad. "The architect has to develop certain skills that up until now have been considered to be the domain of the social scientist," argued the Iranian architect Farokh Afshar. In theory, China seemed well-suited for such experimentation, particularly given the ubiquity of grassroots design methods during the Cultural Revolution. With the advent of the Four Modernizations campaign, however, the government's agenda had changed. Architects were now expected to actively contribute to the integration of industry with agriculture, and town with country. "We are being urged to speed up the development of market towns as one of our national priorities," explained BIAD-affiliated architect Wang Huabin. Echoing the party's new, reform-era principles, Wang explained that only through developing town and country in concert would architects be able to contribute to "new life, a new hope, and a new civilization in China." The conference's international participants remained unconvinced, however. "What we are left with, from examples given by our Chinese colleagues," surmised the Indian architectural and urban designer Charles Correa, "is that they can't change for ways which everyone feels is for the better." Other international observers voiced concern over the relationship between the party's rhetoric and the difficult, understudied practices needed to fulfill its goals. "I think it's important not to separate ideology and process," argued Tunney Lee. "I think when it is separated it becomes impossible to see the goals of the ideology."[28]

In his concluding remarks to the event, the Aga Khan noted that the questions raised required architects themselves "to take cognizance" and "accept the fact that the criteria for designing and planning for the rural habitat are totally different from the traditional criteria of designing for urban buildings."[29] Determining the appropriate nature of design in China's rural versus its urban environments was only one of the issues facing China's architectural community in the face of reform, however. A complex array of problems existed in socialist Chinese architecture, some of which derived from the nature of socialist Chinese design itself, while others were particular to new economic and social pressures produced from reform-era liberalization. Addressing these conditions required new skill sets, new design techniques, and new models of architectural practice.

REDESIGNING THE DESIGN INSTITUTE

As officials tackled the atrophied state of design education, the party also initiated a reassessment of the country's design institutes. In his evaluation of China's architectural education system, Walkley had criticized the limitations of the country's state-run design organs as providing "the only opportunity for student experience" which ultimately "[militates] against the acquisition of an adequate range of experience." His observations underscored the obstacles facing the country's architects as they confronted the design-related responsibilities of economic liberalization. The design institute figured as the only logical vessel for enacting the state-sanctioned process of modernization, even as operational obstacles embedded in the institutional mechanism itself jeopardized the implementation of reform in relationship to architectural practice. The institute's unwieldy size, its strict and inefficient separation of responsibilities, and its lack of effective performance assessment criteria all limited the possibility of innovation, which in turn limited architecture's ability to respond to the economic changes taking place. New organizational prototypes for architectural practice in China were thus vital to the prospects of reform itself.[30]

Additional sets of revised economic policies introduced by party leaders in 1984 hastened the need for requisite shifts in relation to architectural and urban design. A dramatic increase in private business activity within China's cities, for example, where the number of officially registered private enterprises and individual households engaged in small-scale domestic trade had doubled, from 5.9 to 11.7 million, between 1983 and 1985, prompted reformers to launch a second stage of urban-focused economic policies in the belief that the government's control over economic enterprises was too strict. Influenced by Hungary's model of market socialism, the campaign encouraged profit incentives, greater managerial responsibility, and a higher degree of operational autonomy in an effort to better integrate elements of central planning with market-based regulations. Moderates had also begun to circulate an internal party strategy to more actively promote younger, technologically savvy party members. Two-thirds of the party's Central Committee members were over the age of sixty, and reformers recognized they needed to infuse the party with a new generation of leaders if liberalization was going to sustain itself. Between 1984 and 1987, the proportion of party members with at least a senior high school education rose from 17.8 percent to 28.5 percent.[31] Over the same period of time, almost one million college graduates joined the party. The infusion of new talent into the party, coupled with the government's continued commitment to unleashing market-based economic principles, had an immediate impact on architecture.

In November 1984, John Bryant, head of the Oklahoma State University

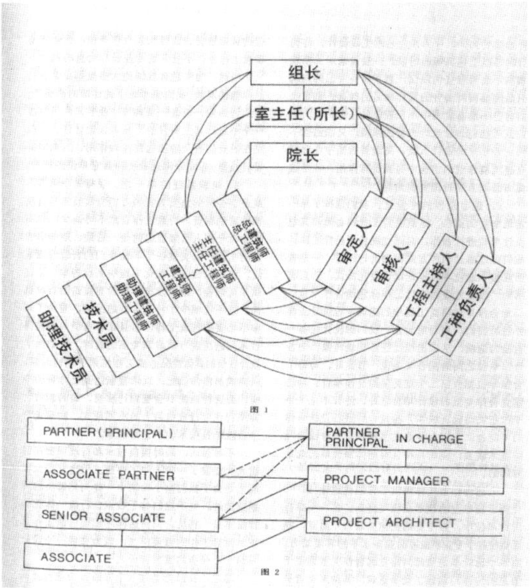

Fig. 71 Comparison of management structures between a typical Chinese design institute (above) and a foreign private practice (below). Originally published in *Architectural Journal* (*Jianzhu Xuebao*), no. 8 (1986).

School of Architecture, penned a letter to I. M. Pei detailing his observations of China following his participation in a recent AIA-sponsored tour. Bryant specifically wanted to draw Pei's attention to the Chinese government's recent decision to let some Chinese architects form private offices. The policy had "not yet been announced fully," reported Bryant, "and our colleagues in central and southern China don't seem to believe that it will happen." Nevertheless, Bryant observed that "the professionals at the Chinese Society of Architects in Beijing are already doing it and are looking for outside partners from Hong Kong or the USA." That autumn, plans were announced for the establishment of a new kind of architectural design office in China. Known as the Beijing Architectural Design Group (BADG) and established under the jurisdiction of the Ministry of Construction, the entity was headed by Wang Tianxi, a Tsinghua University graduate who had worked in Beijing and New York City for Pei on the Fragrant Hill Hotel, among other commissions. BADG was intended to function as a new design armature within the municipality of Beijing, and was tasked with "bringing prosperity to China's architectural production, exploring ways of improving the state of design experimentation, and improving the design industry's economic efficiency."[32]

BADG was distinctive from typical design institute structures in a number of respects. Importantly—and unlike China's state-managed design institutes—the group assumed "sole responsibility for its own profits and losses." Moreover, its professional responsibilities were specifically limited to the practice of design. This made it much smaller than state-administered institutes but theoretically capable of maximizing the full talent of its staff by giving younger architects more opportunity for on-site training. Organizationally, the office was expected to support no more than thirty employees, and would rely on more horizontal and circular transfers of knowledge and expertise among its employees, with a management system that combined what Wang described as "different structures of design institutes in China and in some developed countries" to produce better design practices and built results (fig. 71).[33] Improved workflow, greater efficiency in design production, and a more transparent system for promotion were other notable goals of the new office. These international entwinements of technique and labor management made the enterprise a speculative initiative, though officials reasoned that new models were important and necessary to the country's broader move toward economic liberalization.

By early 1985, the government launched two additional and experimental quasi-private design offices, each to be directed by a Chinese architect with extensive international expertise, to address perceived inadequacies of the design institute amid the mounting pressures of reform. Great Earth Architects & Engineers International constituted socialist China's first "collectively-owned" joint Sino-foreign private architectural firm. The practice was headed by Peng Peigen, a mainland Chinese-born architect living in Canada who moved to Beijing in 1982 to accept a position to teach architecture at Tsinghua University. Peng studied architecture in Taiwan under Wang Dahong, a classmate of I. M. Pei in China, before moving to the United States to earn a master's degree in architecture at the University of Illinois–Champaign-Urbana in 1973.[34] He had initially approached Wang Tianxi about joining him in Great Earth, but Wang declined in order to establish BADG. Similar to that office, Great Earth was intended to operate as a smaller, flexible practice within an existing bureaucratic mechanism, namely, the Construction Bureau. It did not derive its income from state subsidies, as was accustomed design institute policy, but from the profits accrued through government- and foreign-funded projects both inside and outside China. It was expected to pay taxes per Chinese law, and wages would be paid on an adjustable basis dependent upon the amount of work completed by the firm. If the office's revenue exceeded an undisclosed amount, however, it would be regulated accordingly.

Officially launched at a ceremony held in the Great Hall of the People on January 19, 1985, Great Earth was publicly supported by key figures in the central government, including Premier Zhao Ziyang and Vice Premiers Wan Li and Yao Yilin. "Leaders of the government hope that this non-official setup will become an experimental unit of one kind for the reform of architectural designing industry," explained an announcement of the office's opening published in *World Architecture* (*Shijie Jianzhu*). "Collective ownership and private ownership will coexist, compete with each other, help and complement each other." These goals echoed BADG's objectives, though Great Earth was more explicitly designed to replicate foreign design practices in China, with a particular focus on village and town planning models for rural areas. In order to compensate for its unique status and any presumed monetary advantages incurred therein, Great Earth would contribute 100,000 RMB to a foundation devoted to rural architectural development and the promotion of rural architectural expertise. Its staff was expected to total no more than fifty employees headed by eleven major practitioners—six Chinese and five foreign participants—that included a number of senior figures with international experience such as Chen Zhanxiang, an urban planner best known for his collaborations with Liang Sicheng in post-1949 Beijing; Shou Zhenhua, principal architect at BIAD; Tao Ho, a well-known Hong Kong–based practitioner; and Macklin Hancock, a Harvard-educated planner who worked on the design of Don Mills, an early model for postwar suburban design in Toronto.[35]

In February 1985, a third prototype emerged in the form of the Zhongjing Architectural Design Office, which was launched by the ASC in coordination with the Beijing Civil Engineering Society and eventually incorporated into BIAD in 1987 (fig. 72). Zhongjing was placed under the control of ASC member and party stalwart Yan Xinghua, and like China's other new experimental practices, it was not dependent upon funding from the state, but was expected to derive income from contracts made with other work units around China. Like Great Earth, the firm was designed to pursue a range of architectural and urban design work, and it offered a broad range of design services, though Zhongjing did not have its own building and rented space from the Ministry of Construction—a unique situation in a country in which every work unit was otherwise allocated land by the government. Its chief architect, Shen Yadi, had practiced in Singapore and Hong Kong before coming to Beijing to work at the Beijing Planning Department, which was unusual for such a high-level designer in China.

Fig. 72 Staff, Zhongjing Architectural Design Office, Beijing. Originally published in *Building in China* 3, no. 3 (1990).

Non-Chinese foreigners were also hired. Zhongjing's first non-Chinese employee was Joe Carter, a Canadian designer who had taught studios at Tianjin University in 1986 and 1987. Carter described the structure of the Zhongjing office, like both Great Earth and the Beijing Architectural Group, as being unique from standard design institutes. For example, Zhongjing employees all divided up their work among themselves rather than relying upon the standard work unit system of one person/one job, in which design responsibilities belonged to architect and engineers, administration to managers, clerical work to clerks, and maintenance to service staff. This reduced the risk of inefficient hierarchies, improved staff morale, reduced the office's overhead costs, and increased overall awareness of the organization's processes among all staff members. Employees were not provided with housing, as was typical for most work units, but employees were given health insurance, pensions, and the possibility of year-end bonuses. Moreover, all employees, with the exception of Yan and Shen, were under thirty three years of age.[36]

As experiments not simply in the production of design, but in the design of production, these design practices were expected to stimulate design creativity throughout the discipline, facilitate the continued introduction of foreign expertise into China, and contribute to the reconfiguration of architectural practice in China. Importantly, these offices were established not only in the name of inducing new, quality design standards in China, but in introducing new ways of organizing design. The management strategies and economic policies at work in these offices were as significant to their existence as the projects they were expected to produce. The reorganization of socialist China's architectural labor was a daunting, ambitious exercise, yet one that architects and reform-minded officials alike considered essential to the discipline's survival. New strategies were urgently needed.

Reflecting upon the historical development of China's architectural profession, Bu Zhengwei, professor of architecture at Tianjin University, argued that a new architectural age in China had arrived—one in which young architects needed to be allowed to undergo a process of "self-liberation" so that they might find their individual inspiration as designers and more effectively contribute to contemporary architectural production. "No one is satisfied with our contemporary architecture," argued Bu, "and some foreign guests have even argued that 'architecture' doesn't even exist in China. But doesn't the promotion of so-called 'compliant architecture,' 'wind-borne architecture,' 'copy architecture,' and 'high yield, square-meter-variety architecture' destroy individuality and neglect examples of well-designed, high-quality architecture?" Official promotion of individual acts of creativity were not to be misconstrued as an argument against socialism, however. "If there is no 'freedom to create,'" reasoned Bu, "architects cannot present their own work, leading to a situation where they are not benefiting the collective."[37]

Nevertheless, the enaction of new methods, management systems, and scales of practice into the state-run industry offered an explicit critique of the paradigm for design in socialist China. The similar professional profiles shared by each of the office's leaders are important in this regard. International experience, an awareness of professional networks, and, above all, respect within the party were all valued qualities in these new experimental design laboratories. Such a bold undertaking also demanded a familiar language of legitimization. Justification for each group's launching was couched in Mao-era rhetorical flourishes aimed to situate each practice within the party's established ideological framework, but one that over time risked devaluing the ideological foundation of such rhetoric altogether. "Strictly speaking, the all-inclusive design institute is reflective of a feudal, autarkic attitude," argued Wang. "Over the course of the twentieth century, a number of factors have changed social development, necessitating new degrees of specialization capable of facilitating significant development." In rationalizing Zhongjing's establishment, Yan Xinghua argued, "Only through reform is there vitality."[38]

REFORMING DESIGN

Over the course of the mid- to late 1980s, Great Earth, BADG, and Zhongjing earned an array of different architectural commissions around China and abroad. Early Great Earth projects, for example, included master plans for Xiamen, Tianjin, and Hangzhou as well as a boutique restaurant in Taiwan, some of which were undertaken in cooperation with established institutions such as Tsinghua University's Department of Architecture, the Shanghai Institute of Architectural Design and Research, and the Design Institute of the People's Liberation Army's Logistics Department, among others. Zhongjing's early work included a Chinese revolutionary history museum in Shaanxi; the Hong Kong and Macau Trade Center and hotel complex in Beijing, built in coordination with the Hong Kong Engineering and Design Corporation; Beijing's Urban and Rural Trade Center, a redevelopment proposal for the Qingdao railway station; and a Beijing kindergarten. Early BADG projects included the Tianlun Hotel in Beijing, a training center for book editors in Yantai, Shandong, and the Parliament Building in the Republic of Vanuatu.[39]

Collectively, the different scales, sites, and programs on display in these projects offered a range of potential design solutions to the political, economic, and social challenges facing reform-era China. Staff and client satisfaction were considered key attributive components of such results. "We pay particular attention to the attitudes of our staff," reasoned Yan. "We do our best to ensure the design quality is good, and that drawings are produced quickly, and that the client is satisfied. We're constantly working to improve our output."[40] Such work rivaled bodies of work typically handled by much larger design institutes and evinced

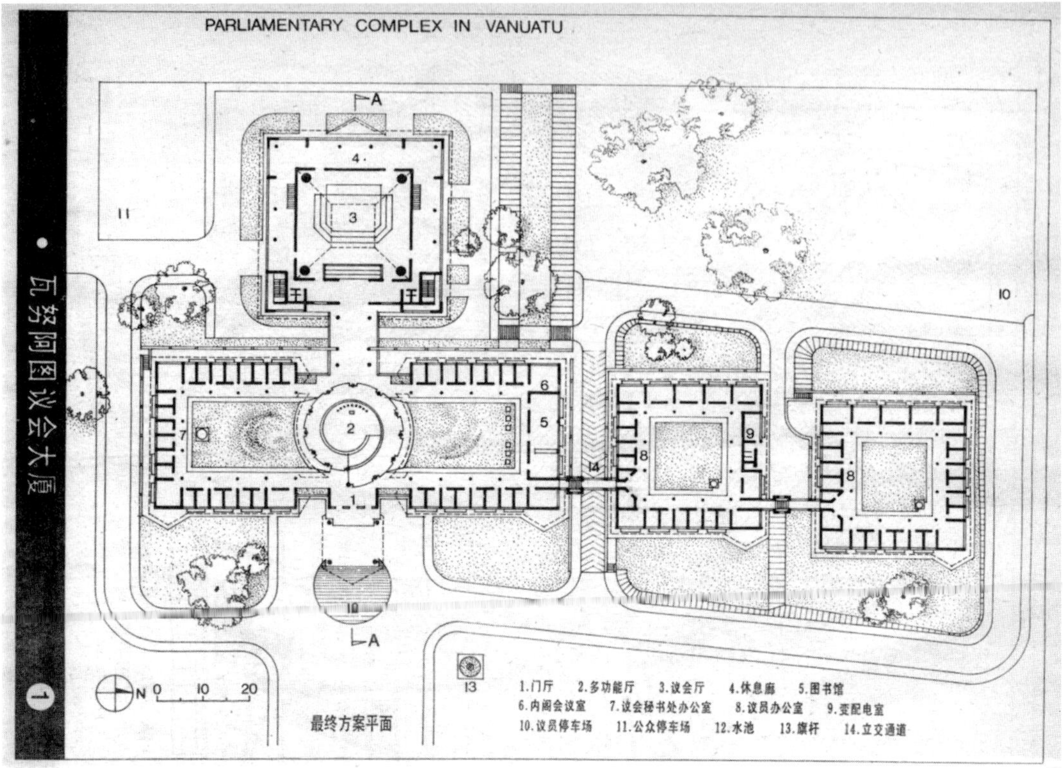

Fig. 73 Plan, Parliamentary complex, Wang Tianxi, Zhang Guanghua, and Lo Jingbo, Beijing Architectural Design Group, Vanuatu, 1987–91. Originally published in *Architectural Journal* (*Jianzhu Xuebao*), no. 1 (1988).

the kind of operational efficiency and elasticity sought by party leaders.

Promotional media associated with the offices also emphasized the improvement of architecture and urban planning throughout China through international-quality production standards and an emphasis on "distinctive Chinese features."[41] What exactly these features were remained undefined, but they gestured toward some unnamed creative impulse with respect to China's architectural past that echoed ongoing architectural discourse in China at the time regarding architectural heritage and the relevance of postmodernism. Such language hinted at tensions not simply between different forms of architectural practice in China, but different kinds of architectural expression.

As attempts to capture the kind of bold architectural language demanded by reform, the work of BADG, Zhongjing, and Great Earth in fact offered mixed results. A BADG project for a parliamentary complex for the Pacific island nation of Vanuatu, for example, illuminates the group's ability to work across contexts and cultures. The newly independent nation was in search of a new political edifice, and BADG was asked to produce a building that would respond to local building traditions, respond to the area's humid, tropical climate, and withstand earthquakes and cyclones. The initial scheme consisted of four main structures, each linked by a series of interior halls, elevated walkways, and exterior paved paths (fig. 73). Despite efforts to engage in vernacular building practices, the firm struggled to mold the project into a convincing expression of

Fig. 74 Parliamentary complex, Wang Tianxi, Zhang Guanghua, and Lo Jingbo, Beijing Architectural Design Group, Vanuatu, 1987–91.

local identity. As realized in 1991, the complex featured two main buildings arranged along a central, east–west axis, with an adjacent structure intended for use as a dining room for legislative members and the general public (fig. 74). The complex's roof structure, which was intended to evoke traditional Vanuatu roof construction methods and materials, in particular the imbricated surface of the natangura palm tree, projected little more than a disappointing abstracted form of Vanuatu's past, rather than elevating it into a statement of the country's future.[42]

Like BADG, Zhongjing also struggled to consolidate the range of uncertain new practices and technologies demanded by the architectural marketplace into a convincing design strategy. In the Beijing Urban and Rural Trade Center, which was expected to facilitate economic partnerships between urban-based, state-run manufacturers and distributors and rural communities, the office proposed two distinctive forms of architectural expression for the building's exterior and interior, respectively. Programmatically, the building consisted of a loosely composed, asymmetrical layout of product displays and showcases, offices, exhibition halls, and a cafeteria (figs. 75, 76). Externally, a mirrored glass curtain wall wrapped itself around the building's first four floors, which composed its main exhibition space, while a staggered series of traditional Chinese roofed towers perched atop the space provided office and administrative activities. The towers attempted to historicize the transactional nature of the building from the outside, while its mirrored surface camouflaged the massive complex relative to its urban surroundings. Internally, the building's main exhibition hall was dominated by a kind of technological performativity, including visible air-conditioning units, a self-controlled fire alarm system, broadcast television, a telecommunications system, and a central atrium interlaced with escalators—a new and coveted technology. Design itself was the vessel for such machinery. "Architectural design should introduce modern equipment into China," explained an accompanying text to the building's plans.[43] The building's assemblage of

Fig. 75 Beijing Urban and Rural Trade Center, Zhongjing Architectural Design Office, Beijing, 1990. Originally published in *Building in China* 3, no. 3 (1990).

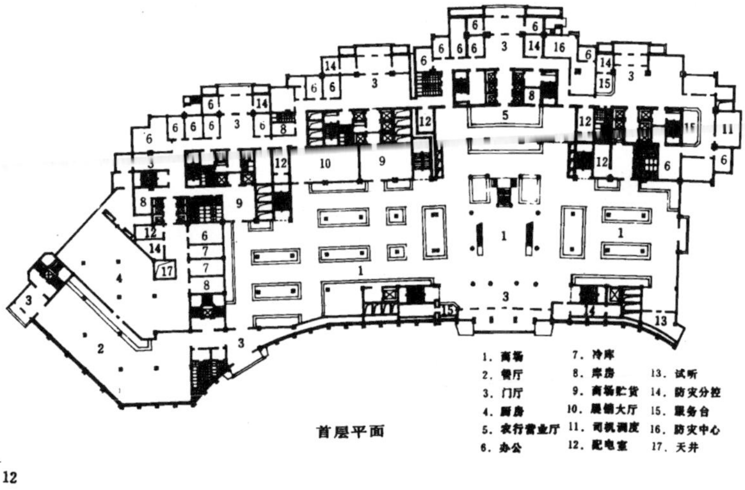

Fig. 76 Plan, Beijing Urban and Rural Trade Center, Zhongjing Architectural Design Office, Beijing, 1990. Originally published in *Architectural Journal* (*Jianzhu Xuebao*), no. 10 (1987).

historical pastiche with signs of technological progress offered an architectural language that echoed several recently completed joint venture projects, including the Great Wall Hotel. Like those projects, it struggled to capture and reconcile reform's multiple, often-conflicting interests into a compelling visual and formal image.

Great Earth, though larger, more international, and better able to offer more design services than either Zhongjing or BADG, also struggled in this regard. The office's anticipated rural work did not materialize as planned, prompting a shift to larger urban-scale architectural plans designed to induce a kind of urban "reordering" at a time in which China's urban planning departments and municipal offices were having difficulties adjusting to the large-scale changes taking place. In a series of urban planning strategies for the Xiamen SEZ, Great Earth proposed an "elastic" system of terraced platforms and "modern" high-rises capable of supporting the city's new special economic activities (fig. 77).[44] The plan eventually took form over the course of the 1990s and early 2000s as a set of concentrated urban clusters linked via an ambitious transportation network. An unrealized zoning strategy proposal for Shenzhen's SEZ

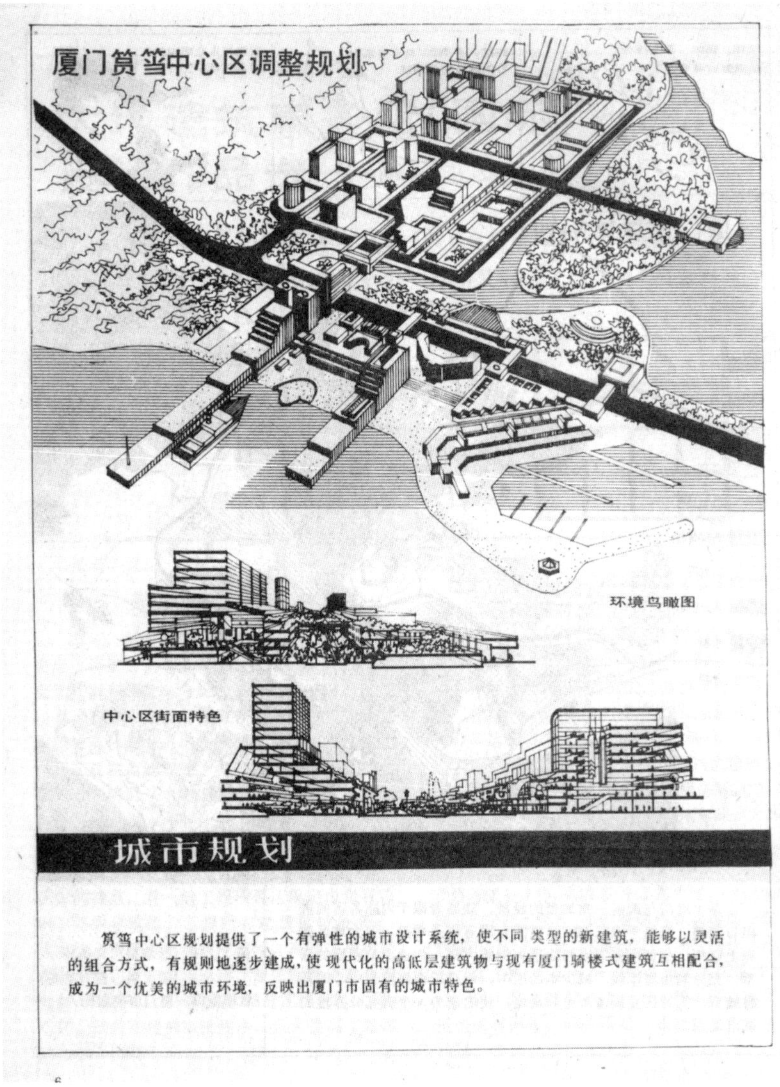

Fig. 77 Proposed development of Xiamen, Great Earth Architects & Engineers, 1987. Originally published in *Architectural Journal* (*Jianzhu Xuebao*), no. 7 (1987).

provided strict areas for residential, industrial, and undeveloped forested land in an effort to control the city's swift growth. Though the proposal was not realized, it aimed to provide a visible and physical structure to the unanticipated forms of urban development taking shape. In an early and ambitious design for the China Travel Service building in Beijing, commissioned in 1986 and completed in 1993, the office attempted to disaggregate and domesticate a massive podium tower into a series of interlocking public spaces and offices by cladding it in a series of imperial-era Chinese ornamental details.

The work of these offices may have been distinct from equivalent production taking place in the country's design institutes, but even more importantly, it was through these and other design projects that each practice began to push the operational, scalar, and conceptual boundaries of architecture as it was practiced in China. Subsequent models emerged, including the well-known designer Dai Nianci's Jianxue Architecture and Engineering Design Institute, which he founded in 1988 following his retirement as chief architect from the Ministry of Urban and Rural Construction and Environmental Protection's design institute.[45] The 1990s saw the establishment of China's first private practices by figures such as Yung Ho Chang and Wang Shu. But it was the work of BADG, Zhongjing, and Great Earth that first enabled new possibilities for design production by prodding the discipline to embrace more reflexive management systems, more merit-based remuneration structures, and a more individualized approach to architectural creation. At the same time, and in part due to the perceived success of these new models, incompatibilities began to emerge with the state-run institutes still responsible for project management and construction. The praise lavished on these new operations gradually denigrated the ideological basis and structural integrity of the design institute itself, exposing new schisms between the country's architectural community and the construction industry within which it remained uneasily positioned. These frictions presaged consequential changes in the conceptual production of Chinese architecture relative to the physical act of construction.

New educational and professional models altered the role of the designer in Chinese society. Lessons gleaned from an expanded international field tested the architect's role in China, particularly vis-à-vis notions of architectural labor and the construction process. Architects struggled to recalibrate notions of disciplinary labor by rationalizing that through the empowerment of such individuality, the collective would ultimately benefit. Issues of taste, style, and discernment were qualitative concerns to which the architect could, and should, contribute his/her expertise. In justifying his own personal involvement with Great Earth, for example, the designer Shen Zhouhua argued that "there is no worthwhile style in any Chinese architecture today because architectural style is something that the administrators who govern our profession do not understand. All these people are concerned about is to save money and they think the only way to do this is by using cheap materials."[46] Architects found themselves arguing for new forms of expertise as brokers of information and expertise in an expanding economy increasingly shaped by flows of capital and international interactivity.

Over time, however, issues of taste produced questions of class. Such explicit and authoritative expressions of power began to be perceived as running counter to the broader interests of the state. An architect's professional responsibility to the state touched upon matters related to the manifold ways architecture participated in Chinese society. "In the coming century, China's economic condition will determine architectural quality, architecture's responsibilities, and architecture's features," Charlie Qiuli (Q. L.) Xue, a doctoral student at Tongji University, reminded *Architectural Journal* readers in March 1989. "The architect still maintains a low position in society . . . and even the most brilliant plan is still little more than a drawing."[47] For all of the advancements made in the profession, Xue argued, architecture was still dependent upon the broader superstructure of the state. Such worries echoed architectural debates in other parts of the world regarding disciplinary autonomy, and the obligation of the architect to society at large—questions that could, in fact, be applied to China's own architectural production abroad, particularly in the African continent, where the growing influence of Chinese design was generating new political, economic, and cultural convergences.

CHAPTER 9

China in Africa

Architecture offered more than simply a means of improving China's domestic conditions. It also presented a means by which the country could recalibrate its foreign policy abroad. Under Mao, architecture had been routinely deployed abroad to convey socialist China's unique contributions to the developing world and the international socialist cause while distinguishing its more strident ideological position from that of the Soviet Union. These projects also provided opportunities for Chinese architects to gain experience in foreign contexts while learning from other engineers and architects active in other parts of the world. This was particularly true in Africa, where Mao's efforts to equate class struggle with racial struggle resonated with numerous leaders of newly decolonized countries, including Ghana's Kwame Nkrumah, Guinea's Sékou Touré, and Mali's Moussa Traoré, at a time in which numerous capitalist and socialist powers were deploying architecture to cultivate new geopolitical alliances, secure access to valuable natural resources, and make new worlds through various institutional, environmental, and economic forces during the Cold War.[1]

China's 1972 rapprochement with the United States and its subsequent embrace of alternative sources of capital after 1978 surprised and disappointed a number of its socialist allies, who found Mao-era anti-imperialist policy and rhetoric compelling.[2] Resolving the contradictions posed by China's abrupt turn toward the free market necessitated finesse and tact. Many of China's international commitments were built upon Mao-era trade and diplomatic agreements dating back decades, at a time in which Chinese aid had offered a valuable, alternative model to both the Soviet Union and the United States. Recalibrating China's domestic efforts at reform for an international audience necessitated a reassessment of party messaging. Architecture's technological and representational multivalence—its ability to project a range of meanings that could be emphasized or obscured as either its designing authority or its client saw fit—was of benefit in this regard.

The Chinese government's early reform-era reorientation toward Western Europe, the United States, and Japan for architectural knowledge, technology, and capital did not preclude the continued circulation of multiple forms of design intelligence between China and allies in Southeast Asia, the Middle East, Latin America, and—the focus of this chapter—Africa. Following the official advent of reforms in 1978, China promoted certain free market–oriented policies even as its economy remained dependent upon commodity rather than currency exchange, meaning that even as the ideological tenor subtending such work began to change, the procedural machinations required to realize such work remained grounded in long-term, low to zero interest loan agreements and agreements involving trades of specific goods and services. Over the course of the 1980s, a number of Chinese-designed and -managed public edifices were constructed in African capitals, including sports stadiums, cultural facilities, and national assembly buildings also known as "people's palaces." As with earlier, Mao-era construction, such as the TAZARA Railway, Chinese and African leaders lauded these projects for the mutually beneficial collaboration they displayed, the public amenities they provided, and the political, cultural, and recreational events they supported. At the same time, however, themes of technical expertise and design proficiency became more dominant. CCP officials were less vocal in touting their country's own post-1949 history of self-reliance as a model for African partners to emulate and downplayed the significance of socialist revolution to China's own development.

A closer look at Chinese architectural production in African countries over the course of the early reform era complements the study of architectural changes taking place within the country over the same period. China's opening up at home reverberated through its prestige-building efforts abroad, and architects were important to both missions. New practices and ideas absorbed by Chinese designers from abroad began to inform China's architectural exports, leading to new kinds of architectural expressions that in turn signaled a distinct ideological turn relative to China's international presence. It was in part through the absorption of architectural lessons across its various geopolitical alliances that China was able to gradually aggregate an international spectrum of design and construction expertise. Such knowledge had a particular if ill-defined currency that enabled the country to begin to reposition itself as a fulcrum for international architectural demand and supply in what was becoming an increasingly dynamic and integrated global market economy.

ARCHITECTURAL EXPORTATION AFTER MAO

For all of the shifts taking place in relation to China's domestic and diplomatic affairs, CCP officials still recognized the political power of engaging people through large-scale, public monuments—an awareness that stemmed in part from the diminishment of China's own architectural history by imperialist powers during the late nineteenth and early twentieth centuries, and architecture's subsequent contributions to the spectacular public pageantry of life under Mao. Spectacularizing socialist China's political edifices was important to concentrating the collective aspirations of the nation around the party, and it subsequently became a valuable strategy through which China helped to fulfill the aspirations of developing nations to be taken seriously as functioning societies. Over the course of the late 1960s and early 1970s, the materialization of political monuments such as Guinea's People's Palace, completed in 1967, and the TAZARA Railway, finished in 1975, channeled shared frustration into physical expressions of mutual empowerment. Consequently, China framed such work as having a certain resonance relative to the desires of its developing partners that other international aid projects completed by the Soviet Union or the United States, for example, did not.

The design and construction of the People's Palace in Kinshasa, Zaire, initiated in 1973 and completed in 1979, spanned the waning days of the Mao era and the official launching of reform and, in so doing, testifies to the ways in which China's international architectural aid both reflected and contradicted China's nascent plans to liberalize (fig. 78). In particular, the Kinshasa project showed the challenges involved in reconfiguring China's international image for the post-Mao age, particularly as the rhetorical power of Mao-era revolution continued to endure in many parts of the developing world. The building's roots may be traced back to a January 1973 trip to China by Zaire President Mobutu Sese Seko, a self-professed U.S. ally and anti-communist leader seeking to normalize relations with the PRC and neutralize Soviet influence within the region. While in Beijing, Mobutu was feted by CCP leaders and dazzled by the choreography of an official state tour, and he returned to Zaire committed to borrowing from China's model of self-reliance as part of his own recently launched nation-building project. The campaign, celebrated as a "Radicalization of the Revolution," urged Zairians to eschew Western suits and ties for Mao-inspired jackets while embracing the spirit of *Salongo,* or hard work and national self-reliance, in apparent reference to China's own renowned work ethic and discipline. A second trip to Beijing

Fig. 78 People's Palace, Zhu Shanquan, Lin Kaiwu, and Qi Zhenya, Beijing Institute of Architectural Design, Kinshasa, Zaire, 1979. Originally published in *Elima,* May 19, 1979.

followed in December 1974, during which plans for the People's Palace were discussed and confirmed.[3]

Sino-Zairian negotiations were taking place as Mobutu promoted Zaire as a wellspring of African cultural authenticity, or *L'Authenticité,* and global "blackness" through a series of extravagant international events and major infrastructural improvements in Kinshasa. These spectacles included Zaire 74, a three-day music festival featuring performers such as James Brown, B. B. King, and the Spinners, and the "Rumble in the Jungle" heavyweight boxing championship between George Foreman and Muhammad Ali. Both events capped a flurry of building activity within the city, including the construction of Parliament, the headquarters of Radio-Télévision Nationale Congolaise, the International Trade Center, and an unfinished tower dedicated to nationalist leader Patrice Lumumba, whom Mobutu himself was responsible for killing.[4] The ambitious modernization program drained the national coffers in an effort to consolidate, in Mobutu's own words, the country's cultural identity in anticipation of greater exposure to the capitalist global economy, though the endeavor also communicated Mobutu's clear desire for recognition in the eyes of Western audiences. In the problematic absence of unifying national Zairian traditions and practices, they represented new traditions, events, and monuments invented to express Zairian identity and legitimize his self-proclaimed role as "Father of the Nation" in the process.[5]

China was an important if less visible influence on Mobutu's campaign. The conflicted aspirations for national autonomy and international recognition at the endeavor's core resonated in the Chinese-designed plans for Kinshasa's People's Palace, just as they subsequently reverberated through China's own post-1978 efforts to redefine Western architectural concepts like postmodernism on terms that were specific to China's reform-era cultural condition. In late 1974, members of BIAD led by Zhu Shanquan, Lin Kaiwu, and Qi Zhenya traveled to Kinshasa to undertake preliminary site studies, eventually producing plans for a forty-thousand-square-meter, four-story structure with Beaux-Arts–informed compositional features also found in Beijing's National Hall of the People and earlier international Chinese design work such as the People's Palace in Conakry, Guinea. Like those projects, the Kinshasa People's Palace featured a neoclassically influenced colonnade facing a large public square. Programmatically, the building's central component was a 3,501-seat auditorium, which was flanked by two interior courtyards—another formal similarity to both Beijing's and Conakry's halls (fig. 79). Various administrative offices and ancillary areas surrounded these spaces, all of which were aligned along a series of circulation axes.[6]

To provide Mobutu with the necessary technological and spatial features needed for his nation-building efforts, the design team equipped the building with numerous lounges, meeting rooms, a six-hundred-seat banquet hall, and an eight-hundred-seat movie theater that doubled as

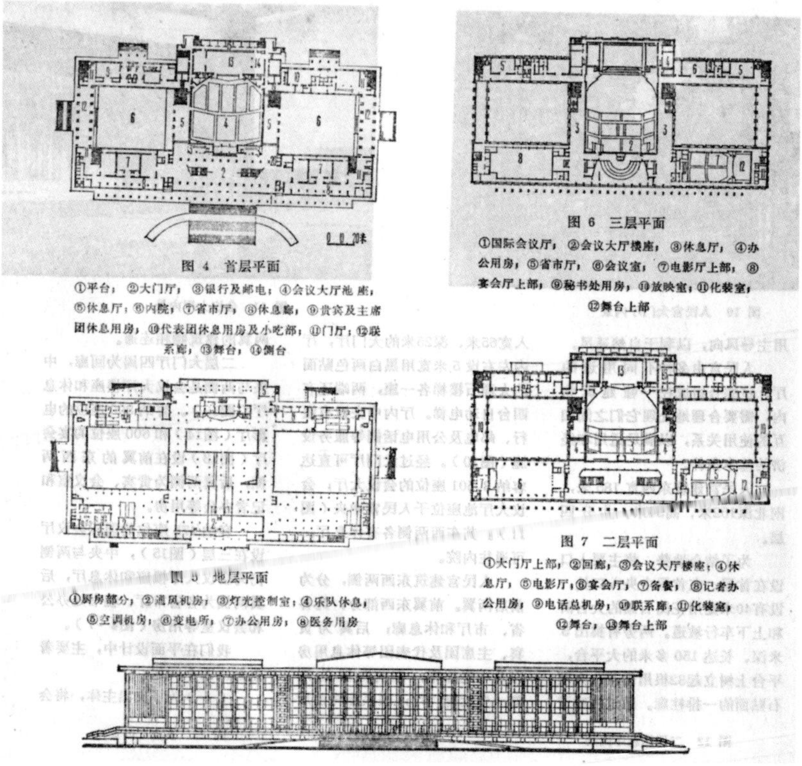

Fig. 79 First floor plan, People's Palace, Zhu Shanquan, Lin Kaiwu, and Qi Zhenya, Beijing Institute of Architectural Design, Kinshasa, Zaire, 1979. Originally published in *Architectural Journal* (*Jianzhu Xuebao*), no. 2 (1980).

a space for live performances. Theater, oration, and dancing were important components of Zaire's invented nationalism; public performances often involved elaborate costumes, singing, and demonstrative celebrations of Mobutu's sacrifices to the state, making the new space a useful venue in the campaign. The building also featured a 475-seat meeting hall with international standard sound equipment, rehearsal rooms, and administrative space. These amenities aimed to accommodate the country's own diplomatic ambitions and underscored the sophistication of China's growing design expertise. Project architects understood that not all of the palace's spaces would be active at once, and they worked to ensure each room had a certain degree of flexibility based on a variety of potential uses.

Climatic sensitivity was another documented concern of the complex's architects, who designed various sunshades, ventilation openings, and rain guards to protect visitors from weather. At the same time, the building's basic formal geometry and massive structural elements echoed the new forms of applied design knowledge emerging through China's recently completed Beijing Hotel and diplomatic residential compound. These features were indicative of the CCP's dovetailing desires to improve its diplomatic infrastructure at home and burnish its own international standing through participating in Africa's development. They also spoke to the conflicted politics underlying Zaire's own nation-building project and China's willingness to accommodate them.

In theory, China's architectural involvement in Kinshasa contradicted Mobutu's calls for Zairians to return to their roots and reject imported ideologies, though there's little evidence to indicate that Mobutu considered these exhortations relevant or necessarily applicable to architecture.[7] Regardless, China's unique geopolitical position and history of oppression at the hands of the West rendered its architectural contributions to Kinshasa's urban environment exempt from such treatment. The building anchored an ambitious Chinese-authored urban plan to redesign the center of Kinshasa through a series of new public monuments, including a telecommunications tower, various government offices, and a new sports stadium, which was eventually completed in 1993. China's efforts to provide Zaire with new public edifices shaped by local specificities and possessive of a certain international visibility embodied China's ideology of shared Third World self-determination, which remained a source of inspiration to Mobutu and resonated with China's own belabored attempts to produce the same kind of architectural expression back home.

As construction began in November 1975, however, political circumstances both in Zaire and China began to shift in ways that threatened to disrupt the architectural and political cooperation taking place. Earlier that June, for example, Mobutu expelled the U.S. ambassador to Zaire and accused the CIA of supporting a coup attempt against him. In November, Zairian troops invaded Angola at the behest of the CIA, a contradiction of Third World solidarity that discredited Mobutu's efforts to craft Zaire's image around anti-colonialism and African autonomy, and risked weakening China's international status in the region. Chinese leaders aggressively and publicly supported Mobutu, which some saw as evidence of a new Chinese diplomatic strategy with respect to Africa, though at least one foreign observer saw the PRC's steadfast support for Zaire as a sign of "weakness and frustration" that it did not have more geopolitical sway to counter the unpredictable course of events. Over the course of late 1976 and 1977, meanwhile, Zairian leaders watched with curiosity as China embarked upon its own convoluted process of "*démaotisation*" through further engagement with capitalist countries such as the United States and Japan and a gradual distancing from historical socialist allies.[8]

Despite each country's uncertain ideological realignment, however, Zairian and Chinese leaders publicly expressed loyalty to the other through visible performances of diplomatic commitment such as medical exchanges, agricultural initiatives, and the construction of the People's Palace, which upon its completion was trumpeted as marking "a symbol of Sino-Zairese cooperation." At the building's inauguration, held on May 19, 1979, Mobutu and Li Qingchao, the vice minister in charge of construction, lauded the building as a harbinger of current and future cooperation. The monument's showy opening also coincided with the twelfth anniversary of the Popular Movement of the Revolution, Mobutu's ruling party and the only de facto political organization in the country, thus

Fig. 80 Bandundu Room, People's Palace, Zhu Shanquan, Lin Kaiwu, and Qi Zhenya, Beijing Institute of Architectural Design, Kinshasa, Zaire, 1979. Originally published in *Elima,* May 20, 1979.

honoring both Mobutu's stewardship and China's patronage. Symbolically, the project satisfied the demands placed upon it by both parties. All of the equipment and building materials used in the edifice's construction were imported from the PRC—an unusual condition given Mobutu's campaign and the fact that China's technological standing remained on par with, if not poorer than, several of the countries with which it was architecturally engaged. Nevertheless, such a gesture satisfied the domestic narrative promoted by CCP leaders that the country remained a technologically advanced benefactor to the developing world. From the perspective of Zairian officials, the inclusion of decorative detailing, including Zairian masks, furniture, and woodwork, both localized the Chinese technology on display and reinforced national discourses on authenticity and Zaire's natural and cultural abundance (fig. 80). These aesthetic gestures reverberated with China's own post-Mao search for an appropriate national architectural style, its own experimentation with architectural heritage, and its early interest in postmodernism, even as it also seemed to embody the successful pursuit of a mutually collaborative modernization.[9]

Other Chinese projects completed over roughly the same period proved similarly productive. Plans for a Cameroonian cultural center and legislative congress building initiated in 1973 but completed in 1981, for example, were intended to provide Cameroon with a unique architectural expression of its cultural identity, and a facility through which both cultural and political activity could take place in the name of a revalorized "national culture."[10] Rhetorically, Chinese and Cameroonian officials also justified such work as evidence of the same shared benefit and mutual empowerment honed through China's earlier, Mao-era architectural design work such as Guinea's People's Palace or the TAZARA Railway, for example. At the same time, studying a country's local conditions and attempting to produce an architecture suitable to that place provided lessons into specific operational and representational challenges—how to accommodate context, for example, and how to capture identity through physical form—at a time in which China was beginning to test the rhetorical and semiotic parameters of its own expanded economic and political activity.

Procedurally, however, these buildings raised questions regarding China's design influence over other parts of the world. China's international commissions were initially assigned or won by specific design institutes in national competitions, at which point teams of Chinese architects and engineers traveled to the country in question to better understand the site and working conditions. They then returned to China to complete preliminary design schemes, which were shared with their African partners and relevant representatives. Suggested revisions were made, but final design decisions lay with Chinese technicians. Following the design process, Chinese foremen and materials were sent to the country to begin construction. Chinese technicians supervised the project's realization, which was largely built of Chinese building materials. In the Cameroon Cultural Center, for example, Cameroonian wood was used only as a surfacing material for walls, the ceilings of specified meeting rooms and offices, and doors and windows, while each of the complex's six thousand pieces of furniture, including chairs, tables, and armchairs, were made in China.[11]

Comprehensive Chinese oversight had certain benefits for China and its partners. It provided a tested management standard that promised efficiency and economy. The provisions of Chinese design knowledge and materials promoted and developed Chinese industry while ensuring African clients were not burdened with unrealistic responsibilities. Yet such mechanics clearly privileged Chinese expertise over the architectural skills available in each country. Despite the official emphasis on the collective nature of each building's making, these were projects that depended upon Chinese expertise, and they signaled the growing influence of Chinese involvement in African economic and political development and cultural expression. They also benefited China's architects and the country's design industry in ways that extended beyond the diplomacy or economics involved in each individual project's realization to produce a broader international framework of Chinese design and construction services.

INTENSIFIED ARCHITECTURAL AMBITIONS

The early 1980s marked a consequential turning point in China's international architectural profile. Chinese supervisors were gradually withdrawn from Mao-era endeavors such as the TAZARA Railway, which had begun to deteriorate due to environmental conditions, physical weaknesses with Chinese-built equipment, performance limitations, and management problems left to local agents who often lacked resources and materials to properly complete repairs. These factors resulted in part from dependencies not only on Chinese financing, but upon Chinese materials, equipment, and technical knowledge.[12] Over roughly the same period of time, however, China gained access to new forms of international capital and financing, which in turn led to new opportunities in design and development around the world. In 1980, for example, China joined the World Bank, followed by the African Development Bank and Fund in 1985, and the Asian Development Bank in 1986. Between 1981 and 1985, contracts between China and foreign countries increased by 60 percent per year on average. By 1985 China was handling 1,600 new contracts with eighty-five countries valued at $4.2 billion USD.[13]

Through these shifts, the nature and scale of China's technical assistance abroad began to change as well. More state-run businesses were encouraged to seek work abroad, resulting in the growth of international contracts held by Chinese construction entities for a range of construction projects, including joint ventures. By the end of 1985, over twenty-seven thousand Chinese experts and workers were engaged in labor service contracts abroad earning China $900 million USD in convertible currency, along with more than thirty-one thousand Chinese workers and technicians involved in foreign contracting businesses. One hundred and eighty-one joint ventures or Chinese-financed enterprises existed in Hong Kong, Macau, and forty-three other countries.[14]

The party's own shifting diplomatic and economic interests transformed its relationship not only to Africa, but to the United States and the Soviet Union, particularly regarding contentious topics such as Taiwan and nuclear proliferation. Maintaining China's diplomatic independence from either of the world's two superpowers, at a time in which its own international profile had begun to take on new proportions, was key. Beginning in 1982, party officials increased their denunciations of U.S. and Soviet policy concerning the so-called Third World in an effort to burnish China's reputation as a developing country committed to anti-imperialism and the defeat of global hegemony. In December of that same year, Premier Zhao Ziyang embarked upon a tour of eleven African countries, including Egypt, Algeria, Morocco, Guinea, Zaire, Congo, Gabon, Zambia, Zimbabwe, Tanzania, and Kenya. It was the first high-ranking Chinese delegation to the continent since Zhou Enlai's visit in 1963, and it marked a consequential, transitional phase in China's international affairs.

Zhao's trip aimed to reassure China's African diplomatic partners that it would continue to support its preexisting friendships, even as these new economic developments continued to reconfigure its international profile. Throughout his month-long tour, Zhao insisted that China considered itself part of the so-called Third World and committed to continued cooperation with its African brothers and sisters based upon mutual respect for sovereignty and noninterference in internal affairs, "with no strings attached."[15] China's financial assistance was also framed as evidence of "cooperation" rather than aid. As in the past, such rhetoric also helped to imbue its architectural ambitions with a certain humility that appealed to the leaders of developing nations eager to limit their dependence upon U.S. and Soviet aid, technology, and expertise.

Throughout Zhao's tour, physical evidence of China's architectural efforts abroad helped to showcase and reinforce claims of its mutually beneficial noninterventionism. In Conakry, the premier laid a wreath at the Monument of November 22, 1970, which was designed and built by Chinese engineers in 1971 to commemorate the deaths of over three hundred Guineans by invading Portuguese and Portuguese-trained Guinean soldiers in an attempted coup on November 22, 1970. Zhao and President Touré also held two days of talks at the People's Palace. In Zaire, meetings between the premier, State Councilor Gu Mu, Foreign Minister Wu Xueqian, and Mobutu were held in the recently completed People's Palace. During Premier Zhao's visit to the Republic of Congo, the country's *Mweti* newspaper trumpeted a massive hydroelectric power station completed in 1979 in partnership with Chinese technicians as "the greatest example of Congolese-Chinese cooperation."[16] Zhao also visited sections of the TAZARA Railway in both Tanzania and Zambia.

In Kenya, Zhao promised funding to continue the construction of an Olympic-standard sports facility capable of hosting the fourth All-Africa Games, which Kenyan President Daniel arap Moi secured in 1979. Plans for a national stadium in Nairobi, the country's capital and largest city, dated back to 1964, and a site was identified, but plans never materialized due to a lack of resources. In 1978, following Kenya's hosting of the second Federation of African University Sports Union games at Nairobi City Stadium, debate resurfaced over Kenya's need for a "more modern stadium."[17] A new site was selected, and Kenyan officials received an offer from the Chinese government to build a new stadium. In September 1980, Moi traveled to Beijing with the intention of securing funding for a new national sports complex through an interest-free soft loan. The Southeast University Institute of Architectural Design, under the leadership of Zhou Fangzhong, won the design commission for the complex, which was sited fifteen kilometers from Nairobi (figs. 81, 82).

That December, architect Xu Shangzhi and other project members traveled to Nairobi to study the site. Kenyan officials were purportedly skeptical concerning the quality of China's design work in Africa and requested their own architects, while the Chinese government representatives insisted the project would have to be designed by Chinese architects. In the end, the Chinese government persevered, and Xu and his team purportedly spent seven months in Kenya.[18] The project included a sixty-thousand-seat outdoor stadium, a five-thousand-seat indoor gymnasium consisting of one international standard swimming pool designed to meet international and Olympic standards, warming-up and children's

Fig. 81 National Sports Complex, Southeast University Institute of Architectural Design, Nairobi, 1987. Originally published in *Architectural Journal* (*Jianzhu Xuebao*), no. 11 (1985).

Fig. 82 Indoor gymnasium, Zhou Fangzhong, Southeast University Institute of Architectural Design, Nairobi, 1987. Originally published in *Architectural Journal* (*Jianzhu Xuebao*), no. 11 (1985).

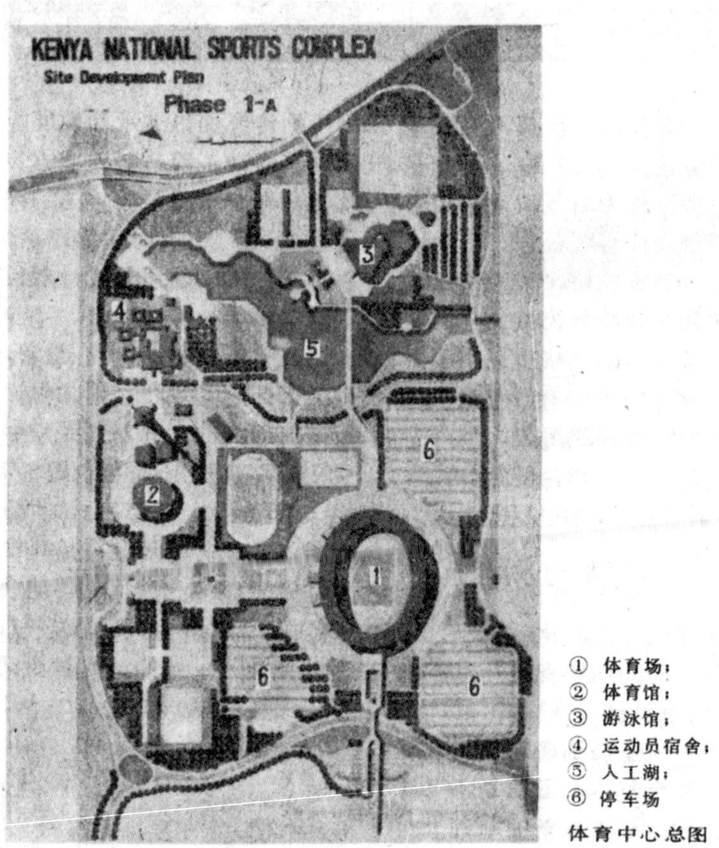

pools, a Tartan track, athletes' housing, and a football field. Ancillary services to be provided included a railway line linking the venue to Nairobi and access roads and a proposed shopping center and supermarket. More than simply a venue for recreation, the scheme was celebrated as a "shining example of President Moi's concern for Kenya's sportsmen and women and a living monument for those departed great sportsmen."[19] Construction began in 1982.

For those Chinese designers engaged in the project, the commission was a unique opportunity to engage with a foreign locale—an experience reflected in some of the project's notable aesthetic and formal features, including both the outdoor stadium and indoor gymnasium's striking cantilevered stands, the addition of abstracted mask relief sculptures above the main stadium, and the exposure of structural elements in the athletes' hostel.[20] Despite each country's lofty goals for the project, however, the design and construction process proved a financial and procedural ordeal. Throughout the surveying and design process, the Kenyan press reported "sharp" differences between Kenyan and Chinese technicians, though an amenable formula was eventually established.[21] As with the majority of China's other architectural work in Africa, the details of all building and construction work were prepared in China and later sent to Nairobi for Kenyan experts to approve or alter where necessary, subject to the approval of the original Chinese designers. Construction was initially expected to take thirty-six months, though an attempted coup and financial difficulties led to a postponement of the project and the games themselves.

By the end of 1984, the Moi regime had reconsolidated power, and initial collaboration between two hundred Chinese and three hundred Kenyan workers had produced a "beehive of masonry."[22] Questions concerning the project's completion lingered, however; in 1985 Kenya decided to renege on its hosting responsibilities due to a lack of funds before recommitting itself to the endeavor. Over the course of construction, Chinese officials also pursued other investment opportunities in Kenya. In January 1987, for example, a delegation traveled to Mombasa and expressed interest in expanding China's trade with the port. That April, a proposal was discussed to open an electronic assembly factory in Mombasa in coordination with a Chinese investor partnership known as the Ken-Shen Electronic Group.[23]

The stadium was eventually completed in April 1987 and hosted the opening of the games in August. Originally identified as the Kasarani Sports Complex, it was renamed the Moi International Sports Centre in honor of Kenya's president just prior to the start of the games. The African Games, then the largest organized sporting event in the history of the continent, had required "bold leadership and a bold nation," and Kenya's president had delivered. The country's ambitions had also been made possible by the stadium itself, which upon its completion had immediately become Kenya's most prestigious sports venue, akin to "what Wembley is to England or Maracana to Brazil." China's role in the complex's realization was understated, though the Kenyan press did commend the complex as "the most ambitious project ever carried out by the Chinese outside the Great Wall of China itself."[24] Such hyperbole underscores the ways in which the stadium operated not merely as a facility for sports, but as a vessel for a new kind of international development narrative—one in which two developing nations had helped each other to reach specific state goals.

Notably, the project was described in the press as an "ultra-modern" sports complex—the same term coincidently used to describe China's Qijiayuan diplomatic residential compound upon its completion in Beijing more than one decade earlier.[25] In both cases, the notion of an ultramodernity seemed designed to evoke a successful transcendence of previous standards of architectural modernity despite the obstacles posed by factors such as historical oppression, economic underdevelopment, and technical constraints. The ultramodern nature of Beijing's diplomatic projects, for example, spoke to structural and scalar qualities above and beyond Mao-era socialist design, while the Moi Sports Centre was understood to have surpassed existing iterations of modern architecture in Kenya originating in its colonial past.

To have advanced beyond these existing modernities confirmed the stadium's fulfillment of a set of national goals uniquely suited to architectural production—the organization of a country around a specific event, at a determined time and place. Other aspects of the stadium's ultramodernism seemed to derive from the project's unprecedented form and ambitious scale relative to its Kenyan context, its contemporary building materials, and the coordinated Sino-Kenyan participation involved in its production. The logistical complexity of such an endeavor had historically eluded Kenya, and its completion established for Kenya a long-sought reputation as a reliable host of complex events of a high international standard, including the Olympics.

More generally, the project's complex, international production links it to the decolonized African milieu and the "*mondialisation*" that had begun to take place in relation to socialist design work throughout the continent over the course of the 1960s and 1970s.[26] The Kenyan press contrasted the quality of the stadium's construction to other commissioned projects associated with the games, including a scoreboard designed by a Hungarian firm and the Nyayo National Stadium's poorly designed basketball gymnasium.[27] As a kind of architectural talisman, the stadium seemed capable of transcending national boundaries to facilitate any number of possible, future continental dreams for Kenya and China alike. It had "restor[ed] Africa's pride," and in so doing, had finally delivered the kind of universalism long espoused as part of the modernist project. Such lofty goals remained dependent upon China's ability to support the facility with technicians and materials, however. "The future is bright if these wonderful facilities are put to good use and kept in a good state of repair," opined Kenya's *Standard.* "Building them is one thing—in fact the easy thing—maintaining them is another matter altogether."[28] The project may have helped to distance Kenya from its own colonial history while countering its own domestic shortcomings and lingering dependence upon foreign expertise, but the country remained bound to a new kind of design knowledge originating from another distant locale.

FROM ULTRAMODERN TO POSTMODERN

In 1986 the architect Gao Shiling published an article in *Architectural Journal* (*Jianzhu Xuebao*) titled "A Style All One's Own: Africa's Tourist Architecture." Gao's review concerned a trip she had made to Tanzania with an unnamed Chinese delegation in early 1983, and featured descriptive aesthetic and spatial analysis of hotels, inns, and lodges visited within several of the country's natural game preserves and beaches. Gao was struck by the way in which these accommodations, each designed by architects from different countries and employing various sets of building and decorative techniques, somehow captured characteristics specific to the place in which they were built. The design of the lodge at the Lobo Wildlife Reserve, for example, offered what Gao considered to be an ingenious adaptation to the site's topography and local limestone that encouraged visitors to walk back and forth between the hillside and the green fields below. At Lake Manyara, Gao encountered accommodations composed of several low-rise wings of guest rooms and restaurant and bar facilities, each arranged in a kind of "picturesque disorder." Bahari Beach, located some twenty-five kilometers from Dar es Salaam, featured an array of hotels, inns, and hostels, including beachside bungalows catering specifically to young people; several of these creatively incorporated the localized aesthetic of the thatched roof. One hotel's extended entranceway resembled an elephant's trunk—an inspired act of "eye-catching" symbolism that, to Gao, also resonated with the identity of the place. In particular, reasoned Gao, China's young architects needed to "take risks, boldly innovate, and fuse together architecture, culture, art, and nature."[29]

Gao's article communicated a romantic fascination with Tanzanian architecture that testified to the extractive value of China's architectural engagement with African countries for many Chinese designers, few of whom had extensive international experience. The localized aesthetics perceived by Chinese visitors seemed to offer a means by which architects could reimagine China's own tourism-related infrastructure back home. Even as party leaders continued to tout the humility at the core of China's contributions to Africa's own economic development, however, certain imbalances had begun to emerge in relation to architectural knowledge exchange that risked destabilizing China's diplomatic ties throughout the continent. African students sent to China to study architecture, for example, often struggled to see in China's cities and imposing monuments architectural and urban models to be followed. Oussouby Sacko, for instance, arrived in Beijing in 1985 from Mali on a government scholarship to study architecture in China. Following a year spent in Beijing immersed in language training, he moved to Nanjing, where he earned a bachelor's degree in architecture from Southeast University in 1990.

Sacko recounted the impressive scale of Beijing's massive public façades and the amenities offered by the Great Wall, Jianguo, and Jinling hotels, which provided foreign students with much-appreciated recreational escape; I. M. Pei's recently completed Fragrant Hill Hotel also left an impression. In general, however, China's architectural messaging seemed difficult to discern, particularly as Southeast University professors promoted the value of architectural heritage within the classroom and yet produced, outside of class, big-roof structures seemingly at odds with the country's rich architectural history. Racism and the overbearing presence of Chinese security also influenced his perceptions of the country and its built environment. Claims of ultramodernity in China's African ventures notwithstanding, for Sacko and his foreign classmates, it was not China that offered a fulfilling, paradigmatic modernity, but Hong Kong.[30]

Tension among African and Chinese students in China was indeed an ever-present concern that increasingly affected the nature of China's engagements with African countries over the course of the 1980s, particularly as the number of African students traveling to China grew. A series of verbal and physical attacks against African students by Chinese students in Tianjin and Beijing in late 1985 and 1986, for example, prompted the Chinese government to redouble its efforts to court African partners. In January 1987, three hundred African students defied authorities and marched through Beijing to protest what they believed to be racist treatment in China. The group marched from the Beijing Foreign Language Institute to meet with the ambassador of Morocco, who also served as the dean of the African diplomatic corps. There, the students demanded that they be allowed to go home following the publication of a letter accusing African students of harassing Chinese girls and demonstrating manners "acquired by life in tropical forests." The letter also demanded that China stop funding the whole of "uncultural" Africa. The Chinese Foreign Ministry declared the letter to be a fraud, while an official at the State Education Commission explained the letter was written by "bad people who wanted to destroy good relations between the Chinese and African people." Other reports surfaced of a Sudanese student being attacked by a group of Chinese people in a Beijing hotel after he danced with a Chinese girl.[31] Two years later, in January 1989, a series of violent clashes between African and Chinese students in Nanjing quickly spread to other cities in China.[32]

On July 1, 1985, China and Ghana commemorated the twenty-fifth anniversary of diplomatic relations. In commemoration of their shared diplomatic history, the two countries reached an agreement to replace the city's playhouse with a national arts theater complex that was to be Chinese-designed, -financed, and constructed. Ghana was one of China's oldest diplomatic partnerships in Africa, and though the relationship had languished following a military coup that overthrew President Kwame Nkrumah in February 1966, its revitalization signaled China's growing influence within the continent. The agreement was reached as party officials struggled to convince African allies of the safety and comfort of their citizenry in China, and in 1988 a team of Chinese experts led by Chen Yiming of the Central Conservatory of Music and Professor Zhang Shiqun of the Central Academy of Fine Arts traveled to Accra to study the site and proposal. A cultural pact was subsequently signed between the two countries that July.[33] Plans for the theater were quickly completed by the Hangzhou Institute of Architectural Design (HIAD) and submitted in February 1989 to the Ghanaian embassy in Beijing. Soon after, however, the violent suppression of nationwide public protests beginning June 4 against the growing inequities taking place in reform-era China risked threatening the project. Nevertheless, a pact to realize the theater was finally signed in July, in recognition of Ghana's unwavering support for China during this time of crisis, and at last enabling the building's realization.[34]

The initial design for the new National Theatre, overseen by chief architect Cheng Taining of HIAD, consisted of three triangular wedges of theater and studio space positioned atop a large podium. This scheme, however, was to be substantially revised, following the Ghanaian government's rejection of it for its overly conservative appearance, and Cheng subsequently committed himself instead to translating the "exaggerated, mystical, and uninhibited qualities of African art" into architectural form, resulting in the curved contours of the final scheme.[35] Although also intended as a new and more liberated form of modern architectural expression, forged through Chinese and Ghanaian cooperation, Cheng's building instead offered an architectural interpretation of "African-ness" based on a set of stereotypes that merely exoticized African cultural expression.

As the main new center for the nation's theater, dance, and performance arts, the building accommodated a 1,500-seat theater and two secondary triangular masses providing additional rehearsal studios (figs. 83, 84). Around these spaces were located practice, dressing, and makeup rooms, as well as supporting office and circulation space. The complex also included a public square and fountain, and a Chinese garden discreetly wedged into a corner next to a VIP room intended for political and cultural emissaries. The mahogany-stained interiors, decorated with examples of contemporary African art, provided ample space for various other public activities, including book launches, commercial promotions, and fashion shows. Externally, the complex's hulking, white-tiled mass jutted out over a granite-faced plinth onto one of Accra's busiest intersections, projecting a formal dynamism that Cheng believed would embody the cultural activities supported by the building while dramatically distinguishing itself from any of Accra's Cold War–era constructions. To accommodate the massive size of this all-purpose cultural center, the city's preexisting drama studio, an open-air amphitheater built in 1961 under the Nkrumah regime (with U.S. funding from the Sloan, Ford, and Rockefeller foundations) was demolished—despite its political and cultural significance as the location of many of the country's first decolonized theater, musical, and dance productions. The construction of a replica of this original theater, by Chinese engineers on the University of Ghana's campus to the north of the city, signified Ghana's acquiescence to China's narrative of mutual and non-Western empowerment.

The new building's construction process also illuminated the extent to which hierarchies at work in China's international architectural production had become fraught with cross-cultural complexities as they worked to accommodate their own sets of architectural and engineering practices within a foreign context. As previously discussed, China sought to distinguish its international influence from any other international aid provider by emphasizing the equitable cooperative nature of the construction process itself. The building's realization, which was launched in June 1990, was spearheaded by a Chinese construction firm, China National Complete Plant Import and Export Corporation. The initial workforce of 520, comprising four hundred Ghanaians and 120 Chinese, shifted over time to 470 Ghanaian laborers under the supervision of eighty-three Chinese foremen.[36] A range of Chinese procedures and techniques were also adopted in an effort to realize the project quickly and efficiently. The Chinese foremen were assigned to the site for spells of time ranging from six months to one year, after which they were sent either to another project in a different country or back to China. They directed teams of Ghanaian laborers in carefully regulated work shifts operating seven days a week and resided in makeshift accommodation constructed across the street from the construction site, where daily whistles registered the workday's start and end as well as lunch breaks. Chinese leaders felt these frameworks would help structure foreign labor in productive ways, suggesting the possibility of broader reconfiguration within Ghanaian society through Chinese cooperation. In keeping with China's Mao-era system of commodity exchange, almost all the building's materials, including cement, marble, granite, wood, and tile facing, originated from China.

Following its completion on December 20, 1992, the theater was trumpeted as marking the first national, "ultra-modern" theater of its kind in all of West Africa, with an "imposing and magnificent" form that would serve as "a lasting monument of Ghana/China friendship and solidarity."[37] Like the Moi International Sports Centre, the National Theatre's ultramodernism was intended to suggest the dawning of a new era in Ghanaian architecture's development distinct from that of the country's previous and pseudo-modern colonial past. As in the sports complex in Kenya, the discursive parameters of such "ultramodern" architecture seemed to derive from the international yet nonaligned nature of the project and its potential for national empowerment. The opening fes-

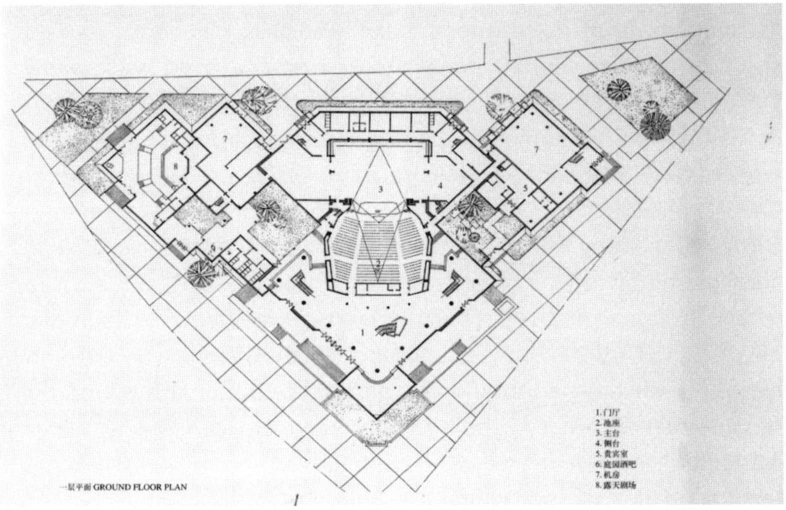

Fig. 83 National Theatre, Cheng Taining, Hangzhou Institute of Architectural Design, Accra, Ghana, 1992.

Fig. 84 Ground floor plan, National Theatre, Cheng Taining, Hangzhou Institute of Architectural Design, Accra, Ghana, 1992. Originally published in *Selected Works of China's 100 First-Class Registered Architects* (*Zhongguo baiming yiji zhuce jianzhushi zuopin xuan,* 1998).

tivities included the launching of a Chinese art exhibition and a joint performance by the Ghana Dance Ensemble, Abibigroma, the National Symphony Orchestra, and the Pan African Orchestra. The National Theatre's opening also signaled the launch of a nationwide theater construction initiative, the aims and objectives of which were to be centered on the promotion and development of the performing arts. Notably, however, the building's opening ceremony did not feature China's ambassador to Ghana, but instead included Mr. Song Luyan, China's vice minister for Machine Building and Electronics Industry, who symbolically handed over the theater's keys. The gesture by China revealed the larger industrial implications at work through the project.

The theater's conception, design, and construction also spanned a period of growing public debate in Ghana over the possibility of Africa's recolonization and the extent to which Ghanaian architecture should more accurately reflect the nation's culture. This is seen, for example, in a speech delivered in June 1986 by Dr. Kofi Sam, secretary for Works and Housing, urging the country's civil engineers to design buildings that "reflected reality" and took into consideration local conditions and indigenous raw materials. The risks posed by Africa's "economic colonialism" were also highlighted in an article in the *Ghanaian Times,* while another urged Africa to bolster its "self-reliance" and dismantle all colonial structures still present in many of its country's societies, and to work toward restoring "cultural identity" and respecting "cultural values" by moving away from popular forms of cultural expression such as drumming and dancing. In fact, a cultural awareness drive was subsequently launched in August 1989 in an attempt to "reawaken the cultural consciousness of the Ghanaian people" and "resuscitate and revive one's way of life." Other newspaper editorials urged Africa's resistance to foreign developmental models and the importation of technological hardware.[38]

Oddly, the National Theatre project evaded all such public criticism. Its omission from these public debates implies a lingering exceptionalism afforded to China's nonaligned patronage, even while exposing the ideological inconsistencies at work in Ghana's drive toward self-modernization. The project's exclusive Chinese garden remained a space for VIPS, and likely inaccessible to most residents. More significantly, Cheng's justification of his building's form through aforementioned clichés concerning Africa's forms of cultural expression as "exaggerated" and "un-inhibited" may have satisfied Ghana's leaders, but such rationales also revealed Cheng's, and by extension the Chinese government's, physical and epistemological distance from Ghanaian reality. Cheng himself never traveled to Africa as part of the National Theatre's design or construction process and so never engaged with Ghanaian culture firsthand.[39] Instead, he relied on a small team of engineers who spent time examining the site conditions before reporting back to Hangzhou. His generalizations echoed colonial-era descriptions of African cultural production, and were offered by Cheng in Chinese-language descriptions of the project as rationale for the swollen physical contours of the building itself. As a result, Ghanaian officials likely did not know about Cheng's comments. Regardless, the possibility of China's subjective reappraisal of their country's architectural history and culture did not publicly register as a major concern.

Following the building's completion, in fact, Ghanaian architect and politician Don Arthur of the Provisional National Defense Council Secretariat thanked China's engineers for inculcating a "Chinese work culture" in those Ghanaians who assisted in the construction.[40] This was despite the fact that few Chinese foremen could speak English upon their arrival in Accra, leaving both them and Ghanaian workers with little choice but to rely on a system of drawn instructions, coupled with miming, to convey what was required. Chinese supervisors would eventually learn to communicate in English, but few stayed in Ghana long enough to capitalize on this. Those Ghanaian workers deemed especially diligent and dedicated were subsequently selected by their Chinese foremen to become members of its management and maintenance crew, but they still lacked fundamental knowledge about the building's construction. Thus, when an earthquake damaged the theater in 2005, thirteen years after its completion, it was Chinese engineers who undertook the repairs rather than entrusting the work to a local firm. Ghanaian architects had no choice but to acquiesce, since all of the documentation of the building's construction was written in Chinese.[41]

REFORM, CHINA, AND THE WORLD

Chinese-designed and -constructed architectural and engineering projects produced in Africa did not in themselves evince some neocolonial or imperialistic impulse. With their emphasis on mutual empowerment, shared sacrifice, and technological exchange, these works fulfilled numerous national and continental objectives, and in so doing, may be understood as a departure from other forms of foreign-derived architectural production taking place there. Nevertheless, they also represented a new strain of international architecture, dependent upon a distinct set of economic and ideological determinants, that remain imbued with the same kinds of coercive disparities and imbalances that were endemic to the modernist project. In this respect, they did more than provide modern facilities to numerous African nations eager to be considered part of the modern world order. They helped China to modernize itself and broadened the country's existing Mao-era experience concerning what it meant to participate in another country's modernization. In so doing, this work formed part of a distinctly Chinese effort at "world-making" through architecture, that is, sets of practices, knowledge, and experience capable of entwining China's own political and economic system within those present in other parts of the world.[42]

Understanding the internationalization of Chinese architecture during the 1980s as a process of exportation as much as one of importation is essential to the history of Reform and Opening Up and challenges the notion that China's liberalization was a passive acceptance of foreign architectural practices, theories, and norms in the name of progress. Reform-era architecture involved a complex interplay of design methods, discursive positions, and production standards that circulated in and out of China, helping to better integrate the country and its architectural production to the world at large. Accounting for this process also reveals connections to the subsequent rise of a so-called China Model for modernization that has become prevalent in analysis of China's foreign policy today.

The exportation of Chinese architecture to Africa during reform illuminates a new, transformative vector in global architectural culture and the basis for what is currently understood as the China Model: one that eschews traditional, Euro-American design knowledge in favor of mutually empowering, collaborative paradigms for development revolving around generous financial arrangements and Chinese expertise. It was the exchange of design and building knowledge and technology that initially offered China an important purchase from which it could participate both in the global economy and in international architectural discourse. It was architecture's representational qualities and its methods of production that allowed China to transmute its diplomatic and economic exchanges into real projects that demonstrated idealistic objectives, while enhancing and internationalizing China's political and economic influence. Through these links, Chinese leaders were able to observe processes of economic liberalization taking shape in other contexts. It was also through such connections that the party attempted to render the abnormalities of their own country's economic liberalization normative both at home and abroad.

The history of these projects problematizes the stubborn notions of center and periphery that persist in our framing and understanding of architecture's diffusion around the postwar, globalized world. Architecture recasts China's engagement with African countries in aesthetic, material, programmatic, scalar, typological, and spatial terms that reveal the conceptual design and physical construction of China's liberalization to be much more than a domestic phenomenon, but rather the formation of a new center toward which the world increasingly turns. Over time, and in large part accelerated by its own embrace of market-oriented economic policy, China's relationship with countries such as Zaire, Kenya, Ghana, and others accelerated a reorientation of African economic and architectural activity toward the PRC that precipitated a broader international shift toward Chinese architectural design and construction. China's reservoir of expertise concerning African architectural design and procedure represented a form of world-making that spanned the late Mao and early reform eras, gradually taking on definition and greater geopolitical significance over the course of the 1990s and early 2000s until today.

This process began prior to the official launching of China's reform, but reform was essential to its development, particularly as China used architecture to shape and refine its new economic reality both at home and abroad. Eventually, such work developed into a Sinocentric, state-subsidized, epistemological system through which technological expertise and economic leverage could be deployed for China's measurable geopolitical gain. Architecture was an important and enabling technology in this process, but it also had influential cultural effects on questions of identity, nation-building, and representation. China's reform-era international architectural production allowed China's designers and the institutes that supported them to experiment with different forms of architectural expression, reimagine their position in the world, and, by extension, reconsider China's role as a source of international architectural expertise. Through acts of design and construction, Chinese architects enacted a new kind of Chinese architectural influence that has spread throughout much of the developing world, and remains characterized by processes of exchange and principles of difference yet bound by reiterative, Mao-era expressions of mutual benefit and shared progress. The buildings produced remain testaments to the new dynamics of architectural production still transforming the world today.

CONCLUSION

Reform and Beyond

In the introduction, and again in Chapters 1 and 6, I highlighted the Beijing Hotel's east addition to show how the building was deployed to reconcile the competing interests at work in the CCP prior to 1978, even as it rendered visible these pressures to a populace unwittingly entangled in a political struggle over China's future. After 1978, following the assertion of Deng Xiaoping's authority over the party, the Beijing Hotel remained an important site for the exchange of ideas and capital, and a symbol of China's opening up to the world. It was one of numerous projects that contributed to the reordering of Chinese society. Buildings like the Beijing Hotel helped the government induce and manage the daunting exercise of reform, even as they also ushered in relationships, knowledge, materials, objects, and atmospheres that threatened the party's control over the process.

Reform may have been a politically sensitive proposition, but as the various buildings, discourses, and practices included in this book suggest, it was, above all, an act of unprecedented creativity. In the rush to debate, experiment, and speculate that characterized the era and its architectural production, vital new ideas about architecture and urbanism took shape within China—ideas that, in turn, gave rise to new contours of public life. Prior to reform, architecture was understood first and foremost as an industrial exercise in collectivity—collective design, collective construction, and collective inhabitation. By the end of the 1980s, it had become an increasingly individualistic pursuit and experience. For a government so dependent upon the appearance of control over its self-image, its territorial sovereignty, its population, and information, among many other examples, the unleashing of these energies was destabilizing but also rejuvenating.

Acknowledging architecture's significance to late and post-Mao China—and the acts of design and construction that composed it—focuses attention on its many links to the politics, economics, and cultural production of the reform era. Assembled together within these previous chapters, architecture's disparate and varied contributions to reimagining China's reality capture both the top-down policy-making at work and bottom-up, everyday experiences involved in change—the drawing and the building of reform. In assessing party policies and principles of action through the production of a concrete wall, or the reorganization of a design office, this book has also illuminated what systemic economic, political, and social transformation entails in relation to the physical environment and, by extension, people's lives. Architecture was expected to facilitate the various forces propelling reform forward, even as the government simultaneously relied on architecture to control public access to reform's benefits. Architecture provided the party with its desired teleology, but it also broadened the public's access to subjectivities of meaning and disrupted established forms of political expression, all of which upset major sources of the party's power.

Few, if any, of the early reform era's most defining images feature an iconic architectural edifice—an indication of the problematic aesthetic judgments and political sensitivities that continue to define the era today. As this study has made clear, however, architecture's historical value to reform does not lie merely in questions of style or appearance, but rather in the broader economic, political, and social circumstances architecture anticipated and reified over time. Much of the architecture designed and built in the name of reform remains, though the distinctive milieu within which the work originated has long since passed. In their endurance, they remind us of the bewilderment, uncertainty, and excitement that coursed through China after Mao, the unprecedented economic, social, and cultural changes that occurred, and the era's transformative importance to Chinese society and the world.

Such persistence, despite changes in political leadership, ideological orientations, and public sentiment, also testifies to architecture's value as history, particularly with respect to the shifting global dynamics of ideology and design during the Cold War and in its aftermath.[1] Reform-era architecture was both larger and costlier than its Mao-era equivalent and required new procedures and financing systems that remain active and influential both in relationship to China's built environment but also throughout Asia, the Middle East, Africa, Europe, and the Americas. In asserting for itself a new position within these systems, China also transformed them. In that sense, an architectural history of reform offers new perspective on the last forty years of globalization, and how we understand China's participation therein. Appreciating the changes that took place in relation to the country's architecture sheds light on how China became so central to the global economy. It also challenges the notion that the process was a seamless integration shaped by neoliberal economic deregulation and free trade.

With reform, buildings produced and revealed truths that were jarring, painful, or otherwise impossible to see. One truth remains particularly indelible—the iconic image of "Tank Man," which shows a single human figure standing in front of a line of mobilized army tanks, and was taken

Fig. 85 "Tank Man," Jeff Widener, June 4, 1989.

by Associated Press photographer Jeff Widener from a sixth-floor balcony in the Beijing Hotel on June 4, 1989, in the aftermath of the government's suppression of public revolt in and around Tiananmen Square (fig. 85).[2] The building's heavily publicized 1974 completion along Chang'an Avenue originally augured the prospects of economic change; in 1989 it helped compress the resultant socioeconomic asynchronies into one unforgettable image of defiance that swiftly prompted an official reconsideration of the government's liberalizing agenda. Comparative images taken on the ground fail to capture both the drama and courage commonly associated with the moment, underscoring the political inconvenience of the hotel's view (fig. 86). Over the course of the events surrounding June 4 and the People's Liberation Army's eventual retreat from the city center, bullets also pierced windows of the diplomatic residential compounds and the Jianguo Hotel, which had been hailed as an embodiment of the government's Open Door policy upon its opening seven years prior.[3] Party leaders, having long utilized hotels as a means of internalizing the world, were aghast to discover that these international spaces and forms had helped to externalize the local. "The lesson from this disturbance is bitter," reported the *People's Daily* (*Renmin Ribao*) on February 20, 1990. "Because we had abandoned our ideological base, bourgeois liberalization flooded to the point of calamity. A microclimate was even formed in China that echoed the international microclimate. Together they set off this storm in our capital and caused undue damage to our nation and people who try hard to maintain stability and prosperity."[4]

The government's decision to open fire on its own people brought an end to the greatest urban mass demonstration in modern Chinese history. The protests themselves were prompted by many factors. The gradual marginalization of reform-minded leaders such as Zhao Ziyang and Hu Yaobang over the course of 1987 and 1988 provided one source of frustration. Hu's sudden death on April 15, 1989, catalyzed a series of

Fig. 86 "Tank Man," Terril Jones, June 4, 1989.

public demonstrations in Beijing that culminated in the protests organized in and around Tiananmen Square. Several months prior, in January 1989, a series of clashes between African and Chinese students in Nanjing quickly spread to other cities in China. Such violence was triggered by additional incidents of Chinese racism directed at visiting African students, and growing Chinese resentment over perceptions of the government's favoritism for students from other parts of the developing world. One month following June 4, however, Ghana and China signed their agreement to construct the National Theatre in Accra in recognition of Ghana's unwavering support for China during its time of crisis.[5]

Although the CCP maintained its hold over the country following the crackdown, the socioeconomic logic underlying its rationale to rule gradually disappeared, necessitating new justifications and mechanisms to exert its authority. Within the realm of architectural discourse, a series of *Architectural Journal* (*Jianzhu Xuebao*) articles published in the months following June 4, 1989, blamed the influence of postmodernism for the destabilization of Chinese architectural culture. In July, Zhang Zaiyuan, professor of architecture and urban planning at Wuhan University, charted the ebb and flow of Chinese architectural discourse over the past ten years to argue that deep confusion over the country's disciplinary objectives and the fickle flow of design trends had resulted in thoughtless and counterproductive debate over modernism, postmodernism, and national architectural characteristics. "China's architectural ecosystem has been thrown into disequilibrium," opined Zhang, resulting in "a very difficult and transitional era" and an ambiguous path forward.

A November 1989 essay titled "The Lessons of Twice Importing Architectural Theory: From National Form to Postmodernism" seconded these fears. In the piece, Zou Denong identified several similarities between what he saw as the careless borrowing of postmodern design theory by China's architectural elite over the course of the 1980s, and the 1950s, another era of widespread conceptual adoption from abroad—specifically, the Soviet Union. Just as Soviet advisors had exerted unchecked sway over China's nascent communist leadership in the promotion of a socialist realist architecture for China, so did Zou perceive undue foreign influence as part of what he termed "postmodernism's theory of addition: the addition of big roofs, the addition of ornament, the addition of fake structural members, the addition of certain tastes, and most importantly, the unavoidable addition of capital."[6] The efficiency embodied through socialist China's historical architecture evinced national characteristics in ways that could not be matched by reform-era design, with its exuberant embrace of imperial-era cliché. In Zou's mind, such excess spoke to an architectural discourse unhinged from the fundamental economic issues Zou considered so pertinent to the survival of socialist Chinese society.

By the late 1980s, it appeared that numerous microclimates throughout the country had begun to form, each contributing to the erosion of the party's authority. In Shekou, the local branch of the Communist Youth League organized a symposium in January 1988 for dozens of local young people featuring several representatives from the China Research Center for the Ideological Education of Youth in Beijing. The event was held on the ninth floor of the former China Merchants' Headquarters Building, one of the many recently constructed buildings designed and built to facilitate development. The panel's introductory comments, which concerned Shenzhen's active role in promoting socialism with Chinese characteristics, were met with incredulous retorts from the audience. "What Chinese characteristics are there actually [in Shenzhen]? The characteristics of Shenzhen are foreign characteristics! In Shenzhen, the architecture, streets, urban structure, and management of enterprises are just the same as those abroad." The symposium, which launched a months-long debate between Beijing officials and Shekou youth known as the "Shekou Storm" (*Shekou Fengbo*), remains an important if forgotten catalyst in the subsequent events in Beijing. The *People's Daily* would later acknowledge that "the so-called 'Shekou Storm' was not just an incident which happened on that tiny plot [Shekou]; it is actually related to or reflects an inevitable and nation-wide debate in the ideological sphere. This debate would have come about sooner or later anyway."[7]

Loosening control of China's economy and physical environment was accompanied by greater governmental oversight over the country's "symbolic environment," an initiative first launched in autumn 1989 with a hasty series of campaigns aimed against the illegal publication of textual material.[8] Rather than continuing its cautious rationing of capitalism's material benefits to a well-positioned few, the government accelerated their distribution while working to control people's opinions of it. In 1990 the party began to promote land-leasing strategies that allowed the assigning of land use rights to individual users. SEZ activity also rapidly expanded, with new and distinct types and forms proliferating throughout the country. In 1992 Deng Xiaoping embarked upon an ambitious tour of southern China's SEZs to demonstrate his unwavering belief in the potential of centrally planned, market-based economic principles.

The central government struggled to reassert control over China's economic life. By the end of 1992, every province in China, excluding Tibet, had sold use rights totaling four thousand pieces of state land equal to two hundred fifty square kilometers, which prompted the government to force the reduction and closure of zones in an effort to slow the speed of their development.[9] By 1993 the government had effectively begun to more closely control flows of communications into and through Chinese society, though by 1994, it had also opened 311 cities and counties as well as 114 open zones to foreign investment, trade, and technology.

Over the past thirty years, architecture has continued to participate in China's economic transformation. The 1980s and its numerous ideological vicissitudes and creative bursts had a formative impact on the intellectual and professional development of many of China's pre-eminent designers today, making an architectural study of Reform and Opening Up useful in assessing the actors, ideas, and conditions shaping Chinese design in the twenty-first century. For example, 1993 marks the establishment of the first professional design practice in China, by Yung Ho Chang, whose father, architect Zhang Kaiji, was one of the country's leading architects before and following reform. Chang was allowed to study architecture in the United States during the early days of reform, and he also worked with Clement Chen & Associates in San Francisco on the designs for the Jianguo Hotel. On the basis of these types of experiences and relationships, Chang was given the opportunity to develop a new kind of private design practice, and it was through these practices that it has been argued a so-called experimental architecture in China emerged, led by the work of figures such as Chang and Pritzker Prize–winner Wang Shu.[10]

This work has been recognized for its efforts to more fully reconcile the political economy of reform to more convincing architectural expressions demonstrative of Chinese identity. Both Chang and Wang in particular have been depicted in Chinese- and English-language scholarship as intellectually and institutionally independent individuals who were exposed to new kinds of architectural forms and practices imported from abroad as students at Southeast University in the 1980s and who incorporated these ideas into their own unique design methods. In many respects, however, the relative freedoms granted to figures such as Chang and Wang can be understood not as the first, but as the final step in China's early architectural reform era. The establishment of offices such as the Zhongjing and the Beijing Architectural Design Group were official, state-supported experiments that nevertheless enabled the creation of these so-called private practices, and it is to these first, experimental platforms that we must look for the first seeds of what Manfredo Tafuri termed the "reorganization of production" necessitated by the free market, and enabled by architecture, in his own study of a so-called avant-garde movement in Europe sixty years prior. Architecture's ability to intercede between "reality and utopia" in the name of capitalist development occurred much earlier in reform-era China than one might believe; these tensions remain at the heart of the intellectual and professional formation of China's current architectural elite.[11]

Reconditioning China to the economic, political, and social vicissitudes of the global market has engendered a number of unique forms of architectural thinking and practice, but it has also produced a degree of estrangement among a handful of China's prominent designers toward the economic forces propelling contemporary Chinese urbanization and the political urgencies pushing such development forward. Among these architects, the deployment of certain material processes or design-build techniques gestures back to the days of revolution that preceded reform. Recent disciplinary interest in amateurism, for example, ripples through the work of figures such as Liu Jiakun or Wang Shu, both of whom came of age during the reform era; Liu spent three years in the countryside as a youth. Buildings such as his Luyeyuan Stone Sculpture Art Museum (2002), or Wang's Ningbo History Museum (completed in 2005), revel in the raw materiality of bricks and concrete in ways that echo the spontaneous, on-site *sanjiehe* interactions between intellectuals and villagers that took place during the Cultural Revolution, though this recent work is drained of the ideological fervor of the past. Rather, Liu's and Wang's work derives its meaning through contrast to the large-scale, glossy, quasi-corporate sheen that proliferated throughout China's cities over the course of the 1980s and 1990s.[12] These designers owe their careers to the many changes initiated within the discipline during the early reform era, even as they maintain their distance from its excesses.

How will the legacy of reform continue to affect Chinese architecture in the years to come? President Xi Jinping's 2014 critique of China's "weird architecture" indicates the discomfort still prevalent within the party that buildings have the potential to signify ideas beyond what the government might intend or sanction. Xi's dismissal of unusual design, and his linking of architectural oddities in China to the influence of vague, foreign forces, begs questions concerning what constitutes the normative in contemporary Chinese architecture. It also offers a dispiriting rejoinder to Yang Yun's 1980 essay regarding postmodernism, in which he expressed wariness regarding undue foreign influence, but ultimately encouraged Chinese architects not to dismiss foreign architecture as nothing more than "strange objects."[13] These two moments of strangeness in China's architectural production serve as reminders, not only that the early reform era remains an essential if controversial period in Chinese history, but of architecture's ability to inform, to inspire, to incite—in short, to tempt change.

Notes

INTRODUCTION

1. "Guoji julebu," *Jianzhu Xuebao*, no. 1 (1973): 48–49.

2. Jamie Monson, "Working Ahead of Time: Labor and Modernization during the Construction of the TAZARA Railway, 1968–1986," in *Making a World after Empire: The Bandung Moment and Its Political Afterlives*, ed. Christopher J. Lee (Athens: Ohio University Press, 2010), 242.

3. Annie Dillard, *Encounters with Chinese Writers* (Middletown, CT: Wesleyan University Press, 1984), 22.

4. Deng Xiaoping was famously quoted as acknowledging that "some people and some regions should be allowed to prosper before others, always with the goal of common prosperity." See Deng, *Deng Xiaoping wenxuan*, 2 vol. (Beijing: Renmin chubanshe, 1993), 155.

5. Zou Denong, *Zhongguo jianzhushi tushuo* (Beijing: Zhongguo jianzhu gongye chubanshe, 2001), 171–72, 180–82; Paul Clark, *The Chinese Cultural Revolution: A History* (Cambridge: Cambridge University Press, 2008), 215–16.

6. Mitchell Dean has argued that power is made manifest in a building's control of human conduct, including who accesses particular spaces and how, and what users do while they inhabit them. See Dean, *Governmentality: Power and Rule in Modern Society* (London: Sage, 1999), 11–12.

7. Yu Shuishan, *Chang'an Avenue and the Modernization of Chinese Architecture* (Seattle: University of Washington Press, 2012), 75–87.

8. Mariusz Czepczynski, *Cultural Landscapes of Post-Socialist Cities: Representation of Powers and Needs* (London: Ashgate, 2008), 67.

9. "Exhibition Hall—China's Gift to Ghana," *Ghana Today* 5, no. 25 (1962): 11.

10. Feng Jicai, *Ten Years of Madness: Oral Histories of China's Cultural Revolution* (San Francisco: China Books and Periodicals, 1996), 9–10; Roderick MacFarquhar and Michael Schoenhals, *Mao's Last Revolution* (Cambridge, MA: Harvard University Press, 2006), 118–21.

11. Beijing shi jianzhu shejiyuan gongyu xianchang sheji xiaozu, "Shiliuceng zhuangpeishi gongyu jianzhu," *Jianzhu Xuebao*, no. 1 (1974): 32.

12. "Beijing zhicheng zisheng taishi qizhongji," *Renmin Ribao*, November 29, 1973, 2.

13. Wang Zhili, "Yi ge lishi de jiaoxun," *Jianzhu Xuebao*, no. 6 (1980): 2.

14. Sam Webb, "The Road to Wisdom Has No End," *Progress in Planning* 8, pt. 2 (1979): 146.

15. Deng Xiaoping, "Emancipate the Mind, Seek Truth from Facts and Unite as One in Looking to the Future," The Selected Works of Deng Xiaoping, December 13, 1978, https://dengxiaopingworks.wordpress.com/2013/02/25/emancipate-the-mind-seek-truth-from-facts-and-unite-as-one-in-looking-to-the-future/ (accessed November 14, 2019).

16. Richard Rose, *Understanding Post-Communist Transformation: A Bottom Up Approach* (London: Routledge, 2000), 1.

17. See, for example, Julian Gewirtz, *Unlikely Partners: Chinese Reformers, Western Economists, and the Making of a Global China* (Cambridge, MA: Harvard University Press, 2017); Andrew J. Nathan, "The New Tiananmen Papers: Inside the Secret Meeting That Changed China," *Foreign Affairs* (July/August 2019): 80–91.

18. Overviews of the era's architectural development can be found in Charlie Q. L. Xue, *Building a Revolution: Chinese Architecture since 1980* (Hong Kong: University of Hong Kong Press, 2005); Zou Denong, *Zhongguo xiandai jianzhu shi* (Beijing: Zhongguo jianzhu gongye chubanshe, 2010), 101–45; Peter Rowe and Seng Kuan, *Architectural Encounters with Essence and Form in Modern China* (Cambridge, MA: MIT Press, 2002), 137–60.

19. See, for example, Rowe and Kuan, *Architectural Encounters*, 141–46; Yu, *Chang'an Avenue*, 165–77.

20. Bei Dao, *City Gate, Open Up* (New York: New Directions, 2017), 293.

21. Yu Guangyuan, Steven I. Levine, and Ezra Vogel, *Deng Xiaoping Shakes the World: An Eyewitness Account of China's Party Work Conference and the Third Plenum (November–December 1978)* (Norwalk, CT: EastBridge, 2004); Ezra F. Vogel, *Deng Xiaoping and the Transformation of China* (Cambridge, MA: Belknap Press of Harvard University Press, 2011), 229–40.

22. "Guanyu jianzhu xiandaihua he jianzhu fengge wenti de yixie yijian," *Jianzhu Xuebao*, no. 1 (1978): 26–30.

23. Richard Baum, *Burying Mao: Chinese Politics in the Age of Deng Xiaoping* (Princeton, NJ: Princeton University Press, 1994), 5. Susan Shirk has summarized oscillations in government policy from moderation (*fang*) in 1979–80, 1984, 1986–87, and 1988 to contraction (*shou*) in 1981, 1985–86, 1987, and 1988–89. See Shirk, "The Political Economy of Chinese Industrial Reform," in *Remaking the Economic Institutions of Socialism: China and Eastern Europe*, ed. Victor Nee and David Stark (Stanford: Stanford University Press, 1989), 328–64.

24. David Gissen, *Manhattan Atmospheres* (Minneapolis: University of Minnesota Press, 2014); Lydia Kallipoli, *The Architecture of Closed Worlds, or What Is the Power of Shit?* (New York: Lars Müller, 2018); Charles Rice, *The Emergence of the Interior: Architecture, Modernity, Domesticity* (London: Routledge, 2007); Andrea Vesentini, *Indoor America: The Interior Landscape of Postwar Suburbia* (Charlottesville: University of Virginia Press, 2018); Max Hirsh, "East-East Architectural Transfers and the Afterlife of Socialist Postmodernism in Japan," in *Second World Postmodernisms: Architecture and Society under Late Socialism*, ed. Vladimir Kulić (London: Bloomsbury, 2019), 198–210; Fredric Jameson, "Postmodernism, or The Cultural Logic of Late Capitalism," *New Left Review* 146 (July/August 1984): 83.

25. In 1982, for example, the U.S. writer Annie Dillard participated in a series of exchanges with the Chinese Writers Association in both China and the United States. Upon gazing outside during one meeting in China to watch a group of men lifting approximately four-meter slabs of concrete with little more than ropes and bamboo poles resting on their bare shoulders, Dillard reconsidered the value of literature to the necessity of architectural production. "It is almost impossible," admitted Dillard, "given the sight outside the window, not to say at this meeting, forget it. Go for fork-lifts." Dillard, *Encounters with Chinese Writers*, 26.

26. Walter Benjamin, "The Work of Art in the Age of Its Technological Reproducibility" (2nd version, 1935–36), in *The Work of Art in the Age of Its Technological Reproducibility, and Other Writings on Media*, ed. Michael W. Jennings, Brigid Doherty, and Thomas Y. Levin, trans. Edmund Jephcott, Rodney Livingstone, Howard Eiland et al. (Cambridge, MA: Belknap Press of Harvard University Press, 2008), 40.

27. Daniel B. Abramson, "A Trans-Pacific Planning Education in Reverse," in *Crossing Borders: International Exchange and Planning Practices*, ed. Patsy Healey and Robert Upton (London: Routledge, 2010), 291.

28. See Julian Gewirtz, "The Futurists of Beijing: Alvin Toffler, Zhao Ziyang, and China's 'New Technological Revolution,'" *Journal of Asian Studies* 78, no. 1 (February 2019): 115–40.

29. Steven Lubar, "Representation and Power," *Technology and Culture* 36, no. 2 [supp.: Snapshots of a Discipline: Selected Proceedings from the Conference on Critical Problems and Research Frontiers in the History of Technology, Madison, Wisconsin, October 30–November 3, 1991] (April 1995): S55.

30. See, for example, Zhang Zhongyi, "Cong xifang jianzhu jie de xianzhuang kan jianzhu yu kexue jishu de guanxi," *Jianzhu Xuebao*, no. 1 (1985): 7–11; Xu Ronglie, "Lun jianzhu kexue jishu de fazhan qushi," *Jianzhu Xuebao*, no. 12 (1986): 2–7.

31. See Aggregate Collaboration, *Governing by Design* (Pittsburgh: University of Pittsburgh Press, 2012).

32. Andrew Leach, "Architecture or Revolution?," in *Architecture and Revolution: Contemporary Perspectives on Central and Eastern Europe*, ed. Andrew Leach (London: Routledge, 1999), 116–17.

33. Ulf Hannerz, *Cultural Complexity: Studies in the Social Organization of Meaning* (New York: Columbia University Press, 1992), 3.

34. Hilde Heynen, "The Most Modern Material of Them All . . . ," in *Forty Ways to Think about Architecture: Architectural History and Theory Today*, ed. Ian Borden, Murray Fraser, and Barbara Penner (London: John Wiley, 2014), 95–99.

35. Reinhold Martin has referred to postmodernism not as a style, but as a discursive formation. See Martin, *Utopia's Ghost: Architecture and Postmodernism, Again* (Minneapolis: University of Minnesota Press, 2010), xiv.

36. F. Sizheng Fan, for example, has argued that "although postmodernism was a popular topic in China, it was not a mainstay in actual design." See Fan, "Culture for Sale: Western Classical Architecture in China's Recent Building Boom," *Journal of Architectural Education* 63, no. 1 (October 2009): 66. See also Gao Minglu, *Total Modernity and the Avant-Garde in Twentieth-Century Chinese Art* (Cambridge, MA: MIT Press, 2011), 9–23; Hao Shuguang, *Dangdai Zhongguo jianzhu sichao yanjiu* (Beijing: Zhongguo jianzhu gongye chubanshe, 2006), 106; Ke Song, "Modernism in Late-Mao China: A Critical Analysis on State-Sponsored Buildings in Beijing, Guangzhou, and Overseas, 1969–1976" (PhD diss., University of Melbourne, 2017), 16–39; Wang Jing, *High Culture Fever: Politics, Aesthetics, and Ideology in Deng's China* (Berkeley: University of California Press, 1996); Ren Xuefei, *Building Globalization: Transnational Architecture Production in Urban China* (Chicago: University of Chicago Press, 2007), 48; Zhang Xudong, *Chinese Modernism in the Era of Reforms: Cultural Fever, Avant-Garde Fiction, and the New Chinese Cinema* (Durham, NC: Duke University Press, 1997).

37. Gong Deshun, Zou Denong, and Dou Yide, *Zhongguo xiandai jianzhu shigang* (Tianjin: Tianjin kexue jishu chubanshe, 1989).

38. See, for example, Wang Dihua, "Du 'Tan jianzhu zhong "Shehuizhuyi neirong, minzu xingshi" de kouhao' de yijian," *Jianzhu Xuebao*, no. 12 (1981): 29–31.

39. Andreas Huyssen, "Introduction: Modernism after Postmodernity," *New German Critique* 33, no. 3 (2006): 1–5; Martin, *Utopia's Ghost*, xxi–xxiv.

40. Donald M. Nonini, "Is China Becoming Neoliberal?," *Critique of Anthropology* 28, no. 2 (2008): 146–76.

41. Liu Chun, *The Transformation of Chinese Socialism* (Durham, NC: Duke University Press, 2006), 2.

42. Rose, *Understanding Post-Communist Transformation*, 47; Immanuel C. Y. Hsu, *China without Mao: The Search for a New Order* (Oxford: Oxford University Press, 1990), x.

43. Li Zhang, "Afterword: Flexible Postsocialist Assemblages from the Margin," *positions* 20, no. 2 (2012): 659–67.

44. Ren Hai, *Neoliberalism and Culture in China and Hong Kong* (London: Routledge, 2010); Bae-Gyoon Park, *Locating Neoliberalism in East Asia: Neoliberalizing Spaces in Developmental States* (Hoboken, NJ: John Wiley, 2012).

45. Ana Miljački, "Cold War Adaptations," in *Terms of Appropriation: Modern Architecture and Global Exchange*, ed. Ana Miljački and Amanda Lawrence (London: Routledge, 2017), 94–115; Kulić, *Second World Postmodernisms;* Ching Kwan Lee, *The Specter of Global China: Politics, Labor, and Foreign Investment in Africa* (Chicago: University of Chicago Press, 2017).

46. See, for example, Lee, *Specter of Global China*.

CHAPTER 1
RECEPTION

1. H. R. Haldeman, *The Haldeman Diaries: Inside the Nixon White House* (New York: G. P. Putnam's, 1994), 413.

2. In late 1973, for example, Mao apparently requested that Deng and Wang Hongwen, a member of the Gang of Four, each tour the country and report back to him. Following their return to Beijing, Mao asked both of them, "After I die, what will happen in China?" Wang replied, "The whole country will certainly follow Chairman Mao's revolutionary line and carry through the revolution to the end!" Deng replied, "Civil war will break out and there will be confusion

throughout the country!" Deng's reply resonated more forcefully with Mao, who appointed him chief of the staff of the People's Liberation Army (PLA). Yan Jiaqi and Gao Gao, *Zhongguo "Wen Ge" Shi Nian Shi* (Xianggang: Xianggang dagong baoshe, 1986), 507–10; cited in John Gittings, *The Changing Face of China: From Mao to Market* (Oxford: Oxford University Press, 2005), 57.

3. "Construction Boom in Peking," *South China Morning Post*, June 25, 1973, 6.

4. Leslie Gelb, "Surging Trade with China," *New York Times*, December 2, 1973, 217; Rosalie L. Tung, *U.S.–China Trade Negotiations* (New York: Pergamon, 1982), 4.

5. Marc James Hersh, "Entering the China Market," in *Doing Business in China: American Trade Opportunities in the 1970s*, ed. William W. Whitson (New York: Praeger, 1974), 433.

6. China National Tourism Administration, *The Chronological Record of the Events in China Tourism Development* (Beijing: China National Tourism Administration, 1995), 10. For a history of the Cultural Revolution, see Frank Dikötter, *The Tragedy of Liberation: A History of the Chinese Revolution, 1945–57* (New York: Bloomsbury, 2013), 257–74.

7. Michael Croft, *Red Carpet to China* (London: Longmans, 1958), 11; cited in Anne-Marie Brady, *Making the Foreign Serve China: Managing Foreigners in the People's Republic* (Lanham, MD: Rowman and Littlefield, 2003), 96.

8. Ke Song, "Modernism in Late-Mao China: A Critical Analysis on State-Sponsored Buildings in Beijing, Guangzhou and Overseas, 1969–1976" (PhD diss., University of Melbourne, 2017), 125.

9. Yu Shuishan, *Chang'an Avenue and the Modernization of Chinese Architecture* (Seattle: University of Washington Press, 2012), 129.

10. Simon Leys, *Chinese Shadows* (New York: Penguin, 1978), 18–19.

11. Jim Mann, *Beijing Jeep: A Case Study of Western Business in China* (Boulder, CO: Westview, 1997), 52.

12. Margaret Macmillan, *Nixon and Mao: The Week That Changed the World* (New York: Random House, 2007), 27–29.

13. Jeremy Friedman, *Shadow Cold War: The Sino-Soviet Competition for the Third World* (Chapel Hill: University of North Carolina Press, 2015), 199.

14. Song Ke and Zhu Jianfei, "Architecture at a Political Turning Point: Diplomatic Buildings in 1970s Beijing," *ABE Journal*, no. 12 (2017): 5, https://journals.openedition.org/abe/3759 (accessed January 21, 2018).

15. See Song, "Modernism in Late-Mao China," 124–65.

16. Yu, *Chang'an Avenue*, 160.

17. Beijing shi jianzhu shejiyuan gongyu xianchang sheji xiaozu, "Shiliuceng zhuangpeishi gongyu jianzhu," *Jianzhu Xuebao*, no. 1 (1974): 32. See also Yu, *Chang'an Avenue*, 160.

18. Beijing shi jianzhu shejiyuan gongyu xianchang sheji xiaozu, "Shiliuceng zhuangpeishi gongyu jianzhu," 19.

19. Beijing shi jianzhu shejiyuan gongyu xianchang sheji xiaozu, "Shiliuceng zhuangpeishi gongyu jianzhu," 31.

20. Beijing shi jianzhu shejiyuan gongyu xianchang sheji xiaozu, "Shiliuceng zhuangpeishi gongyu jianzhu," 32.

21. Michel Foucault, "Of Other Spaces: Utopias and Heterotopias," trans. Jay Miskowjec, *Architecture/Mouvement/Continuité* (October 1984): 46–49.

22. Joseph Kraft, "A Reporter in China: The Right Road and the Wrong Road," *New Yorker*, May 6, 1972, 110.

23. Song, "Modernism in Late-Mao China," 145.

24. See "Beijing youyi shangdian," *Jianzhu Xuebao*, no. 1 (1973): 50–51; David Bruce, *Window on the Forbidden City: The Beijing Diaries of David Bruce, 1973–1974*, ed. Priscilla Roberts (Hong Kong: Centre of Asian Studies Occasional Papers and Monographs No. 145, 2001), 120, 141, 393.

25. David Airey and King Chong, *Tourism in China: Policy and Development since 1949* (London: Routledge, 2011), 153–96.

26. Mann, *Beijing Jeep*, 115.

27. Zhang Bo, *Wode jianzhu chuangzuo daolu* (Beijing: Zhongguo jianzhu gongye chubanshe, 1994), 206.

28. Cao Yue and Yang Weicheng, "Shebei zhuanye huigu," in *Beijing shi jianzhu sheji yanjiuyuan chengli 50 zhounian ji nianji*, ed. Beijing shi jianzhu sheji yanjiuyuan chengli 50 zhounian ji nianji bianweihui (Beijing: Zhongguo jianzhu gongye chubanshe, 1999), 58–59.

29. Zhang, *Wode jianzhu chuangzuo daolu*, 210; Orville Schell, "I-Peking and Shanghai," *New Yorker*, March 7, 1977, 42.

30. Schell, "I-Peking and Shanghai," 42. See also Song, "Modernism in Late-Mao China," 155–62.

31. Bruce, *Window on the Forbidden City*, 253–54.

32. "Construction Boom in Peking," 6.

33. Bruce, *Window on the Forbidden City*, 231.

34. "Peking Builds 'City' for Foreign Residents," *Asian Building and Construction* (July 1974): 16.

35. Bruce, *Window on the Forbidden City*, 231.

36. Schell, "I-Peking and Shanghai," 42.

37. Peter Rowe and Seng Kuan, *Architectural Encounters with Essence and Form* (Cambridge, MA: MIT Press, 2002), 133–34; Yu, *Chang'an Avenue*, 162; Song and Zhu, "Architecture at a Political Turning Point," 5.

38. See "Hongkong to Canton Road Link Planned," *South China Morning Post*, December 31, 1973, 1; "All Eyes on China's Oil Industry at Exhibition," *South China Morning Post*, October 9, 1974, 37; "Shum Chun Resthouse for China Visitors," *South China Morning Post*, January 7, 1974, 6; "China Expands Railway," *South China Morning Post*, February 24, 1975, 1. See also Zhang Bo, "Zai wo yuan chuangzuo shijian zhongde tihui," in *Beijing shi jianzhu s heji yuanjiuyuan chengli 50 zhounian jinian ji*, ed. Beijing shi jianzhu sheji yuanjiuyuan xueshu congshu (Beijing: Zhongguo jianzhu gongye chubanshe, 1999), 36; Song, "Modernism in Late-Mao China," 166–210; Charlie Q. L. Xue and Guanghui Ding, *A History of Design Institutes in China: From Mao to Market* (London: Routledge, 2018), 61–63.

39. Julian Sobin and Lee Sobin, "The PRC as a Trading Partner: A View after Three Fairs," in *Doing Business with China: American Trade Opportunities in the 1970s*, ed. William W. Whitson (New York: Praeger, 1974), 447–48.

40. Bruce, *Window on the Forbidden City*, 401.

41. Joseph Lelyveld, "Mao, 80, and Zhou, 76, Absent from Celebration of 1949 Victory," *New York Times*, October 2, 1974, 3.

42. See Mao Zedong, *Mao Zedong on*

Diplomacy (Beijing: Foreign Languages Press, 1998), 248–49, 308–10, 405.

43. Margaret Pearson, *Joint Ventures in the People's Republic of China: The Control of Foreign Direct Investment under Socialism* (Princeton, NJ: Princeton University Press, 1991), 52.

44. John H. Holdridge, *Crossing the Divide: An Insider's Account of the Normalization of U.S.-China Relations* (Lanham, MD: Rowman and Littlefield, 1997), 117.

45. Henry Kissinger, *The Kissinger Transcripts: The Top Secret Talks with Beijing and Moscow* (New York: New York Press, 1998), 83.

46. "Mayflower 'Embassy,'" *New York Times*, April 22, 1973, 176; Jay Mathews, "10-Man Chinese Party Arrives," *Washington Post*, April 19, 1973, A3.

47. Press Briefing Paper, April 16, 1973, Folder POL 17a, "PRC Liaison Office, 1973, Diplomatic and Consular Representation," RG 59, Subject Files, 1969–1978, A1 5411, National Archives and Records Administration (NARA), College Park, MD.

48. Memorandum for the President, Grant of Diplomatic Privileges and Immunities for the Washington Liaison Office of the People's Republic of China, February 28, 1973, Folder POL 17–2, "Immunities, Privileges, 1973," RG 59, Subject Files, 1969–1978, A1 5411, NARA, College Park, MD.

49. "Embassy Row Area—10 bdr., pool, tennis crt. Excel. space for China: House Hunting," *Washington Post*, July 17, 1973, B1.

50. "Embassy Row Area," B1; "Chinese Buy Windsor Park Hotel," *Washington Post*, November 18, 1973, B1.

51. Joy Billington, "Housing 'Peoples' China," *Washington Star-News*, December 22, 1974, C-3.

52. Linda Charlton, "Chinese Mission Arrives in Washington," *New York Times*, April 19, 1973, 3.

53. Maxine Cheshire, "Chinese Want a Small Hotel," *Washington Post*, December 26, 1971, K1.

54. Marlene Cimons, "Learning to Live a Little Our Way, a Little Theirs," *Washington Post*, March 31, 1974, L10.

55. Billington, "Housing 'Peoples' China," C-3.

56. Billington, "Housing 'Peoples' China," C-3.

57. Nancy Bernkopf Tucker, *China Confidential: American Diplomats and Sino-American Relations, 1945–1996* (New York: Columbia University Press, 2001), 290.

58. See Memorandum, Chinese Guest List at USLO Peking Thank You Party for Chinese Officials Involved in the USLO Compound Construction, September 4, 1976, Folder POL 6, "People, Biographic Data, 1973," RG 59, Subject Files, 1969–1978, A1 5411, NARA, College Park, MD; "The Bruces Show the Flag in China," *Washington Post*, March 10, 1974, G1.

59. Bruce, *Window on the Forbidden City*, 196.

60. Bruce, *Window on the Forbidden City*, 543.

61. Memorandum, East Asia: US-PRC Relations, undated, Folder "1973 Briefing," RG 59, Subject Files, 1969–1978," A1 5411, NARA, College Park, MD.

62. Tucker, *China Confidential*, 372.

63. Tucker, *China Confidential*, 372; Patrick Tyler, *A Great Wall: Six Presidents and China* (New York: PublicAffairs, 1999), 157; James Lilley with Jeffrey Lilley, *China Hands: Nine Decades of Adventure, Espionage, and Diplomacy in Asia* (New York: PublicAffairs, 2004), 175; Memorandum, Chinese Guest List for United States Liaison Office Fourth of July Reception, July 24, 1973, and Memorandum, Chinese Guest List at USLO Peking Thank You Party.

64. "Guoji julebu," *Jianzhu Xuebao*, no. 1 (1973): 48–49.

65. Cited in Warren Weinstein, *Chinese and Soviet Aid to Africa* (New York: Praeger, 1975), 3.

66. Tucker, *China Confidential*, 328.

67. Murrey Marder, "China Tells U.S. Marine Unit to Leave," *Washington Post*, May 25, 1974, A1; Tyler, *Great Wall*, 152, 443n128.

68. Maria Galikowski, *Art and Politics in China, 1949–1984* (Hong Kong: Chinese University Press, 1998), 158–60.

69. Hou Yimin, "Bihua yu shiji," *Meishu*, no. 10 (1981): 5–8, cited in Jane Debevoise, *Between State and Market: Chinese Contemporary Art in the Post-Mao Era* (Leiden: Brill, 2014), 82.

70. Song and Zhu, "Architecture at a Turning Point."

71. John Gittings, "Excess and Enthusiasm," in *Picturing Power in the People's Republic of China: Posters of the Cultural Revolution*, ed. Harriet Evans and Stephanie Donald (Lanham, MD: Rowman and Littlefield, 1999), 27.

72. Bruce, *Window on the Forbidden City*, 126; Weinstein, *Chinese and Soviet Aid to Africa*, 5.

73. Cole Roskam, "Non-Aligned Architecture: China's Designs on and in Ghana and Guinea, 1955–1992," *Architectural History* 58 (2015): 269.

74. See, for example, Jamie Monson, *Africa's Freedom Railway: How a Chinese Development Project Changed Lives and Livelihoods in Tanzania* (Bloomington: Indiana University Press, 2009); Martin Bailey, *Freedom Railway: China and the Tanzania-Zambia Link* (London: Rex Collings, 1976).

75. Jamie Monson, "Working Ahead of Time: Labor and Modernization during the Construction of the TAZARA Railway, 1968–86," in *Making a World after Empire: The Bandung Moment and Its Political Afterlives*, ed. Christopher J. Lee (Athens: Ohio University Press, 2010), 242.

76. Nicholas Ashford, "Chinese-Built Tanzam Railway Trains Run Ontime at £5.50 Fare for 1.162-mile Journey," *The Times*, July 26, 1976, 5.

77. Tiedaobu disan shejiyuan, "Tanzan tielu Daleisi Salamu yi ke zhan jianzhu," *Jianzhu Xuebao*, no. 1 (1976): 32–34.

78. Jacqueline Grapin, "Letter from Dar es Salaam," *The Times*, March 4, 1975, 14.

79. Ashford, "Chinese-Built Tanzam Railway," 5.

80. Bailey, *Freedom Railway*, 65.

81. For historical GDP data, see "Historical GDP Per Capita by Country, Statistics from the World Bank," Knoema, https://knoema.com/jesoqmb/historical-gdp-per-capita-by-country-statistics-from-the-worldbank-1960-2018 (accessed January 12, 2021).

82. George T. Yu, "China and the Third World," *Asian Survey* 17, no. 11 (1977): 1036–48.

83. Deng Xiaoping, "Speech by Chairman of the Delegation of the People's Republic of China at the Special Session of the U.N. General Assembly," April 10, 1974, Marxists Internet Archive, https://www.marxists.org/reference/archive/deng-xiaoping/1974/04/10.htm (accessed March 7, 2020); He Li,

"Mao Zedong guanyu san ge shijie huafen lilun yu ershi shiji qishi niandai Zhongguo waijiaozhan lue tiaozheng," *Zhonggongdangshi Yanjiu,* no. 4 (2010): 14–21; Jiang An, "Mao Zedong's 'Three Worlds' Theory: Political Considerations and Value for the Times," *Social Sciences in China* 34, no. 1 (2013): 35–57; H. S. Yee, "The Three World Theory and Post-Mao China's Global Strategy," *International Affairs* 59, no. 2 (Spring 1983): 239–49.

84. Simon Leys, *Chinese Shadows* (New York: Penguin, 1977), xvii.

85. Sobin and Sobin, "PRC as a Trading Partner," 443–44.

86. See Zhu Tao, "Architecture in China in the Reform Era; 1978–2010," in *A Critical History of Contemporary Architecture, 1960–2010,* ed. Elie G. Haddad and David Rifkind (London: Ashgate, 2014), 401–17.

CHAPTER 2
THE STUDY TOUR AND THE EXHIBITION

1. Memorandum of Conversation, August 6, 1975, Folder "Leg 7," RG 59, Subject Files, 1969–1978, A1 5411, National Archives and Records Administration (NARA), College Park, MD. During President Nixon's February 1972 tour, Zhou expressed regret to Nixon over the decision to send children to the Ming Tombs to "put up a show" and "prettify" the site in anticipation of his arrival. "It was putting up a false appearance," acknowledged Zhou, noting that U.S. "press correspondents have pointed this out to us." See "Memorandum of Conversation," February 26, 1972, National Security Archive, George Washington University, Washington, DC.

2. Kevin C. Dunn, "Imagining Mobutu's Zaire: The Production and Consumption of Identity in International Relations," *Millennium Journal of International Studies* 39 (2001): 235–58; G. Thomas Burgess, "Mao in Zanzibar: Nationalism, Discipline, and the (De)Construction of Afro-Asian Solidarities," *Making a World after Empire: The Bandung Moment and Its Political Afterlives,* ed. Christopher J. Lee (Athens: Ohio University Press, 2010), 196–234.

3. Maria Antonietta Macciocchi, *Daily Life in Revolutionary China* (New York: Monthly Review, 1972), 27.

4. Roland Barthes, *Travels in China,* ed. Anne Herschberg Pierrot, trans. Andrew Brown (Malden, MA: Polity, 2012), 150.

5. See David Bruce, *Window on the Forbidden City: The Beijing Diaries of David Bruce, 1973–1974,* ed. Priscilla Roberts (Hong Kong: Centre of Asian Studies Occasional Papers and Monographs No. 145, University of Hong Kong, 2011), 593–94.

6. In his analysis of cultural production in Cultural Revolution–era China, for example, Paul Clark has argued that "architecture is a field in which politics need not be as obvious as in other arts." See Clark, *The Chinese Cultural Revolution: A History* (Cambridge: Cambridge University Press, 2008), 215.

7. Pierre Bourdieu, "Passport to Duke," *Metaphilosophy* 28, no. 4 (October 1997): 451; Alex Hughes, "Bodily Encounters with China: On Tour with *Tel Quel,*" *Modern and Contemporary France* 14, no. 1 (February 2006): 49–62.

8. Harrison Brown, "Scholarly Exchanges with the People's Republic of China," *Science* 183, no. 4120 (January 11, 1974): 52; David M. Lampton, with Joyce A. Madancy and Kristen M. Williams for the Committee on Scholarly Communication with the People's Republic of China, *A Relationship Restored: Trends in U.S.-China Educational Exchanges, 1978–1984* (Washington, DC: National Academies Press, 1986); Douglas P. Murray, "Exchanges with the People's Republic of China: Symbols and Substance," *Annals of the American Academy of Political and Social Science* 424 (March 1976): 29–42; Richard Kirkby, interview, January 19, 2017.

9. Charlotte Perriand, *A Life of Creation* (New York: Monacelli, 2003), 356; Henry C.K. Liu, "China Today: An Architect's Photographs and Commentary," *Architecture Plus* 1, no. 1 (February 1973): 40–47, 97; "Luomaniya jianzhu kaochatuan lai woguo kaocha," *Jianzhu Xuebao,* no. 2 (1973): 39; Walter Wagner, "A Report ... on Life and Architecture in China," *Architectural Record* 126 (September 1974): 111–24; "Zhong Jia liang guo jianzhushi de youhao huijian," *Jianzhu Xuebao,* no. 2 (1973): 12; Elisabeth Kendall Thompson, "The New China," *Architectural Record* (October 1973), 130; "Architects on Tour of China," *Los Angeles Times,* April 21, 1974, G27; "Meiguo jianzhu daibiaotuan fangwen woguo," *Jianzhu Xuebao,* no. 3 (1974): 21–22; "Rizhong jianzhu jishu jiaoliuhui youhao fang Hua daibiaotuan fangwen woguo," "Silanka gongchengshi xiehui daibiaotuan fangwen woguo," *Jianzhu Xuebao,* no. 4 (1974): 29; "Riben jiansheyejie youhao fang Hua tuan fangwen woguo," *Jianzhu Xuebao,* no. 6 (1974): 25; "Riben zhuzhai jianshe youhao fang Hua tuan ji Riben jianzhu wuli jishu jiaoliu youhao fang Hua tuan fangwen woguo," *Jianzhu Xuebao,* no. 3 (1975): 17; "Chaoxian jianzhujia daibiaotuan fangwen woguo," *Jianzhu Xuebao,* no. 1 (1973): 27; "Zhongguo jianzhushi daibiaotuan fangwen Chaoxian," *Jianzhu Xuebao,* no. 2 (1973): 30.

10. Murray, "Exchanges," 39.

11. Perriand, *Life of Creation,* 357.

12. Bonnie S. McDougall, *Mao Zedong's "Talks at the Yan'an Conference on Literature and Art": A Translation of the 1943 Text with Commentary* (Ann Arbor: University of Michigan Press, 1980), 75.

13. Liu, "China Today," 41.

14. Wagner, "Report," 113–14.

15. Gideon Bachmann and Michelangelo Antonioni, "Antonioni after China: Art versus Science," *Film Quarterly* 28, no. 4 (Summer 1975): 29.

16. Rey Chow, *Writing Diaspora: Tactics of Intervention in Contemporary Cultural Studies* (Bloomington: Indiana University Press, 1993), 10.

17. Wagner, "Report," 112.

18. Thompson, "New China," 130.

19. Liu, "China Today," 40, 97.

20. Wagner, "Report," 114.

21. Kirkby, interview; Nick Jeffrey and Malcolm Caldwell, "Introduction [Planning and Urbanism in China]," *Progress in Planning* [Special Issue on Planning and Urbanism in China] 8, pt. 2 (1977): 100.

22. Sam Webb, "The Road to Wisdom Has No End," *Progress in Planning* 8, pt. 2 (1977): 144.

23. "Introduction," *Progress in Planning,* 101. See also *Architectural Design* [Special Issue on China] 3 (1974): 138–57; *Architectural Design* [Special Issue on China, Part 2] 4 (1974): 218–26.

24. Webb, "Road to Wisdom Has No End," 146.

25. Liang Yulin and Wang Zhixiang, "Shaoxing Lu Xun jinian guan," *Jianzhu*

Xuebao, no. 2 (1977): 8–10, 50–51.

26. Wagner, "Report," 113–14.

27. Archibald C. Rogers, "Some Chinese Principles of Architecture," *Baltimore Sun,* July 6, 1974, A18.

28. Dick Turpin, "Chinese Build for Future, Visitors Say," *Los Angeles Times,* May 23, 1974, A11.

29. Liu, "China Today," 42.

30. Liu, "China Today," 41.

31. Bernard Zumthor, "China Today: Education for Architecture," *Architects' Journal* [Special Issue on China Today] 158, no. 51 (December 19 and 26, 1973): 1547.

32. Wagner, "Report," 114.

33. Zumthor, "China Today," 1546. See also Julia Kristeva, *About Chinese Women,* trans. Anita Barrows (London: M. Boyars, 1977).

34. Wagner, "Report," 114.

35. Julian Gewirtz, *Unlikely Partners: Chinese Reformers, Western Economists, and the Making of Global China* (Cambridge, MA: Harvard University Press, 2017), 70.

36. Jianzhu xuehui *Jianzhu Xuebao* zazhi she, eds., *Zhongguo Jianzhu Xuehui 60 nian* (Beijing: Zhongguo jianzhu gongye chubanshe, 2013), 48.

37. Zhang Bo, *Wode jianzhu chuangzuo daolu* (Beijing: Zhongguo jianzhu gongye chubanshe, 1994), 215.

38. "Chinese Educators End 30-Day US Tour in Hub," *Boston Globe,* December 11, 1977, 22; "Architects from China Tour U.S. Quietly," *Los Angeles Times,* October 19, 1975, I2.

39. See, for example, "Xiandai chengshi de gexing," *Xiandaihua* 4, no. 12 (December 1983): 3–5.

40. One tour of Chinese architects to New York, Boston, Washington, DC, Chicago, Los Angeles, and San Francisco, among other cities, requested minimal press coverage to avoid possible protestors or demonstrations—a reminder of the ideological tensions at work within China and in relation to its international standing. "Architects from China Tour U.S. Quietly," I2.

41. "News Review," *Asian Building and Construction,* January 1973, 9.

42. "Zhongguo jianzhushi daibiaotuan canjia guoji jianxie jianzhu gongyehua disici taolunhui," *Jianzhu Xuebao,* no. 2 (1973): 47.

43. "Zhongguo jianzhu gongcheng jishu daibiaotuan fang Ri," *Jianzhu Xuebao,* no. 1 (1973): 35.

44. "Zhongguo jianzhu gongcheng jishu daibiaotuan fang Ri," 35.

45. "Zhongguo jianzhu kaochatuan fu Yi, Fa canguan kaocha," *Jianzhu Xuebao,* no. 2 (1973): 37; "Zhongguo jianzhushi daibiaotuan canjia guoji jianxie jianzhu gongyehua disici taolunhui," *Jianzhu Xuebao,* no. 2 (1973): 47; Song Ke and Zhu Jianfei, "Architecture at a Political Turning Point: Diplomatic Buildings in 1970s Beijing," *ABE Journal,* no. 12 (2017), https://journals.openedition.org/abe/3759 (accessed January 12, 2021).

46. See Zhongguo jianzhu xuehui zhaokai pi Lin pi Kong tanhui jiyao, "Jiji xiangying Dang de haozhao, ba jianzhu jie de pi Lin pi Kong douzheng jinxing daodi," *Jianzhu Xuebao,* no. 1 (1974): 1.

47. "Zhongguo jianzhu xuehui youhao fang Ri daibiaotuan fang Ri," *Jianzhu Xuebao,* no. 4 (1975): 42.

48. "Delegation of PRC Architects Depart for U.S.," *Xinhua,* trans. *China Foreign Broadcast Information Service (FBIS),* September 18, 1975.

49. "Technology Impresses Chinese Architects," *MEMO,* October 27, 1975, 2.

50. "Chinese Educators End 30-Day US Tour," 22; "Architects from China Tour U.S. Quietly," 12; "Meiguo gaoceng jianzhu daibiao tuan fang Hua," *Jianzhu Xuebao,* no. 6 (1980): 70; Rosemary Brady, "Chinese Tour Buildings in New Haven," *Hartford Courant,* September 17, 1978, 11A.

51. "The Bruces Show the Flag in China," *Washington Post,* March 10, 1974, G1.

52. The Museum of Modern Art to Bureau of East Asian and Pacific Affairs, Department of State, August 21, 1974, International Council and International Program Records, Series I: International Program Exhibition Files 1938–2000, SP-ICE-23-58, I. B. 738, "Art in Embassies, Peking Collection, 1973–1974," Archives of the Museum of Modern Art, New York.

53. Memorandum, "Chronology of American Attempts to Secure an Exhibition of Archeological Finds from the PRC," September 10, 1974, Folder 14A2, "Records of the Office of Public Information General, Exhibition Files, 1941–, Dec. 13, 1974–Mar 30, 1975, The Exhibition of Archaeological Finds of the People's Republic of China, Correspondence, Memos, USIA, CBS, Filing (1973–1974)," National Gallery of Art Archives, Washington, DC, Gallery Archives. See also *Jianzhu Chuangzuo* zazhi, ed., *Jianzhu Zhongguo 60 nian: Shijian juan* (Tianjin: Tianjin daxue chubanshe, 2009), 94; "China Treasures," *New York Times,* July 7, 1974, 5; "Archaeology Delegation Leaves for Exhibition Opening in U.S.," *Xinhua,* trans. *FBIS,* December 6, 1974, A9.

54. Carol M. Fox, "Hosting Our Chinese Guests," December 2, 1974, in Folder 14A2, "Records of the Office of Public Information General, Exhibition Files, 1941–, Dec 13, 1974–Mar 30, 1975, The Exhibition of Archaeological Finds of China, Correspondence, Memos, USIA, CBS, Filing [1973–1974]," National Gallery of Art Archives, Washington, DC.

55. John H. Holdridge, *Crossing the Divide: An Insider's Account of the Normalization of U.S.-China Relations* (Lanham, MD: Rowman and Littlefield, 1997), 119. See also Murray, "Exchanges," 32.

56. Memorandum, Katherine Warwick to Robert Hughes, November 20, 1974, in Folder 14A2, "Records of the Office of Public Information General, Exhibition Files, 1941–, Dec 13, 1974–Mar 30, 1975, The Exhibition of Archaeological Finds of China, Correspondence, Memos, USIA, CBS, Filing [1973–1974]," National Gallery of Art Archives, Washington, DC.

57. Memorandum, Warwick to Hughes.

58. Fox, "Hosting Our Chinese Guests."

59. Jerome A. Cohen, "U.S.-China Relations," *New York Times,* December 18, 1974; Paul Richard, "Chinese Art Press Preview Cancelled," *Washington Post,* December 10, 1974, B1; Letters, J. Carter Brown, December 18, 1974, and December 27, 1974, in Folder 14A2, "Records of the Office of Public Information General, Exhibition Files, 1941–, Dec 13, 1974–Mar 30, 1975, The Exhibition of Archaeological Finds of China, Correspondence, Memos, USIA, CBS, Filing [1973–1974]," National Gallery of Art Archives, Washington, DC.

60. William F. Buckley, Jr., "The Chinese Exhibitionists," *Washington Star-Times,* December 17, 1974, A-10.

61. Buckley, "Chinese Exhibitionists," A-10.

62. "Sulan jianzhu yishu tupian zhanlan,"

Jianzhu Xuebao, no. 1 (1973): 44; *Sulan jianzhu tupian zhanlan, 1961–1971*, brochure, author's collection; "Zhongguo jianzhu tupian zhanlan," *Jianzhu Xuebao*, no. 2 (1973): 39.

63. Ceng Jian, "Ruidian jiaju dengju shinei zhuangshi zhanlanhui," *Jianzhu Xuebao*, no. 4 (1976): 35–36.

64. See Tseng Kwong Chi, *Ambiguous Ambassador* (Tucson: Nazraeli, 2005).

65. I. M. Pei, a member of the 1974 AIA tour who would subsequently return to China to design the Fragrant Hill Hotel, noted that Chinese workers "were fantastically fast in starting, not accurate, but fast." See Christopher S. Wren, "I.M. Pei's Peking Hotel Returns to China's Roots," *New York Times*, October 25, 1982, C13.

66. Edwin A. Winckler, Janet Cady, and the National Committee on U.S. China Relations, "Urban Planning in China: Report of the U.S. Urban Planners Delegation to the People's Republic of China," undated, 3. Kevin Lynch Papers, Folder "China," AC 400, b. 39, MIT Archive, Cambridge, MA.

67. Wang Tan, "SOM—yi zhong jianzhu liupai," *Shijie Jianzhu*, no. 6 (1981): 55.

CHAPTER 3
THE BRICK, THE BLOCK, AND THE PANEL

1. *Jianzhu Xuebao*, no. 2 (1973): 1.

2. Jing Guihua, "Buzhun chouhua wuguo shoudu Beijing de guanghui xingxiang," *Jianzhu Xuebao*, no. 2 (1974): 6–11; Cheng Jian, "Xin Zhongguo de chengshi jianshe burong wumie," *Jianzhu Xuebao*, no. 1 (1974): 7–8.

3. Jing, "Buzhun chouhua wuguo shoudu Beijing de guanghui xingxiang," 6.

4. Guojia jianshe weiyuanhui xiezuo xiaozu, "Sheji gaige shengli de shi nian," *Renmin Ribao*, November 1, 1974, 1; repr. in *Jianzhu Xuebao*, no. 6 (1974): 2–3, 47.

5. Adrian Forty, *Concrete and Culture: A Material History* (London: Reaktion, 2012), 226.

6. Pedro Ignacio Alonso and Hugo Palmarola, *Panel* (London: Architectural Association, 2014).

7. Kang Chao, *The Construction Industry in Communist China* (Chicago: Aldine, 1968), 146–47; "PRC Builds More Small Cement Works during 1972," trans. *China Foreign Broadcast Information Service (FBIS)*, January 3, 1973, B2.

8. Henry C. K. Liu, "China Today: An Architect's Photographs and Commentary," *Architecture Plus* 1, no. 1 (February 1973): 43.

9. Zixian Liu, "Making a New World and a New People: Cold War, Maoist Austere Architecture and the 'Rammed-Earth Campaign,' 1966–76," *Journal of Contemporary Chinese Art* 4, nos. 2, 3 (2017): 269–85.

10. Simon Leys, *Broken Images: Essays on Chinese Culture and Politics*, trans. Steve Cox (New York: St. Martin's, 1980), 122.

11. Yang Xiguang and Susan McFadden, *Captive Spirits: Prisoners of the Cultural Revolution* (Hong Kong: Oxford University Press, 1997), 234.

12. Alonso and Palmarola, *Panel*, 258; Kimberly Elman Zarecor, "The Local History of an International Type: The Structural Panel Building in Czechoslovakia," *Home Cultures* 7, no. 2 (2015): 217–35.

13. Liu, "China Today," 42.

14. Maria Antonietta Macciocchi, *Daily Life in Revolutionary China* (New York: Monthly Review, 1972), 202.

15. "Quanguo zhuzhai sheji tupian zhanlan," *Jianzhu Xuebao*, no. 6 (1974): 6–25.

16. "Quanguo jianzhu qingbao gongzuo zuotanhui," *Jianzhu Xuebao*, no. 3 (1974): 21.

17. James T. Myers, Jürgen Domes, and Erik von Groeling, eds., *Chinese Politics: Ninth Party Congress (1969) to the Death of Mao (1976)* (Columbia: University of South Carolina Press, 1989), 2:293–99.

18. See Richard Baum, *Burying Mao: Chinese Politics in the Age of Deng Xiaoping* (Princeton, NJ: Princeton University Press, 1994), 48–65.

19. "Quanguo kongxin qikuai ji qiangti gaige jingyan jiaoliuhui zai Shanghai zhaokai," *Jianzhu Xuebao*, no. 3 (1975): 25.

20. "Sheng banfa shigong," *Jianzhu Xuebao*, no. 1 (1975): 24.

21. See, for example, Xinan Jianzhu Keyansuo, "Jiaonang chou kong kongxin jichu," *Jianzhu Xuebao*, no. 1 (1973): 47; Zhejiangsheng jiben jiansheju, "Hunningtu kongxin qikuai," *Jianzhu Xuebao*, no. 2 (1974): 26–29, 45.

22. Guojia jianwei jianzhu kexue yanjiu yuan, *Qiangti gaige* (Beijing: Guojia jianwei jianzhu kexue yanjiu yuan, 1976).

23. Guojia jianwei jianzhu kexue yanjiu yuan, *Qiangti gaige*, 1.

24. Zhejiangsheng jiben jiansheju, "Hunningtu kongxin qikuai," 45.

25. Guojia jianshe weiyuanhui xiezuo xiaozu, "Sheji gaige shengli de shi nian," 1.

26. Zhonggong Lüda shi jianzhu shejiyuan zongji weiyuanhui, "Zhuajinzhuahao pi Lin pi Kong, gaohao 'sanjiehe' xianchang sheji," *Jianzhu Xuebao*, no. 3 (1974): 2–4.

27. Guojia jianwei jianzhu kexue yanjiu yuan, *Qiangti gaige*, 1.

28. Guojia jianwei jianzhu kexue yanjiu yuan, *Qiangti gaige*, 1.

29. Yang Zhang, Chun Zhang, William Drake, and Robert Olshansky, "Planning and Recovery Following the Great 1976 Tangshan Earthquake," *Journal of Planning History* 14, no. 3 (2015): 230.

30. Beverley Hooper, *Inside Peking: A Personal Report* (London: MacDonald and Jane's, 1979), 76, 117.

31. See Zhang Kaiji, "Guanhai canjiren, kaituo 'wu zhangai' huanjing," in *Zhuzhai sheji 50 nian: Beijing shi jianzhu sheji yanjiuyuan zhuzhai zuopinxuan* (Beijing: Zhongguo jianzhu gongye chubanshe, 1999), 69–70.

32. Susan Buck-Morss, *Dreamworld and Catastrophe: The Passing of Mass Utopia in East and West* (Cambridge, MA: MIT Press, 2002).

33. Deborah Shapley, "China after Mao: Science Seeks to Be Both Red and Expert," *Science* 197, no. 4305 (August 19, 1977): 739–41.

CHAPTER 4
ARCHITECTURAL HISTORY AND HERITAGE

1. Jean Pasqualini (Bao Ruowang), *Prisoner of Mao* (London: Penguin, 1976), 212, 255; quoted in Simon Leys, *Broken Images: Essays on Chinese Culture and Politics* (New York: St. Martin's, 1979), 68.

2. Shanghai shi minyong jianzhusheji yuan er wu gonggao, "'Sirenbang' pohuai Shanghai tiyuguan gongcheng de zuixing," *Jianzhu Xuebao*, no. 2 (1977): 11; "Cong zhufang kan 'Sirenbang' de

chou'e benzhi," *Jianzhu Xuebao,* no. 2 (1977): 11.

3. Zhang Xupeng, "Historical Writing in the People's Republic of China since 1978," *Revue Tiers Monde* 216, no. 4 (2013): 91. See also Barbara W. Tuchman, *Notes from China* (New York: Collier, 1972), 43–48.

4. Thomas de Monchaux, "Notre-Dame and the Paradoxes of Historical Preservation," *New Yorker,* May 13, 2019, https://www.newyorker.com/culture/cultural-comment/notre-dame-and-the-paradoxes-of-historical-preservation (accessed May 16, 2019); Gabriel Fuentes, "Beyond History: The Aesthetics of Authenticity and the Politics of Heritage in Havana, Cuba," *Future Anterior* 14, no. 2 (Winter 2017): 47.

5. Håkan Hökerberg, "The Past in the Present—Difficult Heritage in the Contemporary Context," in *Architecture as Propaganda in Twentieth-Century Totalitarian Regimes,* ed. Håkan Hökerberg (Florence: Polistampa, 2018), 312; Laurajane Smith, *Uses of Heritage* (London: Routledge, 2006), 6–7; Michael Burawoy and Katherine Verdery, eds., *Uncertain Transition: Ethnographies of Change in the Postsocialist World* (Oxford: Rowman and Littlefield, 1999), 4; Barbara Misztal, *Theories of Social Remembering* (Maidenhead, UK: Open University, 2002), 17.

6. Immanuel C. Y. Hsu, *China without Mao: The Search for a New Order* (Oxford: Oxford University Press, 1990), 103.

7. Anne-Marie Broudehoux, *The Making and Selling of Post-Mao Beijing* (New York: Routledge, 2004), 42–44.

8. *Jianzhu Xuebao* (*Mao zhuxi jiniantang guihua sheji zhuanji*), no. 4 (1977): 1–46.

9. Daniel Leese, "A Place Where Great Men Rest? The Chairman Mao Memorial Hall," in *Places of Memory in Modern China,* ed. Marc Andre Matten (Leiden: Brill, 2011), 91–129; Rudolf G. Wagner, "Reading the Chairman Mao Memorial Hall in Peking: The Tribulations of the Implied Pilgrim," in *Pilgrims and Sacred Sites in China,* ed. Susan Naquin and Chun-Fang Yu (Berkeley: University of California Press, 1992), 378–423; Yu Shuishan, *Chang'an Avenue and the Modernization of Chinese Architecture* (Seattle: University of Washington Press, 2012), 144–58.

10. Wagner, "Reading the Chairman Mao Memorial Hall," 406, 420; Leese, "Place Where Great Men Rest?," 92–129.

11. Jiang Qiansheng, "Qinshou Qiyi Wenjia shi hui jiuzhi chenlieguan," *Jianzhu Xuebao,* no. 2 (1978): 43–45.

12. "Shaoshan jianzhu," *Jianzhu Xuebao,* no. 1 (1977): 1–11; Zunyi shi jiben jianshe weiyuanhui, "Geming lishi mingcheng Zunyi," *Jianzhu Xuebao,* no. 3 (1977): 1–5.

13. See *Jianzhu Xuebao,* no. 4 (1977); Gao Yilan, "Mao Zhuxi jiniantang sheji guocheng zongjie," *Jianzhushi,* no. 1 (2003): 1–25.

14. "Ba Yi" Nanchang qiyi jinianta gongcheng zhihuibu sheji zu, "'Ba Yi' Nanchang qiyi jinianta sheji," *Jianzhu Xuebao,* no. 3 (1979): 1–6.

15. Zhu Yuqing, "Dui 'Ba Yi' Nanchang qiyi jinian ta sheji de jidian kanfa," *Jianzhu Xuebao,* no. 1 (1980): 25. Zhu also critiqued the Monument to Martyrs of the Huaihai campaign, which was also completed in 1979. See Meng Diao and Sun Mingyuan, "Huaihai zhanyi lieshi jinian ta," *Jianzhu Xuebao,* no. 5 (1979): 23–25.

16. Zhu, "Dui 'Ba Yi' Nanchang," 25.

17. John Gittings, *The Changing Face of China: From Mao to Market* (Oxford: Oxford University Press, 2005), 154.

18. Ellen Johnston Laing, *The Winking Owl: Art in the People's Republic of China* (Berkeley: University of California Press, 1988), 95–96; Helmut Martin, *Cult and Canon: The Origins and Development of State Maoism* (Armonk, NY: M. E. Sharpe, 1982), 110–11.

19. See, for example, Julia Andrews, *Painters and Politics in the People's Republic of China, 1949–1979* (Berkeley: University of California Press, 1994), 396; Yoni Braester, *Witness against History: Literature, Film, and Public Discourse in Twentieth-Century China* (Stanford: Stanford University Press, 2003), 146–57.

20. "Guanyu Jianzhu Xiandaihua he Jianzhu Fengge Wenti de yi xie Yijian," *Jianzhu Xuebao,* no. 1 (1979): 26–30.

21. Peter Rowe and Seng Kuan, *Architectural Encounters with Essence and Form in Modern China* (Cambridge, MA: MIT Press, 2002), 143–44.

22. Wang Zhili, "Yi ge lishi de jiaoxun: Liang ge shiqi de jianzhu kexue gong-zuo," *Jianzhu Xuebao,* no. 6 (1980): 1–2, 20.

23. Tong Jun, *Xin jianzhu yu liupai* (Beijing: Zhongguo jianzhu gongye chubanshe, 1980); Rowe and Kuan, *Architectural Encounters,* 142.

24. Ron Knapp, *China's Old Dwellings* (Honolulu: University of Hawai'i Press, 2000), 10.

25. Liang Sicheng, *Liang Sicheng wenji,* 4 vol. (Beijing: Zhongguo jianzhu gongye chubanshe, 1982–86); Liu Dunzhen, *Liu Dunzhen wenji,* 2 vol. (Beijing: Zhongguo jianzhu gongye chubanshe, 1982–84); Liang Sicheng, *A Pictorial History of Chinese Architecture,* ed. Wilma Fairbank (Cambridge, MA: MIT Press, 1984).

26. Bai Zuomin, "Shijue fenxi zai jianzhu chuangzuo zhong de yingyong," *Jianzhu Xuebao,* no. 3 (1979): 9–15, 57.

27. Lin Aimei, "Xianggang zhuzhai jian-she de tedian he leixing," *Shijie Jianzhu,* no. 2 (1980): 49–54; Liu Keqiang, "Taiwan de zhuzhai jianshe," *Shijie Jianzhu,* no. 2 (1980): 45–48; Zhou You, "Xinjiapo xin jianzhu jijin," *Shijie Jianzhu,* no. 2 (1980): 79–83.

28. See Bulunuo Saiwei, "Jianzhu kongjian lun (yi)," trans. Zhang Sizan, *Jianzhushi,* no. 1 (1980): 189–98; Bulunuo Saiwei, "Jianzhu kongjian lun (er)," trans. Zhang Sizan, *Jianzhushi,* no. 3 (1980): 202–22.

29. See, for example, Luyuanyixin, "Waibu kongjian de sheji (yi)," *Jianzhushi,* no. 3 (1980): 223–39; Chen Shaoming and Zhang Mingyu, "Zhong Ri jianzhu qinyuan," *Jianzhushi* 4 (1980): 187–93.

30. "Beijing juban jianzhu huihua zhan-lan," *Jianzhu Xuebao,* no. 6 (1980): 70; "HK-China Architectural Exchange," *Building Journal Hong Kong* (July 1982): 90; "Xianggang jianzhu tupian zhanlan zai Beijing kaimu," *Jianzhu Xuebao,* no. 7 (1982): 16; Shao Huayu, "'Zhongguo chuantong jianzhu tupian zhanlan' zai Xianggang Jiulong Xinshijie Zhongxi kaimu," *Jianzhu Xuebao,* no. 11 (1982): 76; "Xiangang jianzhu tupian zhanlan xianke," *Jianzhu Xuebao,* no. 8 (1982): 73–77; "Beijing juban jianzhu huihua zhanlan," *Jianzhu Xuebao,* no. 6 (1980): 70.

31. Yu, *Chang'an Avenue,* 175; Rowe and Kuan, *Architectural Encounters,* 137–44; Xiang Bingren, "Yuyan, fuhao ji jianzhu," *Jianzhu Xuebao,* no. 8 (1984): 56–61; Yi Dingceng, "Fujaolun meixue he jianzhu yishu," *Jianzhu Xuebao,* no. 10 (1985): 26–29; He Li, "Modernism and China: A Summary from the *People's Daily,*" trans.

Geremie Barmé, *Renditions: A Chinese-English Translation Magazine,* nos. 19–20 (Spring and Autumn 1983): 45.

32. Xiao Tong, "Jiefang sixiang, kaidong jiqi, ba kancha sheji gongzuo tigao dao yi ge xin de shuiping"; Yan Zixiang, "Jiefang sixiang, jiao ta shidi, nuli zuo hao kancha sheji gongzuo"; Gong Deshun, "Dapo jingshen jiasuo, tigao sheji shuiping," *Jianzhu Xuebao,* no. 6 (1979): 1–10.

33. Richard Baum, *Burying Mao: Chinese Politics in the Age of Deng Xiaoping* (Princeton, NJ: Princeton University Press, 1994), 103; "Zhongguo jianzhu xuehui disiju disici changwulishi kuoda huiyi zai Tai'an zhaokai," *Jianzhu Xuebao,* no. 4 (1980): 28.

34. See James A. Flath, "Managing Historical Capital in Shandong: Museum, Monument, and Memory in Provincial China," *Public Historian* 24, no. 2 (Spring 2002): 50.

35. Qi Kang, "Jianzhu huanjing yu gu jianzhu baohu," *Jianzhu Xuebao,* no. 6 (1980): 32–37.

36. Huang Zuyin, "Taishan youlan jia-kongsuodao xianlu de taolun," *Jianzhu Xuebao,* no. 6 (1980): 18–20.

37. Wu Hung, *A Story of Ruins: Presence and Absence in Chinese Art and Visual Culture* (London: Reaktion, 2012), 195–201. See also Wang Wei, *Yuanming Yuan* (Beijing: Beijing Chubanshe, 1980).

38. Wang Zhili, "Zhengqiu Yuanmingyuan yizhi yu shehuizhuyi jingshen wenming jianshe," *Jianzhu Xuebao,* no. 1 (1983): 20–26.

39. See *Le Yuanmingyuan: Jeux d'eau et Palais européens du XVIIIeme siècle à la cour de Chine* (Paris: Éditions Recherche sur les Civilisations, 1987).

40. Lei Gao and Marc Treib, "Making and Remaking the Yuanmingyuan," *Future Anterior* 3, no. 1 (Summer 2006): 17–18, 23n18.

41. Anne-Marie Broudehoux, *The Making and Selling of Post-Mao Beijing* (London: Routledge, 2004), 67–88.

42. Box 2056, "China," Proposals for a Programme of Cooperation in the Field of Architectural Restoration with the State Bureau for the Care of Historical Relics of China, Volume 3, 5, Aga Khan Award for Architecture Archives, Geneva.

43. Minutes of His Highness's Meeting with Vice Premier Gu Mu, Minister for External Finance, Imports and Exports, Oct. 22, 1981, Box 2055, Architectural Restoration Programme(s): China, Folder "Correspondence/Minutes/Agreements/Finance," Aga Khan Award for Architecture Archives, Geneva; James Millward, *Eurasian Crossroads: A History of Xinjiang* (New York: Columbia University Press, 2007), 271, 275, 278.

44. Minutes of His Highness's Meeting with Vice Premier Gu Mu.

45. Maris Boyd Gillette, *Between Mecca and Beijing: Modernization and Consumption among Urban Chinese Muslims* (Stanford: Stanford University Press, 2000), 73. Paul Collard to Guillaume de Spoelberch, November 18, 1982, Preliminary Report on Mission to China, June 18, 1982, Box 2055, Architectural Restoration Programmes(s): China, Folder, "Correspondence/Minutes/Agreements/Finance," Memorandum, Update on China architectural restoration projects, July 12, 1988, Box 2271, AKAA, China, restoration, health, tourism, hotels, Aga Khan Award for Architecture Archives, Geneva.

46. Paul Collard to Guillaume de Spoelberch, July 2, 1982, Box 2055, Architectural Restoration Programmes(s): China, Folder, "Correspondence/Minutes/Agreements/Finance," Aga Khan Award for Architecture Archives, Geneva.

47. Jacques Mullender to Yan Zixiang, August 1981, Georges Pompidou Centre Archives, Paris; Xavier Luccioni to author, April 28, 2017; Frédéric Edelmann, "Léon Hua, architecte entre la Chine et la France," *Le Monde,* January 7, 2013, https://www.lemonde.fr/disparitions/article/2013/01/07/leon-hoa-architecte-entre-la-chine-et-la-france_1813787_3382.html (accessed June 2, 2018).

48. *Environnement quotidien en Chine* (Paris: Centre de Création Industrielle, Centre Georges Pompidou, 1982), 174.

49. In July 1983, for example, Switzerland organized an architectural exhibition in Beijing. See "Ruishi 1970-1980 jianzhu tupian zhanlan zai Jing kaimu," *Jianzhu Xuebao,* no. 9 (1983): 74. In January 1984 the Pompidou Centre organized an exhibition titled *Chinese Television* (*Les journées de la télévision Chinoise*), which consisted of a live feed of state-sponsored Chinese television. See *Les journées de la télévision Chinoise,* January 18–23, 1984, Georges Pompidou Centre Archives, Paris.

50. Hélène Larroche, "Image perçue, image donnée," in *Environnement quotidien en Chine,* 6–7; "'Zhongguo jianzhu, shenghuo, huanjing zhanlan,' zai Faguo Bali kaimu," *Jianzhu Xuebao,* no. 8 (1982): 71–72.

51. Yan Haiming, *World Heritage Craze in China: Universal Discourse, National Culture, and Local Memory* (New York: Berghahn, 2018), 3.

52. Christopher S. Wren, "China Unleashes a Capitalist Tool," *New York Times,* April 25, 1982, 137; "Old Shenzhen Rehabilitation Proposals," *China City Planning Review* (October 1988): 34.

53. "Old Shenzhen Rehabilitation Proposals," 43.

CHAPTER 5
THE JOINT VENTURE AND THE SEZ

1. Gu Mu, *Gu Mu huiyi lu* (Beijing: Zhongyang wenjian chubanshe, 2009), 296–305; Julian Gewirtz, *Unlikely Partners: Chinese Reformers, Western Economists, and the Making of Global China* (Cambridge, MA: Harvard University Press, 2017), 36, 194. See also Carol Lee Hamrin, *China and the Challenge of the Future* (Boulder, CO: Westview, 1990), 11; F. Chi, "China's Newborn SEZs and Their Strategic Significance," *Economic Reporter,* August 1981, 11.

2. David Zweig, *Internationalizing China: Domestic Interests and Global Linkages* (Ithaca, NY: Cornell University Press, 2002), 60; Aradhna Aggarwal, "SEZ-Led Growth in Taiwan, Korea, and India: Implementing a Successful Strategy," *Asian Survey* 52, no. 5 (September/October 2012): 874.

3. C. K. Leung, "Spatial Redeployment and the Special Economic Zones in China," in *China's Special Economic Zones: Policies, Problems, and Prospects,* ed. Y. C. Jao and C. K. Leung (Oxford: Oxford University Press, 1986), 9; Zweig, *Internationalizing China,* 60; Aggarwal, "SEZ-Led Growth," 874.

4. For histories of Shenzhen that emphasize top-down planning, see Margaret Pearson, *Joint Ventures in the People's Republic of China: The Control of Foreign Direct Investment under Socialism* (Princeton, NJ: Princeton University Press, 1991); Susan Shirk, "The Political

Economy of Chinese Industrial Reform," in *Remaking the Economic Institutions of Socialism: China and Eastern Europe*, ed. Victor Nee and David Stark (Stanford: Stanford University Press, 1989); Mee Kam Ng and Wing-Shing Tang, "The Role of Planning in the Development of Shenzhen China: Rhetoric and Realities," *Eurasian Geography and Economics* 45 (2004): 190–211; Constance Clark, "The Politics of Place Making in Shenzhen, China," *Berkeley Planning Journal* 12, no. 1 (1998): 103–25; Michael J. Bruton, Sheila G. Bruton, and Yu Li, "Shenzhen: Coping with Uncertainties in Planning," *Habitat International* 29 (2005): 227–43; Anthony Gar-on Yeh and Fulong Wu, "The Transformation of the Urban Planning System in China from a Centrally-Planned to Transitional Economy," *Progress in Planning* 51, no. 3 (1999): 167–252; Julie Auyeung, "Local Experts to 'pave the way' for China," *South China Morning Post*, September 25, 1979, 54; Julie Auyeung, "HK to Design 'giant' Shumchun," *South China Morning Post*, October 24, 1979, 1; "City Planners Survey Shumchun Potential," *South China Morning Post*, June 19, 1980, 16. Alternative perspectives can be found in Mary Ann O'Donnell, Winnie Wong, and Jonathan Bach, eds., *Learning from Shenzhen: China's Post-Mao Experiment from Special Zone to Model City* (Chicago: University of Chicago Press, 2017); Juan Du, *The Shenzhen Experiment* (Cambridge, MA: Harvard University Press, 2020).

5. Douglas Spencer, "The Architecture of Managerialism: OMA, CCTV, and the Post-Political," in *Architecture against the Post-Political: Essays in Reclaiming the Critical Project*, ed. Nadir Lahiji (New York: Routledge, 2014), 155.

6. Tony Walker and Roger Flanagan, *China: Building for Joint Ventures* (Hong Kong: Levett and Bailey Chartered Quantity Surveyors, 1987), 13.

7. Jonathan Bach, "Shenzhen: From Exception to Rule," in O'Donnell, Wong, and Bach, eds., *Learning from Shenzhen*, 23–38.

8. Kwei-Jeou Wang, "Economic and Social Impact of Export Processing Zones in the Republic of China," *Industry of Free China* 54, no. 6 (December 25, 1980): 28; Xiangming Chen, "The Evolution of Free Economic Zones and the Recent Development of Cross-National Growth Zones," *International Journal of Urban and Regional Research* 19, no. 4 (December 1995): 593–621; Ji Chongwei, "Why China Has Opened Special Economic Zones," *China Reconstructs* (September 1984): 14; Pearson, *Joint Ventures*, 53. Deng Xiaoping purportedly based his approval of the SEZ model in part on the logic that Yan'an, the communists' temporary headquarters during China's civil war, had served as a kind of special zone during the conflict. See Hamrin, *China and the Challenge of the Future*, 54n4.

9. Taiwan's EPZs depended upon walls, barbed wire, locked gates, and special security clearance to physically separate them from the rest of the territory in which they were located and limit the public's exposure to the forms and impact of production taking place. Despite these constraints, however, the EPZ's boundary remained porous, and workers bicycled to and from their jobs within the EPZ and their homes outside the zone's boundaries. In fact, most of the economic growth attributed to the EPZ manifested outside the zone itself as new boulevards, high-rise office buildings, department stores, Gaoxiong's international airport, and its port facilities, which became the world's tenth most active entrepôt in 1979. "Kaohsiung to open airport," *South China Morning Post*, August 28, 1971, 25; Wang, "Economic and Social Impact," 9; Clayton Jones, "Tax-Free Lure for Foreign Factories Draws in Technology and Peasants," *Christian Science Monitor*, April 28, 1981, https://www.csmonitor.com/1981/0428/042845.html (accessed May 14, 2018). See also Neil H. Jacoby, *U.S. Aid to Taiwan: A Study of Foreign Aid, Self-Help, and Development* (New York: Frederick A. Praeger, 1966), 143; Gustav Ranis, "Industrial Development," in *Economic Growth and Structural Change in Taiwan: The Postwar Experience of the Republic of China*, ed. Walter Galenson (Ithaca, NY: Cornell University Press, 1979), 225–27.

10. "Development at Shumchun," *South China Morning Post*, May 5, 1933, 2.

11. Kwan Yiu Wong, David K. Y. Chu, Mo Kwan Lee Fong, Kin Che Lam, Yan Tak Ng, and See Lou Too, "Economic Development of Shenzhen Municipality—Plans and Progress," Occasional Paper No. 13, Chinese University of Hong Kong, January 1981, 51; FCO 40/48, "Hong Kong Political Affairs—Internal; Kowloon Disturbances, May 1967," National Archives, Kew, London.

12. China Resources, the party's Hong Kong–based corporate investment body, was responsible for managing the party's real estate holdings in Hong Kong, which were estimated to provide the party with more than $300 million USD in annual income. See *Far Eastern Economic Review* (July 30, 1976): 44; "New Chinese Investment," *South China Morning Post*, April 23, 1978, 10. See also Agenda Minutes for a meeting between Sir Lawrence Kadoorie, Mr. Alan Williams, and Sir Peter Carey, March 30, 1977, PREM 16/2204, National Archives, Kew, London.

13. Agenda Minutes for a meeting between Sir Lawrence Kadoorie, Mr. Alan Williams, and Sir Peter Carey.

14. See Huang Weiwen, "The Tripartite Origins of Shenzhen," in O'Donnell, Wong, and Bach, eds., *Learning from Shenzhen*, 71. Over the course of 1978, China Merchants Steam Navigation Company, a PRC-owned, Hong Kong–based shipping corporation, actively and unsuccessfully sought locations for a ship-breaking plant in Hong Kong. Company representatives subsequently approached Guangdong party officials with a proposal to use Shekou as the base for their operations. Officials agreed, and a one-square-kilometer industrial estate was formed under the China Merchants Steam Navigation Company, under the direct supervision of the Ministry of Communications in Beijing. China Merchants agreed to provide an initial $20 million USD investment, and the party made available land for a long-term lease of generally twenty-five years, at approximately four to eight dollars per square meter, with workers' wages within the site fixed between the average wage scales for Guangdong and Hong Kong.

15. Julie Auyeung, "Massive Plan for Shumchun," *South China Morning Post*, May 20, 1980, 37; Yu Guangyuan, Steven I. Levine, and Ezra F. Vogel, *Deng Xiaoping Shakes the World: An Eyewitness Account of China's Party Work Conference and the Third Plenum (November–December 1978)* (Norwalk, CT: EastBridge, 2004), 136.

16. Yi-min Lin, *Between Politics and Markets: Firms, Competition, and Institutional Change in Post-Mao China* (Cambridge: Cambridge University Press, 2001), 30; Adi Ignatius, "U.S. Companies Going It Alone in China Find Road Bumpy but Have Few Regrets," *Wall Street Journal*, October 24, 1988, 1.

17. Sara Stevens has argued for the significance of expertise in relation to postwar U.S. building culture. My own analysis of expertise in relation to reform-era China is indebted to her work. See Stevens, *Developing Expertise: Architecture and Real Estate in Metropolitan America* (New Haven, CT: Yale University Press, 2016).

18. Anthony Walker, *Land, Property, and Construction in the People's Republic of China* (Hong Kong: Hong Kong University Press, 1991), 81.

19. The statute legalized foreign direct investment into the country through several foreign and Chinese ownership scenarios, each of which presumed foreign capital would account for at least 25 percent of any total deal. See Fox Butterfield, "Peking Issues Rules to Lure Investment," *New York Times*, July 9, 1979, A1. See also Preston M. Torbert and Judith A. Thomson, "China's Joint Venture Law: A Preliminary Analysis," *Vanderbilt Journal of Transnational Law* 12, no. 4 (Fall 1979): 848; Walker, *Land, Property, and Construction*, 79.

20. See Bach, "Shenzhen: From Exception to Rule," 29. Rosalie L. Tung, *U.S.–China Trade Negotiations* (New York: Pergamon, 1982), 35. CITIC had forty-four directors, including five from Hong Kong and Macau, including Liao Chengzhi (1908–1983), first director of the Hong Kong and Macau Affairs Office, Rong Yiren (1915–2005), first director of CITIC, and Vice Premier Gu Mu (1914–2009).

21. "Greater Opportunities for Tourists to China," *South China Morning Post*, April 14, 1978, 49; "New Chinese Investment," *South China Morning Post*, April 23, 1978, 10. See also Victor Su, "China to Build Resort for Us," *South China Morning Post*, March 13, 1979, 1; "Shenzhen Joint Ventures Boom," *South China Morning Post*, December 30, 1980, 23.

22. "China News Report No. 31: Housing Estate Projects in China by Hong Kong Businessmen over the Last Five Years," Public Relations Sub-Division, Government Information Services, January 1981, CO 129/626/11, National Archives, Kew, London.

23. Peter Loke, "Mirs Bay to Boost Tourists' Image," *South China Morning Post*, June 2, 1975, 6.

24. Charlie Q. L. Xue and Guangding Hui, *A History of Design Institutes in China: From Mao to Market* (London: Routledge, 2018), 68–69.

25. Wei Xiutang, "A Shenzhen Joint Venture: Bamboo Garden Hotel," *China Reconstructs* (September 1984): 18–24. See also Xu Mingtian, *Chuntian de gushi: Shenzhen chuangye shi, 1979–2009* (Beijing: Zhongxin chubanshe, 2008), 1:21–22; Du, *Shenzhen Experiment*, 166.

26. Wei, "Shenzhen Joint Venture," 23; Du, *Shenzhen Experiment*, 166.

27. Wei, "Shenzhen Joint Venture," 23.

28. Ji Chongwei, "Why China Has Opened Special Economic Zones," *China Reconstructs* (September 1984): 17; Weiping Wu, *Pioneering Economic Reform in China's Special Economic Zones: The Promotion of Foreign Investment and Technology Transfer in Shenzhen* (London: Routledge, 2018), 95.

29. "Development of Tung Wui District in Shumchun," *Building Journal Hong Kong* (March 1980): 37–38; "Accord on Huge Housing Project," *South China Morning Post*, May 14, 1980, 39; "Advertisement for Cogi Estates," *South China Morning Post*, December 4, 1980, 12. See also Mary Ann O'Donnell, "Heroes of the Special Zone," in O'Donnell, Wong, and Bach, eds., *Learning from Shenzhen*, 45.

30. "Donghu Liyuan—Zhongguo shangpinfang de yuandian," Quan Jing Wang, September 27, 2019, http://www.p5w.net/news/cjxw/201009/t3214056.htm (accessed June 26, 2019); "Deep Bay Airport Gets the Nod from Peking," *South China Morning Post*, September 13, 1981, 11.

31. Kevin B. Bucknall, "Implications of the Recent Changes in China's Foreign Trade Policies," *Australian Journal of Chinese Affairs*, no. 5 (January 1981): 18.

32. Kevin Sinclair, "Leo Builds up China Links," *South China Morning Post*, December 9, 1984, 18. The six-week course, which featured lectures from other Hong Kong–based designers such as Tao Ho, Barry Wills, C. K. Wong, Patrick Lau, and Chung Wah Nan, focused particularly on the design and construction of hotels and other tourist facilities. See also Chiu Kit-Ying, "China Woos HK Architects," *South China Morning Post*, November 27, 1984, 18.

33. "Deep Bay Airport Gets the Nod," 11.

34. David Chen, "Deng 'in Canton to wield axe,'" *South China Morning Post*, February 7, 1982, 1; Christopher Wren, "Deng, Gone 37 Days, Back in Peking," *New York Times*, February 19, 1982, 3; Wren, "Corrupt Officials Draw Peking's Ire," *New York Times*, February 10, 1982, 9; Wren, "China Unleashes a Capitalist Tool," *New York Times*, April 25, 1982, 137; "Twenty-Year Development Plan for Shenzhen," *Building Journal Hong Kong* (October 1982): 76; "Sewage Equipment for Shenzhen," *Building Journal Hong Kong* (December 1983): 37.

35. Orville Schell, *To Get Rich Is Glorious: China in the Eighties* (New York: Pantheon, 1984), 39.

36. Walter Cheung, "Shumchun Barrier Nearly Complete," *South China Morning Post*, November 17, 1983, 14.

37. Advertisement for Shenzhen International Commercial Building, *South China Morning Post*, April 23, 1981, 26. See also "Shenzhen 'Sells' Office Space," *South China Morning Post*, October 21, 1980, 29.

38. Wren, "China Unleashes a Capitalist Tool," 137; Du, *Shenzhen Experiment*, 170; "Book Closes on Goodyear, Subsidiaries," *South China Morning Post*, February 21, 1984, 27; Robert Mayerson, "Mandarin Acquires Goodyear Offshoots," *South China Morning Post*, July 11, 1984, 25; Olivia Sin, "Creditors Take over Millie's China Ventures," *South China Morning Post*, January 24, 1985, 27; Olivia Sin and Suzanne Sim, "Millie's Debts Set at $200 Million," *South China Morning Post*, December 4, 1984, 37. The sale of Goodyear Estates to Mandarin Resources for $9.25 million HKD represented the first time a joint venture equity stake in Shenzhen was successfully transferred from one owner to another. See "Goodyear Hotel Stake Sold," *South China Morning Post*, September 29, 1984, 30.

39. Ezra F. Vogel, *One Step Ahead in China: Guangdong under Reform* (Cambridge, MA: Harvard University Press, 1989), 136.

40. Zong Bize, "Guanyu gaige woguo chengshi jiegou wenti de tanlun," *Jianzhu Xuebao*, no. 11 (1983): 23–27.

41. Ji Chongwei, "Why China Has Opened Special Economic Zones," *China Reconstructs* (September 1984): 17.

42. Wang Zheng and Wang Weidong, eds., *Shenzhen jianzhu yishu* (Xi'an: Shaanxi renmin meishu chubanshe, 1989).

43. Shenzhen jianzhu congshu bianji weiyuanhui, ed. *Gaoceng jianzhu* (Beijing: Zhongguo jianzhu gongye chubanshe, 1988); Peter Hall, "Economic and Location Factors in Enterprise Zones," in *The Enterprise Zone Concept: British Origins, American Adaptations*, Working Paper No. 350 (Berkeley: Institute of Urban and Regional Development, University of California Berkeley, 1981), 38; Du, *Shenzhen Experiment*, 171; David Harvey, *Condition of Postmodernity: An Enquiry into the Origins of Cultural Change* (Oxford: Blackwell, 1989), 200–30).

44. See, for example, O'Donnell, Wong, and Bach, eds., *Learning from Shenzhen*, 1, 24–38.

45. Zweig, *Internationalizing China*, 81–86.

CHAPTER 6
THE INTERNATIONAL HOTEL

1. Zhongguo Jianzhu Xuehui and Guojia Jianwei Jianyanjiusheji Yanjiusuo, eds., *Lüguan jianzhu* (Beijing: Zhongguo jianzhu xuehui chuban, 1979), 4. See also Zhongguo Jianzhu Xuehui, *Jianzhu Xuebao* zazhishe, ed., *Zhongguo Jianzhu Xuehui liushi nian* (Beijing: Zhongguo jianzhu gongye chubanshe, 2013), 51; Guangzhou shi shejiyuan, "Guangzhou Liuhua He pan xin jianzhu," *Jianzhu Xuebao*, no. 2 (1976): 42–44; Baiyun binguan sheji xiaozu, "Guanzhou Baiyun Binguan," *Jianzhu Xuebao*, no. 2 (1977): 18–23; Beijing shi jianzhu shejiyuan wushi, "Lüyou jianzhu sheji de ji ge wenti," *Jianzhu Xuebao*, no. 3 (1977): 8–13, 27; Sichuan sheng gongye jianzhu sheji yuan, "Sichuan Weinilun chang waiguo jishurenyuan zhaodaisuo," *Jianzhu Xuebao*, no. 3 (1978): 44–46; Guojia jianwei jianzhu kexue yanjiuyuan jianzhu sheji yanjiusuo, "Lun lüguan jianzhu sheji de jige wenti," *Jianzhu Xuebao*, no.4 (1978): 7–12.

2. Christine Richter, "Tourism Services," in *The Emerging Service Economy*, ed. Orio Giarini (New York: Pergamon, 1987), 213–44.

3. Beijing shi jianzhu shejiyuan wushi, "Lüyou jianzhu sheji de ji ge wenti," *Jianzhu Xuebao*, no. 3 (1977): 8; Jim Mann, *Beijing Jeep: A Case Study of Western Business in China* (Boulder, CO: Westview, 1997), 115.

4. Beijing shi jianzhu sheji yuan wu shi, lüguan diaocha yanjiu xiaoxu, "Lüguan jianzhu sheji de ji ge wenti," *Jianzhu Xuebao*, no. 3 (1977): 8; James P. Sterba, "China's Crash Hotel Program," *New York Times*, February 7, 1979, D1; Gregory M. B. Tong, "Designing Hotels for the People's Republic of China," *Asian Architect and Builder* (August 1979): 15.

5. Tong, "Designing Hotels," 16, 19.

6. Tong, "Designing Hotels," 16; Rosalie L. Tung, *U.S.–China Trade Negotiations* (New York: Pergamon, 1982), 102.

7. Ezra F. Vogel, *Deng Xiaoping and the Transformation of China* (Cambridge, MA: Belknap Press of Harvard University Press, 2011), 336; Jay Matthews and Linda Matthews, *One Billion: A China Chronicle* (New York: Random House, 1983), 18.

8. Ann Crittenden, "The Financial Ills of Cyrus Eaton Jr.," *New York Times*, May 12, 1981, D1. A March–April 1980 issue of *China Business Review* states that in addition to the Great Wall Hotel, two of the first three joint ventures that received approval from the Foreign Investment Commission included a Xinjiang wool factory with Tung Yang Fang (East Sea Textiles) and an airport catering service for Boeing 747s. The omission of the Jianguo Hotel from this list may have been due to the fact that it represented an informal joint venture signed prior to the advent of the law. See Tung, *U.S.–China Trade Negotiations*, 110.

9. Clement Chen III, interview, January 14, 2014; Solveig Jansson, "Getting a Foot in China's Door," *Institutional Investor* 11, no. 3 (March 1986): 122; Randall E. Stross, *Bulls in the China Shop and Other Sino-American Business Encounters* (New York: Pantheon, 1991), 199. See also "Wo waiguo shezi guanli weiyuan hui pizhun san ge hetong," *Renmin Ribao*, April 23, 1980, 1; Liu Li, "Yinxiang yu qishi," *Jianzhu Xuebao*, no. 9 (1982): 35–37.

10. Tiziano Terzani, *Behind the Forbidden Door: Travels in an Unknown China* (New York: Henry Holt, 1984), 53; Clement Chen III, interview; Orville Schell, "An Oasis of Privilege in China: The Jianguo, Capitalism in Peking," *New York Times*, November 27, 1983, 9.

11. Schell, "Oasis of Privilege," 9; Felicity Scott, *Architecture or Techno-Utopia: Politics after Modernism* (Cambridge: MIT Press, 2007), 2.

12. Schell, "Oasis of Privilege," 9; Margaret Pearson, *Joint Ventures in the People's Republic of China: The Control of Foreign Direct Investment under Socialism* (Princeton, NJ: Princeton University Press, 1991), 147; Jansson, "Getting a Foot in China's Door," 122.

13. Mann, *Beijing Jeep*, 210.

14. Wang Mingxian and Zhang Xudong, "Notes on Architecture and Postmodernism in China," *boundary 2*, 24, no. 3 (Autumn 1997): 167; "Beijing Huadu, Jianguo liang fan dian sheji zuotan," *Jianzhu Xuebao*, no. 9 (1982): 21–23.

15. Jansson, "Getting a Foot in China's Door," 122.

16. "Deng fuzongli chuxi Meiguo youhao tuanti he huaqiao de zhaodaihui," *Renmin Ribao*, February 1, 1979, 4; Nancy Langston, "Racking It up in the Last of the Seller's Markets," *Far Eastern Economic Review* (February 28, 1985): 52. "Wushi jia lüyou fandian jiang tuiguang Beijing Jianguo fandian jingyan," *Renmin Ribao*, April 28, 1984, 2; Tung, *U.S.–China Trade Negotiations*, 108; Zhang Xudong, *Chinese Modernism in the Era of Reforms: Cultural Fever, Avant-Garde Fiction, and the New Chinese Cinema* (Durham, NC: Duke University Press, 1997), 14. See also Frank Ching, "Peking, Recognizing Yankee Know-How in Tourism, May Seek Help of U.S. Firms," *Wall Street Journal*, September 20, 1978, 48; Alan Smart and Jinn-Yuh Hsu, "The Chinese Diaspora, Foreign Investment and Economic Development in China," *Review of International Affairs* 3, no. 4 (Summer 2004): 546.

17. Keller Easterling, *Enduring Innocence: Global Architecture and Its Political Masquerades* (Cambridge, MA: MIT Press, 2005), 5. See also David Wen-Wei Chang, *China under Deng Xiaoping: Political and Economic Reform* (New York: St. Martin's, 1988), 196–236; Chuihua Judy Chung, Jefrey Inaba, Rem Koolhaas, and Sze Tsung Leong, eds., *Great Leap Forward: Harvard Design School Project on the City* (Koln: Taschen, 2001).

18. Peng Peigen, "Cong Bei Yuming de Beijing 'Xiangshan fandian' sheji

tan xiandai Zhongguo jianzhu zhi lu," *Jianzhu Xuebao*, no. 4 (1980): 14–19.

19. Peng, "Cong Bei Yuming de Beijing," 14–19; Dong Yugan, "Yuyan yu yuyan: Bei Yuming de Zhongguo xiandai jianzhu," *Shidai Jianzhu*, no. 5 (September 2007): 60–65.

20. Marjorie Yang, interview, November 14, 2013; Calvin Tsao, interview, March 12, 2014; I. M. Pei, presentation to Tsinghua University delegation in New York City, 1980, Box 11, I. M. Pei Papers, Library of Congress, Washington, DC.

21. Following a visit to the hotel, the French architect and furniture designer Charlotte Perriand mentioned the hotel's "spirit screen," or *zhaobi*, to a Chinese architect, who criticized Pei for not understanding anything about tradition and piercing a large, round hole into a screen that blocked the hotel's entrance. Perriand, *A Life of Creation* (New York: Monacelli, 2003), 362.

22. Zhu Changzhong, "Fengjing huanjing yu lüyou binguan: Ping Xiangshan fandian de guihua sheji," *Jianzhu Xuebao*, no. 4 (1983): 59–60.

23. Perriand, *Life of Creation*, 362. See also Correspondence, Y. L. Yang to I. M. Pei, August 24, 1983, Box 11, I. M. Pei Papers, Library of Congress, Washington, DC. See also Ji Zhen, "Dui woguo lüyou lüguan jianzhu jingji xiaoyi de chubu fenxi," *Jianzhu Xuebao*, no. 6 (1983): 26–30; Mo Bozhi, "Huanjing, kongjian yu gediao," *Jianzhu Xuebao*, no. 9 (1983): 45–55. For a description of the hotel's deterioriation, see Denys Roberts, *Another Disaster: Hong Kong Sketches* (London: Radcliffe, 2006), 303–4.

24. Gu Mengchao, "Cong Xiangshan fandian taolun Bei Yuming de sheji sixiang," *Jianzhu Xuebao*, no. 4 (1983): 61–64; "Beijing Xiangshan fandian jianzhu sheji zuotanhui," *Jianzhu Xuebao*, no. 3 (1983): 58.

25. "Beijing fandian jianchi zhua fanfushi jiaoyu," *Beijing Ribao*, May 26, 1981; cited in Stross, *Bulls in the China Shop*, 201.

26. Jim Kinoshita, interview, January 23, 2014. See also Kinoshita, *From Slocan to Hong Kong* (Victoria, BC: Trafford, 2005), 197–206. See also Liu Binyan, "Sanshiqi ceng loushang de Zhongguo," *Renmin Wenxue* 8 (1986): 39–54.

27. Tung, *U.S.–China Trade Negotiations*, 93, 105.

28. By 1977 the firm maintained offices in Lebanon, Tehran, Doha, Jedda, Abu Dhabi, Muscat, Moscow, and Seoul. MacDonald Becket, *Leadership in Architecture: My Passion in Life* (Bloomington, IN: AuthorHouse, 2014), 130.

29. Tung, *U.S.–China Trade Negotiations*, 95; Pearson, *Joint Ventures in the People's Republic of China*, 53.

30. Tung, *U.S.–China Trade Negotiations*, 106.

31. Andy Andreasen, interview, September 20, 2016.

32. "U.S. Firms Bow Out on CM," *Engineering News-Record* (July 15, 1982): 34.

33. Preliminary design scheme, The Great Wall Hotel of Beijing, Becket International Architects/Engineers, 1982.

34. Frederic Jameson, "Postmodernism, or the Cultural Logic of Late Capitalism," *New Left Review*, 146 (July/August 1984): 83. See also Siegfried Kracauer, "The Hotel Lobby," originally published in *The Mass Ornament: Weimar Essays* (1922–25); republished in *The City Cultures Reader Second Edition*, ed. Malcolm Miles and Tim Hall (London: Routledge, 2003), 145–48; Annabel Jane Wharton, *Building the Cold War: Hilton International Hotels and Modern Architecture* (Chicago: University of Chicago Press, 2001).

35. Fredric Jameson, interview, February 7, 2014.

36. Orville Schell, *To Get Rich Is Glorious* (New York: Pantheon, 1984), 116.

37. Bruce Marcus, interview, May 8, 2014; Lucy Hobgood-Brown, interview, April 5, 2014; Frieda Kronegg, interview, June 8, 2014.

38. Wang Yaocheng, "Zhuang Yanlin yu gaige kaifeng chuqi de hezi fandian jianshe," *Renwu*, no. 2 (2009): 43–48; "Sweet Is Turning to Sour: Foreign Capitalists in China Run into a Host of Troubles," *Time*, June 2, 1985, 56; Tung, *U.S.–China Trade Negotiations*, 115.

39. Han Kehua, "Jianjue jiuzheng zai xing shi xia lüyou xitong chuxian de buzheng zhi feng zhengqu lüyou shiye geng da geng jiankang de fazhan" (report issued by the National Tourism Bureau [Guojia Luyou Ju], March 1–7, 1985); Zhao Baoshan, "Development Budget for Joint-Venture Projects in the Beijing Region," *Building in China* 4, no. 1 (March 1991): 2; David Airey and King Chong, *Tourism in China: Policy and Development since 1949* (London: Taylor and Francis, 2011), 166, 180.

40. The project's roots lay in the 1979 establishment of the firm's first international office in Hong Kong by Portman's son John III (Jack), who visited numerous Chinese cities before settling on Shanghai. There, he initially sought sites along the city's famed Bund, although the government proposed a parcel of land symbolically positioned across the street from a Soviet-gifted exhibition center. Working there in coordination with the Kajima Corporation and the American International Group (AIG) insurance conglomerate, the firm proposed one tower, later expanded to three, within which the project's hotel and residential space would be housed. Jack Portman III, interview, September 18, 2013.

41. John Portman, "An Architecture for Contemporary China," *Building in China* 3, no. 4 (December 1990): 25; Jack Portman III, interview; Walter Jackson, interview, October 18, 2013. See also schematic design presentation book, John Portman and Associates, 1984, John Portman and Associates Archives, Atlanta. See also Jane Woo, "Slim Pickings in Shanghai," *Hong Kong Business* (September 1991): 68.

42. Woo, "Slim Pickings in Shanghai," 68.

43. "A Giant Awakes in Beijing," *Asian Architect and Contractor* (January 1989): 13.

44. Liu, "Sanshiqicenglou shang de Zhongguo," 39–54.

45. Craig Calhoun, *Neither Gods nor Emperors: Students and the Struggle for Democracy in China* (Berkeley: University of California Press, 1994), 248.

46. Ronald Skyme, *Hotel Specification International* (London: Pennington, 1986), 18–19.

47. Beijing Workers' Union, "Notice to All Chinese Compatriots," May 17, 1989, in *Cries for Democracy: Writings and Speeches from the 1989 Chinese Democracy Movement*, ed. Han Minzhu (Princeton, NJ: Princeton University Press, 1990), 275.

CHAPTER 7
POSTMODERNISM

1. Yang Yun, "You xifang xiandai jianzhu xin sichao yinqi de lianxiang," *Jianzhu Xuebao*, no. 1 (1980): 26–34. See also Zhou Buyi, "Dangdai shijie jianzhu sichao," *Shijie Jianzhu*, no. 1 (1980): 5. Roger Hong, a Chinese-American member of the team responsible for the failed Metropolitan Hotel, noted the presence of Robert Venturi's *Complexity and Contradiction in Architecture* in the Beijing Institute of Architectural Design's offices during his time there in 1980. See Hong, "Joint Venture in Beijing," *Architecture California* 3, no. 4 (October/November 1981): 22.

2. See, for example, Fredric Jameson, "Postmodernism, or The Cultural Logic of Late Capitalism," *New Left Review* 146 (July/August 1984): 53–92; Jameson, "The Brick and the Balloon: Architecture, Idealism, and Land Speculation," *New Left Review* 228 (March/April 1998): 25–46.

3. Zou Denong, "Yi ge si ceng xiangshi de lilun—guanyu houxiandaizhuyi," originally published in 1986; republished in Zou, *Zou Denong wenji* (Beijing: Huazhong keji daxue chubanshe, 2012), 212–14.

4. Johann P. Arnason, "Theory: Modernity, Postmodernity, and the Japanese Experience," in *Japanese Encounters with Postmodernity*, ed. Johann P. Arnason and Yoshio Sugimoto (London: Kegan Paul, 1995), 23.

5. Timothy Hyde has engaged in the history of these formations in relationship to British architecture; see Hyde, *Ugliness and Judgment: On Architecture in the Public Eye* (Princeton, NJ: Princeton University Press, 2019), 4.

6. Joseph Fewsmith, *Dilemmas of Reform in China: Political Conflict and Economic Debate* (Armonk, NY: M. E. Sharpe, 1994), 69. See also Julian Gewirtz, *Unlikely Partners: Chinese Reformers, Western Economists, and the Making of Global China* (Cambridge, MA: Harvard University Press, 2017), 44.

7. Fewsmith, *Dilemmas of Reform in China*, 69–70. See also Lu Zhenmao, "A Summary of Discussions over the Past Three Years on the Problems of Planned Economy and Regulation by Market Mechanism," *Guangming Ribao*, May 29, 1982, trans. *China Foreign Broadcast Information Service (FBIS)*, June 8, 1982, K6–K9; "Appropriate Development of Individual Economy Is a Necessity of the Social Economic Life," *Renmin Ribao*, January 9, 1983, 1, trans. *FBIS*, January 11, 1983, K1–K2.

8. Jiang Feng, "Yishu wei renmin dazhong fuwu," *Meishu*, no. 1 (1980): 5–6; Jane Debevoise, *Between State and Market: Chinese Contemporary Art in the Post-Mao Era* (Leiden: Brill, 2014), 23; Julia Andrews, *Painters and Politics in the People's Republic of China, 1949–1979* (Berkeley: University of California Press, 1994), 389–400.

9. He Li, "Modernism and China: A Summary from the People's Daily," trans. and intro. Geremie Barmé, *Renditions: A Chinese-English Translation Magazine*, nos. 19–20 (Spring and Autumn 1983): 47.

10. Fewsmith, *Dilemmas of Reform in China*, 69.

11. Xiang Qiyuan, "Economic Development and Income Distribution," in *China's Search for Economic Growth: The Chinese Economy since 1949*, ed. Xu Dixin et al., trans. Andrew Watson (Beijing: New World, 1982), 111.

12. Xiang, "Economic Development," 121.

13. Paul Goldberger, "Tract House, Celebrated," *New York Times Magazine*, September 14, 1975, 68–69, 74; Goldberger, "80's Design: Wallowing in Opulence and Luxury," *New York Times*, November 13, 1988, H1, H32; Robert A. M. Stern, *New Directions in American Architecture* (New York: George Braziller, 1977), 117; Charles Jencks, "Postmodern vs. Late-Modern," in *Zeitgeist in Babel: The Postmodernist Controversy*, ed. Ingesborg Hoesterey (Bloomington: Indiana University Press, 1991), 4–21. See also Ying Wang and Hilde Heynen, "Transferring Postmodernism to China: A Productive Misunderstanding," *Architectural Theory Review* 22, no. 3 (2018): 338–63. For theorizations of postmodernism, see Hans Bertens, *The Idea of the Postmodern: A History* (London: Routledge, 1995), 20–81; Reinhold Martin, *Utopia's Ghost: Architecture and Postmodernism, Again* (Minneapolis: University of Minnesota Press, 2010); Jorge Otero-Pailos, *Architecture's Historical Turn* (Minneapolis: University of Minnesota Press, 2010); Emmanuel Petit, *Irony; or the Self-Critical Opacity of Postmodern Architecture* (New Haven, CT: Yale University Press, 2013).

14. Yang, "You xifang xiandai jianzhu xin sichao yinqi de lianxiang," 28.

15. Yang, "You xifang xiandai jianzhu xin sichao yinqi de lianxiang," 33–34.

16. Yang, "You xifang xiandai jianzhu xin sichao yinqi de lianxiang," 28; Ai Dingzheng, "Jianzhu chuangzuo zhong de ji zhong cuowu qingxiang," *Jianzhu Xuebao*, no. 1 (1980): 21–22. See also Peter Rowe and Seng Kuan, *Architectural Encounters with Essence and Form in Modern China* (Cambridge, MA: MIT Press, 2002), 139–41; Yu Shuishan, *Chang'an Avenue and the Modernization of Chinese Architecture* (Seattle: University of Washington Press, 2012), 173.

17. See "Guanyu Post-Modernism de yi fa," *Shijie Jianzhu*, no. 4 (1981): 78.

18. Yoshinobu Ashihara and Terunobu Fujimori, "Yougan yu Zhongguo guanyu 'Houxiandai jianzhu' de taolun"; originally published in *Japan Architect* (November 1985); republished in Gu Mengzhao and Zhang Zaiyuan, eds., *Zhongguo Jianzhu: Pingxi yu Zhanwang* (Tianjin: Tianjin kexue jishu chubanshe, 1989), 24–26.

19. Ashihara and Fujimori, "Yougan yu Zhongguo guanyu 'Houxiandai jianzhu' de taolun," 24–26; Kevin Lynch, Tridib Banerjee, and Michael Southworth, *City Sense and City Design: Writings and Projects of Kevin Lynch* (Cambridge, MA: MIT Press, 1990), 226–31; Charles Jencks, interview, February 11, 2014; Jack Portman III, interview, September 18, 2013.

20. John Bryant to I. M. Pei, November 20, 1984, Box 11, I. M. Pei Papers, Library of Congress, Washington, DC.

21. For a discussion of the politics of language associated with postmodernism, see Gilles Deleuze and Félix Guattari, *A Thousand Plateaus: Capitalism and Schizophrenia*, trans. Brian Massumi (Minneapolis: University of Minnesota Press, 1987), 76; Martin, *Utopia's Ghost*, 65. See also Chen Zhihua, "Guanyu 'Jianzhu shi ninggu de yinyue,'" *Jianzhushi*, no. 2 (1980): 171–72; Wu Yonghui, "Shi cong bijiao wenxue kan Zhongguo jianzhu," *Xin Jianzhu*, no. 4 (1985): 41–43; Xiong Ming, "Jianzhu chuangzuo yu shidai jingshen," *Jianzhu Xuebao*, no. 1 (1985): 2–6; Li Baihao,

"Houxiandai jianzhu hechu qule?," *Huazhong Jianzhu*, no. 2 (1988): 5.

22. Ezra Vogel, *Deng Xiaoping and the Transformation of China* (Cambridge, MA: Belknap Press of Harvard University Press, 2011), 566; Richard Baum, *Burying Mao: Chinese Politics in the Age of Deng Xiaoping* (Princeton, NJ: Princeton University Press, 1994), 150.

23. "Zhongguo jianzhu xuehui yi ji ba san nian chunli xueshu zuotanhui jiyao," *Jianzhu Xuebao*, no. 3 (1983): 3.

24. Andre Mendelsohn, "Alvin Toffler in China: Deng's Big Bang," *New Republic* (April 4, 1988): 15–17; Julian Gerwitz, "The Futurists of Beijing: Alvin Toffler, Zhao Ziyang, and China's 'New Technological Revolution,' 1979–1991," *Journal of Asian Studies* 78, no. 1 (February 2019): 115–40.

25. Martin, *Utopia's Ghost*, xi.

26. Shu-Shin Wang, "The Rise and Fall of the Campaign against Spiritual Pollution in the People's Republic of China," *Asian Affairs: An American Review* 13, no. 1 (1986): 47–62.

27. Wu An-chia, "Whither Mainland China: On the Theoretical Study Campaign," in *Changes and Continuities in Chinese Communism*, ed. Yu-ming Shaw (Boulder, CO: Westview, 1988), 1:155. See also Wang, "Rise and Fall of the Campaign against Spiritual Pollution," 47–62.

28. Baum, *Burying Mao*, 156; "Jinian Zhongguo jianzhu xuehui chengli sanshi zhou nian dahui jiyao," *Jianzhu Xuebao*, no. 1 (1984): 1–3.

29. Gong Deshun, "Yi jiu ba si nian quanguo youxiu jianzhu sheji pingshu," *Jianzhu Xuebao*, no. 9 (1984): 23–29, 82–83; Wu Guoli, "Shouci Xiandai Zhongguo Jianzhu Chuangzuo Xueshu yantaohui zai Wuhan juxing," *Jianzhu Xuebao*, no. 7 (1985): 11; "Jiwang kailai, renzhong daoyuan," *Jianzhu Xuebao*, no. 1 (1989): 23–24. See also Wang Xingtian, Yang Yu, and Dai Chun, "Huayu liubian yu qunti gengdie: Xiandai Zhongguo Jianzhu Chuangzuo Luntan 30 nian," *Shidai Jianzhu*, no. 1 (2015): 160–63.

30. Liu Erming and Yi Feng, eds., *Zhongguo dangdai zhuming jianzhushi zuopinxuan* (Beijing: Zhongguo jihua chubanshe, 1999), 2:100.

31. Liu and Feng, eds., *Zhongguo dangdai zhuming jianzhushi zuopinxuan*, 100; Sun Guocheng and Gao Qinglin, "Fuyu chuantong xingshi yish shidai qixi," *Jianzhu Xuebao*, no. 4 (1986): 39–41.

32. Zhang Jinqiu, "Shaanxi lishi bowuguan sheji," *Jianzhu Xuebao*, no. 9 (1991): 24.

33. Zhang Ping, "Houxiandai zhuyi yu Zhongguo dangdai jianzhu wenhua," *Jianzhu Xuebao*, no. 11 (1986): 67.

34. Fu Kecheng, "Sheji de lu yingai hen kuai—cong Beijing Xidan zonghe shangye dalou sheji tanqi," *Jianzhu Xuebao*, no. 7 (1985): 19–23; Marlowe Hood, "Search for Concrete Ideas," *South China Morning Post*, December 3, 1988, 39.

35. Zeng Zhaofen, "Houxiandai zhuyi yi lai dao Zhongguo," *Shijie Jianzhu*, no. 2 (1987): 61.

36. Baum, *Burying Mao*, 189.

37. Wang Hui, "The New Criticism," in *One China, Many Paths*, ed. Chaohua Wang (London: Verso, 2003), 55–86.

38. Jameson, "Postmodernism," 74; Jameson, interview, February 7, 2014.

39. Xu Shangzhi, "Wo guo jianzhu xiandaihua yu jianzhu chuanzuo wenti," *Jianzhu Xuebao*, no. 9 (1984): 12.

40. Zhou Buyi, "Du Meiguo jianzhushi xianhui 1986 nian rongyu jiang zuopin yougan," *Jianzhu Xuebao*, no. 4 (1987): 71.

41. "Qing pingxuan nin xihuan de 'Beijing bashi niandai shi da jianzhu,'" *Beijing Ribao*, April 3, 1988, 2; "Bashi niandai shi da jianzhu pingxuan jiexiao," *Beijing Ribao*, April 29, 1988, 1; Hood, "Search for Concrete Ideas," 39.

42. "Bashi niandai shi da jianzhu pingxuan jiexiao," 1; Hood, "Search for Concrete Ideas," 39.

43. "Bashi niandai shi da jianzhu pingxuan jiexiao," 1; Hood, "Search for Concrete Ideas," 39.

44. Huang Kewu and Di Zongfan, "Beijing tushuguan xinguan sheji," *Jianzhu Xuebao* 1 (1988): 26–32; Rowe and Kuan, *Architectural Encounters*, 153–54.

45. Hood, "Search for Concrete Ideas," 39.

46. See Mary McLeod, "Architecture and Politics in the Reagan Era: From Postmodernism to Deconstructivism," *Assemblage*, no. 8 (February 1989): 22–59.

47. See Ding Guanghui, *Constructing a Place of Critical Architecture in China: Intermediate Criticality in the Journal Time + Architecture* (London: Routledge, 2016), 97–136.

48. Henry A. Kissinger, "China Now Changing Rules and Ruling Party," *Los Angeles Times*, October 25, 1987, 18.

49. Hood, "Search for Concrete Ideas," 39.

CHAPTER 8
ARCHITECTURAL EDUCATION AND THE PROFESSION

1. Gu Daqing, "An Outline of Beaux-Arts Education in China: Transplantation, Localization, and Entrenchment," in *Chinese Architecture and the Beaux-Arts*, ed. Jeffrey W. Cody, Nancy S. Steinhardt, and Tony Atkin (Honolulu: University of Hawai'i Press), 82.

2. Michael Joroff to Kevin Lynch, February 27, 1984, Kevin Lynch Papers, MIT Archives, Cambridge, MA.

3. For examples within fields of cultural production, see Jane Debevoise, *Between State and Market: Chinese Contemporary Art in the Post-Mao Era* (Leiden: Brill, 2014), 15–40; Ying Zhu, *Chinese Cinema during the Era of Reform* (Westport, CT: Praeger, 2003), 73.

4. Qian Feng and Wu Jiang, *Zhongguo xiandai jianzhu jiaoyu shi (1920–1980)* (Beijing: Zhongguo jianzhu gongye chubanshe, 2008), 218–20; Gu, "Outline of Beaux-Arts Education," 83.

5. Gao Yilan, "Teaching Students to Design for People," trans. John K. C. Liu, *Journal of Architectural Education* 35, no. 1 (Autumn 1981): 40.

6. Gao, "Teaching Students to Design for People," 40.

7. For a history of China's one-child policy, see Susan Greenhalgh, *Just One Child: Science and Policy in Deng's China* (Berkeley: University of California Press, 2008).

8. Gao, "Teaching Students to Design for People," 40.

9. Committee on Overseas Professional Qualifications, Expert Panel in Architecture, "Questionnaire on the Organization of the Profession in Overseas Countries, China," May 5, 1978, American Institute of Architects Archives, Washington, DC.

10. Gavin Walkley to National Council of Architectural Registration Boards (U.S.), August 1, 1978, American Institute of Architects Archives, Washington, DC; Committee on Overseas Professional Qualifications, "Questionnaire."

11. "Guanyu jianzhu xiandaihua he jianzhu fengge wenti de yixie yijian," *Jianzhu Xuebao*, no. 1 (1979): 26–30.

12. Xiao Tong, "Jiefang sixiang, kaidong jiqi, ba kancha sheji gongzuo tigao dao yi ge xin de shuiping"; Yan Zixiang, "Jiefang sixiang, jiao ta shidi, nuli zuo hao kancha sheji gongzuo"; Gong Deshun, "Dapo jingshen jiasuo, tigao sheji shuiping," *Jianzhu Xuebao*, no. 6 (1979): 1–10.

13. Committee on Overseas Professional Qualifications, "Questionnaire." See also "Jiaqiang Zhongwai jianzhu jie de xueshu jiaoliu," *Jianzhu Xuebao*, no. 4 (1978): 35; *MEMO*, March 16, 1979, 5; Martha M. Davis, "United States City Planners in China," *Urban Planning Update* (May 1980): 52, in Kevin Lynch Papers, Folder "China," AC400 b. 39, MIT Archives, Cambridge, MA.

14. See, for example, "Agreement Concerning the Exchange Program between the Department of Architecture of the Swiss Federal Institute of Technology, Zurich (ETHZ), and the Architecture Department of Southeast University (SEU), Nanjing, 2001–2003," ETH-Bibliothek, Hochschularchiv der ETH Zurich, AKZ. 2011–08, D-ARCH; Herbert Kramel, interview, June 7, 2014; Franz Oswald, interview, June 3, 2014; Wang Jinwen to Monika Coray, April 25, 1983, ETH-Bibliothek, Hochschularchiv der ETH Zurich, AKZ. 2011–08, D-ARCH; interview, Peter and Johanna Diethelm-Grauer, June 6, 2014.

15. Gary Hack, interview, August 19, 2013.

16. Dennis Frenchman, interview, August 13, 2013; Hack, interview. See also Kevin Lynch, Tridib Banerjee, and Michael Southworth, *City Sense and City Design: Writings and Projects of Kevin Lynch* (Cambridge, MA: MIT Press, 1990), 226–31.

17. Daniel B. Abramson, "A Trans-Pacific Planning Education in Reverse," in *Crossing Borders: International Exchange and Planning Practices*, ed. Patsy Healey and Robert Upton (London: Routledge, 2010), 299.

18. Anthony Vacchione, interview, July 30, 2013.

19. Vacchione, interview.

20. Vacchione, interview.

21. Vaccione, interview; Cui Kai, interview, August 19, 2015. See also Wang Tan, "Meiguo de jianzhu jiaoyu," *Shijie Jianzhu*, no. 3 (1981): 39–42; Cheng Guangxian, "Jianada jianzhu jiaoyu (1)," *Shidai Jianzhu*, no. 1 (1984): 32–35, and "Jianada jianzhu jiaoyu (2)," *Shidai Jianzhu*, no. 2 (1985): 18–21.

22. Roger Hong, "Joint Venture in Beijing," *Architecture California* 3, no. 4 (October/November 1981): 21.

23. Hong, "Joint Venture in Beijing," 22.

24. Hong, "Joint Venture in Beijing," 22–23. See also Xiong Ming, Liu Li, and Geng Zhangfu, "Kunlun fandian shinei sheji gousi," *Jianzhu Xuebao*, no. 9 (1985): 2–8; "Beijing Kunlun fandian," *Jianzhu Xuebao*, no. 10 (1988): 66.

25. Hong, "Joint Venture in Beijing," 21, 22, 23; Xiong, Liu, and Geng, "Kunlun fandian shinei sheji gousi," 2–8.

26. Participants included Farokh Afshar, Takefumi Aida, Mohammed Arkoun, Brian Brace-Taylor, Jacques Bugnicourt, Roger Carmignani, Pierre Clément, Charles Correa, Balkrishna Doshi, Hassan Fathy, Oleg Grabar, Klaus Herdeg, Renata Holod, Hasan-Uddin Khan, Tunney Lee, William Lim, Otto Koenigsberger, William Porter, Mildred Schmertz, and the Aga Khan himself. Chinese representatives included Cao Wanhua, Chen Zhi, Han Suyin, Hou Renzhi, Jin Oubu, and Yang Tingbao, among others. *The Changing Rural Habitat: Proceedings of Seminar Six in the Series Architectural Transformations in the Islamic World* (Singapore: Concept Media, 1982); "Aka han jianzhu jiang diliuci guoji xueshu taolunhui zai Zhongguo juxing," *Jianzhu Xuebao*, no. 1 (1982): 1–6.

27. Transcript, China Seminar, Tape 1, Side 2, Tape 3, Side 2, Aga Khan Archives, Geneva.

28. Transcript, China Seminar, Tape 5, Side 2, Tape 6, Side 1, Tape 6, Side 2, Tape 7, Side 1, Aga Khan Archives, Geneva.

29. His Highness the Aga Khan, "Concluding Remarks," in *Changing Rural Habitat*, 1:153.

30. Committee on Overseas Professional Qualifications, "Questionnaire." See also Charlie Q. L. Xue and Guangding Hui, *A History of Design Institutes in China: From Mao to Market* (London: Routledge, 2018), 58–94.

31. Zhongyang weiyuanhui, *Zhonggong Zhongyang guanyu jingji tizhi gaige di juding* (Beijing: Renmin chubanshe, 1984), 4–6; Immanuel C. Y. Hsu, *China without Mao: The Search for a New Order* (Oxford: Oxford University Press, 1990), 184. Anxiety over the effects of the market on retail prices also led to a brief run on China's banks, unsettling party leaders in the process. Richard Baum, *Burying Mao: Chinese Politics in the Age of Deng Xiaoping* (Princeton, NJ: Princeton University Press, 1994), 170, 189.

32. John Bryant to I. M. Pei, November 20, 1984, Box 11, I. M. Pei Archives, Library of Congress, Washington, DC. See also Wang Tianxi, "Xinlu chutan: Guanyu jianshe bu Beijing jianzhu sheji shiwusuo," *Jianzhu Xuebao*, no. 8 (1986): 2–5. See also Wang Weimin, "Xin Zhongguo diyi jia jianzhu sheji shiwusuo de qianshi jinsheng—Beijing Jianzhu Sheji Shiwusuo jishi," *Zhonghua Jianzhubao*, no. 4 (July 18, 2011): 1–3.

33. Wang Tianxi, "Finding a New Way," *Building in China*, no. 3 (1987): 28.

34. Mary Lee, "More by Design," *Far Eastern Economic Review* (January 24, 1985): 34; Li Jia, "Guonei diyi jia Zhongwai hezuo shejigongsi dansheng ji," *Zhonghua Jianzhubao*, no. 1 (July 22, 2008): 1.

35. "Dadi jianzhu shiwusuo zai Beijing chengli," *Shijie Jianzhu*, no. 1 (1985): 23; Jin Oubu, "Sheji gaige shidian liang nian," *Jianzhu Xuebao*, no. 7 (1987): 2; Lee, "More by Design," 34; Liu Xiaoting, "Chen Zhanxiang de chengshi guhua sixiang yu shixian" (PhD diss., Wuhan Ligong Daxue, 2012), 30.

36. Yan Xinghua, "Zhiyou gaige, caiyou shengmingli," *Jianzhu Xuebao*, no. 10 (1987): 3; Joe Carter, interview, November 6, 2012.

37. Bu Zhengwei, "Dajia douyaou you ziji de!," *Jianzhu Xuebao*, no. 4 (1985): 27.

38. Wang, "Xinlu chutan," 5; Yan, "Zhiyou gaige, caiyou shengmingli," 2; "Dadi jianzhu shiwusuo zai Beijing chengli," 23.

39. See "Dadi jianzhu shiwusuo (guoji) sheji zuopin xuan," *Jianzhu Xuebao*, no. 7 (1987): 5–32; "Zhongjing sheji zuopin xuan," *Jianzhu Xuebao*, no. 10 (1987): 4–30; "Jianshe bu Beijing Jianzhu sheji shiwusuo sheji jinzuo," *Jianzhu Xuebao*, no. 1 (1988): 14–25.

40. "Zhongjing sheji zuopin xuan," *Jianzhu Xuebao*, no. 10 (1987): 2.

41. Tao Dejian, "Sheji tizhi gaige de xianfeng," *Xin Jianzhu*, no. 3 (1986): 9.

42. Wang Tianxi, "Wana'atu yihui dasha," *Jianzhu Xuebao*, no. 4 (1992): 63.

43. "Chengxiang maoyi zhongxin (jianzao fang'an)," *Jianzhu Xuebao*, no. 10 (1987): 12.

44. "Xiamen zhongxin qu tiaozheng guihua," *Jianzhu Xuebao*, no. 4 (1987): 5.

45. Xue and Hui, *History of Design Institutes in China*, 75.

46. Lee, "More by Design," 34.

47. Xue Qiuli, "Shiji zhi jiaokan Zhongguo jianzhu," *Jianzhu Xuebao*, no. 3 (1989): 23.

CHAPTER 9
CHINA IN AFRICA

1. Cole Roskam, "Non-Aligned Architecture: China's Designs on and in Ghana and Guinea, 1955–1992," *Architectural History* 58 (2015): 161–91. Łukasz Stanek has argued that the multiple Cold War–era alliances, antagonisms, and mobilities involving architectural production be understood as a kind of world-making, within which globalization constitutes one part. Stanek, *Architecture in Global Socialism: Eastern Europe, West Africa, and the Middle East in the Cold War* (Princeton, NJ: Princeton University Press, 2020), 29–33.

2. Jeremy Friedman, *Shadow Cold War: The Sino-Soviet Competition for the Third World* (Chapel Hill: University of North Carolina Press, 2015), 200–203.

3. "L'exemple d'une coopération sincere," *Elima*, May 20–21, 1979, 1.

4. David Borman, "Acting Authentically: Performance and Transnational Authenticity in Tchicaya U Tam'si's The Glorious Destiny of Marshall Nnikon Nniku," *Research in African Literatures* 44, no. 3 (Fall 2013): 87–100; Johan Lagae and Kim De Raedt, "Building for 'l'Authenticité': Eugène Palumbo and the Architecture of Mobutu's Congo," *Journal of Architectural Education* 68, no. 2 (2014): 178–89.

5. Kevin C. Dunn, "Imagining Mobutu's Zaire: The Production and Consumption of Identity in International Relations," *Millennium Journal of International Studies* 39 (2001): 235–58.

6. Zhu Shanquan, Lin Kaiwu, and Qi Zhenya, "Zhayi'er Renmingong sheji," *Jianzhu Xuebao*, no. 2 (1980): 18–20.

7. Lagae and De Raedt, "Building for 'l'Authenticité'," 178–89.

8. Fox Butterfield, "Where Moscow Goes, Can Peking Be Far Behind?," *New York Times*, June 25, 1978, E4; Kakinda Mbwende, "Le réveil chinois," *Elima*, January 30, 1979, 1, 7; Kalonji Kal, "La Chine et l'unité de movement non-aligné," *Elima*, February 21, 1979, 5.

9. Nzonzila Ndonzuau, "Coopération tous azimuts entre le Zaïre et la Chine," *Elima*, May 11, 1979, 1; Angelo-Mobateli, "Le Président-Fondateur a inauguré le Palais du Peuple," *Elima*, May 20, 1979, 1–7.

10. "Kamailong wenhuagong jianzhu sheji," *Jianzhu Xuebao*, no. 1 (1983): 71; "L'immeuble serait disponible en Octobre," *Cameroon Tribune*, July 12 and 13, 1981, 1; "Le Chef de l'État a reaffirmé le Non-Alignement du Cameroun," *Cameroon Tribune*, July 5 and 6, 1981, 1; "Presentation des lettres de creance des Ambassadeurs du Libéria et de Chine au Chef de l'État," *Cameroon Tribune*, July 5 and 6, 1981, 2–3; Casimir Datchoua Soupa, "Le Palais de la Culture de Yaoundé en voie d'achèvement: Les journalistes de C. T. l'ont visité," *Cameroon Tribune*, July 12 and 13, 1981, 2.

11. Soupa, "Palais de la Culture de Yaoundé," 2.

12. See Jamie Monson, *Africa's Freedom Railway: How a Chinese Development Project Changed Lives and Livelihoods in Tanzania* (Bloomington: Indiana University Press, 2009), 100–103.

13. Organization for Economic Cooperation and Development, *The Aid Programme of China* (Paris: Organization for Economic Cooperation and Development, 1987), 22.

14. Organization for Economic Cooperation and Development, *Aid Programme of China*, 22. See, for example, "A Chinese Official Plans Africa Visit," *New York Times*, December 19, 1982, 15.

15. "Zhao Speaks at Mass Rally," *Xinhua*, trans. in *China Foreign Broadcast Information Service (FBIS)*, December 30, 1982, I3.

16. Quoted in "Zaire President Welcomes Zhao," *Xinhua*, trans. in *FBIS*, January 2, 1983, I16; Zhu Shanquan, Lin Kaiwu, and Qi Zhenya, "Zhayi'er Renmingong sheji," *Jianzhu Xuebao*, no. 2 (1980): 16–20; "Economic Aid to Congo," *Xinhua*, trans. in *FBIS*, January 2, 1983, I10.

17. "Hunt for a Site," *Daily Nation*, August 1, 1987, 15; "No More Hurdles on Road to Nairobi," *Daily Nation*, August 1, 1987, 17.

18. Charlie Q. L. Xue, Ding Guanghui, Chang Wei, and Wan Yan, "Architecture of 'Stadium Diplomacy'—China-Aid Sports Buildings in Africa," *Habitat International* 90 (August 2019): 3–11.

19. "Hunt for a Site," 18; "No More Hurdles," 17.

20. Xue, Ding, Chang, and Wan, "Architecture of 'Stadium Diplomacy,'" 5.

21. "The Big Kick-Off," *Daily Nation*, August 1, 1987, 9.

22. "Big Kick-Off," 9.

23. "Big Welcome for Chinese Officials," *Coastweek*, January 23–29, 1987, 4; "The Chinese Connection!," *Coastweek*, March 27–April 2, 1987, 1. Mombasa parliamentary representative Shariff Nassir subsequently traveled to Shenzhen to secure a business agreement with the Shenzhen Electronic Group. "Nassir Flies Off to China," *Coastweek*, April 3–9, 1987, 3.

24. "Twenty-One-Gun Blasts Greet Games," *Sunday Standard*, August 2, 1987, 1. See also "Africa's Pride Has Been Restored," *Standard*, August 12, 1987, 6; "A Bright Future for Kenya Sport," *Standard*, August 15, 1987, 18; "Games May Lead to Hosting Olympics," *Coastweek*, July 31–August 6, 1987, 1; "What Can We Learn from These Games?," *Daily Nation*, August 13, 1987, 6.

25. "It's All Systems Go," *Daily Nation*, August 1, 1987, 1.

26. See Łukasz Stanek, "Architects from Socialist Countries in Ghana (1957–67): Modern Architecture and Mondialisation," *Journal of the Society of Architectural Historians* 74, no. 4 (December 2015): 416–42.

27. "Basketball Gymnasium Dangerous—Namake," *Daily Nation*, July 15, 1987, 23. See also "Another Snag Hits the Games," *Standard*, July 17, 1987, 3.

28. "Bright Future for Kenya Sport," 18.

29. Gao Shiling, "Bieju yizhong de Feizhou lüyou jianzhu," *Jianzhu Xuebao*, no. 9 (1986): 76–78.

30. Oussouby Sacko, interview, May 22, 2020.

31. "African Students in China Protest," *Standard*, January 8, 1987, 2.

32. Accusations were made that over thirty African students in Nanjing were beaten with cattle prods during a raid of their guesthouse. Chinese students accused African male students of molesting Chinese women and employing Chinese prostitutes. See "Chinese, Africans Conflict," *Ghanaian Times*, January 4, 1989, 2; "OAU Condemns Students Conflict in China," *Ghanaian Times*, January 5, 1989, 1; "Ghana Has Confidence in China—Annan," *Ghanaian Times*, January 17, 1989, 1; "Traore for China," *Ghanaian Times*, January 20, 1989, 2.

33. "Chinese Team Here," *Ghanaian Times*, April 6, 1988, 1; Charles Neequaye, "Ghana, China Sign Cultural Pact," *Ghanaian Times*, July 29, 1988, 1. See also Gillian Heathcote and Oscar Bruce, "The Chinese, Ethiopians Are Providing It," *Ghanaian Times*, September 23, 1985, 1; Peter Schwab, *Designing West Africa: Prelude to 21st-Century Calamity* (New York: Palgrave Macmillan, 2004), 100; Kwame Nkrumah and June Milne, *Kwame Nkrumah: The Conakry Years, His Life and Letters* (London: Panaf, 1990), 9.

34. Gayheart Edem Mensah, "Ghana, China $15m National Theatre Pact," *Ghanaian Times*, July 6, 1989, 1.

35. Dangdai Zhongguo Jianzhushi Congshu Bianweihui, ed., *Dangdai Zhongguo jianzhu shi: Cheng Taining* (Beijing: Zhongguo jianzhu gongye chubanshe, 1997), 72; Cheng Taining, interview, June 1, 2013.

36. Gillian Heathcote, "National Theatre Project Takes Off," *Ghanaian Times*, June 20, 1990, 8.

37. S. O. Amevor, "National Theatre to Be Completed by Sunday," *Ghanaian Times*, December 14, 1992, 1.

38. See, for example, Muhammad A. Mongu, "The Counter-Offensive to Re-Colonize Africa," *Ghanaian Times*, April 18, 1988, 4; John Owusu, "Building Designs Must Reflect Nation's Culture," *Ghanaian Times*, June 25, 1986, 1; "Banker Warns Africa of Economic Colonialism," *Ghanaian Times*, June 2, 1988, 1; "Colonial Shackles Still Holding Africa—Lecturer," *Ghanaian Times*, May 28, 1988, 1; Adwoa Aseidu, "Africa Must Restore Her Cultural Identity," *Ghanaian Times*, May 13, 1988, 1; Jerry John Rawlings, "We Must Respect Our Cultural Values," *Ghanaian Times*, October 25, 1988, 4; R. Harry Reynolds, "Self-Reliance Provides Solutions to Problems," *Ghanaian Times*, January 2, 1989, 8; "Foreign Investors and Africa's Economies," *Ghanaian Times*, March 24, 1990, 4; "Technological Industry in Developing Countries," *Ghanaian Times*, July 21, 1989, 4; Editorial, "Mysteries of Technology Transfer (1)," *Ghanaian Times*, August 30, 1989, 2; Baffour Opoku, "Cultural Awareness Drive Launched," *Ghanaian Times*, August 15, 1989, 1.

39. Cheng, interview.

40. Alfred Tamakloe, "National Theatre Complex Completed on Schedule," *Ghanaian Times*, December 22, 1992, 1.

41. Samuel Darko, interview, May 22, 2014; Stella N. D. Arthiabah, interview, May 28, 2014.

42. Stanek, *Architecture in Global Socialism*, 29.

CONCLUSION

1. See Vladimir Kulić, ed., *Second World Postmodernisms: Architecture and Society under Late Socialism* (London. Bloomsbury, 2019); Łukasz Stanek, *Architecture in Global Socialism: Eastern Europe, West Africa, and the Middle East in the Cold War* (Princeton, NJ: Princeton University Press, 2020).

2. Jeff Widener, email to author, January 22, 2014.

3. "How Stuart Franklin Took His Tank Man Photograph," Phaidon, http://www.phaidon.com/agenda/photography/articles/2016/april/05/how-stuart-franklin-took-his-tank-man-photograph/ (accessed August 1, 2018). See also Te-Pang Chen, "The Other 'Tank Man' Photographs, *Wall Street Journal*, May 30, 2014, https://blogs.wsj.com/chinarealtime/2014/05/30/the-other-tank-man-photographs/ (accessed August 1, 2018). Jim Mann, *Beijing Jeep: A Case Study of Western Business in China* (Boulder, CO: Westview, 1997), 20, 304.

4. Lu Zhengcao, "Thoughts after Reading *A Day in Martial Law*," *Renmin Ribao*, February 20, 1990, 3, trans. *China Foreign Broadcast Information Service* (*FBIS*), March 16, 1990; republished in *China Since Tiananmen: Political, Economic, and Social Conflicts*, ed. Lawrence R. Sullivan (Armonk, NY: M. E. Sharpe, 1995), 7–8.

5. Gayheart Edem Mensah, "Ghana, China $15m National Theatre Pact," *Ghanaian Times*, July 6, 1989, 1.

6. Zhang Zaiyuan, "'Houxiandai' yu Zhongguo jianzhu minzu xingshi zhi zhengming," *Jianzhu Xuebao*, no. 7 (1989): 39–40; Zou Denong, "Liang ci yinjin waiguo jianzhu lilun de jiaoxun: Cong 'minzu xingshi' dao 'hou xiandai jianzhu,'" *Jianzhu Xuebao*, no. 11 (1989): 47–50.

7. Editorial note, *Renmin Ribao*, August 8, 1988, 3; cited in Xu Luo, "The 'Shekou Storm': Changes in the Mentality of Chinese Youth Prior to Tiananmen," *China Quarterly* 142 (June 1995): 543, 545.

8. Daniel C. Lynch, "Dilemmas of 'Thought Work' in Fin-de-Siècle China," *China Quarterly* 157 (March 1999): 174.

9. Lowell Dittmer, "China in 1989: The Crisis of Incomplete Reform," *Asian Survey* 29, no. 1 (January 1990): 22; David Zweig, *Internationalizing China: Domestic Interests and Global Linkages* (Ithaca, NY: Cornell University Press, 2002), 94.

10. See, for example, Guanghui Ding, "'Experimental Architecture' in China," *Journal of the Society of Architectural Historians* 73, no. 1 (March 2014): 28–37; Guanghui Ding, *Constructing a Place of Critical Architecture in China: Intermediate Criticality in the Journal Time + Architecture* (London: Routledge, 2016), 97–136.

11. Manfredo Tafuri, *Architecture and Utopia: Design and Capitalist Development* (Cambridge, MA: MIT Press, 1976), 100.

12. Austin Williams, "The Simplicity of Liu Jiakun's Work," *Architectural Review* (February 20, 2017), https://www.architectural-review.com/buildings/the-simplicity-of-liu-jiakuns-work/10016529.article (accessed February 15, 2019). This position was also prefigured within Japanese postmodern discourse during the 1980s. See, for example, Arata Isozaki, "Of City, Nation, and Style," in *Postmodernism and Japan: Post-Contemporary Interventions*, ed. Masao Miyoshi and Harry D. Harootunian (Durham, NC: Duke University Press, 1989), 54. Isozaki's essay originally appeared in *Shinkenchiku* in November 1983 and was translated into English in *The Japan Architect* (January 1984).

13. "Xi Jinping Isn't a Fan of Weird Architecture in China," *Wall Street Journal*, October 17, 2014, http://blogs.wsj.com/chinarealtime/2014/10/17/xi-jinping-isnt-a-fan-of-weird-architecture-in-china/ (accessed December 3, 2019); Yang Yun, "You xifang xiandai jianzhu xin sichao yinqi de lianxiang," *Jianzhu Xuebao*, no. 1 (1980): 33.

Illustration Credits

The photographers and the sources of visual material other than the owners indicated in the captions are as follows. Every effort has been made to supply complete and correct credits; if there are errors or omissions, please contact Yale University Press so that corrections can be made in any subsequent edition.

Courtesy *Jianzhu Xuebao* (figs. 3, 8, 10, 12, 13, 18, 26–28, 30–33, 47, 48, 58, 59, 62, 63, 70, 71, 73, 76, 77, 79, 81, 82)

People's Republic of China, 1973 MEMCONS, Subject Files, 1969–78, Records of the Department of State, 1763–2002, Record Group 59, National Archives and Record Administration, College Park, MD (fig. 6)

Courtesy China Architecture and Building Press (figs. 7, 9, 11, 21, 44, 45, 60, 61, 66, 84)

Photograph No. 59-OBO-168-HIS_1456; "Beijing—Chancery Office Building—1979," Photographs Related to Embassies, Consulates, and Other Overseas Buildings, ca. 1945–ca. 2006, General Records of the Department of State, 1763–2002, Record Group 59, National Archives and Records Administration, College Park, MD (fig. 15)

© Wu Yinxian (fig. 16)

© Cole Roskam (figs. 17, 19, 67, 83)

© Walter F. Wagner (fig. 20)

Courtesy National Gallery of Art, Washington, D.C., Gallery Archives (fig. 22)

Courtesy Ellen Johnston Laing (fig. 34)

© AP Photo (fig. 35)

© Bibliothèque Kandinsky, MNAM/CCI, Centre Pompidou—Dist. RMN-Grand Palais (fig. 36)

© Bibliothèque Kandinsky (Eustache Kossakowski), MNAM/CCI, Centre Pompidou—Dist. RMN-Grand Palais (figs. 37, 38)

Reproduced with the permission of HSBC Holdings plc. (figs. 39, 40)

© C. C. Pei/Pei Cobb Freed & Partners (fig. 50)

© Pei Cobb Freed & Partners (figs. 51, 52)

© 1991 Michael Portman, The Shanghai Centre Collection, The Portman Archives (fig. 56)

© 1988 John Portman and Associates, The Shanghai Centre Collection, The Portman Archives (fig. 57)

© Phillip Capper/https://www.flickr.com/photos/42033648@N00/1014925647 (fig. 74)

© AP Photo/Jeff Widener (fig. 85)

© AP Photo/Terril Jones (fig. 86)

Index